New Business Frontiers in the Metaverse

Shivani Inder
Chitkara Business School, Chitkara University, India

Shuchi Dawra
Chitkara Business School, Chitkara University, India

Kyla Latrice Tennin
College of Doctoral Studies, University of Phoenix, USA

Sandhir Sharma
Chitkara Business School, Chitkara University, India

IGI Global
PUBLISHER of TIMELY KNOWLEDGE

A volume in the Advances in E-Business Research
(AEBR) Book Series

Published in the United States of America by
IGI Global
Business Science Reference (an imprint of IGI Global)
701 E. Chocolate Avenue
Hershey PA, USA 17033
Tel: 717-533-8845
Fax: 717-533-8661
E-mail: cust@igi-global.com
Web site: http://www.igi-global.com

Library of Congress Cataloging-in-Publication Data

Names: Inder, Shivani, 1984- editor. | Dawra, Shuchi, 1981- editor. | Tennin, Kyla Latrice, 1982- editor. | Sharma, Sandhir, 1974- editor.
Title: New business frontiers in the metaverse / edited by Shivani Inder, Shuchi Dawra, Kyla L. Tennin, Sandhir Sharma.
Description: Hershey, PA : Business Science Reference, [2024] | Includes bibliographical references and index. | Summary: "This book will focus on conceptualizing the landscape of metaverse while exploring myths and challenges that would play the dynamics while defining the future of metaverse. Further, it would explore the state of businesses from perspectives of different stakeholders and addresses its implication on public policy significance"-- Provided by publisher.
Identifiers: LCCN 2024002066 (print) | LCCN 2024002067 (ebook) | ISBN 9798369324226 (hardcover) | ISBN 9798369324233 (ebook)
Subjects: LCSH: Technological innovations--Economic aspects. | Metaverse--Economic aspects.
Classification: LCC HC79.T4 N467 2024 (print) | LCC HC79.T4 (ebook) | DDC 338/.064--dc23/eng/20240418
LC record available at https://lccn.loc.gov/2024002066
LC ebook record available at https://lccn.loc.gov/2024002067

This book is published in the IGI Global book series Advances in E-Business Research (AEBR) (ISSN: 1935-2700; eISSN: 1935-2719)

British Cataloguing in Publication Data
A Cataloguing in Publication record for this book is available from the British Library.

Advances in E-Business Research (AEBR) Book Series

In Lee
Western Illinois University, USA

ISSN:1935-2700
EISSN:1935-2719

Mission

Technology has played a vital role in the emergence of e-business and its applications incorporate strategies. These processes have aided in the use of electronic transactions via telecommunications networks for collaborating with business partners, buying and selling of goods and services, and customer service. Research in this field continues to develop into a wide range of topics, including marketing, psychology, information systems, accounting, economics, and computer science.

The **Advances in E-Business Research (AEBR) Book Series** provides multidisciplinary references for researchers and practitioners in this area. Instructors, researchers, and professionals interested in the most up-to-date research on the concepts, issues, applications, and trends in the e-business field will find this collection, or individual books, extremely useful. This collection contains the highest quality academic books that advance understanding of e-business and addresses the challenges faced by researchers and practitioners.

Coverage

- Mobile Business Models
- Web advertising
- Virtual organization
- E-business systems integration
- Global e-business
- Semantic Web
- Intelligent Agent Technologies
- Electronic Supply Chain Management
- Sustainable E-business
- Valuing e-business assets

IGI Global is currently accepting manuscripts for publication within this series. To submit a proposal for a volume in this series, please contact our Acquisition Editors at Acquisitions@igi-global.com or visit: http://www.igi-global.com/publish/.

The Advances in E-Business Research (AEBR) Book Series (ISSN 1935-2700) is published by IGI Global, 701 E. Chocolate Avenue, Hershey, PA 17033-1240, USA, www.igi-global.com. This series is composed of titles available for purchase individually; each title is edited to be contextually exclusive from any other title within the series. For pricing and ordering information please visit http://www.igi-global.com/book-series/advances-business-research/37144. Postmaster: Send all address changes to above address.

Titles in this Series

For a list of additional titles in this series, please visit: http://www.igi-global.com/book-series/advances-business-research/37144

Revolutionizing Customer-Centric Banking Through ICT
Dharmendra Singh (Modern College of Business and Science, Oman) Garima Malik (Birla Institute of Technology Management, India) and Swati Bhatnagar (New Delhi Institute of Management, India)
Business Science Reference • copyright 2024 • 304pp • H/C (ISBN: 9798369320617) • US $315.00 (our price)

Cases on Social Media and Entrepreneurship
Syed Far Abid Hossain (BRAC Business School, BRAC University, Dhaka, Bangladesh)
Information Science Reference • copyright 2024 • 323pp • H/C (ISBN: 9798369317815) • US $255.00 (our price)

Digital Business and Optimizing Operating Strategies
Gökhan Akel (Antalya Belek University, Turkey) and Mustafa Atahan Yılmaz (Pamukkale University, Turkey)
Business Science Reference • copyright 2024 • 313pp • H/C (ISBN: 9798369304280) • US $250.00 (our price)

Building Smart and Sustainable Businesses With Transformative Technologies
Hamed Nozari (Department of Management, Azad University of the Emirates, Dubai, UAE)
Business Science Reference • copyright 2024 • 306pp • H/C (ISBN: 9798369302101) • US $250.00 (our price)

Metaverse Applications for New Business Models and Disruptive Innovation
Muhammad Anshari (Universiti Brunei Darussalam, Brunei) Muhammad Syafrudin (Sejong University, South Korea) and Ganjar Alfian (Universitas Gadjah Mada, Indonesia)
Business Science Reference • copyright 2023 • 265pp • H/C (ISBN: 9781668460979) • US $250.00 (our price)

Digital Technologies for Entrepreneurship in Industry 4.0
Elena G. Popkova (MGIMO University, Russia)
Business Science Reference • copyright 2022 • 270pp • H/C (ISBN: 9781668442654) • US $250.00 (our price)

Driving Transformative Change in E-Business Through Applied Intelligence and Emerging Technologies
Hamed Taherdoost (University Canada West, Canada)
Business Science Reference • copyright 2022 • 307pp • H/C (ISBN: 9781668452356) • US $250.00 (our price)

Virtual Technologies and E-Collaboration for the Future of Global Business
Jingyuan Zhao (University of Toronto, Canada) and Joseph Richards (California State University, Sacramento, USA)
Business Science Reference • copyright 2022 • 273pp • H/C (ISBN: 9781668450277) • US $250.00 (our price)

IGI Global
PUBLISHER of TIMELY KNOWLEDGE

701 East Chocolate Avenue, Hershey, PA 17033, USA
Tel: 717-533-8845 x100 • Fax: 717-533-8661
E-Mail: cust@igi-global.com • www.igi-global.com

To the pioneers and innovators shaping the metaverse,

To the entrepreneurs and visionaries who dare to dream big,

To the researchers and scholars who seek to understand and demystify the complexities of this digital frontier,

To the policymakers and leaders who strive to harness the metaverse's potential for the greater good,

And to the future generations who will inherit the transformative power of the metaverse,

This book, New Business Frontiers in the Metaverse, is dedicated to you.

May it serve as a guiding light on your journey into the uncharted territories of the metaverse, and may it inspire you to seize the opportunities and overcome the challenges that lie within.

Together, let us shape the future of the metaverse and create a world that is more connected, more innovative, and more transformative than ever before.

Table of Contents

Detailed Table of Contents

The idea of the metaverse has drawn a lot of interest as the possible next big thing in the digital world. This chapter shows the underlying technologies guiding the development and uptake of various metaverse platforms through a thorough investigation of those platforms. It looks at how mixed reality, augmented reality, and virtual reality are coming together in the metaverse and explains how these platforms are promoting a smooth transition between the real and virtual worlds. It looks at how these platforms might completely change how consumers interact with products, content, and other crossing national borders and reinventing the digital economy. This chapter concludes by making a strong case for the metaverse's role as a spark for the digital age's revolutionary shift. It promotes a comprehensive comprehension of the metaverse's transformational potential and calls for more investigation into the complex effects it has on technology, society, and the world economy.'

The metaverse, a term coined to describe a collective virtual shared space that merges aspects of physical and digital realities, is rapidly evolving as a transformative concept in the realm of technology. This interconnected digital universe goes beyond traditional virtual reality, offering a seamless integration of immersive experiences, social interactions, and economic activities. As technology advances and connectivity deepens, the metaverse holds the promise of redefining how people work, socialize, and engage with the digital landscape, presenting both opportunities and challenges that resonate across various sectors of the interconnected world. The chapter will examine the idea of the metaverse through a thorough analysis of the literature and an examination of some of the fundamental elements of the metaverse, such as awareness and expectation levels and the expected domains to be covered in the metaverse in Indian culture along the extent of the metaverse awareness among Indians.

The fourth wave of computer innovation is now being driven by virtual reality (VR) and augmented reality (AR), two spatial, immersive technologies. The resulting pervasive computing paradigm, which this wave is expected to produce, can change (online) commerce, entertainment, distant employment, and education. This new paradigm is called the Metaverse. Although the metaverse is still in its infancy, history demonstrates how swiftly new technology can advance, potentially leaving those who lag. Digital reality technologies can transform the entertainment industry, remote work, education, marketing, and economics. Additionally, these technologies are starting to create a new paradigm for information exchange. The concept of the Metaverse has given rise to a new paradigm. While it appears that it will take years for the metaverse to reach its full potential, it is currently a phenomenon marked by the activity of hundreds of entrepreneurs who are making noise but producing no noteworthy results. According to many observers, the current uptick in activity by large tech businesses is assisting in bringing some order to the market's volatility by providing startup companies with the dependable mainstream customer bases they lack. In order to provide better and more integrated business processes, metaverse will provide a far more immersive experience to an organization's whole ecosystem of clients, staff, and partners. In light of this, the study's objectives are to comprehend the business prospects in the metaverse, identify relevant business strategies, and forecast future business developments in the metaverse. The study also looks at the challenges that companies have while integrating the metaverse, taking into account different scenarios.

There has been huge industry buzz and excitement for the metaverse. Metaverse is considered as a hyper-connected digital universe fundamentally changing business practices, including how consumers, brands, and firms will transact and interact in a space of virtual realities. Metaverse is beyond gaming, and now it is a 3D virtual world with rich and immersive experiences. It involves a digital economy where people can create, buy, and sell goods and services. Industry can also use the metaverse for educational purposes, collaboration, and social interactions. It's reasonable to assume that most consumers will eventually move to the metaverse, given that more than 75% of consumers worldwide rely on technology in their daily lives. Additionally, as new forms of content, consumption, and commerce become available, consumer behaviors will also change. While there is already some overlap between digital commerce and video games, the metaverse introduces virtual goods and services that elevate purchasing beyond the ordinary, opening up new revenue streams for companies and providing a means of reaching out to younger customer demographics. According to earlier research, most younger customers desire the ability to purchase their preferred brands online wherever they go, including on metaverse platforms. This research presents a multidisciplinary analysis of the metaverse, with an emphasis on how it can affect consumer behavior. The authors are putting forth a conceptualization model of the metaverse in this study, which includes the following essential components: it is digitally mediated, spatial, immersive, shared, and functions in real-time. They also discuss how these components affect consumer behavior. The knowledge of the metaverse marketplace and how it affects customer behavior has expanded as a result of this study. This research aids in determining how consumers' shopping habits are altered by the metaverse, a virtual environment, and how businesses might benefit from it.

Metaverse is an innovative and collective virtual shared space and internet application that integrates varied new technologies and has thereby impacted all diverse sectors. It has brought a disruption by integrating features of sociality, multi-technology, virtual reality (VR), augmented reality (AR), interoperability, and immersive technologies. It seems like an iteration of the internet, a 3D virtual space where humans experience virtual world beyond the imagination of reality. The intersection of Metaverse and Industry 4.0 represents a potential disruption across varied sectors like education, healthcare, travel, digital payments, digital currency, IT sector, and many other business services. In this chapter, a survey and study will be done on how metaverse and Industry 4.0 have disrupted these sectors and redefined their method to operate, innovate, collaborate, and flourish. Also, a study will be done on its challenges related to data security, privacy, and ethical use of advanced technologies, and a model framework will be proposed accordingly.

Architecture, throughout history, has reflected humanity's progress and cultural values. This chapter explores the exciting new frontier of architectural design in the metaverse. The metaverse offers a boundless canvas for architects, free from physical constraints. Imagine towering, organic structures or underwater cities. This digital realm also holds immense potential for functionality, from virtual classrooms to interactive retail spaces. However, challenges exist. User experience, bridging the gap between virtual and real, and ethical considerations all require thoughtful navigation. As the metaverse evolves, architects stand poised to shape virtual landscapes and potentially the future of real-world design and human interaction. This chapter also proposes the term ArchiVerse, an amalgamation of architecture and metaverse.

By offering customers a satisfying shopping experience, Hidesign has effectively expanded its market and taken the lead in the Indian luxury market within the framework of the experience economy. Some luxury brands are venturing into the metaverse platform to broaden their brand influence and distribution

The concept of the metaverse and immersive virtual reality experiences has gained significant attention in recent years. Metaverse refers to a parallel digital universe that combines both the physical and digital worlds, allowing multiple users to interact and engage in various activities. Immersive virtual reality experiences, on the other hand, involve users interacting with the virtual world through avatars that replace physical existence. Metaverse applications are designed to provide immersive online experiences by leveraging technologies such as virtual reality and augmented reality. Behavioural analysis is crucial in various fields. It aims to analyse human behaviour patterns, motive and mental health disorders. The chapter proposed a SaaS platform in order to meet the growing demand for accurate behavioural analysis in the metaverse. This platform aims to provide comprehensive behavioural analysis and insights within the metaverse, enabling them to make data-driven decisions and optimize their interactions with users in virtual environments.

Chapter 11
Challenges of a Metaverse Shaping the Future of Entrepreneurship 155
Muhammad Usman Tariq, Abu Dhabi University, UAE & University of Glasgow, Glasgow, UK

The chapter thoroughly examines the various barriers that affect how entrepreneurial endeavours develop in the ever-changing metaverse. Entrepreneurs face never-before-seen obstacles as the metaverse, defined by virtual surroundings and cutting-edge technology like augmented reality and virtual reality, develops as a revolutionary platform for business. The chapter thoroughly explores these issues, which include social and cultural factors, economic complexity, ethical problems, and technical limitations. The last section of the chapter offers a forward-looking outlook on potential developments and breakthroughs in the metaverse, highlighting the need for ongoing collaboration and adaptation between engineers, entrepreneurs, legislators, and legal experts to traverse this rapidly changing digital landscape successfully. It emphasizes how critical it is to resolve these issues to fully realize the metaverse's potential for creative and prosperous enterprise.

Chapter 12
Role of Blockchain Technology for User Data Security in Metaverse 174
Babita Jha, Christ University, India
Sushant Garg, Christ University, India
Tushar Singhal, Christ University, India

The metaverse is generating widespread interest among organizations of various scales, as companies acknowledge its capacity for profound transformation. Prominent organizations are actively adopting the metaverse concept to improve their operations and interact with clients in innovative and captivating manners. This chapter examines the vital function that blockchain plays in bolstering user data security as it explores the urgent problem of data breaches in the metaverse sector. The authors also carefully examine recent data breach cases in the metaverse sector, such as sandbox incursions, deepfake attacks, and digital avatar assaults. By outlining these practical difficulties, they make clear how urgent it is to come up with reliable ways to safeguard user data in the metaverse. The study findings have emphasized the dynamic and evolving nature of the metaverse industry, which is now undergoing substantial development and continuous exploration. They have also focused on significant blockchain technologies that demonstrate potential in ensuring data security.

Preface

Welcome to *New Business Frontiers in the Metaverse*, a pioneering exploration of the uncharted territories of the metaverse and its profound impact on entrepreneurship, society, and humanity. As the metaverse revolution gains momentum, it's crucial to move beyond the hype and delve into the complexities, challenges, and opportunities that lie within.

This book is designed to be a comprehensive guide for researchers, industry experts, academicians, policymakers, and students seeking to understand the metaverse's multifaceted dimensions. By addressing the myths and challenges head-on, we aim to provide a detailed roadmap for navigating the metaverse's entrepreneurial landscape.

Through a unique blend of technological, cultural, and ethical perspectives, we explore the integrated technologies that shape the metaverse, including NFTs, Web 4.0, augmented reality, virtual reality, and mixed reality. We examine the implications for public policy and unveil opportunities for entrepreneurial ventures across various industries, from business and services to education, healthcare, travel, tourism, hospitality, entertainment, digital payments, and digital currency.

As the metaverse continues to evolve, we invite scholars and visionaries to join us on this thought-provoking journey, as we explore the future pathways for entrepreneurial ventures and the revolutionary digital paradigm shift that is reshaping our world.

Let us embark on this exciting adventure together, as we uncover the new business frontiers in the metaverse. With its far-reaching impact on humanity, the metaverse holds the potential to reshape the fabric of our existence. It is our hope that this book will inspire entrepreneurs, policymakers, and individuals to harness the metaverse's transformative power and create a brighter future for all.

The metaverse is a revolutionary concept that has the potential to transform the way we live, work, and interact with each other. As we delve into the depths of this digital frontier, it's essential to understand the complexities and challenges that lie within. This book is designed to be a comprehensive guide, providing a detailed roadmap for navigating the metaverse's entrepreneurial landscape.

Through a unique blend of technological, cultural, and ethical perspectives, we explore the integrated technologies that shape the metaverse. From NFTs and Web 4.0 to augmented reality, virtual reality, and mixed reality, we examine the implications of these innovations on various industries and sectors. Our aim is to provide a holistic understanding of the metaverse's dimensions, enabling entrepreneurs, policymakers, and individuals to harness its transformative power.

As we venture into the metaverse, it's crucial to address the myths and challenges that shape its entrepreneurial landscape. From technological intricacies and cultural dynamics to ethical considerations and public policy implications, we tackle the complex issues head-on. Our goal is to provide a thought-provoking exploration, inspiring scholars and visionaries to join us on this exciting journey into the unknown.

Chapter 1: The idea of the metaverse has ignited considerable interest, positioning itself as a potential transformative force in the digital sphere. This chapter delves into the foundational technologies steering the development of various metaverse platforms, offering a comprehensive exploration of their emergence and adoption. It elucidates the convergence of mixed reality, augmented reality, and virtual reality within the metaverse, showcasing how these platforms facilitate seamless transitions between the physical and digital realms. Furthermore, it examines the potential ramifications of the metaverse on consumer interactions, product engagement, and the global digital economy, transcending national borders. The chapter advocates for a nuanced understanding of the metaverse's transformative potential and calls for further inquiry into its multifaceted impacts on technology, society, and the global economy.

Chapter 2: The metaverse, a conceptual fusion of physical and digital realities, is rapidly evolving as a pivotal technological concept. This chapter embarks on a thorough examination of the metaverse, shedding light on its immersive experiences, social dynamics, and economic implications. Through a comprehensive analysis of existing literature and critical elements such as awareness levels and cultural domains, the chapter illuminates the multifaceted nature of the metaverse. It underscores the potential to redefine societal interactions, work dynamics, and digital landscapes, presenting both opportunities and challenges across diverse sectors. With a focus on Indian culture and awareness, the chapter provides insights into the expanding domain of the metaverse and its profound impact on global connectivity.

Chapter 3: Digital reality technologies are poised to revolutionize numerous industries, from entertainment to economics. This chapter investigates the burgeoning phenomenon of the metaverse, which promises immersive experiences and integrated business processes. Through an exploration of business prospects, strategies, and future developments, the chapter navigates the evolving landscape of the metaverse. It delves into the challenges and opportunities facing organizations as they integrate the metaverse into their operations, offering valuable insights into potential scenarios and strategic considerations.

Chapter 4: Amidst the industry buzz surrounding the metaverse, this chapter presents a multidisciplinary analysis focusing on its impact on consumer behavior. Through a conceptualization model, it delineates essential components of the metaverse and their influence on consumer habits. By examining how virtual environments reshape shopping behaviors and brand interactions, the chapter provides valuable insights for businesses seeking to leverage the metaverse's potential. It contributes to a deeper understanding of consumer dynamics within virtual spaces and the opportunities they present for innovative marketing strategies.

Chapter 5: Building upon the discourse surrounding the metaverse, this chapter offers a comprehensive exploration of its impact on consumer behavior. By dissecting essential components of the metaverse and their implications for consumer interactions, the chapter provides valuable insights into the evolving digital landscape. Through an analysis of consumer shopping habits and virtual experiences, it elucidates the transformative potential of the metaverse for businesses. This research contributes to a nuanced understanding of consumer behavior within virtual environments and its implications for future market trends.

Chapter 6: Architecture enters a new frontier in the metaverse, offering boundless possibilities for design and functionality. This chapter explores the transformative potential of architectural design within digital realms, free from physical constraints. From towering structures to interactive spaces, the metaverse presents unprecedented opportunities for architectural creativity. However, challenges such as user experience and ethical considerations necessitate careful navigation. The chapter introduces the concept of ArchiVerse, envisioning a fusion of architecture and the metaverse, shaping virtual landscapes and potentially influencing real-world design paradigms.

Chapter 7: Luxury brands venture into the metaverse to expand their market reach and engage with a younger demographic. This chapter examines the strategic communication efforts of luxury firms in the metaverse, using Hidesign as a case study. Through an analysis of scene marketing strategies, the chapter offers actionable recommendations for luxury brand metaverse marketing. It underscores the importance of adapting to the evolving digital landscape and leveraging immersive experiences to enhance brand influence and market penetration.

Chapter 8: The integration of the metaverse in higher education heralds a transformative shift in pedagogies and entrepreneurial opportunities. This chapter explores the metaverse's influence on education, emphasizing integration, challenges, and ethical considerations. By immersing students in augmented and virtual reality experiences, the metaverse fosters collaboration and personalized learning. The chapter addresses technological barriers and ethical concerns, advocating for innovative approaches and collaborative partnerships between academia and industry. It underscores the transformative potential of the metaverse in higher education and the importance of ethical considerations in a rapidly evolving landscape.

Chapter 9: Phygital and metaverse strategies are reshaping various sectors, including tourism, by enhancing customer experiences. This chapter explores the emerging phenomenon of phygital tourism and its implications for the hospitality industry. Through a review of marketing literature, it identifies new opportunities for hotels and travel agencies to leverage metaverse technologies. By blending physical and digital experiences, tourism practitioners can create unique customer journeys, tapping into shifting consumer behaviors and preferences. The chapter offers insights into the evolving landscape of phygital tourism and its potential for innovation and growth.

Chapter 10: The metaverse presents unprecedented opportunities for immersive online experiences and behavioral analysis. This chapter introduces a Software-as-a-Service (SaaS) platform designed to meet the growing demand for accurate behavioral analysis within virtual environments. By leveraging technologies such as virtual reality and augmented reality, the platform offers comprehensive insights into user behavior, facilitating data-driven decision-making. The chapter underscores the importance of behavioral analysis in diverse fields and the potential of SaaS platforms to optimize interactions within the metaverse.

Chapter 11: Entrepreneurs navigate unique challenges in the dynamic landscape of the metaverse, marked by virtual environments and cutting-edge technologies. This chapter explores the barriers that entrepreneurs encounter, ranging from social and cultural factors to technical limitations. By examining these obstacles and offering forward-looking insights, the chapter highlights the importance of collaboration and adaptation in the metaverse. It emphasizes the need for interdisciplinary cooperation to realize the metaverse's potential for creative enterprise and prosperity.

Chapter 12: As organizations embrace the metaverse, safeguarding user data becomes imperative to prevent data breaches and ensure trust. This chapter explores the vital role of blockchain in enhancing data security within the metaverse sector. By analyzing recent data breach cases and emerging blockchain technologies, the chapter underscores the urgency of addressing data security challenges. It highlights the dynamic nature of the metaverse industry and the potential of blockchain solutions to mitigate risks and foster trust among users.

Chapter 13: The integration of digital strategies and the metaverse presents unique opportunities for Indian businesses in the post-COVID paradigm. This chapter constructs a comprehensive strategy for navigating the intricate Indian industry landscape, emphasizing the transformative potential of the metaverse. By connecting digital strategies to the evolving metaverse, the chapter offers stakeholders actionable insights for driving innovation and growth. It underscores the dynamic relationship between digital adoption and metaverse applications, paving the way for a new business paradigm in India.

Chapter 14: The metaverse holds immense potential for reshaping digital marketing strategies and consumer interactions. This chapter explores the synergy between the metaverse and digital marketing, highlighting opportunities for brands to engage with consumers in virtual spaces. By analyzing consumer participation and technological advancements, the chapter underscores the transformative role of the metaverse in shaping the future of digital marketing. It offers insights into the evolving digital landscape and the strategic implications for brands seeking to leverage immersive experiences and virtual interactions.

Chapter 15: The metaverse emerges as a transformative platform with vast potential across diverse industries, from gaming to healthcare. This chapter examines the possibilities and challenges associated with the metaverse for Industry 4.0, exploring its social, educational, scientific, and economic implications. By addressing key challenges such as resource management and decentralization, the chapter offers insights into harnessing the metaverse's potential for innovation and collaboration. It underscores the transformative impact of the metaverse on Industry 4.0 and the opportunities it presents for driving growth and advancement.

The metaverse holds the potential to reshape the fabric of our existence, and its impact on humanity will be far-reaching. As we explore the future pathways for entrepreneurial ventures, we uncover opportunities for growth, innovation, and transformation. From business and services to education, healthcare, travel, tourism, hospitality, entertainment, digital payments, and digital currency, the metaverse's influence will be felt across various sectors.

Join us on this pioneering adventure into the metaverse, as we uncover the new business frontiers and explore the endless possibilities that await us. With its revolutionary digital paradigm shift, the metaverse holds the key to a brighter future, and we invite you to be a part of this exciting journey. Together, let's shape the metaverse and create a world that's more connected, more innovative, and more transformative than ever before.

Shivani Inder
Chitkara Business School, Chitkara University, India

Shuchi Dawra
Chitkara Business School, Chitkara University, India

Kyla Latrice Tennin
College of Doctoral Studies, University of Phoenix, USA

Sandhir Sharma
Chitkara Business School, Chitkara University, India

Acknowledgment

Editorial Advisory Board

Shelli Brunswick, *Jharkhand Rai University, India*
Eve Logunova-Parker, *MIT Sloan School of Management, USA*
Jane Thomason, *University College London, UK & Centre for Blockchain, Dubai, UAE*

The creation of this book, *New Business Frontiers in the Metaverse*, would not have been possible without the contributions and support of numerous individuals and organizations.

First and foremost, we extend our gratitude to the researchers, industry experts, academicians, policymakers, and students who have shared their insights and expertise, shaping the content and direction of this book.

We acknowledge the pioneering work of metaverse developers, innovators, and entrepreneurs who are pushing the boundaries of this digital frontier.

We thank our editors, reviewers, and proofreaders for their meticulous efforts in refining the manuscript and ensuring the accuracy and clarity of the content.

We appreciate the support of our publishers, who have believed in the significance of this project and have provided the necessary resources to bring it to fruition.

Lastly, we dedicate this book to the visionaries and trailblazers who are shaping the metaverse and its entrepreneurial landscape, and to those who will join us on this exciting journey into the unknown. Thank you.

Shelli Brunswick, *Jharkhand Rai University, India*

Eve Logunova-Parker, *MIT Sloan School of Management, USA*

Jane Thomason, *University College London, UK & Centre for Blockchain, Dubai, UAE*

The metaverse has arrived, and it's transforming the world as we know it. This revolutionary digital frontier is redefining the fabric of business, society, and humanity at large. As entrepreneurs, policymakers, and individuals, we are faced with both unparalleled opportunities and unprecedented challenges. *New Business Frontiers in the Metaverse* is a timely and groundbreaking book that demystifies the complexities of this emerging landscape.

In this book, the authors take us on a journey through the uncharted territories of the metaverse, exploring its vast potential and addressing the myths and challenges that shape its entrepreneurial landscape. From the intricacies of integrated technologies like NFTs, Web 4.0, and augmented reality to the implications for public policy and entrepreneurial ventures across various industries, this book offers a comprehensive understanding of the metaverse's transformative power.

The metaverse is not just a technological shift; it's a cultural and societal revolution. It's a new dimension where human connection, creativity, and innovation converge. As we navigate this digital paradigm shift, it's essential to have a guide that not only illuminates the path ahead but also provides a deep understanding of the metaverse's underlying dynamics. *New Business Frontiers in the Metaverse* is that guide.

The authors' expertise and vision shine through in every chapter, offering a unique perspective on the metaverse's potential to reshape our world. Their exploration of blockchain applications, cyber fraud, data and identity security, digital twin technology, and future pathways for entrepreneurial ventures in the metaverse is both insightful and thought-provoking.

This book is not just a theoretical exploration; it's a practical guide for entrepreneurs, policymakers, and individuals seeking to navigate the metaverse's complexities. It's a call to action for those who want to seize the opportunities and overcome the challenges that lie within. The author's passion for the metaverse and its potential to transform humanity is contagious, inspiring readers to join the conversation and shape the future of this digital frontier.

New Business Frontiers in the Metaverse is more than just a book – it's an invitation to join a community of visionaries and innovators shaping the future of the Metaverse. It's a testament to the power of human creativity, innovation, and collaboration in the face of uncertainty and change.

As we embark on this exciting journey into the unknown, let us be guided by the wisdom and expertise shared in these pages. Let us embrace the metaverse's transformative power and shape its future with courage, creativity, and compassion. The metaverse is not just a technological revolution; it's a human revolution – a chance to redefine our relationships, our businesses, and our world.

In conclusion, *New Business Frontiers in the Metaverse* is a groundbreaking book that demystifies the complexities of the metaverse and offers a comprehensive understanding of its transformative power. It's a must-read for researchers, industry experts, academicians, policymakers, and students seeking to grasp the metaverse's far-reaching impact on business, education, healthcare, travel, tourism, hospitality, entertainment, digital payments, and digital currency. Join the conversation, and let the exploration begin!

Chapter 1
Metaverse Platforms:
New Age Revolution in Digital World

Sanjay Taneja
https://orcid.org/0000-0002-3632-4053
Graphic Era University (Deemed), India

Rishi Prakash Shukla
https://orcid.org/0000-0003-0854-7302
Chandigarh University, India

ABSTRACT

The idea of the metaverse has drawn a lot of interest as the possible next big thing in the digital world. This chapter shows the underlying technologies guiding the development and uptake of various metaverse platforms through a thorough investigation of those platforms. It looks at how mixed reality, augmented reality, and virtual reality are coming together in the metaverse and explains how these platforms are promoting a smooth transition between the real and virtual worlds. It looks at how these platforms might completely change how consumers interact with products, content, and other crossing national borders and reinventing the digital economy. This chapter concludes by making a strong case for the metaverse's role as a spark for the digital age's revolutionary shift. It promotes a comprehensive comprehension of the metaverse's transformational potential and calls for more investigation into the complex effects it has on technology, society, and the world economy.'

INTRODUCTION

A communal virtual shared place generated by the confluence of virtual and physical reality is referred to as the "Metaverse." Users may engage in real-time interaction with digital items and each other in this completely immersive and interactive digital world. Although the idea of the Metaverse has been around for a while, the development of virtual reality and technological breakthroughs in recent years have brought it a lot of attention.

DOI: 10.4018/979-8-3693-2422-6.ch001

A new research defines the Metaverse as a three-dimensional virtual and augmented reality environment representation where users may work, play, and interact synchronously with one another using personal avatars (Ali, 2023; Narin, 2021). Nevertheless, there isn't a synthesis of the research or agreement across studies on the the Metaverse's definition. The literature that has already been written about the metaverse is contradictory, presenting varying interpretations and attributes of the metaverse idea.

Customers and companies throughout the world may take advantage of the transformative opportunities and experiences provided by the Metaverse. It has the power to completely transform a number of industries, including healthcare, entertainment, and education. Nevertheless, there are drawbacks to the Metaverse as well, including worries about security, privacy, and morality. This is the allure of the metaverse – a place where the boundaries of possibility (Dionisio, Burns, & Gilbert, 2013)are pushed to their limits, and the digital and physical realms converge in a harmonious dance. But before we delve into the heart of this virtual wonderland, let's explore the genesis of this revolutionary concept.

HISTORICAL BACKGROUND AND EVOLUTION

Though it has garnered a lot of attention lately, the idea of the metaverse originated in early computer science and science fiction literature. Neal Stephenson first used the word "metaverse" in his 1992 book "Snow Crash," in which he imagined a virtual reality-based internet replacement. This made-up universe provided a venue for trade, social interaction, and entertainment, among other things. Since then, a lot of futurists, technologists, and businesspeople have been intrigued by the concept.

Virtual worlds like Second Life, which allowed users to build and interact with each other in a digital environment, first started to appear in the early 2000s. Although these platforms could not completely grasp the notion of the metaverse, they did provide the foundation for online social interactions and the creation of virtual economies In the 2010s, when advances in virtual reality (VR) and augmented reality (AR) technology started to offer more immersive and participatory experiences, the term "metaverse" attracted renewed interest. Businesses like Facebook, Google, and Microsoft began making significant investments in virtual reality and augmented reality with the goal of building global user-accessible, networked virtual environments.

Gaming, entertainment, and even finance have all turned their attention to the metaverse in recent years. Businesses like Roblox Corporation and Epic Games have created virtual places where people can engage in a variety of activities, such as gaming, socializing, and content production. Additionally, the development of decentralized virtual worlds where users may own and trade digital goods has been facilitated by the rise of blockchain technology. The COVID-19 pandemic expedited the advancement and assimilation of metaverse technology, as individuals pursued substitute means for remote socialization, employment, and leisure pursuits.

The metaverse was still in its infancy in 2022, when I last updated my knowledge, and a number of businesses and organizations were vying for prominence in this newly developing field. Future technological developments and greater funding for the metaverse are probably going to continue to influence how it develops, maybe creating a digital environment that is more immersive and linked than what is possible in the virtual world now.

Companies like Meta (formerly Facebook), Microsoft, and Epic Games have been at the forefront of this virtual renaissance, pouring billions of dollars into metaverse development. Their efforts have paved the way for the creation of immersive digital worlds, where users can interact, collaborate, and even conduct business in ways that transcend physical boundaries (Park & Kim, 2022).

IMPORTANCE OF THE METAVERSE IN THE DIGITAL WORLD

With its revolutionary paradigm change in how people connect, socialize, and do business in virtual settings, the metaverse is a prominent player in the digital world. The metaverse is an immersive and networked digital world that provides users with previously unheard-of chances to go beyond geographic borders and enjoy improved forms of entertainment, cooperation, and communication. It provides an environment that is conducive to creativity, enabling the development of dynamic and adaptable experiences that can accommodate a wide variety of tastes and interests. Furthermore, the metaverse offers new opportunities for distant cooperation, learning, and leisure activities, potentially upending conventional ideas of employment, education, and leisure. The gaming, entertainment, and retail industries are just a few of the areas that stand to change as more and more organizations incorporate the metaverse into their business plans. In the end, the metaverse marks a critical turning point in the development of the digital landscape by promoting a dynamic and networked virtual environment that has the capacity to revolutionize how people view and engage with the digital world. At the heart of the metaverse lies a convergence of cutting-edge technologies, each playing a crucial role in shaping this digital frontier (Lee et al., 2021). Blockchain technology offers a decentralized framework that is essential for the creation and management of digital assets (Ning et al., 2021), ensuring transparency and security in transactions. The use of blockchain enables users to have ownership and trade digital assets in a trustless environment, which is crucial for the economic viability of the metaverse. Furthermore, blockchain supports the implementation of smart contracts (Duan et al., 2021; Narin, 2021), which automate transactions and agreements, reducing the need for intermediaries and increasing efficiency and trust among participants.

UNDERSTANDING THE METAVERSE

Key Concepts: Virtual Reality, Augmented Reality, and Mixed Reality

1. **Virtual Reality (VR):** A computer-generated simulation of an environment that enables people to interact and fully submerge themselves in a synthetic, digital world is referred to as virtual reality. In order to experience virtual reality (VR), a user usually has to wear goggles or a head-mounted display (HMD) that covers their eyes and ears and blocks out the real environment in favor of a virtual one. VR technology provides a sensation of presence by monitoring the user's motions, enabling them to explore and interact with this virtual world as though they were there in person. Virtual reality (VR) finds widespread use in immersive gaming, training simulations, virtual tours, and other interactive experiences that attempt to replicate real-world settings or construct wholly imaginary ones.
2. **Augmented Reality (AR):**Augmented reality is the superimposition of digital data on top of real life or digital components over the physical environment. Using a smartphone, tablet, or AR glasses, users of AR technology can see computer-generated visuals, sounds, or other sensory upgrades integrated into their perspective of the real world. By adding more context, data, or interactive

digital pieces that mix in perfectly with the real environment, this technology enhances the user's perspective of the real world. Applications for augmented reality (AR) are wide-ranging and can encompass everything from interactive gaming and advertising to instructional resources, navigational assistance, and complicated data visualization.

3. **Combining Reality (MR):** A more sophisticated version of augmented reality called mixed reality allows users to interact with both the actual environment and digital material at the same time. MR makes it possible for virtual things to communicate with the actual world in real time, fusing the greatest features of the virtual and physical worlds to create a seamless, engaging experience. More complex and immersive interactions are made possible by this technology because digital items may be attached to real-world settings and react to occurrences. In a variety of industries, including design, engineering, healthcare, and education, mixed reality (MR) is widely employed to provide sophisticated simulations, training scenarios, and interactive visualizations that necessitate the fusion of virtual and physical aspects.

TECHNOLOGICAL UNDERPINNINGS

A convergence of cutting-edge technology forms the foundation of the metaverse, allowing for the construction of linked and immersive digital worlds. These technical underpinnings include blockchain, fast internet connectivity, artificial intelligence (AI), augmented reality (AR), virtual reality (VR), and virtual reality (VR), because it offers users a completely immersive and interactive digital experience and allows them to perceive and interact with virtual settings as if they were physically there, virtual reality plays a crucial role in the metaverse. Contrarily, augmented reality superimposes digital data on the real environment to improve the user's experience of reality and enable smooth transitions between the real and virtual worlds. An essential element of the metaverse is artificial intelligence, which makes it possible to create dynamic, lifelike virtual worlds. Algorithms powered by AI may improve user interaction and provide more realistic virtual environments, which improves the metaverse experience as a whole.

The decentralized and secure ledger system of blockchain technology promotes the growth of virtual economies in the metaverse. It gives consumers a sense of value and ownership within the virtual ecosystem by enabling the production, ownership, and exchange of virtual assets such as virtual currencies, virtual real estate, and virtual collectibles. Moreover, smooth and low-latency communication inside the metaverse is made possible by high-speed internet access, especially with the rollout of 5G networks. This allows for real-time interactions and data transfer across geographically distributed virtual settings.

Together, these technical foundations make up the metaverse's framework, allowing for the development of immersive, interactive, and networked digital places that might completely change the way people interact, communicate, and work together in virtual settings. With boundless opportunities for creativity, cooperation, and amusement, the metaverse is set to become an ever-more-essential component of the digital environment as these technologies develop.

CHARACTERISTICS OF A METAVERSE

A metaverse's immersive and linked nature, which redefines the digital experience for users, is characterized by a number of essential elements:

1. **Virtual Environment:** Generally, a metaverse provides a fully functional virtual environment that users may explore and engage with instantly. Various terrain, buildings, and other virtual constructions that mimic the actual world or wholly imagined settings are frequently included in this environment.
2. **Connectivity and Durability:** The capacity of a metaverse to effortlessly link several users in a permanent virtual area is one of its distinguishing characteristics. This facilitates ongoing exchanges, activities, and transactions, fostering a feeling of shared presence and allowing for real-time cooperation and communication.
3. **Configuration and User Development:** Users may design, alter, and customize their virtual personas, virtual worlds, and virtual items in metaverses. This feature encourages users to actively engage in their creativity and sense of ownership.
4. **Economics and Virtual Assets:** A lot of metaverses have their own economies in which users may buy, sell, and exchange virtual assets including virtual currency, digital commodities, and even land. The dynamics of the virtual economy frequently resemble those of actual markets, which has led to the creation of online marketplaces and the development of a special environment for virtual trade and entrepreneurship.
5. **Collaboration and Social Interaction:** The metaverse places a strong focus on collaborating and interacting with others. Within the virtual realm, users may participate in a range of social activities such as gaming, communication, and sharing of experiences, which helps to build a feeling of community and connectivity.
6. **Integration Across Platforms:** Metaverses frequently strive to be integrated with other digital platforms and technologies, such as conventional computing devices, augmented reality (AR), and virtual reality (VR). This incorporation enables smooth access for users across a variety of media, providing a more adaptable and welcoming user experience.
7. **Growth and Availability:** Metaverses are made to be easily navigable by users with different degrees of technological proficiency and to support a sizable user population. Because of its scalability, the virtual environment can accommodate a wide range of worldwide audiences while being inclusive and active.

THE IMPACT OF THE METAVERSE

Transforming Industries and Sectors

The rise of the metaverse has fundamentally changed a number of sectors and industries, including how companies run and engage with their clientele. The gaming business is one prominent sector undergoing significant change. The metaverse has made it possible to create extremely dynamic and immersive virtual worlds, which have promoted interesting gameplay and creative monetization strategies. Moreover, virtual concerts, events, and immersive narrative experiences have been made possible by the entertainment industry's use of the metaverse, completely changing how viewers interact with media.

The metaverse has created new opportunities for virtual shopping experiences in the retail sector, enabling customers to browse and buy goods in a vibrant and interactive online setting. This has widened the market and made things easier.

Furthermore, the establishment of virtual property and land ownership within virtual worlds is made possible by the metaverse, which is starting to permeate the real estate market. This might completely transform the real estate industry by offering a platform for online property development and investment possibilities. The metaverse has opened up new avenues for immersive and interactive learning in the field of education. It has made it possible to transmit educational information outside conventional time and space limits and to create virtual classrooms and training simulations.

Furthermore, the metaverse is affecting communication and cooperation across many industries by offering new venues for virtual meetings, remote collaborations, and international networking. This will have an impact on the nature of work in the future by enabling more inclusive and flexible employment models that can improve international cooperation by overcoming spatial constraints.

In general, the way companies and organizations interact with their consumers is changing fundamentally as a result of the integration of the metaverse across sectors and industries. This is encouraging innovation and opening up new avenues for growth and development in the digital age.

Entertainment and Gaming

Within the metaverse, gaming and entertainment are essential elements that greatly influence the immersive digital experiences that users can have. Within the metaverse, entertainment comprises a wide array of activities such as virtual performances, live events, and interactive storytelling that surpasses the confines of time and space. Through the utilization of cutting-edge virtual reality (VR) and augmented reality (AR) technology, the metaverse facilitates unparalleled user engagement with a diverse range of multimedia material, hence promoting a heightened feeling of immersion and involvement.

As a cornerstone of the metaverse, gaming gives users the chance to engage in intricate and captivating virtual worlds that go beyond conventional games. These digital spaces enable the development of complex, user-driven stories, encouraging a feeling of autonomy and social exchange amongst participants. In addition, the metaverse makes it easier for large-scale gaming communities to grow, where members may interact, compete, and explore enormous virtual worlds. The metaverse has made it possible for decentralized gaming economies to arise, wherein users may purchase, sell, and exchange in-game assets, obfuscating the distinction between virtual and actual economies. This is made possible by the incorporation of blockchain technology.

The metaverse's combination of gaming and entertainment has produced inventive and engaging experiences that appeal to a wide range of consumers, breaking down conventional barriers and opening up new avenues for sociability, interactive storytelling, and revenue generation. The combination of gaming and entertainment is set to completely change the digital leisure market as the metaverse develops, providing users a captivating and dynamic environment for artistic creation, interpersonal interaction, and interactive discovery.

Education and Training

Training and education in the metaverse provide a revolutionary method of teaching that makes use of immersive technology to produce engaging and dynamic learning environments. Through the integration of virtual reality (VR), augmented reality (AR), and mixed reality (MR) settings, the metaverse provides educators with an immersive and dynamic platform to impart knowledge, enable role-playing, and encourage learners to actively participate in learning. Students may escape the confines of conventional classrooms thanks to this immersive learning environment, which gives them access to interactive instructional modules, virtual labs, and realistic simulations that improve understanding and retention. Additionally, the metaverse promotes worldwide connectedness, making it possible for instructors and students to work together and share ideas without difficulty across large geographic distances. This encourages cross-border information sharing and cultural interaction, fostering a more inclusive and connected world. Furthermore, gamification and interactive components within the metaverse encourage motivation and active engagement, which makes learning more interesting and pleasurable for pupils. With its transformational and adaptable approach to learning that meets the many requirements and learning styles of students in the digital era, the metaverse has the potential to completely change the educational environment as it develops.

METAVERSE PLATFORMS

Key Players in the Metaverse Industry

Many major companies, from IT giants to creative entrepreneurs, are actively participating in the rapidly growing metaverse business. These entities have a significant impact on the metaverse's development, infrastructure, and user experience.

With their Oculus VR subsidiary, digital behemoths like Meta Platforms (previously Facebook) have contributed significantly to the advancement of virtual reality technology and are aiming to incorporate the metaverse into their social media networks. They have a distinct edge in establishing interactive and linked virtual places for people to engage in due to their substantial resources and skill in social networking.

In the metaverse market, businesses like as Epic Games—developers of the well-known game Fortnite—have also made a name for themselves. Their proficiency in creating They are in a position to investigate the metaverse's possibilities for gaming, social engagement, and virtual events thanks to its highly interactive and captivating virtual surroundings.

Roblox Corporation, a prominent participant in the metaverse, particularly when it comes to producing user-driven experiences and content, is best known for its user-generated game platform Roblox. Their platform has shown the value of user-generated content in reshaping virtual environments and establishing a thriving player and creator community.

In the metaverse market, cryptocurrencies and blockchain-based platforms have also advanced significantly. Blockchain technology is being used by projects like Decentraland and The Sandbox to facilitate the ownership and trade of virtual assets, giving users a feeling of digital ownership inside the metaverse. These platforms are creating the foundation for user-driven, decentralized virtual finances.

Additionally, businesses that specialize in mixed reality (MR) and augmented reality (AR), like Microsoft with its HoloLens and Magic Leap, are advancing the metaverse by fusing virtual and real-world aspects to create seamless mixed reality experiences.

Important participants in this developing sector include startups that concentrate on different facets of metaverse infrastructure, such as virtual asset exchanges, virtual world building tools, and virtual economy administration. Their inventions are crucial for laying the groundwork for a varied and welcoming metaverse environment.

Together, these major actors are propelling the metaverse's growth and uptake, influencing its technological environment, user interface, and possible industries for application. Their efforts are crucial to achieving the metaverse's full potential as a revolutionary digital world that will have a significant impact on how people interact with technology and engage with it in the future.

Comparing Metaverse Platforms

When comparing metaverse platforms, one must consider a number of important factors, such as technological prowess, user base, diversity of content, and accessibility. As of my most recent knowledge update in 2022, the top platforms in the metaverse included:

1. **Roblox**: Roblox is well-known for its concentration on games and user-generated content. It provides a wide range of virtual experiences that appeal to a broad user demographic, with kids and teens being its target audience. It fosters a thriving ecosystem powered by the community and offers easily accessible tools for content development.
2. **Instagram**: Fortnite, created by Epic Games, is now a diverse metaverse platform that mixes live events, social media, and gaming. With a large user base, it's well-known for its interesting in-game content, virtual concerts, and inventive gaming elements.
3. **Decentraland**: Using cutting-edge technology, Decentraland lets people develop, purchase, trade, and profit from virtual assets and land. Within its digital environment, it promotes user ownership and decentralization, enabling the creation of distinctive and adaptable virtual experiences.
4. **Horizon Facebook**: This Facebook-backed network emphasizes virtual reality experiences and social engagement. With a focus on social networking and communication, it seeks to offer a smooth and user-friendly interface that enables users to connect, create, and explore a variety of virtual settings.
5. **Microsoft Mesh**: Microsoft Mesh is a mixed reality platform that combines virtual and augmented reality technologies to enable users to engage in immersive and cooperative experiences. With an emphasis on corporate applications, its spatial computing capabilities enable remote collaboration, training, and productivity increase.

It is critical to evaluate these platforms' user interfaces, content production tools, device compatibility, privacy and security features, and capacity to promote communities and diverse types of engagement when contrasting them. Furthermore, taking into account the platform's monetization methods, scalability, and integration with cutting-edge technology might offer insightful information about their long-term sustainability and influence on the changing metaverse scene.

Building and Developing Within the Metaverse

Creating and sculpting virtual worlds, experiences, and digital assets that promote communication, cooperation, and trade within this immersive virtual world is the process of building and developing within the Metaverse. A variety of tasks are included in this process, such as the development of virtual currencies and assets, the design and implementation of virtual places, and the production of dynamic and captivating content that appeals to a wide range of user demographics.

Using cutting-edge technology like virtual reality (VR), augmented reality (AR), and 3D modeling tools to create immersive and interactive settings that give users a sense of presence and engagement is one of the most important parts of developing inside the Metaverse. Using these technologies, developers frequently create virtual landscapes, structures, avatars, and other digital assets that improve the overall user experience and enable smooth communication between users in the Metaverse.

Additionally, social and collaborative capabilities must be integrated into the Metaverse's development process in order to allow users to co-create, interact, and communicate in shared virtual places. This promotes a feeling of community and makes it possible for group projects, get-togethers, and enjoyment in the digital sphere.

A key component of the Metaverse is the growth of virtual markets and economies, which enable users to purchase, sell, and exchange virtual products and services as well as digital assets. Users may now take part in a dynamic digital economy and companies can monetise their goods in innovative ways thanks to this.

Challenges and Opportunities for Metaverse Platforms

As metaverse systems develop and change the digital world, they provide special problems as well as exciting opportunities. Safeguarding users' privacy and security in these virtual settings is a major concern. With the increasing integration of the metaverse into everyday life, worries about cybersecurity risks, identity theft, and data protection are becoming more and more relevant. In addition, striking a balance between user-generated content and platform policies is difficult since platforms have to deal with problems like copyright violations, content monitoring, and creating a welcoming and safe online community.

Metaverse platforms need to overcome extra obstacles like interoperability and standards. A coherent and integrated metaverse experience depends on the smooth integration of diverse virtual settings and technology. Nonetheless, attaining compatibility across various platforms and technologies continue to be a logistical and technological hurdle that calls for coordinated industry cooperation and the creation of uniform standards.

Conversely, the metaverse offers a plethora of prospects that have the potential to stimulate innovation and expansion in various industries. Businesses have the chance to interact with customers in fresh and meaningful ways thanks to the possibilities of immersive advertising and e-commerce, which may result in the creation of new marketing plans and income streams. The metaverse also presents opportunities for the development of virtual real estate, making it possible to create and make money from online venues for social events, events, and virtual commerce.

Metaverse systems have the potential to enhance education and remote collaboration by offering dynamic and immersive settings for learning, coaching, and remote teaming. These online resources can help worldwide cooperation and information exchange, promoting a more linked and approachable educational process. Furthermore, the metaverse has the power to completely transform games and entertainment by providing users with never-before-seen chances for interactive adventures, immersive narrative, and group virtual travels.

Overall, the metaverse offers a promising frontier for innovation and growth across various industries, presenting special opportunities for businesses, creators, and users to interact in a dynamic and interconnected digital world, even though issues like security, interoperability, and content management still exist.

LITERATURE REVIEW

A thorough analysis of the body of research on the metaverse indicates a rapidly developing topic with a wide range of multidisciplinary studies and discussions. A comprehensive understanding of the conception, evolution, and consequences of the metaverse has been facilitated by the contributions of scholars from a variety of fields, including computer science, sociology, psychology, economics, and media studies.

The literature that now exists frequently explores the metaverse's historical development, following its inception from early science fiction to modern applications in virtual and augmented reality. Scholars have conducted an analysis of the metaverse's cultural, social, and economic ramifications, emphasizing its capacity to transform interpersonal relationships, consumer conduct, and societal frameworks. Additionally, they have looked at the psychological effects of extended use of virtual worlds, examining how identity development, social interactions, and general wellbeing may be affected.

Additionally, the literature highlights the metaverse's technological foundations, concentrating on developments in virtual reality, augmented reality, blockchain technology, and artificial intelligence that have aided in the creation of the metaverse. Scholars have examined aspects including scalability, interoperability, security, and user experience while evaluating the technological potential and problems of building and managing immersive and networked virtual worlds.

The assessment also emphasizes how the metaverse is being used in a variety of fields, including as business, education, gaming, entertainment, and healthcare as mentioned in Fig. 1. Research has looked at how the metaverse can change various industries and how it may help provide new opportunities for consumer interaction, learning, and teamwork. Researchers have also examined the metaverse's ethical and legal ramifications, addressing issues with data privacy, digital rights management, and virtual environment governance.

Overall, the thorough analysis of the body of research highlights the metaverse's complexity and significant influence on modern life. It provides a comprehensive knowledge of the potential, problems, and consequences connected with the ongoing growth and integration of the metaverse into our digital world and acts as a basis for future scholarly investigation.

EXPLORATION OF KEY CONCEPTS, DEVELOPMENTS, AND DEBATES

For a thorough grasp of the metaverse's complex structure and ramifications, it is important to explore significant ideas, innovations, and discussions around it. The integration of immersive technology to construct linked digital worlds, as well as virtual reality (VR) and augmented reality (AR), are key concepts in the metaverse setting. These ideas highlight the fundamental ideas behind developing a smooth, interactive virtual environment that replicates interactions and experiences in the real world.

Technological innovations like as the widespread use of high-fidelity VR headsets, haptic feedback systems, and spatial computing have propelled the metaverse's fast progress. Because of these advancements, virtual experiences are now more realistic and immersive, which has resulted in the creation of complicated virtual economies, digital asset ownership, and other virtual socializing models. The metaverse has also spurred discussions on a range of moral, societal, and financial problems. These discussions center on issues like data security and privacy, digital ownership rights, the viability of virtual economies, and the effects of extended digital immersion on social dynamics and mental health. Furthermore,

Figure 1. Virtual commerce technology
Source: Authors Compilations

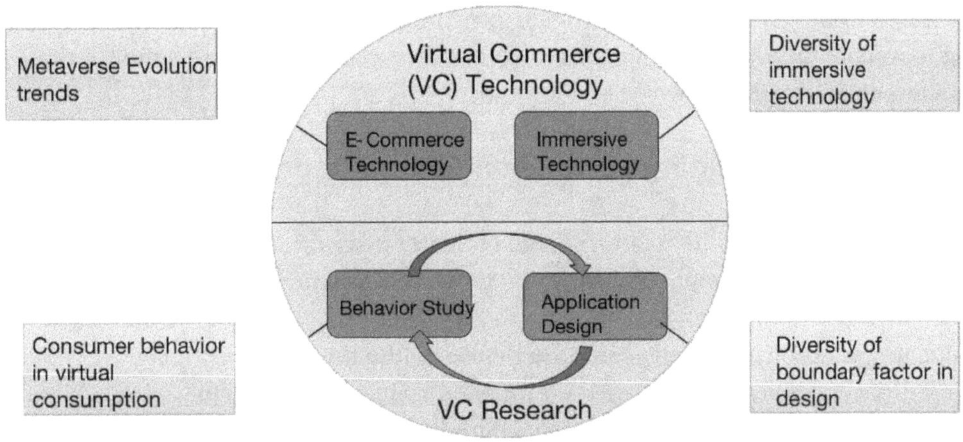

conversations concerning inclusion, accessibility, and the digital divide have surfaced, emphasizing the necessity of guaranteeing fair access to the metaverse and its advantages for a variety of demographics.

Furthermore, discussions on the metaverse's possible effects on established businesses and social mores have been sparked. These include changes to work environments, altered leisure and media consumption habits, and a blurring of lines between the real and virtual worlds. These conversations highlight the necessity of thorough legal frameworks, moral principles, and industrial standards to traverse the complicated effects of the metaverse's extensive use and incorporation into many aspects of modern life.

In summary, delving into these fundamental ideas, advancements, and discussions surrounding the metaverse offers a sophisticated comprehension of its revolutionary capacity, obstacles, and consequences for people, enterprises, and the community at large; consequently, it establishes the foundation for knowledgeable choices and conscientious growth in this ever-changing digital terrain.

Explanation of the Chosen Research Approach (Qualitative, Quantitative, or Mixed Methods)

The choice of research methodology for metaverse studies is critical in determining the scope and depth of the investigation. Applying a qualitative research methodology would be very advantageous for examining the intricate and multifaceted facets of the metaverse. This method gives researchers a deep grasp of the social, cultural, and psychological ramifications of interacting with the metaverse by allowing them to explore the subjective experiences, perceptions, and actions of people within virtual worlds.

Interviews, focus groups, and ethnographic studies are examples of qualitative research techniques that can help with a thorough investigation of users' experiences, motives, and difficulties navigating the metaverse. Researchers can uncover new themes, patterns, and cultural dynamics through qualitative data analysis, which advances our understanding of the metaverse phenomena as a whole. This method also allows for the collection of many viewpoints and voices from users, artists, and stakeholders by academics, which makes it possible to present the effects of the metaverse on culture, society, and personal well-being in a comprehensive and contextually rich way.

Scholars can get important insights into the social interactions, identity development, and community dynamics that occur inside virtual worlds by placing an emphasis on qualitative research. Additionally, qualitative research makes it possible to investigate intricate occurrences that quantitative methods could miss, leading to a more thorough and nuanced understanding of the metaverse's multifarious character and its ramifications for the digital world and beyond.

Summarization of Key Findings and Their Implications

A metaverse-based summary of the main findings indicates a significant influence on many facets of industry and society. The study emphasizes how the metaverse has the power to completely change how people interact with one another by providing a vibrant, immersive virtual environment where people may communicate, work together, and share experiences without being constrained by geography. The results also highlight how the metaverse will significantly influence how business and entertainment are conducted in the future, with virtual economies and digital assets emerging as viable market alternatives. These findings imply a paradigm shift in the way organizations approach customer interaction, requiring a reassessment of conventional approaches in order to take use of the metaverse's potential for creative and customized customer experiences. The study also emphasizes how important it is to include ethical and legal frameworks in guarantee user security, privacy, and safety in the metaverse while highlighting the necessity of appropriate management and supervision. It is imperative that stakeholders from many sectors comprehend these crucial discoveries and their ramifications in order to successfully and sustainably leverage the metaverse's transformational potential.

Recommendations for Future Studies and Practical Applications

Suggestions for further research and useful uses in the metaverse field are essential for its continuous advancement and incorporation into other industries. First and foremost, studies in the future need to concentrate on comprehending the social and psychological ramifications of extended participation in the metaverse, including how it affects relationships, conduct, and general wellbeing. This might entail doing multidisciplinary study combining sociology, psychology, and human-computer interaction studies to guarantee a thorough grasp of how the metaverse affects people individually and as a society.

It's also crucial to investigate the metaverse's possible uses outside of entertainment and games. This means looking into its application in real-world settings including professional training, healthcare, and education. Future research might focus on creating immersive learning environments that use the metaverse to establish dynamic and captivating learning spaces. Further study might focus on using the metaverse for remote patient care and telemedicine, which would allow medical professionals to give individualized, easily accessible treatment to anyone anywhere in the globe.

Furthermore, it is critical to overcome the technological problems posed by the metaverse, such as those pertaining to data security, interoperability, and scalability. Future research should focus on creating strong frameworks and standards that enable smooth interaction and integration between diverse virtual worlds, guaranteeing users across a range of platforms and devices a consistent and integrated metaverse experience.

The metaverse may find useful applications in fields including digital asset management, e-commerce, and virtual collaboration. Companies might investigate how the metaverse can be used to develop creative marketing and sales tactics, providing immersive and engaging encounters with clients. Furthermore, the incorporation of blockchain technology into the metaverse has the potential to enable safe ownership and exchange of digital assets, hence promoting the emergence of virtual economies and decentralized markets.

In general, the ethical, sociological, and technological aspects of the metaverse should be given priority in future research and practical implementations. This will promote responsible and inclusive growth that benefits people, communities, and industries equally.

REFERENCES

Ali, S. A. (2023). *Metaverse Marketing vs Digital Marketing*. Academic Press.

Dionisio, J. D. N., Burns, W. G., & Gilbert, R. (2013). 3D virtual worlds and the metaverse: Current status and future possibilities. *ACM Computing Surveys*, *45*(3), 1–38. Advance online publication. doi:10.1145/2480741.2480751

Duan, H., Li, J., Fan, S., Lin, Z., Wu, X., & Cai, W. (2021). Metaverse for Social Good: A University Campus Prototype. *MM 2021 - Proceedings of the 29th ACM International Conference on Multimedia*, 153–161. 10.1145/3474085.3479238

Duan, H., Li, J., Fan, S., Lin, Z., Wu, X., & Cai, W. (2021). Metaverse for social good: A university campus prototype. *Proceedings of the 29th ACM International Conference on Multimedia*, 153–161. 10.1145/3474085.3479238

LeeL.-H.BraudT.ZhouP.WangL.XuD.LinZ.HuiP. (2021). *All One Needs to Know about Metaverse: A Complete Survey on Technological Singularity, Virtual Ecosystem, and Research Agenda*. Retrieved from http://arxiv.org/abs/2110.05352

Narin, N. G. (2021). A Content Analysis of the AIDS Media. *Journal of Metaverse*, *1*(1), 17–24. https://lens.org/132-852-388-772-732

NingH.WangH.LinY.WangW.DhelimS.FarhaF.DaneshmandM. (2021). A Survey on Metaverse: the State-of-the-art, Technologies, Applications, and Challenges. Retrieved from http://arxiv.org/abs/2111.09673

Park, S. M., & Kim, Y. G. (2022). A Metaverse: Taxonomy, Components, Applications, and Open Challenges. *IEEE Access : Practical Innovations, Open Solutions*, *10*, 4209–4251. doi:10.1109/ACCESS.2021.3140175

ADDITIONAL READING

Bina, O., Inch, A., & Pereira, L. (2020). Beyond techno-utopia and its discontents: On the role of utopianism and speculative fifiction in shaping alternatives to the smart city imaginary. *Futures*, *115*, 102475. doi:10.1016/j.futures.2019.102475

Chapter 2
Introduction to Metaverse:
Concept and Evolution

Oindrila Chakraborty
J.D. Birla Institute, India

ABSTRACT

The metaverse, a term coined to describe a collective virtual shared space that merges aspects of physical and digital realities, is rapidly evolving as a transformative concept in the realm of technology. This interconnected digital universe goes beyond traditional virtual reality, offering a seamless integration of immersive experiences, social interactions, and economic activities. As technology advances and connectivity deepens, the metaverse holds the promise of redefining how people work, socialize, and engage with the digital landscape, presenting both opportunities and challenges that resonate across various sectors of the interconnected world. The chapter will examine the idea of the metaverse through a thorough analysis of the literature and an examination of some of the fundamental elements of the metaverse, such as awareness and expectation levels and the expected domains to be covered in the metaverse in Indian culture along the extent of the metaverse awareness among Indians.

INTRODUCTION

The metaverse is becoming more and more of a reality as technology develops. The distinctions between the real world and the virtual world are getting more hazy as augmented reality and virtual reality grow in sophistication. People will be able to design and alter their own virtual environments, communicate with others in real time, and even take part in virtual marketplaces in this new metaverse. There is an infinite amount of possibilities and boundless opportunity for creativity. But this new territory also presents new difficulties. For example, how will security and privacy be handled in the metaverse? What laws will be required to guarantee morality and justice in virtual economies? As we advance into this new digital era, all of these questions will need to be answered. However, one thing is certain: the metaverse has the power to alter how we work, live, and engage with the world. The future has countless possibilities as the lines separating the real and virtual worlds becoming increasingly blurry and we get closer to realizing this with every new technical development and incredible visions.

DOI: 10.4018/979-8-3693-2422-6.ch002

Imagine a society in which juggling work, recreation, socializing, and property ownership comes naturally to us. a stunning and engrossing virtual world where it is impossible to tell the difference between reality and the virtual world. This is what the metaverse is all about - the next big thing in internet that has the power to completely turn around the way we live.

The term "Metaverse" refers to a conceptual version of the internet that allows users to access persistent online 3-D virtual environments using both virtual and augmented reality headsets and traditional personal computers.

While metaverses are already existing in some limited form, such as virtual worlds and video games, a fully developed metaverse is still some ways off. Science fiction writer Neal Stephenson first used the word "Metaverse" in his 1992 book Snow Crash. According to the book, the metaverse is a communal virtual environment where users can communicate with one other and with virtual items. Although Stephenson's metaverse vision is still mostly unmet, the idea has gained popularity as technology has evolved in recent years. As evident, the metaverse is still in its nascent stages of development, but it is already having an impact on our lives (Beckmann and Böhm, 2022). For example, many companies are using virtual reality and augmented reality to train their employees (Walmart, Chipotle, US Army etc.) or to give customers a preview of their products (IKEA, Amazon, Gucci, Sephora, Google, Disney, L'Oréal etc.). The metaverse is also being used to create new forms of entertainment, such as virtual concerts and sporting events. Many people refer to the metaverse as the next stage of the internet's development. With virtual reality (VR) and augmented reality (AR) headsets, users will be able to fully immerse themselves in the metaverse as an alternative to communicate with the internet through a screen. This will make it possible to work, play, and socialize in new and more engaging ways. Although the idea of the metaverse has been around for many years, it has only lately gained popularity as a topic of conversation. Numerous causes contribute to this, such as the growing acceptance of VR and AR, the emergence of new technologies like blockchain and non-fungible tokens (NFTs), and the growing curiosity about virtual worlds. Facebook switched its name as a part of their rebranding and reposition decision to Meta in 2021 to reflect its dedication to creating the Metaverse. In addition to making significant investments in VR and AR technologies, Meta is developing new strategies for generating income from the metaverse, like virtual goods and advertising. In the metaverse, other businesses are also making investments. For instance, Microsoft is creating HoloLens, a VR platform of its own. Google is also developing AR and VR. In this manner, if the metaverse continues to develop, it is likely to become even more integrated into our daily lives with the intertwined corporate interventions in every spheres with or without realising it. We may one day use the metaverse to work, go to school, shop, socialize and beyond. The metaverse could also provide new and innovative ways to learn and create with interactive and participative arbitration.

METAVERSE IN EVERYDAY LIVES

There could be numerous ways to assimilate metaverse in everyday lives of people in the coming future, starting from childhood needs to geriatric pedestal. Some of the possibilities are given below and depicted further through Figure 1:

(a) Education

Students could take virtual field trips to historical sites or museums. They could also participate in virtual labs and simulations (Mystakidis, 2022).

(b) Work

Employees could collaborate on projects in virtual workspaces. They could also attend virtual meetings and training sessions. As Narin (2021) noted, the metaverse could help individuals work more productively and successfully by offering new tools and platforms for collaboration.

(c) Socializing

Friends and family could meet up in virtual worlds to chat, play games, or watch movies together. As Damar (2021) implied, the metaverse may offer new and more immersive methods to communicate and connect with friends and family.

(d) Shopping

Customers could try on clothes or furniture virtually before they buy them. They could also visit virtual stores from all over the world.

(e) Entertainment

People could attend virtual concerts, sporting events, and other live performances. They could also play virtual games and explore virtual worlds.

(f) Reduced Environmental Impact

The metaverse could reduce the need for travel and other activities that have a negative impact on the environment, as Stephenson (1992) envisioned in his novel *Snow Crash.*

BACKGROUND OF THE CONCEPT: METAVERSE AND ITS EVOLUTION

The concept of the metaverse, an online environment that links our digital and physical realms, has been simmering for many years, encouraged by science fiction and technical developments. However, pinpointing its precise origin becomes like to navigating a maze of related concepts and inventions. Below is an approximate and chronological idea of the probable historical backdrop for the metaverse:

Figure 1. Showing the integration of metaverse in everyday lives
(Source: Author)

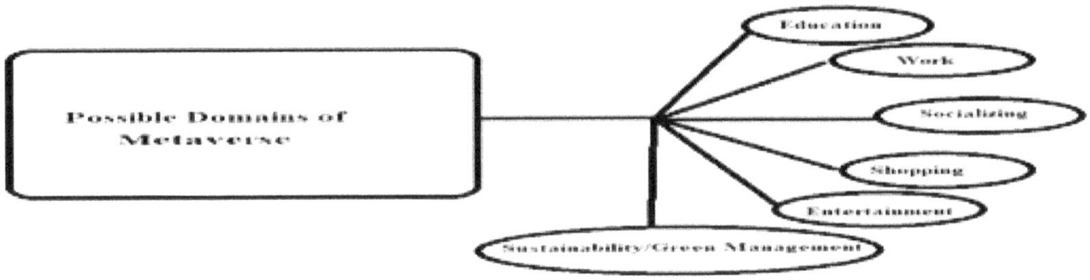

A) Early Seeds (1960s-1980s)

In science fiction arena, Neal Stephenson's 1992 novel "Snow Crash" and Vernor Vinge's 1981 short story "True Names" are often credited with popularizing the term "Metaverse" and depicting immersive virtual worlds. The earliest virtual reality (VR) and augmented reality (AR) have been documented with the developments of technologies, like the VPL Research Eyegear (1989) and Nintendo Virtual Boy (1995) and laid the groundwork for immersive experiences in the similar field. Afterwards, online platforms like Second Life (2003) and massively multiplayer online games (MMOGs) like World of Warcraft (2004) also offered early glimpses into virtual communities and economies.

B) Convergence and Acceleration (1990s-2010s)

User-generated content and interconnectedness — two fundamental and key facets of the metaverse — were made possible by the widespread adoption, growth, and development of the internet and Web 2.0. The boundaries between the actual and virtual worlds became increasingly hazy with the introduction and steady ascent of social media sites like Facebook and the developments in online gaming, such as cloud computing and virtual reality headsets like Oculus Rift (2012). Decentralized ownership and economies were introduced with the rise of blockchain technology and cryptocurrencies such as Bitcoin, which could have implications for the Metaverse.

C) Metaverse Mania (2020s Onwards)

With Facebook's 2021 rebranding to Meta, business and public interest in the development of a metaverse platform surged. With platforms like Decentraland, The Sandbox, and Roblox gaining popularity, investments in metaverse - related technology and businesses are also booming. There are still disagreements concerning the metaverse's boundaries, governance, and technology. Talks centre on combining different technologies—such as haptics, VR, AR, and AI — to seamlessly combine digital and real-world experiences.

It is difficult to identify the exact genesis of metaverse, yet it is the result of numerous technology developments, societal movements, and imaginative concepts. Future developments are expected to be dynamic and ever-changing, influenced by user preferences, advances in technology, and moral issues. The metaverse is still under development, but it's generally described as a network of interconnected

3D virtual worlds that people can access through avatars. These worlds can be anything from realistic simulations of our own planet to fantastical alien landscapes. Within the metaverse one can:

A) ***Interact with others:*** Meet up with friends and family from anywhere in the world, attend virtual concerts and conferences, or even collaborate on projects in real-time.
B) ***Explore and Experience:*** Visit virtual replicas of famous landmarks, embark on epic quests in fantasy worlds, or simply relax on a virtual beach.
C) ***Work and Create:*** Attend virtual meetings, conduct business transactions, or unleash your creativity by building your own virtual spaces and experiences.
D) ***Own and Trade:*** Purchase virtual land, clothing, and other digital assets using cryptocurrencies, and even create your own businesses within the metaverse. Figure 2 summarises the activities carried out with the metaverse.

Figure 2. Showing the activities carried out through metaverse
(Source: Author)

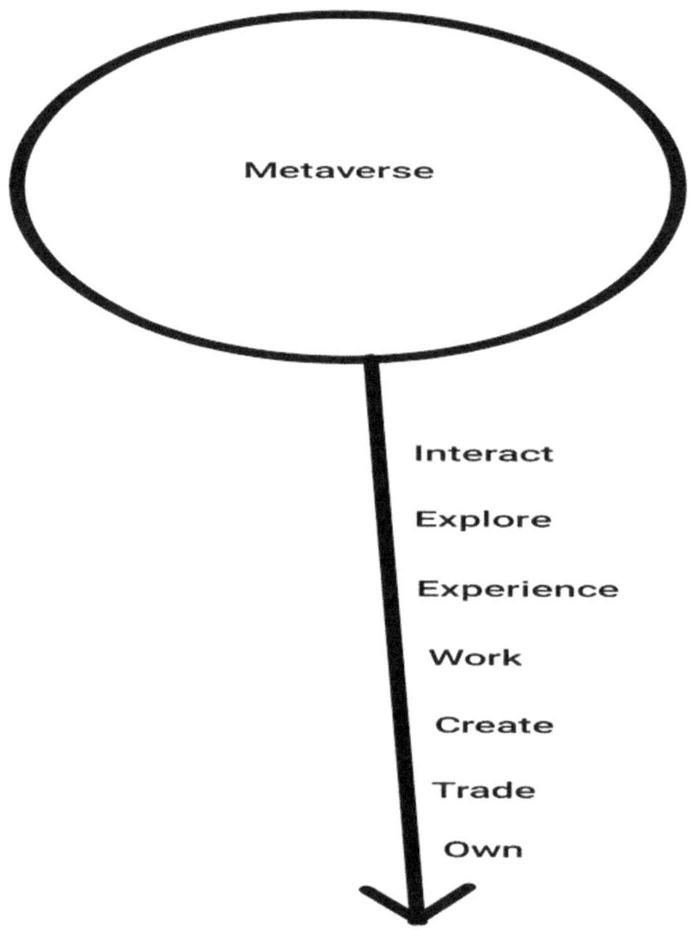

FUNDAMENTAL CONCEPTS OF METAVERSE

As already highlighted, the term "Metaverse" has transcended the realm of science fiction, captivating headlines and igniting fervent discussions across diverse disciplines. This chapter delves into the contemporary literature along with diverse definitions surrounding the metaverse, unearthing both its alluring promises and potential perils.

The metaverse is an evolving digital realm that combines augmented reality (AR), virtual reality (VR), and the internet to create immersive, interconnected experiences. In this expansive virtual space, users can interact with computer-generated environments and each other in real-time, transcending traditional boundaries of physical space. The concept of the metaverse is gaining traction as technology advances, offering a multifaceted landscape for social interaction, gaming, commerce, education, and beyond. As discussions and developments in the metaverse continue to unfold, it holds the potential to redefine how we perceive and engage with the digital world. Within the metaverse, individuals can create personalized avatars, explore diverse landscapes, and participate in collaborative activities. This digital frontier is not limited to entertainment; it's becoming a platform for innovative business solutions, decentralized economies, and new modes of communication. As companies invest in metaverse development and technology continues to evolve, the metaverse is poised to reshape our online experiences, offering a glimpse into a future where the boundaries between the physical and virtual worlds blur, providing new possibilities for human connection and creativity. Moreover, the metaverse raises intriguing questions about identity, privacy, and governance in this evolving digital space. As users contribute to and shape the metaverse, discussions around standards, ethics, and regulations become crucial. The metaverse is not just a singular entity but a tapestry of interconnected virtual spaces, each with its unique characteristics and possibilities. It beckons as a canvas for innovation, inviting individuals and industries to explore uncharted territories and collaborate in ways that were once unimaginable. As we navigate this transformative landscape, the metaverse stands as a testament to the ongoing fusion of technology and human imagination.

A) Defining the Elusive

Pinning down a precise definition of the metaverse remains a contentious issue as it is defining the elusive. It is often envisioned as a hyper-immersive 3D online world, as it is multifaceted in nature with the interplay between immersive technologies, block chain-based economies, and evolving social interactions that constitute the metaverse experience. The term "Metaverse" has been defined in various ways across literature, often emphasizing a collective virtual shared space.Researchers like Castronova (2005) and Damer (2008) have contributed to conceptualizing the metaverse as a persistent, immersive, and user-driven digital environment.

B) Transformative Visions

The potential applications of the metaverse paint a tantalizing picture which is envisioned as an immersive learning environments, fostering deeper engagement and personalized learning for students and revolutionizing other sectors like healthcare through virtual surgeries, remote consultations, and AI-powered medical diagnostics. Even in advertising and performing arts related industries, it is painting a vibrant future for the creative segments with virtual concerts and interactive storytelling experiences blurring the lines between audience and participant.

C) Looming Shadows

But amidst so much of the excitements, it comes with a caution . The digital divide threatens to exacerbate existing inequalities, potentially rendering the metaverse a playground for the privileged. Excessive immersion raises concerns about addiction, there is a vulnerability of privacy and the potential for manipulation in persistent virtual worlds.

D) Navigating the Uncharted

The nascent nature of the metaverse necessitates robust regulatory frameworks. Existing legal frameworks may not suffice for issues like virtual crime and hate speech. Collaborative efforts between governments, tech companies, and researchers are crucial to bridge this gap and establish responsible governance mechanisms.

THE TECHNOLOGIES BUILDING THE METAVERSE

The metaverse is being powered by a convergence of cutting-edge technologies. Researchers have investigated the technological requirements and challenges associated with building and maintaining the metaverse (Sarwar et al., 2021). The role of augmented reality (AR) and virtual reality (VR) technologies in shaping the user experience within the metaverse has been explored (Milgram & Kishino, 1994).

A) ***Virtual Reality (VR):*** Creates immersive experiences that make people feel like they are physically present in the virtual world. Virtual Reality (VR) is a simulated experience that immerses a person in a completely computer-generated environment. Unlike augmented reality, VR doesn't blend with the real world; it replaces it entirely. It is completely immersive. VR uses headsets or goggles to shut out the real world and create a convincing illusion of being in a virtual environment. VR can create the sensory experience by stimulating the multiple senses, including sight, sound, and even touch, further enhancing the feeling of immersion. One can interact with the virtual environment in various ways, depending on the technology and application. One might move around, manipulate objects, or have other experiences within the virtual world. VR simulations can transport one to fantastical landscapes, historical periods, or even outer space. It is generally used in gaming, training, education, and various other fields. It works through VR headsets with screens close to the eyes, displaying different images for each eye to create a 3D effect. Some of these VR headsets also have trackers to follow the head movements of the users and adjust the view accordingly. VR software generates the 3D environment and responds to the interactions of the users in real-time. It may require additional equipments like gloves, suits, or treadmills to enhance the feeling of immersion by providing haptic feedback or tracking of the full body movements of the users. VR applications can revolutionize gaming and immersive entertainment industries. It can also have academic, training and therapeutic usage.

B) ***Augmented Reality (AR):*** Augmented reality, or AR for short, is a technology that overlays computer-generated content onto the real world. This creates an interactive experience where the digital and physical worlds blend seamlessly, combining both. AR doesn't replace the real world, but rather enhances it with digital elements like images, sounds, and other sensory data. One can interact with the virtual content in real-time, manipulating it or responding to it within the physical environment. For example, if in Pokemon Go, virtual creatures appear in the real-world surroundings through the phone camera, or IKEA Place, where one can see how furnitures would look in their home before they buy them. AR needs devices like smartphones, tablets, or specialized headsets to display the digital content and track the movements in the real world. Also, it needs software support like Apps and programmes to use sensors, cameras, and processing power to understand the present environment and to position the virtual content accurately. It helps in enhanced learning, improved productivity and engaging entertainment.

C) ***Artificial Intelligence (AI):*** Powers virtual assistants, generates realistic environments and characters, and personalizes the metaverse experience. AI refers to the intelligence exhibited by machines, as opposed to the natural intelligence of living beings. It involves the ability to perform tasks typically associated with human intelligence, such as reasoning, learning, problem-solving, and decision-making through machine learning, deep learning and symbolic AI.

D) ***Blockchain:*** Enables secure ownership and trade of digital assets within the metaverse. The Figure 3 shows the diverse technological advancements contributing to metaverse.

Figure 3. Showing the key technologies building the metaverse
(Source: Author)

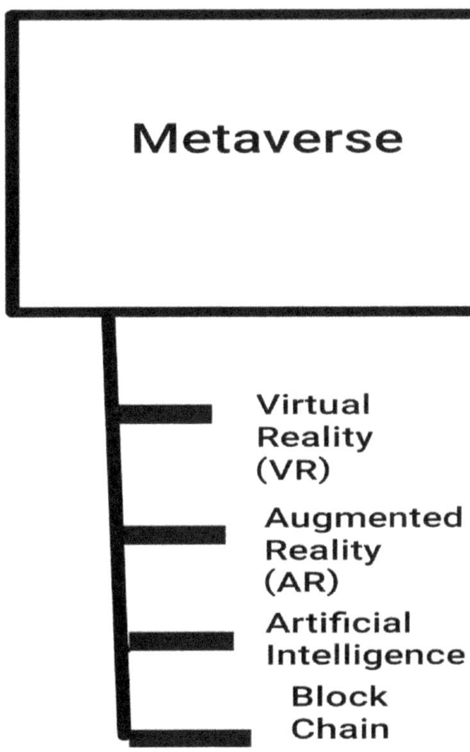

FOCUS OF THE CHAPTER

The chapter would look into the concept of metaverse through intensive literature review along with investigation of some basic aspects of metaverse like awareness level, expectation level, expected domains to be covered for metaverse in Indian society, scope of metaverse with Indian population . The chapter would investigate the following questions the following questions:

1. What is the background and basic concept of metaverse?
2. What is the awareness level of metaverse in India?
3. What are the expectations from metaverse in India ?
4. What are the are the area of interest related to metaverse in India?
5. What are the issues and challenges of metaverse, as in literature as well as in real life in India?
6. What could be the probable solutions to overcome the challenges?
7. What is the scope of growth in India?

RESEARCH DESIGN

The chapter would primarily explore the conceptual background of metaverse through literature review along with a small qualitative survey with the users and potential users of metaverse through pattern coding in India. Figure 4 shows the research design through a flowchart. There are two phases to the research project. To assess awareness and understanding about the metaverse, a focus group interview with a group of people from various fields was done in phase one. In phase two, a survey was undertaken. using a semi-structured survey to examine many connected metaverse topics. In order to obtain a cross-sectional perspective on the subject and to gauge general awareness of the metaverse, a larger age range, a variety of professional specializations, and an income range have all been included in the survey. The survey was administered via in-person interviews, online using Google Forms, video calls over WhatsApp, and messaging .To provide a certain degree of comfort to the respondents and encourage them to voice their ideas, anonymity has been preserved. The respondents' profile is shown through Table 1, Table 2 and Table 3 for different demographic determinants (age, Occupation and per capita income per month).

ISSUES AND CHALLENGES RELATED TO THE CONCEPT METAVERSE

There are a number of challenges to developing the metaverse. One challenge is that the technology required to create a fully realized metaverse is still in its early stages of development. Another challenge is that there is no single company or organization that is leading the development of the metaverse. Achieving interoperability and seamless integration across various virtual platforms and technologies is a challenge. Establishing common technical standards can be essential for a cohesive and interconnected metaverse. There is currently no single standard for the metaverse, which could make it difficult for different platforms and experiences to be compatible with each other, Chen and Zhou (2022) noted. This means that there is a risk that the metaverse could become fragmented, with different platforms and experiences that are not compatible with each other. The current risk of a single dominant entity

Table 1. Showing the age group of the respondents

Serial No.	Number of Respondents	Occupation
1	23	Below18
2	93	18-25
3	102	26-33
4	78	34-41
5	54	42-49
6	46	Above 50
Total	396	

Table 2. Showing the occupation of the respondents

Serial No.	Number of Respondents	Age Groups
1	102	Student
2	149	Service
3	20	Retired
4	91	Professional
5	34	Housewives
Total	396	

Table 3. Showing the income groups of the respondents

Serial No.	Number of Respondents	Income Groups
1	105	Less than 40,000
2	146	40,001-60,000
3	145	Above 60,000
Total	396	

Figure 4. Showing the flow of the research
(Source: Author)

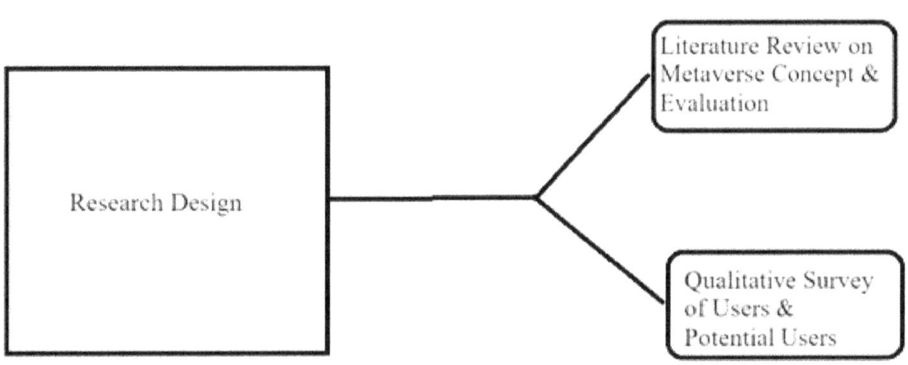

controlling a significant portion of the metaverse raises concerns about monopolistic practices and the concentration of power, potentially limiting diversity and innovation.

Also, the metaverse raises a number of privacy and security concerns, such as how to protect users' data and prevent online harassment, Huang and Dai (2022) observed. As the metaverse involves extensive user interaction and data sharing, maintaining privacy becomes a significant challenge. Protecting personal information and preventing unauthorized access are crucial considerations. Researchers have spoken about the ethical implications of security, privacy, and virtual property rights in the metaverse (Reeves & Malone, 2017). With the increasing integration of financial transactions and sensitive data within the metaverse, the risk of cyber attacks, fraud, and virtual asset theft becomes a prominent challenge as it poses a real threat towards security of the clients.

Another challenge is digital inequality. Access to the metaverse requires reliable internet connections and advanced hardware, which may lead to digital divides, excluding individuals or communities with limited resources from participating in this virtual space. The metaverse operates across international borders, posing challenges for regulatory frameworks. Establishing and enforcing consistent rules for virtual environments, user interactions, and digital assets can be complex. Legal experts have studied the changing legal environment with regard to jurisdictional concerns in virtual worlds and intellectual property (Lessig, 1999).Content Moderation is another challenge. Managing and moderating user-generated content in the metaverse to ensure a safe and inclusive environment is challenging. Preventing harassment, hate speech, and inappropriate behaviour requires effective moderation tools and policies.

Also, extensive use of virtual reality in the metaverse may lead to health issues such as eye strain, motion sickness, and even to the extent of addiction. Balancing immersive experiences with user well-being is an ongoing challenge which should be addressed with utmost importance. Also, one must remember the cultural sensitive side of the global aspects of the metaverse. The metaverse brings together people from diverse backgrounds, cultures, and societies. Ensuring cultural sensitivity and avoiding unintentional cultural appropriation or offense requires careful consideration and community engagement. Despite the challenges, there is a lot of excitement about the potential of the metaverse. Many experts believe that the metaverse will have a major impact on our lives in the upcoming years. Figure 5a summarises the key challenges related to metaverse.

The survey raised a few issues that are pertinent to India, such as the need for technological and infrastructural development. The country needs to make substantial strides in this area in order to support the robust and demanding requirements of the metaverse, which include high-speed broadband, low latency, and wide accessibility. It also requires hardware and software developments like affordable and readily available VR/AR headsets and other accessories for mass adoption of hardware and building robust platforms and virtual environments tailored to Indian cultural contexts for software development.

A number strategies have been proposed as answers to the issues raised, such as closing the digital gap and ensuring that all societal segments have fair access to the metaverse in order to address the issue of digital inequality. In order to secure privacy and mitigate security concerns, it is imperative to implement strong data protection frameworks and provide user education. To guard against moral, legal, and societal conundrums and malpractices as the metaverse develops, clear regulations must be developed and ethical considerations regarding virtual identities, content moderation, and user interactions must be addressed. Figure 5b summarises the proposed solutions to the challenges of the metaverse.

Figure 5. (a) Showing the significant challenges of the metaverse (b) Showing the probable solutions to the challenges of the metaverse
(Source: Author)

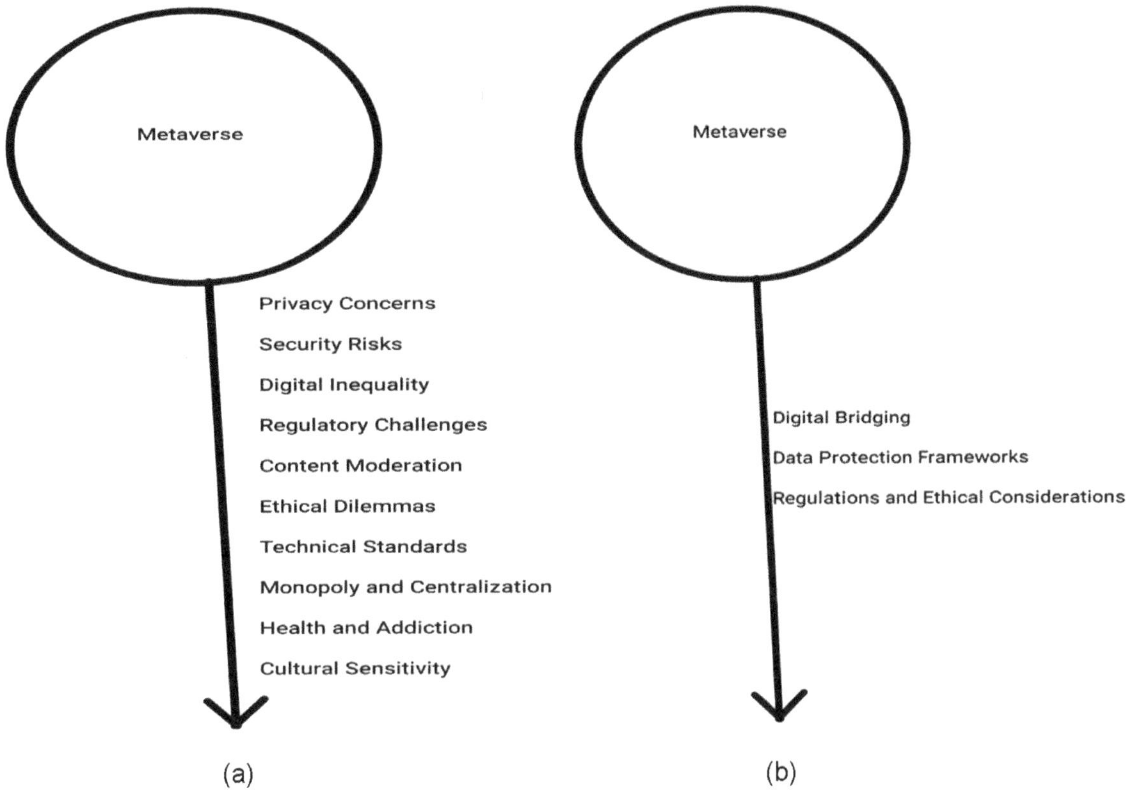

EXPLORATION OF THE EVOLVING LANDSCAPE OF THE METAVERSE- THE RECENT TRENDS IN THE FIELD OF METAVERSE

Metaverseand Web3: A Symbiotic Relationship

Dwivedi et al. (2023) highlighted the synergy between the metaverse's immersive experiences and Web3 principles like decentralization and tokenization. They propose novel applications in areas like DAO governance, decentralized marketplaces, and immersive learning experiences powered by NFTs.

Beyond Entertainment: The Metaverse for Social Impact

Abbate et al. (2023) argued for the potential of the metaverse to address social challenges like global connectivity, educational access, and cultural preservation. They propose initiatives utilizing virtual communities, immersive training programmes, and decentralized platforms to empower marginalized communities. Research by Steinkuehler and Duncan (2008) has delved into the social dynamics within virtual worlds, discussing the emergence of virtual communities and their impact on real-world social interactions. Studies (Nowak et al., 2020) have examined how the metaverse influences cultural expressions, providing a new medium for artistic and creative endeavours.

The Metaverse and AI: A Dynamic Duo

Singh et al. (2023) explored the convergence of AI and the metaverse, with AI driving intelligent avatars, personalized experiences, and dynamic content generation. Castronova (2005) explored the economic aspects of the metaverse, likening it to a digital economy with real-world economic consequences. Virtual currencies, such as Bitcoin and Ethereum, have been examined for their role in facilitating economic transactions within the metaverse (Yelowitz, 2014). They emphasized the need for ethical considerations around bias, transparency, and user control in this increasingly AI-powered virtual world. The metaverse is still developing rapidly. The most popular trends influencing its future are listed below as categories for the ease of understanding:

A) Tech and Accessibility

VR and AR Boom: More affordable and advanced VR/AR headsets are fuelling wider adoption, making the metaverse more accessible to the masses. Expect lighter, sleeker, and more powerful devices in the near future.

AI Integration: Artificial intelligence is enhancing avatars, powering virtual assistants, and driving dynamic content creation. Look for AI-powered NPCs, adaptive environments, and personalized experiences.

Web3 and Decentralization: Blockchain technology is enabling virtual economies, secure ownership of digital assets (NFTs), and democratizing governance in the metaverse. It is expected to have a steep rise in decentralized metaverse platforms and DAOs.

B) Experiences and Applications

Metaverse Gaming: Gaming remains a major driver, with immersive worlds, play-to-earn economies, and social interaction attracting millions. It has full potential of integration with other genres beyond fantasy and sci-fi.

Work and Education: Virtual offices, training simulations, and collaborative platforms are transforming work and education. It is expected to have integration with real-world tools, leading to increase in adoption by businesses and institutions.

Fashion and Entertainment: Virtual fashion shows, concerts, and art galleries are creating new avenues for expression and revenue. It is supposed to blur the lines between physical and digital identities and ownership.

C) Other Key Trends

Focus on Privacy and Security: As user data becomes more valuable, robust security measures and data ownership protection are crucial. It is expected to have stricter regulations and user-centric data management to strengthen the encryption process.

Sustainability Concerns: The environmental impact of metaverse technology is under scrutiny. It is expected to have more energy-efficient solutions and sustainable data centres.

Metaverse Marketing: Brands are creating virtual storefronts, hosting events, and building influencer communities in the metaverse. It is expected to come up with more innovative marketing strategies and immersive shopping experiences through metaverse.

Just a handful of the fascinating developments reshaping the metaverse have been listed in this chapter, despite many others. Future technology is anticipated to have a greater degree of innovation and a wider range of applications as user adoption increases and technology advances for metaverse.

DISCUSSION

The first research question about the background and the basic concept of the metaverse has been already elaborated in the earlier portion of the chapter. The second question explores the awareness status of the Indian potential user of the metaverse. In the first phase of research, the focus group interviews revealed a lack of awareness and knowledge regarding the metaverse and the survey has validated the same in the second phase, across all sections of the society . The respondents' level of awareness is seen in Tables 4, 5, and 6 as per demographic cohorts. The fallacy lies in the defining metaverse part by the respondents. Approximately, only 33% of people know exactly what the phrase "Metaverse" means and could define it in the closest possible terms, as per the ideal definitions of metaverse to make it perfect. When asked to define metaverse in their own words, just 68 respondents were able to define confidently and could raise the percentage to 17% using more meaningful terms, with examples like WhatsApp, Facebook, Gamification etc., which is depicted through Table 8. When defining the phrase, many respondents included terms like gaming, block chains, augmented reality, virtual reality, and technology simulations etc. In case, the respondents were knowledgeable about the term, they often associated the term with Facebook and WhatsApp because of the wise renaming strategy of the brand-Meta. The respondents mentioned about gaming(as per some of the respondents, India has a booming gaming industry, and the metaverse is expected to revolutionize it with immersive experiences and social interactions), education(as per respondents, immersive learning environments in the metaverse can enhance engagement and provide access to quality education even in remote areas), entertainment(as per some of the music enthusiasts in the respondents set, virtual concerts, events, and social spaces offer new avenues for entertainment and community building), Work and Collaboration(as per respondents, remote work and virtual offices can be further enhanced with realistic avatars and interactive virtual spaces)manufacturing & design industries (as per some business enthusiasts and people from manufacturing industry, in the respondents set, the virtual prototyping and simulations can improve efficiency and innovation in various industries) are the areas where metaverse has a chance to grow. The pattern coding for the suggestive areas of metaverse with a scope of growth have been given with some common themes in Table 7, which is indicative of research question eight. The students community and young generations have been seen to have better awareness regarding metaverse because of obvious reasons of them to be associated with the gaming & virtual networking domains more than others. The older generation and people from household were the least informed ones, demanding a holistic, robust and inclusive awareness generation campaign about the concept.

The research question three and four on expectations and interests from metaverse among Indian potential users have been explored later on. The survey revealed some of the expectations and opportunities linked to metaverse like job creation (as per respondents, the metaverse development and supporting ecosystem offer various job opportunities in technology, content creation, design, and more), boosting IT and IT-enabled services(as per respondents, India's strong IT sector can leverage its expertise to become a global leader in developing metaverse solutions), promoting cultural exports(as per respondents, Indian art, music, and film can find new audiences and revenue streams through immersive experiences in the metaverse) etc. The Indian government has recognized the potential of the metaverse and launched initiatives like the "Metaverse Innovation Lab" and the "Digital India Bhash Initiative" to promote its development and ensure responsible and inclusive growth through metaverse.

The research question five and six on the issues and challenges related to Metaverse and the resolving strategies for it have been elucidated in the issues and challenges portion of the chapter. The biggest challenge in India is the technological and infrastructural development, which needs immediate attention to make it perfect to accommodate metaverse and potential usage in India. It includes minimizing the digital gap and also to strengthen the data protection to keep the security high for the users. The legal regulatory frameworks also need to be reworked to reduce the lacuna in legal bindings against the cyber crimes.

CONCLUSION

In summary, the dynamic character of metaverse offers an enthralling exploration of the nexus between technology and human communication. The metaverse has evolved dramatically from the first virtual worlds to the immersive, networked digital worlds of today. Its rise is a reflection of our shared ambition

Table 4. Showing the awareness level of the respondents age group wise

Serial No.	Number of Respondents	Age Groups	Awareness	Percentage
1	23	Below18	20	86.96
2	93	18-25	86	92.47
3	102	26-33	12	11.76
4	78	34-41	10	12.82
5	54	42-49	0	0.00
6	46	Above 50	2	4.35
Total	396		130	32.83

Table 5. Showing the awareness level of the respondents occupation wise

Serial No.	Number of Respondents	Occupation	Awareness	Percentage
1	102	Student	82	80.39
2	149	Service	34	22.82
3	20	Retired	2	10.00
4	91	Professional	12	13.19
5	34	Housewives	0	0.00
Total	396		130	32.83

Table 6. Showing the awareness level of the respondents income group wise

Serial No.	Number of Respondents	Income Groups	Awareness	Percentage
1	105	Less than 40,000	14	13.33
2	146	40,001-60,000	58	39.73
3	145	Above 60,000	58	40.00
Total	396		130	32.83

Table 7. Showing the category coding for metaverse to grow in India

<table>
<tr><th>Serial No.</th><th>Number of Respondents</th><th>Areas to Grow</th><th>Category Coding</th></tr>
<tr><td rowspan="3">1</td><td rowspan="3">67</td><td rowspan="3">Gaming & Social Networking</td><td>Immersive experience</td></tr>
<tr><td>Better interaction</td></tr>
<tr><td>Enhanced integration</td></tr>
<tr><td rowspan="4">2</td><td rowspan="4">34</td><td rowspan="4">Education</td><td>Immersive learning</td></tr>
<tr><td>Better collaborations</td></tr>
<tr><td>Better engagement</td></tr>
<tr><td>Elevated standards of education</td></tr>
<tr><td rowspan="7">3</td><td rowspan="7">98</td><td rowspan="7">Work</td><td>Integration and collaboration</td></tr>
<tr><td>Best for virtual environments/spaces like virtual office/ WFH</td></tr>
<tr><td>Time saving</td></tr>
<tr><td>Better productivity</td></tr>
<tr><td>Better control</td></tr>
<tr><td>Convenience</td></tr>
<tr><td>Comfort</td></tr>
<tr><td rowspan="4">4</td><td rowspan="4">26</td><td rowspan="4">Entertainment</td><td>Virtual concerts & events</td></tr>
<tr><td>Better reach</td></tr>
<tr><td>Easy access</td></tr>
<tr><td>Convenience for performer & audience</td></tr>
<tr><td rowspan="4">5</td><td rowspan="4">12</td><td rowspan="4">Manufacturing & Design</td><td>Virtual prototyping</td></tr>
<tr><td>Easy innovation</td></tr>
<tr><td>Technology simulations</td></tr>
<tr><td>Improved efficiency</td></tr>
</table>

Table 8. Showing the responses for knowledgeable respondents to define metaverse in proper terms

Serial No.	Number of Respondents	Knowledgeable	Percentage
1	396	68	17

for more immersive online experiences that go beyond conventional limits and redefine the ways in which we communicate, work together, and produce content. The metaverse's potential effects on a range of industries, including business, education, entertainment, and social interaction, are becoming more and more apparent as we watch it develop. This virtual space's collaborative nature brings up new possibilities for shared experiences, creativity, and innovation. But along with enormous potential are significant drawbacks, such as concerns about security, privacy, and fair access to these immersive settings. Striking a balance between technological advancement and ethical governance will be crucial in ensuring that the metaverse evolves into a space that enhances human connection and expression while respecting the values and rights of its users. Therefore, in order to promote the responsible and inclusive growth of the metaverse, it is imperative that we keep the societal, ethical, and technological consequences in mind as we navigate this dynamic environment. The concept's continuous development holds the potential to influence how people interact digitally in the future, presenting both thought-provoking issues and exciting opportunities for both individuals and society. The journey of the metaverse is still unfolding as the awareness level is extremely poor in most of the countries including developing countries like India, but it depends on us that how we navigate its development, will undoubtedly shape the digital landscape for generations to come. The enormous scopes of metaverse will be proved either a boon or bane is to the time to reveal.

FURTHER SCOPE OF RESEARCH

The study is completely based on literature review along a small qualitative survey, hence any kind of conclusion could not be drawn with certainty, without any statistical analysis and concrete inference. Therefore any further descriptive or causal research could enrich the inference with more confirmatory investigation.

REFERENCES

Abbate, M. A., Aghdam, N. K., & Mirjalili, S. A. (2022). Systematic Review on Metaverse: And its Future Considerations. *Webology*, *19*(2), 10179.

Beckmann, C., & Böhm, M. (2022). The Metaverse: A New Era of Human-Computer Interaction. *Computers in Human Behavior*, *126*, 107021.

Castronova, E. (2005). *Synthetic Worlds: The Business and Culture of Online Games*. University of Chicago Press.

Chen, L., & Zhou, C. (2022). The Metaverse: A New Frontier for Brands. *Journal of Business Research*, *144*, 113–121.

Damar, E. (2021). The Metaverse: Concepts, challenges, and opportunities. *Technology in Society*, *66*, 101649.

Damer, B. (2008). Avatars, Explorations in Synthetic Consciousness and Cognition. In M. H. Schifreen (Ed.), Digital arts and culture 2009. Academic Press.

Dwivedi, R. K., Singh, S., & Mahapatra, S. (2022). Metaversein Business Research: A Systematic Literature Review. *Journal of Global Information Technology Management*, *25*(4), 525–551.

Herrman, T. M., & Browning, S. (2021). *The Metaverse: A Primer*. Stanford University Press.

Huang, L., & Dai, Q. (2022). The Metaverse: A New Paradigm for Social Interaction. *IEEE Transactions on Computational Social Systems*, *9*(2), 437–446.

Lessig, L. (1999). *Code and other laws of cyberspace*. Basic Books.

Milgram, P., & Kishino, F. (1994). A taxonomy of mixed reality visual displays. *IEICE Transactions on Information and Systems*, *77*(12), 1321–1329.

Mystakidis, S. (2022). The Metaversebetween Utopia and Dystopia: Towards A Critical Understanding of the Emerging Virtual World. *Futures*, *138*, 102965.

Narin, O. (2021). The Metaverse: An Overview of the Future of the Internet. *Journal of Technology Management & Innovation*, *16*(2), 1–15.

Nowak, K. L., Fox, J., & Ralston, R. A. (2020). *Imagined Futures in Digital Media: Navigating the Unknown through Technology*. Routledge.

Petrigna, E., & Musumeci, M. (2022). Metaverseand Its Impact on Healthcare: A Systematic Literature Review. *Journal of Healthcare Engineering*, *12*(1), 20220002.

Reeves, B., & Malone, T. (2017). Leadership in the Age of the Quick Fix. *Harvard Business Review*.

Sarıtaş, T. (2023). Systematic Literature Review on the Use of Metaversein Education. *International Journal of Technology in Education and Science*, *6*(1), 215–229.

Sarwar, M. A., Soomro, T. R., & Pervaiz, H. (2021). Decentralized Identity Management for Metaverse: Opportunities and Challenges. *IEEE Access : Practical Innovations, Open Solutions*, *9*, 32200–32210.

Steinkuehler, C., & Duncan, S. (2008). Scientific Habits of Mind in Virtual Worlds. *Journal of Science Education and Technology*, *17*(6), 530–543. doi:10.1007/s10956-008-9120-8

Stephenson, N. (1992). *Snow Crash*. Bantam Books.

Wu, P., & Ho, A. T. (2022). Full article: Metaverse: Literature Review, Synthesis and Future Research Agenda. *Journal of Management Analytics*, *11*(3), 521–544.

Ye, Y., & Xu, Z. (2022). The Metaverse: A New Paradigm for the Internet. *IEEE Network*, *36*(2), 28–33.

Yelowitz, A. (2014). Bitcoins as An Investment or Speculative Vehicle? A First Look. *Applied Economics Letters*, *21*(6), 406–409.

ADDITIONAL READING

Boellstorff, T. (2008). *Coming of Age in Second Life: An Anthropologist Explores the Virtually Human*. Princeton University Press.

Castronova, E. (2005). *Synthetic Worlds: The Business and Culture of Online Games*. University Of Chicago Press.

Castronova, E. (2020). *Virtual Economies: Design and Analysis*. Edward Elgar Publishing.

Chen, J., Zhu, L., & Zhou, Y. (2021). MetaverseResearch: A Review. *IEEE Access : Practical Innovations, Open Solutions*, *9*, 75967–75978.

Damer, B. (2008). *Avatars! Exploring and Building Virtual Worlds on the Internet*. Peachpit Press.

Huang, H. (2021). Metaverse: A comprehensive survey. *Journal of Network and Computer Applications*, *183*, 102933.

Lanier, J. (2010). *You Are Not a Gadget: A Manifesto*. Vintage.

Lanier, J. (2017). *Dawn of the New Everything: Encounters with Reality and Virtual Reality*. Henry Holt and Co.

Lehdonvirta, V., & Reitman, R. (2018). *Virtual Economies: A Guide to Design, Implementation, and Application*. MIT Press.

McCosker, A., Wilken, R., & Wilken, R. (2017). Playing the Quantified Self: Video Games and the Metropolis. *Digital Health*, *3*, 2055207617710085.

Rehmeyer, J. (2021). Navigating the Metaverse: A Roadmap for Accessibility. *IEEE Spectrum*.

Rosedale, P. (2008). *Second Life: The Official Guide*. Wiley.

Shadbolt, N., Hall, W., & Berners-Lee, T. (2006). The Semantic Web Revisited. *IEEE Intelligent Systems*, *21*(3), 96–101. doi:10.1109/MIS.2006.62

Snow, C. P. (1993). *The Two Cultures*. Cambridge University Press. doi:10.1017/CBO9780511819940

Stephenson, N. (1992). *Snow Crash*. Bantam Books.

Stephenson, N. (1999). Cryptonomicon. Avon.

Susskind, R., & Susskind, D. (2015). *The Future of the Professions: How Technology Will Transform the Work of Human Experts*. Oxford University Press. doi:10.1093/oso/9780198713395.001.0001

Werbach, K. (2021). *The Blockchain and the New Architecture of Trust*. MIT Press.

Zuckerberg, M. (2021). *Building the Metaverse*. Facebook.

KEY TERMS AND DEFINITIONS

Artificial Intelligence (AI): It refers to the development of computer systems that can perform tasks that typically require human intelligence. These tasks include learning, reasoning, problem-solving, understanding natural language, and perception. AI technologies aim to replicate or simulate human cognitive functions, enabling machines to analyze data, adapt to new situations, and improve their performance over time.

Augmented Reality (AR): It is a technology that combines computer-generated information or imagery with the user's real-world environment in real-time, enhancing their perception and interaction with the surroundings.

Bitcoin: It is a decentralized digital currency that operates on a peer-to-peer network, utilizing blockchain technology to secure and verify transactions. Introduced in 2009 by an unknown person or group using the pseudonym Satoshi Nakamoto, Bitcoin is not controlled by any central authority, such as a government or financial institution. It relies on a public ledger, the blockchain, to record and validate all transactions. Bitcoin can be used for various online transactions and is often considered a store of value or a form of digital gold. Its underlying technology, blockchain, ensures transparency, security, and immutability of the transaction history.

Blockchain: It is a decentralized and distributed ledger technology that records transactions across a network of computers in a secure and transparent manner. Each block in the chain contains a list of transactions, and once a block is completed, it is linked to the previous one, forming a chain. This creates a tamper-resistant and transparent record of transactions, commonly associated with cryptocurrencies like Bitcoin, but with potential applications in various industries.

Technological simulations: It refers to computer-based models or representations that mimic real-world processes, systems, or scenarios. These simulations are designed to imitate the behavior of specific technologies, allowing users to explore, analyze, or learn about them in a virtual environment.

Virtual Reality (VR): It refers to a computer-generated simulation of an immersive, three-dimensional environment that can be interacted with and explored by an individual through electronic devices, typically with the aid of specialized headsets and input devices.

Virtual Space: It refers to a computer-generated environment that simulates aspects of the real world or creates entirely imaginary settings. It is commonly experienced through virtual reality (VR) or augmented reality (AR) technologies.

Work From Home (WFH): It refers to the practice of performing one's job or tasks remotely, typically from one's residence, using digital communication tools and technology to connect with colleagues and employers. This arrangement allows individuals to carry out their professional responsibilities without being physically present at a traditional office location.

Chapter 3
Why Should Businesses Care About the Metaverse

J. Joshua Selvakumar
Christ University, India

Sathish Pachiyappan
Christ University, India

G. Suganya
https://orcid.org/0000-0002-1669-5041
Kumaraguru College of Liberal Arts and Science, India

ABSTRACT

The fourth wave of computer innovation is now being driven by virtual reality (VR) and augmented reality (AR), two spatial, immersive technologies. The resulting pervasive computing paradigm, which this wave is expected to produce, can change (online) commerce, entertainment, distant employment, and education. This new paradigm is called the Metaverse. Although the metaverse is still in its infancy, history demonstrates how swiftly new technology can advance, potentially leaving those who lag. Digital reality technologies can transform the entertainment industry, remote work, education, marketing, and economics. Additionally, these technologies are starting to create a new paradigm for information exchange. The concept of the Metaverse has given rise to a new paradigm. While it appears that it will take years for the metaverse to reach its full potential, it is currently a phenomenon marked by the activity of hundreds of entrepreneurs who are making noise but producing no noteworthy results. According to many observers, the current uptick in activity by large tech businesses is assisting in bringing some order to the market's volatility by providing startup companies with the dependable mainstream customer bases they lack. In order to provide better and more integrated business processes, metaverse will provide a far more immersive experience to an organization's whole ecosystem of clients, staff, and partners. In light of this, the study's objectives are to comprehend the business prospects in the metaverse, identify relevant business strategies, and forecast future business developments in the metaverse. The study also looks at the challenges that companies have while integrating the metaverse, taking into account different scenarios.

DOI: 10.4018/979-8-3693-2422-6.ch003

INTRODUCTION

The New Business Environment of Multiple Spaces

We are currently witnessing the co-development of an electronic space that interacts with the physical space and place of our physical world thanks to several developments, including the telephone, computer networks, the Internet, and mobile phones (Li et al., 2001). These developments have had a significant impact on the business and social environment. The rapid advancement of e-commerce and e-business, as well as changes in how people live, work, interact, study, and play, are all signs of the emergence of these interconnected "two spaces" - the physical and the electronic space (Li, 2007). A new generation of organization and management theory has emerged due to the proliferation of activities associated with e-commerce, e-business, e-government, and e-learning that the expansion of the electronic environment has brought about. The 'e' prefix was used to distinguish the business activity in the electronic space from that carried out in the physical world. Metaverses are virtual worlds that add dimensions and domains for various purposes, thus expanding the existing physical universe (Papagiannidis et al., in press). Since they result from human activity, these are frequently called synthetic worlds (Malaby, in press). Combining the real world, the digital world, and various virtual environments creates a new environment.

Metaverse is more than just marketing speak and a lot more than just a platform for consumer interaction; it's a fusion of technologies that will change and have important business ramifications, affecting the operational details and cross-functional tasks essential to company performance. Even if some businesses have already made sizable expenditures, it's still not too late for others to begin their path.

METHODOLOGY

The purpose of this chapter is to identify the business opportunities and problems associated with the metaverse. In order to achieve the goal, the study's methodology has been developed using a systematic process that guarantees a thorough and perceptive evaluation of the previous studies. Initially, case studies and a comprehensive and methodical evaluation of the literature were conducted using the academic database. In order to preserve the quality and applicability of the chosen literature, inclusion and exclusion criteria have been set. In the end, research articles that are relevant to the subject are included and summarized to create a coherent narrative that highlights the metaverse's evolution and unresolved challenges. Additionally, the potential for two relevant cases from the fashion and real estate industries have been examined. Hence, the systematic review ensures that this research provides a comprehensive, well-structured, and insightful overview of the present state of knowledge on the selected topic.

Business Opportunities in the Metaverse

The advantages of the Metaverse extend beyond business-to-consumer settings. Businesses that deal with other businesses will have enormous opportunities thanks to the metaverse. Consider a manufacturer who is purchasing new parts for its machinery. Currently, the procedure is getting a printed brochure or a PDF with 2D still images via email. Users might more affordably test the products in a simulated setting in the metaverse. Envision how robotics systems interact with the natural world by creating a sophisticated digital duplicate of a factory or other industrial place on a colossal scale.

Customers from emerging and marginal economies will have much easier access to the market thanks to the metaverse, which presents many exciting opportunities. The internet has already made access to previously unavailable goods and services possible. Workers in developing countries, for instance, might now be able to get employment in Western businesses without leaving their own country. There will be more options for education, and virtual reality (VR) environments offer an efficient and affordable means of receiving instruction. A comprehensive governance framework will also be required in light of these developments.

Using new technologies like the Internet, Tiernan (2000) believes that e-retailing has changed how retailing is done. According to Chaston (2001), this transformation has impacted many essential facets of the buying experience. According to De Kare-Silver (2001), traditional food retailing is a good example of how the three main characteristics of product atmospherics—smell, taste, and touch—are widely used. When consumers can try a product, their confidence increases, especially if they are unfamiliar with it. Since consumers in e-retailing do not have that option, products are frequently returned because they are dissatisfied with their features or quality. The metaverse is anticipated to drastically alter how customers engage with the digital environment and the retail industry (Austin, 2021). "Metaverse retailing," or in collaborative virtual environments, enables customers to interact with other avatars, including those of other customers and store employees, and navigate an immersive virtual space. Frequently, customers use an avatar or digital representation of themselves (Donath, 1999).

Metaverse retailing is a phenomenon that could start the subsequent development of retailing in a three-dimensional environment, opening up prospects for both existing and new shops. Metaverse commerce is a progression of online shopping. Like e-commerce, shops can reach a wider audience by cultivating a solid metaverse presence that allows customers to visit virtually from far away. Retailers should, therefore, consider how they may modify their tactics to compete in the "virtual" future in the metaverse, as the market for metaverse products is predicted to reach $800 billion by 2024 (Source: Bloomberg Intelligence). From a business standpoint, there exist prospects for significant expansion. Rather than opening stores in every city, a large retailer might construct a multi-million-dollar global hub within the metaverse.

In order to create highly immersive and captivating shopping experiences that appeal to early adopters, some trailblazing retailers have started working with video game developers, who were early movers in the metaverse retailing space. For instance, apparel company Uniqlo collaborated with Mojang Studios, the creators of the computer game Minecraft, to create a collection of T-shirts with a Minecraft motif that was subsequently sold in both physical and digital Uniqlo stores (Waters, 2020). In addition, to show how profitable these collaborations can be, the fashion label Gucci charged $4,000 for a digital replica of its Dionysus Bag on the Roblox marketplace—much more than the retail price for the actual one (Barry, 2021). Retailers gain from their capacity to provide immersive experiences through such agreements, in addition to targeting the enormous and quickly growing audience of video game players—the number of gamers is predicted to surpass three billion by 2023 (Gilbert, 2022). Research shows that when shoppers are in immersive settings as opposed to standard or mobile websites, they stay interested longer and are more likely to make purchases (Dogadkina, 2022).

The metaverse will accelerate the transition from cash to cryptocurrency in gaming, sports betting, and gambling, going beyond traditional retailers. Businesses that have developed the infrastructure to enable cashless digital gambling for live sports and casinos, like Sightline Payments, are well-positioned to benefit from the opportunity as these sectors quickly shift to providing gaming experiences in the metaverse.

Case Study 1: Design Home Inspired - Blurring the Lines Between Video Games and Retail

Design Home, a famous apartment design game boasting over 90 million downloads, has revolutionized mobile gaming and set a new precedent in retail collaboration within video games. Glu Mobile, the parent company of Design Home, used a creative strategy to successfully combine interior design's virtual and physical worlds, turning a mobile game into a retail giant.

Players of the Design Home Mobile game create and decorate virtual apartments, using a digital store to purchase in-game furniture and décor items. Renowned brands like Williams-Sonoma, West Elm, and Pottery Barn have partnered with Design Home to feature virtual versions of their products in the game. Players can purchase these items for their virtual apartments using in-game currency or real money.

Glu Mobile expanded the concept of in-game retail partnerships by launching Design Home Inspired. This innovation involves sourcing real-life, white-label products and making them available for purchase directly through the game. Players can acquire the real-life counterpart without leaving the game when they fall in love with a virtual item. This transformation effectively turned the iOS game into a fully operational furniture store.

Traditionally, retail brands have integrated themselves into video games by introducing their products into the virtual world. For instance, Gucci and Moschino offered outfits in Sims 4, while Uniqlo and Minecraft created Minecraft-themed t-shirts. This concept expanded into popular games like Animal Crossing, where fashion brands such as Net-a-Porter, Gucci, Dior, and Burberry provided clothing for players' avatars. However, these collaborations merely mimicked the introduction of retail products into video game spaces. Design Home took the concept further by developing a white-label store that directly offers real-life products within the game. Rather than merely integrating existing retail products into the Design Home universe, the company created versions of in-game furniture and decor items, turning the game into a retailer.

Figure 1. Design Home's white label store

A groundbreaking aspect of Design Home Inspired is its fully shoppable white-label store. Players can purchase real-life furniture and décor items without exiting the game, creating a frictionless shopping experience. The approach of Design Home Inspired is unparalleled in its direct connection to the brand universe. The white-label products created for the game align closely with the virtual versions, enhancing player engagement and brand immersion.

The metaverse plays a transformative role in reshaping the intersection of virtual and physical retail. The metaverse, as exemplified by Design Home and Design Home Inspired, serves as a dynamic platform that goes beyond traditional in-game product placements. It enables a novel retail model where virtual and physical retail seamlessly coexist, offering players a fully integrated and immersive experience.

Find out more:

https://www.modernretail.co/retailers/why-video-games-are-the-next-retail-frontier/

Enhanced Customer Engagement

The way consumers see and interact with the metaverse is directly influenced by each of the four elements of the metaverse: digital identities, unique digital assets, high consumer immersion, and online collaboration. Customers' social capacities are expanded through online collaboration made possible by the metaverse (both real and temporary ones), which combines the creation of intricate non-dyadic interactions with localized, homogenous groups. Consumers with similar interests tend to congregate and interact in groups due to the metaverse's experience-driven design. Similar to early 2000s online forums and in accordance with the conceptual and technological underpinnings of social media (Kaplan & Haenlein, 2010). In contrast to conventional social media platforms, the immersive quality of these spaces characterizes this collaboration through considerably deeper shared experiences.

In a true metaverse, high levels of consumer immersion enable responsive feedback across all senses and digital replication of customers' real-world activities. Assuming technological limitations, interactions in the metaverse ought to emulate real-world interactions as precisely as feasible. Specifically, users' hand gestures, facial expressions, and eye movements are tracked by Meta's AR/VR headset, Quest Pro, enabling precise and real-time interaction with other users and the 3D environment (Meta, 2022b). High immersion, typically attained by VR and AR technologies, gives users a remarkably high degree of control over how they interact and work in the environment. Due to the integration of several senses (such as touch, sight, and sound), these methods allow users to simulate their interactions with digital and physical environments. Customers feel in control thanks to this resemblance, which maximizes environmental immersion. Furthermore, high immersion enables users to receive comments more authentically and directly than they could with conventional social networking apps. Customers can feel their interactions with businesses, other consumers, and the environment more entirely because of timely feedback, which also increases the influence of these interactions on their future behaviour.

Specialized digital assets signify a new distinct from conventional digital items kind of virtual goods. They enable users to engage with digital real estate and exercise (and feel) full ownership of digital products. According to Strahilevitz and Loewenstein (1998), consumers' perceptions of physical goods' attractiveness and perceived valuation rise over time when they legally own them. Similarly, owners of exclusive digital assets may feel more deeply connected to these products on an emotive and cognitive level than owners of conventional digital goods. Consequently, over time, consumers who genuinely own digital items may feel them to be more valuable and appealing. High levels of personalization are also possible for digital commodities since the user's digital character, or avatar, eventually co-owns them. Digital assets enable businesses and consumers to own digital real estate in addition to true ownership of digital commodities. This promotes high levels of consumer immersion and is essential for how users engage with a true metaverse. Additionally, businesses have financial incentives that directly affect how customers engage with the metaverse because they can buy and create digital real estate (Mileva, 2022). Moreover, while engaging with elements of the metaverse, using digital personas shortens the psychological gap separating users and their surroundings. Temporal, spatial, and social components comprise psychological distance (Liberman et al., 2007). Because digital identities play a significant part in the metaverse, consumers interacting with the digital environment should encounter fewer social and spatial barriers.

The metaverse differs significantly from other digital platforms in that it offers more options for economic interaction and is more realistic. While there are e-commerce options on other digital platforms, the complexity of the economic systems developed in the metaverse is distinct. The emergence and development of digital economic exchange presents retailers with a wealth of opportunities due to the convergence of factors such as online collaboration that creates non-dyadic social networks, unique digital assets that yield actual ownership and digital real estate, and digital personas that enable the use of digital goods for self-expression. The metaverse allows for a considerably more comprehensive range of direct ways customers connect with the digital world, making this the most apparent amplified touchpoint. In particular, the opportunities for retailers in this space are nearly limitless, as distinctive digital assets encourage businesses to use their digital real estate for profound experiences, high consumer immersion enables users to receive immediate feedback from their surroundings, and digital personas enable psychologically closer experiences.

On careful examination of Figure 2, it can be observed that each of the four elements of the metaverse—online collaboration, high consumer immersion, distinctive digital assets, and digital personas—directly

Figure 2. Consumer impact of the metaverse

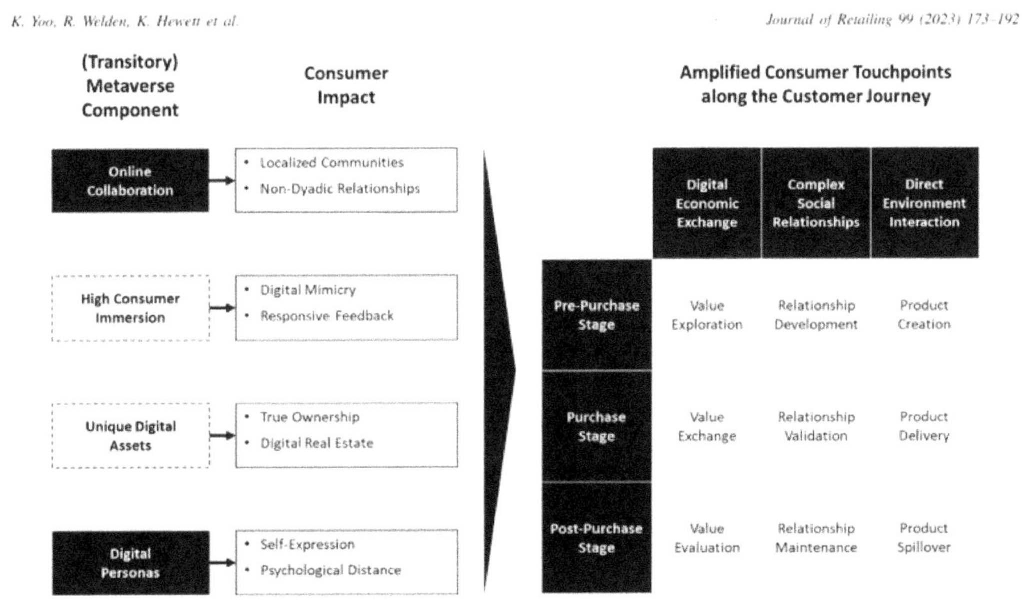

affects how users perceive and interact with the metaverse. Retailers can better map out their role in this new virtual environment by better understanding these relationships and how they work together to make the metaverse stand out among digital platforms. The metaverse modifies the intensity and availability of consumer-retailer touchpoints through its effects on customers. The study utilizes Lemon and Verhoef's (2016) customer journey paradigm, which includes the pre-purchase, purchase, and post-purchase stages, to capture the temporal aspects of the retailing and consumption experience in this domain. In particular, the study suggests three consumer touchpoints in the digital experience—digital economic exchange, complex social relationships, and direct environment interaction.

The metaverse offers customers a 3D environment in which to engage with and experience products. More product information is provided via these interactions, and the experience is more tailored than just browsing a homepage with several product photos (McDannald, 2022). Blockchain technology also allows the creation of exclusive digital goods in the metaverse, such as Fortnite's Balenciaga skins and Burberry's NFT line. According to George-Parkin (2022), the generated digital assets are proprietary to the customers, unlike conventional digital offerings like music downloads.

Case Study 2: The Fashion Industry's Metaverse and NFT Evolution

Fashion, an industry that has always been obsessed with staying at the forefront of innovation, witnessed a significant shift in 2022. The buzzwords of this year were the "metaverse" and "NFTs" (non-fungible tokens). Gucci and Ralph Lauren created virtual pop-up shops within the digital realm, drawing in millions of visitors. Simultaneously, brands like Adidas and Burberry splashed by launching NFT collections and introducing digital assets with unique ownership rights. The metaverse became the stage for innovation, with Decentral and hosting the inaugural Metaverse Fashion Week, featuring digital fashion shows, retail installations, and other virtual experiences.

The evolving metaverse and NFT space might perplex the average person. Questions arise about the future of digital wardrobes, the preference for NFT sneakers over physical ones, and the authenticity of metaverse projects. To address these queries, it is essential to understand that the metaverse is not a single entity; it encompasses the convergence of digital, physical, and augmented realities. It is still a work in progress, much like the early days of the internet or social media. Despite being in its infancy, the metaverse is a potentially lucrative market, with projected global revenues of up to $800 billion by 2024, as reported by Bloomberg Intelligence.

Online multiplayer games like Fortnite, with their tens of millions of tech-savvy players, have become popular entry points for brands to venture into the metaverse. In Fortnite, players could visit a Balenciaga pop-up store and purchase virtual avatars' outfits at a fraction of the real-world cost. This approach mirrored real-life limited-edition releases, attracting fashion enthusiasts and speculators seeking future resale value.

Fashion brands are not merely replicating their physical strategies in the digital world. They are exploring new avenues. Brands have the opportunity to create community spaces within metaverse realms where fans can engage, interact, and access exclusive brand benefits. These virtual hubs may also help drive traffic to brick-and-mortar stores, where most fashion brands still generate the bulk of their revenue.

The metaverse introduces fresh ways for consumers to interact with brands and connect with fellow enthusiasts. Gucci, for instance, developed a virtual space within the gaming ecosystem, The Sandbox, using platforms like Discord to reach an exclusive and in-the-know audience. These servers facilitate

Figure 3. Roblox virtual universe

Courtesy of Ralph Lauren

peer-to-peer communication and community-building, creating a more intimate and dedicated space for brand interactions.

The metaverse presents social opportunities and fosters a new generation of creators. Examples include digital design studio RTFKT collaborating with an 18-year-old artist to create virtual sneakers that sold out within minutes, netting millions in cryptocurrency sales. Beyond virtual goods tied to physical products, this emerging space piqued the interest of fashion giant Nike, leading to the acquisition of RTFKT. Virtual worlds like Roblox form a significant part of the metaverse, providing users with digital spaces for socialization, play, community formation, game creation, and participation in growing economies. Brands like Ralph Lauren have recognized the potential and hosted holiday-themed experiences within these platforms.

Fashion's foray into the metaverse and NFTs is just the beginning. As the metaverse continues to evolve, the industry is poised to adapt and thrive in this new digital landscape. By embracing virtual spaces, fostering community engagement, and exploring the creative potential of the metaverse, fashion brands are positioning themselves for a dynamic and prosperous future in this rapidly expanding digital realm.

Find out more:

https://www.thezoereport.com/fashion/metaverse-nft-fashion

Business Strategies for the Metaverse

Companies can benefit from the economic advantages of the metaverse by providing more innovative and proactive marketing and service strategies than they did in the past (Karampourniotis & Fafaliou, 2022). Modern marketing tools, for instance, include infographics, pictures, and videos used in passive content marketing. Their alignment with the metaverse, wherein enterprises' positioning and offerings are influenced by marketing and service initiatives, is low (Akkucuk & Asugman, 2022).

These prospects are related to the rise in popularity of Generation Z among business-to-business (B2B) consumers, who have a persistent need for distinctive services and immersive, captivating marketing. Businesses must drastically alter their marketing strategies in light of the metaverse's overall developments (Davis & Thorson, 2021). Businesses can employ virtual reality to create immersive experiences or set up online stores to sell digital products. This will guarantee user engagement and boost revenue.

These opportunities constitute the essential components of the Industry 5.0 shift, defined by an emphasis on human-centered technologies, heightened human-machine collaboration, and new opportunities for businesses to innovate and improve their business models. Businesses can boost user engagement and sales by utilizing digital technologies like virtual reality experiences and online stores.

The most apparent distinction between first-generation metaverses (like Second Life) and current metaverses is the existence of distinct digital assets with a marketable value that can be transferred between users, features made possible by the increasingly popular blockchain technologies. Despite being first made widely known by the bitcoin cryptocurrency, blockchain's unique ability to create a sharing economy—a business model in which companies and individuals offer high-security short-term rentals of goods and services—led to its rise in popularity (Euromoney 2022; Kumar, Lahiri & Dogan 2018; Rodeck and Curry 2022). In short, a blockchain is a decentralized digital ledger that enables safe transaction storage in sharing economies. Every transaction is sent to every peer in a peer-to-peer network, and it is only approved once most of the network has verified it. Following validation, the transaction is added to a block of related transactions and chained together to produce a consensus history of all the transactions. Since most of the network's nodes would need to be controlled by hostile actors to hack the ledger successfully, this procedure offers high levels of security. Building on this blockchain technology, the majority of goods and services provided in the metaverse are made and made available as non-fungible tokens (NFTs), which are distinct goods and services with unique identifiers that set them apart from duplicates (Ante, 2022; Nadini et al., 2021; Sharma, 2022). Consequently, NFTs enable users to own digital products and have distinct ownership across the series of these transactions.

In order to promote their brands in the metaverse and increase sales, businesses started to think about creating their own branded Non-Fungible Tokens (Shen et al., 2021). Customers and businesses like Adidas, Taco Bell, and Nike have much interest in Non-Fungible Tokens (NFTs), according to Statista.com (Harris Poll, 2021). Nike's latest efforts in digital transformation extend beyond the realm of virtual and digital environments. Additionally, the company's physical, brick-and-mortar stores are evolving into displays showcasing its innovative use of technology. The company's flagship store in New York is based on the idea that engaging consumers with the brand via technology and sports is just as important as encouraging them to make purchases. Customers can shoot baskets on the in-store baseball court with cameras and television screens to record and playback highlights in real-time. Alternatively, they can use a treadmill simulating outdoor running to burn calories. In addition to receiving guidance from coaches and trainers, customers can personalize the shoes before purchasing them (Seattle, 2022). Businesses can expand their digital assets through marketing opportunities provided by users' capacity to exchange and exhibit real estate and artwork using blockchain-backed NFTs in the metaverse. Furthermore, the prospect of providing services like advice, insurance, or specific types of healthcare encourages new company ventures.

Retail businesses have started to use augmented and virtual reality to allow customers to try on items before making a purchase or to use the metaverse as a test environment for product prototypes (Maleki Vishkaei, 2022). In addition to other operational benefits, these methods of communicating with customers activate the production systems only when items are truly needed, producing a massive advantage in terms of material savings, production cycles, set-up cycles, and inventory (Queiroz et al., 2023).

Financial institutions' interactions with the more conventional Web 2.0 metaverse and their experiments in Web3-enabled metaverse settings differ. Financial services companies are using Web 2.0 technology for a variety of purposes, including employee training (Bank of America, for example) and the creation of virtual "financial towns," telecommuting centers, and interaction spaces (KB Kookmin

Bank, South Korea). They also provide virtual investment advisory services (NH Investment & Securities, for example). Despite being highly developed, these applications have had very little impact on the core financial services business model.

A breakdown of the industries and the rationale behind their use of Metaverse for operations is provided in the above table. The data suggests that 82% and 95% of the media and telecoms industries, as well as the consumer retail sector, have included Metaverse in their marketing campaigns. Additionally, it is evident that the Metaverse platform has been embraced by 85% and 78% of the energy and minerals, tourism, and logistics sectors, respectively, for the purpose of employee learning and development. Over 70% of meetings and conferences on the metaverse have been held by the healthcare industry.

Businesses from various sectors are experimenting with the metaverse for various purposes, including marketing, education, and commerce. Here are a few notable examples:

Education: The Rady School of Management at the University of California, San Diego, offers in-the-moment lectures, breakout rooms, and outdoor spaces via a virtual campus.

Digital twins: BMW is experimenting with modeling entire factories digitally and using Nvidia's Omniverse technology to build items.

Customer service: Helpshift is launching VR support, virtual identity verification, and user feedback, among other customer-help technologies in the metaverse.

Public services: Seoul hopes to set a new record by hosting the world's first metaverse platform for public services by 2023.

Virtual Tourism: The Wunderland platform from Ariva Digital aims to let users visit imagined or recreated locations.

Table 1. Metaverse initiatives implemented to date, by industry, % of senior executives in each industry

Adoption level: High (>70%) | Medium (40–70%) | Low (<40%)

Industry	Marketing campaign or initiatives	Learning and devel-opment for employees	Meetings in the metaverse	Events or conferences	Product design or digital twinning	Recruiting or onboard-ing new employees	Customers can pay with crypto currency
Technology	68	64	54	64	54	39	23
Media and telecommunications	82	36	36	43	54	18	25
Advanced industries	64	55	36	64	64	36	9
Financial sector and insurance	67	63	56	49	56	25	31
Consumer, AF&L, and retail	95	56	59	41	50	41	14
Energy and materials	54	85	69	46	69	31	8
Healthcare and public sector	10	59	79	72	59	38	34
Tourism, transport, and logistics	56	78	56	78	56	44	22
Total sample	67	63	53	52	52	31	22

Source: McKinsey & Company Senior Executive Survey, April 2022

Brand loyalty: By giving consumers access to real streetwear drops, Adidas' Bored Ape Yacht Club NFT release fostered brand loyalty and built a community around its digital products.

Next-generation commerce: AnamaxR develops cloud-based, virtual e-commerce platforms using game-engine technology for 3-D immersive retail experiences.

Businesses currently using the metaverse could gain an enduring advantage over competitors. Business leaders should take a strategic approach by outlining their goals for the metaverse and the role they hope to play; testing, learning, and adopting through the launch of pilot projects, results monitoring, and user behavior analysis; and getting ready to scale through the identification of required capabilities and integration of the metaverse into their operating model.

Future of Business in the Metaverse

The Metaverse, seen in its broadest sense, is a digital universe of linked virtual worlds, settings, and areas where people can engage in social interactions, work, play, and engage in various other activities using digital avatars that represent them. With the integration of VR, AR, and MR as immersive technologies, the Metaverse represents a technologically sophisticated version of the Internet. VR, AR, and MR are the primary realities of XR(Extended Reality) technology. Rather than having separate gadgets for each dimension, XR devices are a part of all three realities. It offers a persistent and immersive virtual world where users can quickly move between various activities and platforms, making distinguishing between the actual and virtual worlds harder. It provides opportunities for fresh approaches to business, social engagement, education, and entertainment. Businesses are investigating how the Metaverse might be used to create virtual gatherings, interactive seminars, dynamic markets, and other innovations that could create new urban digital economies and cultural environments. Similarly, cities are incorporating the Metaverse into many facets of city life to provide virtual events and spatial forms, immersive digital experiences, and interactive simulations for urban planning and design. Though significant ethical and societal ramifications exist, the Metaverse is used to reinvent metropolitan areas and test new ways of living (Bibri et al., 2022).

AI enables intelligent decision-making and autonomous behavior in IoT devices and systems, which is why it is vital in the IoT-embedded metaverse. The quantity of data produced by linked devices and their number are increasing (Huynh et al., 2023). In order to improve the overall effectiveness and performance of IoT systems, AI may be utilized to assess and understand this data. AI has a lot of potential applications in the IoT-embedded metaverse, one of which is machine learning (Cao, 2022).

The metaverse will probably affect how firms function and engage with their clients. Human resources will be able to conduct recruiting and learning in new ways. Teams working on strategy will be able to look at new business models and sources of income. The metaverse's potential is already being utilized by marketing. Sales teams can hold talks and negotiations and host and attend events. Customer service can use the metaverse to answer questions and provide direct action demonstrations. Digital twins and innovative design tools will speed research and development. The operations department could also utilize the metaverse for routine and managerial duties. The Metaverse has been developing; as ideas and technology advance, its precise characteristics may also alter, and as projected possibilities may not come to pass.

There will be a spike in investment across additional industries as the Metaverse expands. The market for virtual goods will continue to grow as a result. Virtual goods are currently valued at about US$50 billion, and by 2025, that amount is predicted to reach US$190 billion. Metaverse has the potential to propel AR/VR's quick development. The total number of AR/VR devices shipped reached 5.12 million units in 2020 and is predicted to reach 43.2 million in 2025. The worldwide AR/VR market is expected to have related expenditures of US$12 billion in 2020 and to increase at a CAGR of 54% over the five years of 2020–2024. It will accelerate the growth of cloud computing since the realization of Metaverse will necessitate greater computer power and data storage. The content or platform creators can create an immersive virtual environment combining advertising, social media, e-commerce, and other features. As a result, their commercial value is expected to grow geometrically as the user value chain is extended. Eventually, the Metaverse will create a physical and digital economy worldwide. The Metaverse will allow for the transfer of all currently existing digital assets, virtual content, intellectual property, and digital currencies. Additionally, this world will be capable of complete autonomy and iteration.

Challenges in Business by Adopting Metaverse

Though the metaverse is becoming increasingly prevalent in our culture and economy, experts and industry professionals cannot agree on properly utilizing its potential (Park & Kim, 2022). While research firms like McKinsey and Gartner have predicted that the metaverse will represent a trillion-dollar revenue opportunity (McKinsey, 2022; Gartner, 2022), others are still skeptical. Journalists and researchers alike wonder if metaverse platforms can be successfully realized (Isaac, 2022; Stokel-Walker, 2021) and their appeal (Falchuk et al., 2018). JP Morgan notes that "metaverses will likely infiltrate every sector in some way in the coming years" (Moy & Gadgil, 2022, p. 2), despite the potentially positive improvements that metaverse platforms might bring about. Prior to their realization, we must recognize and comprehend the obstacles now in the way (Nickerson et al., 2022). By doing this, one may consider how value is created in a metaverse platform (Marabelli & Newell, 2022). This can help practitioners modify their platforms to make them more compatible with the metaverse idea. Thus, to further our understanding of the nature and logic of the metaverse, research must examine the promise and difficulties presented by metaverse platforms in organizational contexts (Torraco, 2005). Through conquering challenges to bring metaverse platforms to life, practitioners can fully utilize them and add value. Four categories of issues were highlighted by Gioia et al. (2013): challenges posed by society, challenges resulting from technology, challenges facing organizations, and challenges facing individuals.

The construction of the Metaverse presents several possible difficulties despite the usage of cutting-edge technologies. The first issue is artificial intelligence ethics, or the prejudice that leads to discrimination against individuals (Baeza-Yates, 2022). In addition to technological difficulties, there are social and ethical difficulties. Social issues include the influence on social structure and the policy environment, while ethical issues include privacy and morality (Allam, 2022). People can work, socialize, learn, and have fun at home using the internet. The original social and economic framework has profoundly touched the contemporary political climate and is even threatened. Since the Metaverse and other digital cities promote decentralization, which opposes the policies of many contemporary governments, its popularity will indeed affect the political system (Bibri & Allam, 2022). The ethics and morality imposed by regulations of the real world cannot be fully replicated in the Metaverse because, in some ways, it is a manufactured universe that is distinct and autonomous from reality. Given the numerous privacy breaches on the internet these days, the issue of personal privacy is even more critical because of the anonymity of blockchain technology. The regulations should take more moral considerations into account in order to improve how the Metaverse's use supports human development. A significant approach to address specific issues is to upgrade infrastructure concurrently.

CONCLUSION

The co-development of electronic and physical spaces has given rise to the transformative metaverse, a complex amalgamation of the real world, digital realms, and virtual environments. This convergence, driven by technological advancements, has reshaped societal and business landscapes, fostering the growth of e-commerce and e-business. The metaverse, far more than a marketing term, represents a paradigm shift influencing not only consumer interactions but also fundamental operational aspects and cross-functional tasks within companies. Amidst this evolution, businesses still have ample opportunities to embrace the metaverse, emphasizing the ongoing dynamic interplay between physical and electronic spaces at the forefront of technological progress.

The metaverse offers significant advantages beyond consumer interactions, creating opportunities for B2B transactions and global market accessibility. "Metaverse retailing" transforms the retail industry, with the market for metaverse products predicted to reach $800 billion by 2024. Collaborations between retailers and video game developers enhance customer engagement, tapping into the vast gamer audience. Additionally, the metaverse accelerates the shift from cash to cryptocurrency in gaming, sports betting, and gambling, benefiting businesses with digital transaction infrastructure. A comprehensive governance framework is essential to navigate the evolving challenges and opportunities presented by the dynamic metaverse landscape. Four fundamental components of the metaverse—distinctive digital assets, high levels of consumer immersion, online collaboration, and digital identities—essentially shape consumer experiences. Digital cooperation broadens social exchanges among enthusiasts, echoing the first online discussion boards. User engagement is improved by realistic feedback and increased control that come with high consumer immersion, which is fueled by VR and AR technology. One emerging kind of virtual product is unique digital assets, which promote individualized experiences and emotional ties. The metaverse, which sets itself apart from other digital platforms, presents intricate economic structures and gives shops a plethora of options for engaging and customized consumers. Ultimately, it appears that the metaverse is transforming space, changing how businesses interact with customers and produce significant virtual experiences.

Companies can harness the economic advantages of the metaverse by adopting innovative marketing and service strategies tailored to the preferences of Generation Z consumers. As the metaverse evolves, businesses can utilize virtual reality experiences and online stores to enhance user engagement and drive revenue growth, marking a shift towards Industry 5.0 principles with a focus on human-centered technologies. Blockchain technology, particularly the use of non-fungible tokens (NFTs), distinguishes current metaverses from their predecessors, enabling secure transactions and unique ownership of digital assets. Businesses like Adidas, Taco Bell, and Nike are exploring branded NFTs to promote their brands and engage consumers in the metaverse. Augmented and virtual reality transform retail operations, allowing customers to try products virtually and optimizing production cycles. Financial institutions are experimenting with Web3-enabled metaverse settings, indicating potential shifts in their business models. Overall, adapting to the metaverse offers businesses diverse opportunities for growth, innovation, and enhanced customer interactions.

In summary, the Metaverse, a digital universe blending virtual worlds through VR, AR, and MR technologies, offers a sophisticated version of the Internet. It creates immersive and persistent virtual spaces, challenging the distinction between real and virtual worlds. The Metaverse presents opportunities for innovative approaches in business, social engagement, education, and entertainment. AI plays a vital role in the IoT-embedded Metaverse, enhancing decision-making and autonomous behavior. Its impact extends to various business functions, including human resources, strategy development, marketing, sales, customer service, and operations. The evolving Metaverse is set to drive investment across industries, with the virtual goods market predicted to reach $190 billion by 2025. This growth is expected to accelerate the development of AR/VR technologies, cloud computing, and the global economy, allowing for the transfer of digital assets and currencies. Ultimately, the Metaverse holds the potential to reshape the physical and digital world, creating a globally connected and autonomous economy.

REFERENCES

Akkucuk, U., & Asugman, G. (2022). Metaverse marketing: Exploring the potential of metaverse for marketing. *Int. J. Mark. Stud.*, *14*, 52–63.

Allam, Z. (2022). The Metaverse as a Virtual Form of Smart Cities: Opportunities and Challenges for Environmental, Economic, and Social Sustainability in Urban Futures. *Sustainability*, *5*(3), 40. https://www.mdpi.com/2624-6511/5/3/40/htm

Ante, L. (2022). The non-fungible token (NFT) market and its relationship with Bitcoin and Ethereum. *FinTech*, *1*(3), 216–224. doi:10.3390/fintech1030017

Austin, S. (2021). The New Wave of Web 3.0 Metaverse Innovations. *Entrepreneur*. https://www.entrepreneur.com/article/380250

Baeza-Yates, R. (2022). Ethical Challenges in AI. *ACM Transactions on Computing Logic, 1*(1), Article 1. . doi:10.1145/3488560.3498370

Bank of America. (2021, October 7). *Bank of America is First in Industry to Launch Virtual Reality Training Program in Nearly 4,300 Financial Centers*. Author.

Barry, C. (2021). Gucci Digitally Outfits Gen-Z in Metaverse Foray with Roblox. *USA Today*. https://www.usatoday.com/ story/tech/gaming/2021/06/09/gucci-meets-roblox-designer-rolls-outdigital-only-collection/7616940002/

Bibri, S. E., & Allam, Z. (2022). The Metaverse as a Virtual Form of Data-Driven Smart Urbanism: On Post-Pandemic Governance through the Prism of the Logic of Surveillance Capitalism. *Sustainability*, *5*(2), 37. https://www.mdpi.com/2624-6511/5/2/37

Bibri, S. E., Allam, Z., & Krogstie, J. (2022). The Metaverse as a virtual form of data-driven smart urbanism: Platformization and its underlying processes, institutional dimensions, and disruptive impacts. *Computational Urban Science*, *2*(1), 24. doi:10.1007/s43762-022-00051-0 PMID:35974838

Chaston, I. (2001). e-Marketing Strategy. McGraw-Hill

Davis, S. M., & Thorson, E. (2021). The metaverse: Promise, peril, and paradigm shift. *Journal of Advertising*, *50*, 279–288.

De Kare-Silver, M. (2001). e-shock: the new rules, e-strategies for retailers and manufacturers: Palgrave. *Developmental Review*, *4*(3), 356–367.

Dogadkina, O. (2022). *Metaverse Shopping: Retailers' New Reality*. VentureBeat. https://venturebeat.com/datadecisionmakers/ metaverse-shopping-retailers-new-reality/

Donath, J. S. (1999). Identity and deception in the virtual community. *Communities in Cyberspace,* 29-59.

Euromoney. (2022). *What is Blockchain?* https://www.euromoney.com/learning/blockchain-explained/whatis-blockchain

Falchuk, B., Loeb, S., & Neff, R. (2018). The social metaverse: Battle for privacy. *IEEE Technology.*

George-Parkin, H. (2022). *How The Metaverse & NFTs are Changing Fashion*. The Zoe Report. https://www.thezoereport.com/ fashion/metaverse-nft-fashion

Gilbert, N. (2022). *Number of Gamers Worldwide 2022/2023: Demographics, Statistics, and Predictions*. FinancesOnline. https://financesonline.com/number-of-gamersworldwide/

Gioia, D. A., Corley, K. G., & Hamilton, A. L. (2013). Seeking qualitative rigor in inductive research: Notes on the Gioia methodology. *Organizational Research Methods, 16*(1), 15–31. doi:10.1177/1094428112452151

Harris Poll, A. (2021). *Interest in NFTs from Certain Major Brands in the United States in March 2021, by Age and Gender* [Graph]. Available online: https://www.statista.com/statistics/1265870/us-nft-branding

Intelligence, B. (2021). *Metaverse may be $800 Billion Market, Next Tech Platform*. Bloomberg Intelligence. https: //www.bloomberg.com/professional/blog/metaverse-may-be-800-billionmarket-next-tech-platform/

Isaac, M. (2022). 6 reasons meta is in trouble. *The New York Times*. Retrieved from https://www.nytimes.com/2022/02/03/technology/facebook-meta-challenges.html

Kamenov, K. (n.d.). *Immersive Experience—The 4th Wave in Tech: Learning the Ropes*. Available online: https://www.accenture.com/ gb-en/blogs/blogs-immersive-experience-wave-learning-ropes

Kaplan, A. M., & Haenlein, M. (2010). The Fairyland of Second Life: Virtual Social Worlds and How to Use Them. *Business Horizons, 52*(6), 563–572. doi:10.1016/j.bushor.2009.07.002

Karampourniotis, P., & Fafaliou, I. (2022). The Metaverse: A Sustainable Way for Companies to Compete. In *Competitive Intelligence and Strategic Management* (pp. 169–184). Springer.

Khandelwal, J. (2022). A Research Study of Businesses that are Thriving in the Virtual World of Metaverse. In PRIMA (Vol. 10, No. 2, p. 29). Publishing India Group.

Li, F. (2007). *What is e-Business? How the Internet Transforms Organisations*. Blackwell.

Li, F., Whalley, J., & Williams, H. (2001). Between the Electronic and Physical Spaces: Implications for Organisations in the Networked Economy. *Environment & Planning A, 33*, 699–716. doi:10.1068/a33161

Liberman, N., Trope, Y., & Stephan, E. (2007). Psychological distance. Social psychology: Handbook of basic principles, 2(2), 353-383.

Malaby, T. (2006, April). Parlaying Value: Capital in and beyond Virtual Worlds. *Games and Culture, 1*(2), 141–162. doi:10.1177/1555412006286688

Maleki Vishkaei, B. (2022). Metaverse: A New Platform for Circular Smart Cities. In *Cases on Circular Economy in Practice* (pp. 51–69). IGI Global. doi:10.4018/978-1-6684-5001-7.ch003

Marabelli, M., & Newell, S. (2022). Everything you always wanted to know about the metaverse* (*but were afraid to ask). *Proceedings of the Academy of Management Annual Meeting*. 10.5465/AMBPP.2022.11559abstract

McDowell, M. (2022). What Teen Brands can Teach Us About Fashion in the Metaverse. *Vogue Business*. https://www.voguebusiness.com/technology/what-teen-brands-can-teach-us-about-fashionin-the-metaverse

McKinsey Digital. (2022, March 29). *What is the metaverse—and what does it mean for business?* McKinsey. https://www. mckinsey.com/capabilities/growth-marketing-and-sales/our-insights/value-creation-in-the-metaverse

Medium. (2022, March 16). *HSBC to become the first global financial services provider to enter The Sandbox*. Author.

Meta. (2022b). *This is Meta Quest Pro*. https://www.meta.com/quest/quest-pro/tech-specs/#tech-specs

Mileva, G. (2022). *The Ultimate Guide to Metaverse Virtual Real Estate*. Influencer Marketing Hub. https://influencermarketinghub. com/metaverse-virtual-real-estate/

Moy, C., & Gadgil, A. (2022). *Opportunities in the metaverse: How businesses can explore the metaverse*. Academic Press.

Mystakidis, S. (2022). Metaverse. *Metaverse. Encyclopedia*, *2*(1), 486–497. doi:10.3390/encyclopedia2010031

Nadini, M., Alessandretti, L., Di Giacinto, F., Martino, M., Aiello, L. M., & Baronchelli, A. (2021). Mapping the NFT revolution: Market trends, trade networks, and visual features. *Scientific Reports*, *11*(1), 20902. doi:10.1038/s41598-021-00053-8 PMID:34686678

Park, S.-M., & Kim, Y.-G. (2022). A metaverse: Taxonomy, components, applications, and open challenges. *IEEE Access : Practical Innovations, Open Solutions*, *10*, 4209–4251. doi:10.1109/ACCESS.2021.3140175

Queiroz, M. M., Fosso Wamba, S., Pereira, S. C. F., & Chiappetta Jabbour, C. J. (2023). The metaverse as a breakthrough for operations and supply chain management: Implications and call for action. *Int. J. Oper. Prod. Manag*. Retrieved from https://www.statista.com/statistics/1290160/projected-metaverse-use-reach-globalconsumers-businesses/

Roblox Corporation. (2022, February 15). *Roblox reports fourth quarter and full year 2021 financial results*. Author.

Rodeck, D., & Benjamin, C. (2022). What is Blockchain? *Forbes*. https://www.forbes.com/advisor/investing/cryptocurrency/ what-is-blockchain/

Scientist. (n.d.). Retrieved from https://www.newscientist.com/article/2295438-why-has-facebook-changedits-name-to-meta-and-what-is-the-metaverse/

Seattle, S. (2022, June 20). *Nike's New Flagship Store is a Powerhouse of Experience-Driven Retail.* Retrieved from Future stores: https://futurestores.wbresearch.com/blog/nikenew-flagship-powerhouse-experience-driven-retail

Sharma, R. (2022). *Non-Fungible Token (NFT): What it Means and How it Works.* Investopedia. https://www.investopedia.com/non-fungible-tokens-nft-5115211

Shen, B., Tan, W., Guo, J., Zhao, L., & Qin, P. (2021). How to promote user purchase in the metaverse? A systematic literature review on consumer behavior research and virtual commerce application design. *Appl. Sci., 11*, 11087.

Stephenson, N. (1992). *Snow Crash.* Bantam Book.

Stokel-Walker, C. (2021). *Why has Facebook changed its name to Meta and what is the metaverse?* Academic Press.

Strahilevitz, M. A., & Loewenstein, G. (1998). The Effect of Ownership History on the Valuation of Objects. *The Journal of Consumer Research, 25*(3), 276–289. doi:10.1086/209539

Tiernan, B. (2000). E-tailing. Chicago.

Torraco, R. J. (2005). *Writing integrative literature reviews: Guidelines and examples.* Human Resource.

Waters, M. (2020). Why Video Games are the Next Retail Frontier. *Modern Retail.*

Yoo, K., Welden, R., Hewett, K., & Haenlein, M. (2023). The merchants of meta: A research agenda to understand the future of retailing in the metaverse. *Journal of Retailing, 99*(2), 173–192. doi:10.1016/j.jretai.2023.02.002

Zelealem, F. (2021, November 30). *South Korea's KB Bank enters metaverse space.* Academic Press.

Chapter 4
How Is Metaverse Impacting Consumers' Behaviour?

Sumit Agarwal
Delhi Institute of Higher Education, India

Neha Varma
Delhi Institute of Higher Education, India

Vandana Gupta
Delhi Institute of Higher Education, India

Ajit Bansal
Chitkara Business School, Chitkara University, India

ABSTRACT

There has been huge industry buzz and excitement for the metaverse. Metaverse is considered as a hyper-connected digital universe fundamentally changing business practices, including how consumers, brands, and firms will transact and interact in a space of virtual realities. Metaverse is beyond gaming, and now it is a 3D virtual world with rich and immersive experiences. It involves a digital economy where people can create, buy, and sell goods and services. Industry can also use the metaverse for educational purposes, collaboration, and social interactions. It's reasonable to assume that most consumers will eventually move to the metaverse, given that more than 75% of consumers worldwide rely on technology in their daily lives. Additionally, as new forms of content, consumption, and commerce become available, consumer behaviors will also change. While there is already some overlap between digital commerce and video games, the metaverse introduces virtual goods and services that elevate purchasing beyond the ordinary, opening up new revenue streams for companies and providing a means of reaching out to younger customer demographics. According to earlier research, most younger customers desire the ability to purchase their preferred brands online wherever they go, including on metaverse platforms. This research presents a multidisciplinary analysis of the metaverse, with an emphasis on how it can affect consumer behavior. The authors are putting forth a conceptualization model of the metaverse in this study, which includes the following essential components: it is digitally mediated, spatial, immersive, shared, and functions in real-time. They also discuss how these components affect consumer behavior. The knowledge of the metaverse marketplace and how it affects customer behavior has expanded as a result of this study. This research aids in determining how consumers' shopping habits are altered by the metaverse, a virtual environment, and how businesses might benefit from it.

DOI: 10.4018/979-8-3693-2422-6.ch004

INTRODUCTION

The Metaverse offers a singular chance to rethink consumer behavior by upending ideas about identity, authenticity, and digital ownership. awareness the impact on consumer decision-making processes requires an awareness of its revolutionary implications for consumer research and practice, as well as its capacity to deliver value and promote well-being. Additionally, the examination of consumer consciousness and sensory acceptance is essential. There are still issues with guaranteeing inclusive and seamless delivery across demographics, using data in an ethical manner, and striking a balance between impartiality and justice while still providing rewarding customer experiences (Amorim et al., 2014; Goyal et al., 2019; Navarro et al., 2022).

The Metaverse is revolutionizing consumer experiences in a variety of industries by bringing adventure, personalization, and interactivity to business-customer relationships.

What Actually Is Metaverse?

The metaverse is a newly developed 3-D digital environment that enables lifelike online personal and professional experiences through the use of augmented reality, virtual reality, and other cutting-edge semiconductor and internet technologies.

The latest McKinsey research indicates that the metaverse has the potential to generate up to $5 trillion in value by 2030. It's an opportunity that is too big to ignore. Some people believe the metaverse to be a digital playground for friends, while others believe it has the potential to be a commercial space for companies and customers. In 2021, metaverse-related companies reportedly raised more than $10 billion, more than twice what they did in 2020. And so far in 2022, more than $120 billion has flowed into the metaverse.

Value creation in the metaverse is a new report published by McKinsey in June 2022. It is based on surveys completed by over 3,400 executives and customers and 13 senior leaders who were interviewed. This research leads us to conclude that the metaverse is best described as a development of the modern internet, something we interact with on a deep level rather than just viewing. It is an example of how digital technology is coming together to expand the application and reach of cryptocurrencies, virtual and augmented reality, artificial intelligence, and spatial computing, among other things. Furthermore, the "enterprise metaverse" might come together in a way that opens up far more possibilities than just acting as a virtual space for social interaction.

Fundamentally, the Metaverse Has 3 Characteristics

- user agency
- a sense of immersion
- real-time interactivity

Lastly, the following will be a part of the metaverse's complete vision:

Platforms and gadgets that communicate with one another without any problems, enabling simultaneous interaction with thousands of individuals, Multiple uses beyond gaming

Definition of Metaverse

A virtual world or group of virtual worlds that are accessible online and reside in a common digital realm are referred to as the "metaverse." Virtual reality, augmented reality, and other immersive technologies are usually included. Although its scope is broad and includes chances in education, entertainment, health and fitness, and even distant job, it is most frequently linked to gaming and ecommerce. All products that can be disseminated and bought both inside and outside of the metaverse are included in the ecommerce market. All games that are either directly related to categorized metaverse applications or cooperative open-world games are included in the category of gaming (Appel et al., 2020; Bessière et al., 2007; Messinger et al., 2008).

What Are AR and VR?

In a nutshell, augmented reality, or AR, is the use of technology to enhance or add a computer-generated image to a person's perception of reality. You've experienced augmented reality (AR) if you've used the IKEA furniture installation software or Pokémon Go on your smartphone. Players can capture characters in the game by using a map to determine their actual whereabouts. It is simultaneously virtual and physical.

The metaverse is delivering a more realistic virtual experience thanks to advanced AR headsets and new and enabling technologies like 5G, edge computing, and cloud capable of delivering massive volumes of data. This is in contrast to the online gaming platforms that have been around since the early 2000s (and were the early forebears of the metaverse), where users could create avatars through which they could move beyond recreation.

HISTORY OF METAVERSE

A loosely defined word, "metaverse," refers to virtual worlds where people interact through avatars, typically in three dimensions and with an emphasis on social and economic interaction The words "meta" and "universe" were combined to create the phrase "metaverse," which first appeared in the science fiction book Snow Crash in 1992. The metaverse is portrayed in Snow Crash as a fictitious version of the Internet that is made possible by the usage of virtual reality (VR) and augmented reality (AR) headsets. It is a single, ubiquitous, and immersive virtual universe. The word "metaverse" is frequently associated with Web3, blockchain, and virtual reality technologies. Businesses have adopted the phrase as a buzzwordto inflate, for the sake of public relations, the development progress of different linked technologies and projects.

Metaverse is evolving as a multidimensional, dynamic, and growing continuum with three primary components:

A variety of technologies, such as edge computing, digital twins, blockchain, artificial intelligence, extended reality, and smart things like factories and automobiles

It includes the "virt-real," which is a spectrum of experiences that vary from entirely virtual to partially virtual and physical.

Variety of new customer experiences as well as enterprise-wide business apps and models that will be reinvented and changed

PURPOSE OF THE STUDY

The Metaverse has the power to fundamentally alter consumer experiences, behavior, and decision-making. But issues like diversity, using data ethically, and striking a balance between fulfilling experiences need for serious thought. The study was done on objectives given below to study the Indian Customers on various aspects of Metaverse Industry. Following are the major objectives of study.

I. To study the adoption of Metaverse in various industries
II. To study the age wise adoption of Metaverse Industry
III. To study the Consumer Understanding of the Metaverse

METAVERSE BUSINESS OPPORTUNITIES IN THE UPCOMING VIRTUAL SPACE

Talking about application of metaverse in the upcoming virtual space it is considered as one of the prominent technology with application in many industries. Using virtual, augmented, and mixed reality technologies to build networked, immersive virtual worlds for particular commercial goals is known as the metaverse in business.

By taking use of metaverse business potential, one can break free from physical constraints, discover new digital realms of engagement, and communicate in previously unheard-of ways with stakeholders and customers (Alaimo and Kallinikos, 2017; Baker et al., 2019).

Amusement and Gaming

Gaming is probably the first thing that comes to mind when you hear the terms "metaverse" and "entertainment." But it's crucial to avoid confusion. Social VR exists in addition to VR games. These may cross over. Recall that the immersive connection of the metaverse defines it. Beat Saber is not a metaverse game; it is mostly an offline game.

In the computer game Fortnite, millions of fans attended Marshmello's virtual concert in 2018. For many, this was a wake-up call that although they may not take place in virtual reality locations, massive, immersive virtual events do happen. More than 33 million people watched Lil Nas X's four Roblox concerts over the span of two days. Sites like VRChat further provide

Online Shopping and Retail

Businesses now have the chance to expand their offerings into the virtual world thanks to the metaverse. Through the creation of virtual showrooms and storefronts, marketers may enthrall audiences globally by presenting their products in captivating three-dimensional formats.

Moreover, the metaverse enables retailers to provide customers with customized experiences. The shopping experience is improved with virtual assistants and chatbots powered by artificial intelligence, virtual try-ons and fittings, and virtual tours of spaces. Furthermore, companies can use gamification strategies and NFTs into their online storefronts to maintain customer interest and involvement (Aggarwal et al., 2018, Aichne and Gruber, 2017; Sharma and Bansal 2023).

Real Estate (Physical and Virtual)

Real estate in the actual world and virtual real estate are the two aspects of real estate use cases for metaverse technologies.

Apple was well-positioned for success following Meta's substantial investments. Their 3D scanning and augmented reality (AR) technology for mobile devices—specifically, the LiDAR sensor featured in the most recent iPhone and iPad models—are among their most potent weapons.

With the help of Apple's RoomPlan Swift API, applications can make use of the iPhone's potent LiDAR sensor to take 3D pictures of entire rooms in order to generate floor plans. This covers the size of the room and the furniture. It can be used by real estate firms to make VR-ready virtual tours. It's possible that in the not too distant future, astute real estate companies could meet with prospective customers in virtual reality and take them on a 3D tour of an apartment. One app that makes use of this API is called RoomScan by Locometric, which enables real estate companies to quickly and simply build floor layouts for their clients.

Online Social Media Networks

Virtual social platforms are becoming more and more popular as people turn to the virtual world to supplement the real one. Socialization and communication are becoming more and more significant parts of our life. Consider creating a social network or platform where users may interact in a virtual environment, explore virtual places, chat, communicate, hang out, and play in order to take advantage of this commercial opportunity in the metaverse.

Conduct in-depth research to determine the target audience and their unique business requirements prior to constructing the platform. Alternatively, you may think about developing a specialized virtual social network or platform that serves companies within a specific sector or industry and provides them with features and functionalities that are specifically designed to improve their networking and collaboration experiences.

Virtual Real Estate

Investors find Decentraland's platform to be an attractive option due to the increasing value of digital assets. Due to the platform's decentralized format, this modification allowed virtual deeds to land to be kept in the blockchain rather than in a centralized database, making it even more beneficial for investors.

It is likely that in the future, users of decentralized immersive VR platforms will be able to purchase "virtual real estate," which would enable them to build worlds in that area that will draw visitors and bring in money. As a result, virtual and physical real estate would have comparable utilitarian values.

Education

Through immersive teaching, surgeons and students can practice surgical procedures using VR and AR technologies. By using digital twins of organs, this is conceivable not only for training incoming medical professionals but also for preparing seasoned physicians for challenging surgeries. This enables medical professionals to comprehend a patient's potential danger prior to surgery.

Working Remotely

Many workers today find it difficult to imagine going back to the old office and working there for the full day. Even while there are advantages to working remotely, it's still important to stay in touch with co-workers for communication and to increase productivity as a whole.

Businesses can create virtual workplaces where employees can join a shared immersive space for successful collaboration by leveraging AR/VR technologies thanks to the metaverse's potential. This makes it possible for companies to close the gap between remote work and teamwork, encouraging productive teamwork and offering workers a fun and fulfilling work environment.

Sales and Marketing

Marketing is another application that is finding success in the metaverse. Immersion and connected spaces offer a number of benefits, chief among which is the ability to interact with goods and services from home in a more high-quality manner than one might from a computer or smartphone. Retail establishments, for instance, have already started to let customers try on virtual try-on augmented reality technologies to demo items like clothing and makeup. Real estate was the previous example used to show how realtors might market their properties using 3D models.

Virtual Tourism

It has long been believed that travel inspires and enriches the mind and soul. But not everyone has the resources or opportunities to travel to new places, and there are those who have travelled far and are hard to impress.

In these situations, companies in the travel and tourism industry can use the metaverse to build fascinating new worlds and tourist destinations. Regardless of geographical restrictions or travel limits, they can create realistic recreations of well-known historical places and landmarks or virtual landscapes, providing immersive experiences that draw tourists and inspire awe. Additionally, travelers can be accompanied by virtual guides from the metaverse who can offer educational tours of various locations.

Production

With the use of metaverse technology, Honeywell is using its Immersive Field Simulator (IFS) to teach employees. Employees can receive training in a simulated version of an actual production facility or in mixed reality. Digital twin's technology, which can faithfully reproduce the plant in the real world, is used to do this.

Honeywell's solution may prepare employees and supervisors for machine breakdowns and other difficulties that need to be fixed by simulating manufacturing facilities.

Medical

Telemedicine and education are now the two main applications of immersive metaverse technologies in the healthcare sector.

Telemedicine

VR is usually not required for telehealth to occur, according to most healthcare providers. Usually, phone conversations or video chats work well for client consultations and discussions. More immersive technologies can be helpful in some situations, nevertheless, in unexpected ways. Diagnosis can be performed with the same technology that tracks an individual's bodily movements and even eye movements. Eye movements can be utilized to identify conditions such as glaucoma. "Neurological markers" can be used in conjunction with eye-tracking devices and software to diagnose conditions such as Alzheimer's.

In March 2022, iMining Technologies acquired virtual land on Decentraland in order to establish the first metaverse pharmacy globally. The purpose of the virtual location was to assist patients with prescription drug delivery to their homes and medication reminders. At the virtual facility, they also provided online consultations with a qualified pharmacist.

METAVERSE STATISTICS WORLDWIDE

By 2024, the Metaverse market is expected to be worth US$74.4 billion.By 2030, this market is predicted to have grown to a projected volume of US$507.8 billion at a compound annual growth rate (CAGR) of 37.73%. With a projected market volume of US$23.0 billion in 2024, the United States leads the world in Metaverse market value generation (Cacioli and Mussap, 2014; Ducheneaut et al., 2009; Plangger and Campbell, 2022).

The Metaverse market is predicted to have 2,633.0 million users by 2030. By 2030, the user penetration rate is projected to reach 39.7%, up from 14.6% in 2024.It is anticipated that the average Value per user (ARPU) will be $79.5 USD. Globally, the Metaverse market has enormous potential and globally countries like China, the United States, and Japan are leading the way in terms of technological advancements and user adoption.

Source: Metaverse - Worldwide | Statista Market Forecast

Metaverse Trends 2024

By 2024, there will be over 600 million active users on Metaverse globally.

Thirteen or younger make up 51% of Metaverse users.

By 2024, the metaverse market is projected to be worth $74.4 billion.

By 2030, the user penetration rate is projected to reach 39.7%, up from 14.6% in 2024.

By 2026, 25% of People Will Visit the Metaverse at Least Once a Day.

According to 54% of experts, by 2040, half a billion people's everyday life would revolve around the Metaverse.

Roblox has 70.2 million active players per day, making it the most popular game on Metaverse. Source: Metaverse Statistics In 2024 (Users & Market Trends) (demandsage.com)

As per report of Statista there is high growth in market size of Metaverse market from around 74.4 billiondollars in 2024 to more than507 billion dollarsin 2030.

Table 1. Market size of Metaverse's market recorded over the years.

Year	Metaverse Market Size
2030*	$507.8 billion
2029*	$415.2 billion
2028*	$312.4 billion
2027*	$219.6 billion
2026*	$150.1 billion
2025*	$103.6 billion
2024*	$74.4 billion
2023	$56.6 billion
2022	$46.1 billion

Source: Statista.

Table 2. Contribution of different countries in the metaverse market worldwide.

Country	Metaverse Market Value
United States	$23 billion
China	$15.9 billion
Japan	$3.9 billion
United Kingdom	$3 billion
Germany	$2.9 billion
India	$2.1 billion
France	$2 billion
South Korea	$1.5 billion
Canada	$1.5 billion
Italy	$1.4 billion

Source: Statista

How Metaverse Can Be Used for Customer Experience and Retail

While the metaverse seems interesting, how will it impact your brand? It's crucial to understand that the metaverse is rapidly evolving from a platform for hobbyists to an ecosystem where people live, work, and purchase online. Additionally, your brand must be present online wherever clients are (Dwivedi et al., 2023; Eladhari, 2007; Gupta et al., 2024; Lee et al., 2021).

- Retailers should be aware of the metaverse for a number of reasons, in addition to being up to date with technology.
- It makes conversational marketing possible. The metaverse provides a means of having large-scale, two-way interactions with customers in place of yelling at them.
- You can trace it. Are you depressed about cookies dying? Not an issue. You own all of your first-party data when you use rich data from the metaverse, which simplifies tailored marketing.

Table 3. Penetration rate of metaverse market worldwide

Year	Metaverse User Penetration Rate
2030*	39.7%
2029*	35.8%
2028*	31%
2027*	25.9%
2026*	21.2%
2025*	17.4%
2024	14.6%
2023	12.5%
2022	10.9%

Source: Statista

- It is engrossing. On social media, you are in competition for customers' attention. However, keeping someone's interest in a virtual changing room or while playing a sponsored game is far simpler.

High growth is seen from current rate of 10.9% in 2022 to projected penetration rate of 39.7% in 2030.

APPROACHES MAY BUSINESS OWNERS TAKE TO GET INTO THE METAVERSE?

While the exact nature of the metaverse is yet unknown, it is obvious that this is the global trend for immersive shopping. You must use non-traditional selling venues, develop NFTs, and market to avatars if you want to stay ahead of the competition (Sharma and Bansal, 2023; Yee and Bailenson, 2007; Zimmermann et al., 2023).

i) **Promote to virtual people:** Most likely, you're currently using a business-to-consumer (B2C) business strategy. However, you'll encounter a business-to-avatar (B2A) paradigm in the metaverse. Amazing progress has been made in creating avatars that are more relatable and reflect regular customer (Agarwal et al., 2022).

You'll need to become an expert at marketing to avatars in an online setting because every user creates an avatar in order to explore the metaverse. B2A is an inexpensive way to communicate with customers in an online environment that emulates in-person encounters. Avatar-friendly marketing tools like virtual tours, events, and games can even go one step further. Disney is already developing a fully virtual recreation of its theme parks for avatars to enjoy in the metaverse. Since the metaverse defies the laws of reality, you have the opportunity to develop innovative experiences that clients will want to tell their friends about (Quintana and Fernández, 2015; Ratan et al., 2020; Roach 2021).

ii) **Create NFTs:** Despite their seeming complexity, non-fungible tokens (NFTs) are actually quite straightforward. They are digital goods that people in the metaverse possess. • NFTs will be the foundation of the metaverse economy; sometimes they are a digitalized version of a physical product, like garments for Roblox, and other times they are a digital product all by themselves. Customers will therefore not only purchase your products but also want digital versions of them. To stay up to date with the metaverse's evolution, now is the ideal moment to learn how to construct an NFT.

iii) **Think about non-traditional channels for selling:** While Facebook, Instagram, and TikTok are just a few of the metaverse platforms that many businesses have readily adopted in recent years, there are a few more that are also worthwhile to take into account.

Horizon; Microsoft Mesh; Clubhouse; DressX; Twitch; Rec Room; Clubhouse; Microsoft Mesh.

STUDY ON INDIAN CUSTOMERS RELATED WITH METAVERSE

A study was done on 500 customers between the months of December 2023 to February 2024 on various issues related with metaverse market in India.

Metaverse will be largely adopted for Education. Over 42% of people said they are looking forward to using Metaverse for educational usage. 53% people are looking forward to joining Metaverse for work reasons while, 45% wanted to join Metaverse for arts and entertainment.

As per the research generation of Gen Z and Millennials are more inclined towards metaverse industry as compare to other age groups.

Though e the Metaverse is a new industry but surprisingly 25% of respondents have a strong understanding of the Metaverse, while 25% reported having a mild understanding while 50% have poor knowledge.

Table 4. Metaverse adoption industry wise

Metaverse's Adoption Sector Wise	Percentage
Education	42%
Adult entertainment	18%
Money investment	45%
Work possibilities	53%
Art and live entertainment	45%
Gaming	28%
Online dating and socializing	35%

Source: Self Research

Table 5. Age group of the metaverse gamers

Age Group	Percentage of Metaverse Gamers
10 to 20 years	37%
21 to 35 years	37%
36 to 50 years	21%
51 to 60 years	5%

Source: Self Research

Table 6. Consumer understanding of the metaverse

Understanding Level	Percentage
Strong	25%
Mild	25%
Poor	50%

Source: Self Research

A good percentage of respondents around 46% are willing to shop on Metaverse but percentage of respondents not willing is quite high around 52%. It suggests that awareness regarding Metaverse is still low.

As per the respondents the overall opinion on meta verse is 32% respondents feels it is not as good as real time experience. 25% feel that its future of world technology. Also 25% respondents are in the opinion that metaverse is mainly for young generations.

As per the study few strong benefits of Metaverse Industry include enhancement of creativity and imagination, overcoming obstacles preventing people from doing things in real life, exploring virtual world, helps in increasing technological literacy, connecting with new people, providing new job opportunities and opportunities for self-expression.

Table 7. Willingness to shop on the metaverse

Willingness to Shop on the Metaverse	Percentage
Yes	46%
No	50%
Already Experienced	04%

Source: Self Research

Table 8. Indian opinions on metaverse

Opinion on Metaverse	Percentage of People
Not as good as real	32%
The future of world technology	25%
New Way to expand profit	22%
Threat to personal privacy	25%
Exciting way to play and socialize	16%
A fad that will not last long	11%
Only Young people interested	25%
A better alternative to real life	12%
A scam or predatory financial scheme	10%

Source: Self Research

Table 9. Top benefits people looking in metaverse

Metaverse's Top Potential Benefits	Percentage of People
Overcoming obstacles preventing people from doing things in real life	40%
Enhancing creativity and imagination	35%
Exploring virtual world	35%
Helps in increasing technological literacy	32%
Connecting with new people	32%
New job opportunities	31%
Opportunities for self-expression	25%

Source: Self Research

Table 10. Are Indian customers ready for metaverse

Metaverse's Top Potential Benefits for Indian Customers	Percentage of People
Easy-to-use interfaces	70%
wide variety of applications	65%
flashy headsets	55%
ability to personalize avatars	52%

Source: Self Research

As per the study now Indian customers are ready for Metaverse experience. As per the study easy-to-use interfaces (70%) and a wide variety of applications (65%) are among the top metaverse features they care about along with some other features.

As per the study Media and Fitness are the two major industries where consumers want a solution that improves their home workouts. Other industries include Retail, Medical and Travel.

As per the study three major concern areas of respondents which may be challenge to Metaverse Industry includes it may result into isolation and alienation from friends, family and the real world, also respondents are facing privacy concern and also may result into monetization of personal information.

Table 11. Top industry areas consumers want to engage with in the metaverse

Industry	Percentage of People
Media	55%
Fitness	41%
Retail	42%
Medical	38%
Travel	35%

Source: Self Research

Table 12. Metaverse issues

Issues	Percentage of People
isolation and alienation from friends, family and the real world	40%
privacy concerns	38%
monetization of personal information	30%

Source: Self Research

FINDINGS

Following are the findings of the study as per the objectives of the research study.

- Metaverse will be largely adopted for Education. Over 42% of people said they are looking forward to using Metaverse for educational usage. 53% People are looking forward to joining Metaverse for work reasons While, 45% wanted to join Metaverse for arts and entertainment.
- As per the research generation of Gen Z and Millennials are more inclined towards metaverse industry as compare to other age groups with more than 60% in total.
- Though the Metaverse is a new industry but surprisingly 25% of respondents have a strong understanding of the Metaverse, while 25% reported having a mild understanding while 50% have poor knowledge. But still there is requirement of more awareness about this industry among the users.
- A good percentage of respondents around 46% are willing to shop on Metaverse but percentage of respondents not willing is quite high around 52%. It suggests that awareness regarding Metaverse is still low.
- As per the respondents the overall opinion on meta verse is 32% respondents feels it is not as good as real time experience. 25% feel that its future of world technology. Also 25% respondents are in the opinion that metaverse is mainly for young generations.
- As per the study few strong benefits of Metaverse Industry include enhancement of creativity and imagination, overcoming obstacles preventing people from doing things in real life, exploring virtual world, helps in increasing technological literacy, connecting with new people, providing new job opportunities and opportunities for self-expression.
- As per the study now Indian customers are ready for Metaverse experience. As per the study easy-to-use interfaces (70%) and a wide variety of applications (65%) are among the top metaverse features they care about along with some other features.
- As per the study Media and Fitness are the two major industries where consumers want a solution that improves their home workouts. Other industries include Retail, Medical and Travel.
- As per the study three major concern areas of respondents which may be challenge to Metaverse Industry includes it may result into isolation and alienation from friends, family and the real world, also respondents are facing privacy concern and also may result into monetization of personal information.

CONCLUSION

India, with its young, technologically savvy population, is poised to become the third largest economy by 2030 and is prepared for the metaverse. The nation produces the most science, technology, engineering and mathematic graduates worldwide, with more than half of its population under 30. It is ideally situated demographically to provide digital labour to the metaverse, particularly given that it is already a popular location for IT offshore worldwide and is quickly becoming into a hub for product development. Although there is no labour shortage in the nation, brain drain is becoming a bigger worry.

Since two out of every three Indian emigrants have advanced degrees, the growth of the metaverse in India could aid in talent retention by giving highly qualified Indians greater options in the digital sphere. Beyond its demographics, its people have more positive views than people around the world on the metaverse. Major Indian companies that have established metaverse divisions include Infosys and Tech Mahindra. Furthermore, India's metaverse products may have a distinctive flavour due to its distinctive cultural notions in language, religion, and entertainment. But before India can fully profit from the metaverse, several issues like technology equity must be resolved. Only then will the metaverse's full potential be realized.

The future of Metaverse in India is great but need is for better understanding of technology and best use of Metaverse in various industries.

REFERENCES

Agarwal, S., Bhardwaj, G., Saraswat, E., Singh, N., Aggarwal, R., & Bansal, A. (2022, February). Insurtech fostering automated insurance process using deep learning approach. In *2022 2nd International conference on innovative practices in technology and management (ICIPTM)* (Vol. 2, pp. 386-392). IEEE. 10.1109/ICIPTM54933.2022.9753891

Aggarwal, A., Dhaliwal, R. S., & Nobi, K. (2018). Impact of structural empowerment on organizational commitment: The mediating role of women's psychological empowerment. *Vision (Basel)*, *22*(3), 284–294. doi:10.1177/0972262918786049

Aichner, T., & Gruber, B. (2017). Managing customer touchpoints and customer satisfaction in b2b mass customization: A case study. *International Journal of Industrial Engineering and Management*, *8*(3), 131–140. doi:10.24867/IJIEM-2017-3-114

Alaimo, C., & Kallinikos, J. (2017). Computing the everyday: Social media as data platforms. *The Information Society*, *33*(4), 175–191. doi:10.1080/01972243.2017.1318327

Amorim, T., Tapparo, L., Marranghello, N., Silva, A. C., & Pereira, A. S. (2014). A multiple intelligences theory-based 3D virtual lab environment for digital systems teaching. *Procedia Computer Science*, *29*, 1413–1422. doi:10.1016/j.procs.2014.05.128

Appel, G., Grewal, L., Hadi, R., & Stephen, A. T. (2020). The future of social media in marketing. *Journal of the Academy of Marketing Science*, *48*(1), 79–95. doi:10.1007/s11747-019-00695-1 PMID:32431463

Baker, E. W., Hubona, G. S., & Srite, M. (2019). Does "being there" matter? The impact of web-based and virtual world's shopping experiences on consumer purchase attitudes. *Information & Management*, *56*(7), 103153. doi:10.1016/j.im.2019.02.008

Bessière, K., Seay, A. F., & Kiesler, S. (2007). The ideal elf: Identity exploration in World of Warcraft. *Cyberpsychology & Behavior*, *10*(4), 530–535. doi:10.1089/cpb.2007.9994 PMID:17711361

Cacioli, J. P., & Mussap, A. J. (2014). Avatar body dimensions and men's body image. *Body Image*, *11*(2), 146–155. doi:10.1016/j.bodyim.2013.11.005 PMID:24394638

Ducheneaut, N., Wen, M. H., Yee, N., & Wadley, G. (2009, April). Body and mind: a study of avatar personalization in three virtual worlds. In *Proceedings of the SIGCHI conference on human factors in computing systems* (pp. 1151-1160). 10.1145/1518701.1518877

Dwivedi, Y. K., Hughes, L., Wang, Y., Alalwan, A. A., Ahn, S. J., Balakrishnan, J., Barta, S., Belk, R., Buhalis, D., Dutot, V., Felix, R., Filieri, R., Flavián, C., Gustafsson, A., Hinsch, C., Hollensen, S., Jain, V., Kim, J., Krishen, A. S., ... Wirtz, J. (2023). Metaverse marketing: How the metaverse will shape the future of consumer research and practice. *Psychology and Marketing*, *40*(4), 750–776. doi:10.1002/mar.21767

Eladhari, M. (2007). The player's journey. *The players' realm: Studies on the culture of video games and gaming*, 171-87.

Goyal, J., Singh, M., Singh, R., & Aggarwal, A. (2019). Efficiency and technology gaps in Indian banking sector: Application of meta-frontier directional distance function DEA approach. *The Journal of Finance and Data Science, 5*(3), 156-172.

Gupta, V., Agarwal, S., & Bansal, A. (2024). Entrepreneurship in the World of Metaverse: Opportunities and Challenges. *Entrepreneurship and Creativity in the Metaverse*, 1-19. https://connect.comptia.org/blog/metaverse-statistics-facts-stats-market-size-and-future

Lee, L. H., Braud, T., Zhou, P., Wang, L., Xu, D., Lin, Z., . . . Hui, P. (2021). All one needs to know about metaverse: A complete survey on technological singularity, virtual ecosystem, and research agenda. *arXiv preprint arXiv:2110.05352*.

Messinger, P. R., Ge, X., Stroulia, E., Lyons, K., Smirnov, K., & Bone, M. (2008). On the relationship between my avatar and myself. *Journal of Virtual Worlds Research*, *1*(2). Advance online publication. doi:10.4101/jvwr.v1i2.352

Navarro, J., Peña, J., Cebolla, A., & Baños, R. (2022). Can avatar appearance influence physical activity? User-avatar similarity and Proteus effects on cardiac frequency and step counts. *Health Communication*, *37*(2), 222–229. doi:10.1080/10410236.2020.1834194 PMID:33054371

Plangger, K., & Campbell, C. L. (2022). Managing in an era of falsity: Falsity from the metaverse to fake news to fake endorsement to synthetic influence to false agendas. *Business Horizons*, *65*(6), 713–717. doi:10.1016/j.bushor.2022.08.003

Quintana, M. G. B., & Fernández, S. M. (2015). A pedagogical model to develop teaching skills. The collaborative learning experience in the Immersive Virtual World TYMMI. *Computers in Human Behavior, 51*, 594–603. doi:10.1016/j.chb.2015.03.016

Ratan, R., Beyea, D., Li, B. J., & Graciano, L. (2020). Avatar characteristics induce users' behavioral conformity with small-to-medium effect sizes: A meta-analysis of the proteus effect. *Media Psychology, 23*(5), 651-675.S. G. Moore and K. C. Lafreniere, 'How online word-of-mouth impacts receivers'. *Consumer Psychology Review*, *3*(1), 34–59.

Roach, J. (2021). Mesh for Microsoft Teams aims to make collaboration in the 'metaverse'personal and fun. *Microsoft*, (November), 2.

Sharma, A., & Bansal, A. (2023). An Assessment of Money Laundering and Terrorism Financing on the Indian Economy. In *Smart Analytics, Artificial Intelligence and Sustainable Performance Management in a Global Digitalised Economy* (Vol. 110, pp. 123–130). Emerald Publishing Limited. doi:10.1108/S1569-37592023000110B007

Sharma, A., & Bansal, A. (2023). Digital Marketing in the Metaverse: Beginning of a New Era in Product Promotion. In Applications of Neuromarketing in the Metaverse (pp. 163-175). IGI Global. doi:10.4018/978-1-6684-8150-9.ch012

Yee, N., & Bailenson, J. (2007). The Proteus effect: The effect of transformed self-representation on behavior. *Human Communication Research*, *33*(3), 271–290. doi:10.1111/j.1468-2958.2007.00299.x

Zimmermann, D., Wehler, A., & Kaspar, K. (2023). Self-representation through avatars in digital environments. *Current Psychology (New Brunswick, N.J.)*, *42*(25), 21775–21789. doi:10.1007/s12144-022-03232-6

Chapter 5

Metaverse and Industry 4.0:
An Effective Integration for Disruption in Varied Sectors and Business Services

Palak Gupta
https://orcid.org/0000-0001-6583-7803
Delhi Institute of Higher Education, India

Mini Verma
Delhi Institute of Higher Education, India

ABSTRACT

Metaverse is an innovative and collective virtual shared space and internet application that integrates varied new technologies and has thereby impacted all diverse sectors. It has brought a disruption by integrating features of sociality, multi-technology, virtual reality (VR), augmented reality (AR), interoperability, and immersive technologies. It seems like an iteration of the internet, a 3D virtual space where humans experience virtual world beyond the imagination of reality. The intersection of Metaverse and Industry 4.0 represents a potential disruption across varied sectors like education, healthcare, travel, digital payments, digital currency, IT sector, and many other business services. In this chapter, a survey and study will be done on how metaverse and Industry 4.0 have disrupted these sectors and redefined their method to operate, innovate, collaborate, and flourish. Also, a study will be done on its challenges related to data security, privacy, and ethical use of advanced technologies, and a model framework will be proposed accordingly.

INTRODUCTION

The integration of the Metaverse and Industry 4.0 technologies indeed holds substantial potential for disrupting various sectors and business services. This integration could unfold disruption in diverse sectors by useful techniques like-:

DOI: 10.4018/979-8-3693-2422-6.ch005

- **Enhanced Virtual Collaboration**: With the metaverse providing immersive virtual environments and Industry 4.0 enabling advanced connectivity and automation, businesses can facilitate more effective collaboration among remote teams. Virtual reality (VR) and augmented reality (AR) technologies can simulate physical presence, making remote collaboration more natural and boosting productivity.
- **Customer Engagement and Marketing**: Brands can leverage the immersive nature of the metaverse to create unique and engaging marketing experiences. With data analytics and AI from Industry 4.0, they can personalize these experiences for individual customers. For example, virtual showrooms can provide customers with personalized product recommendations based on their preferences and browsing history.
- **Smart Manufacturing and Supply Chain Management**: Technologies for Industry 4.0 like IoT sensors, AI, and big data can enhance manufacturing processes and supply chain process. When integrated with the metaverse, manufacturers can visualize and interact with digital twins of their factories and supply chains in real time. This enables better monitoring, predictive maintenance, and optimization of operations.
- **Entertainment and Media**: The entertainment industry can leverage the metaverse to create immersive gaming experiences, virtual concerts, and interactive storytelling. Industry 4.0 technologies can enhance these experiences by enabling real-time rendering, dynamic content generation, and personalized user interactions.
- **Immersive Training and Education**: The metaverse offers immersive learning experiences, while Industry 4.0 technologies enable personalized and adaptive training programs. By combining these, businesses can create highly effective training simulations for employees. For instance, manufacturing workers can undergo virtual training sessions on operating complex machinery or troubleshooting equipment failures.
- **Retail and E-Commerce**: Virtual shopping experiences within the metaverse can revolutionize the retail industry. By integrating Industry 4.0 technologies such as RFID tagging and automated inventory management, retailers can offer seamless virtual shopping experiences with accurate product information, inventory availability, and personalized recommendations.
- **Healthcare and Telemedicine**: The metaverse can facilitate virtual consultations and medical simulations in healthcare. Integrating Industry 4.0 technologies allows for remote monitoring of patients through connected devices and real-time analysis of health data. This fusion enables more efficient healthcare delivery, especially in remote or underserved areas.

Overall, the integration of the metaverse and Industry 4.0 technologies presents exciting opportunities for disrupting various sectors and redefining how businesses operate, collaborate, and engage with customers. However, it also raises important considerations around data privacy, cybersecurity, and inclusivity that must be addressed for widespread adoption and success.

LITERATURE REVIEW & THEORETICAL FRAMEWORK

The concept of the metaverse has been explored by many authors like in science fiction novel "Snow Crash" (Neal Stephenson, 1992). Industry 4.0 has its roots in the work of Klaus Schwab and his team at the World Economic Forum (Schwab, 2016). Media ecology theory, as proposed by Marshall, provides insights into the impact of virtual environments on human behavior and society (Marshall McLuhan, 1964). Theories of cyber-physical systems, offer frameworks for understanding the incorporation of digital technologies with systems in Industry 4.0 (Michael E. Porter and James E. Heppelmann, 2014). Industry 4.0's impact on manufacturing is well-documented, with authors like Klaus Schwab discussing its potential to transform traditional production processes (Schwab, 2017). The metaverse's role in enhancing supply chain visibility and collaboration is highlighted by a study on digital supply chain management (Lee and Bagheri, 2021). The transformative potential of virtual environments in education, including simulations and immersive learning experiences was worked on (Dede, 2009). Industry 4.0's impact on workforce training and skills development is explored by researchers who emphasized the importance of continuous learning in the era of digital transformation (Schuh et al., 2019).

Tapscott and Tapscott, 2019 explored the potential of blockchain technology to disrupt traditional financial services. The metaverse's implications for virtual banking and decentralized finance (DeFi) are discussed by researchers such as Sun et al. (2021) and Wang et al. (2021), who highlighted the role of digital assets and smart contracts. The potential of virtual reality and AI in healthcare is explored by authors like Rizzo and Koenig (2017, 2019), who discussed applications in medical training and therapy. The integration of the metaverse with healthcare delivery is also discussed by Li et al. (2023) who highlighted the benefits of telemedicine and remote patient monitoring. The metaverse's implications for retail are discussed by authors like Yoo et al. (2023) who explored the use of virtual reality in creating immersive shopping experiences. Industry 4.0's impact on e-commerce logistics and supply chain management is examined by researchers such as Wang et al. (2020) and Kerry et al. (2023) who discussed the role of IoT and big data analytics.

Authors like Castronova (2005) explored the economic and social implications of virtual worlds in gaming and entertainment. Industry 4.0's role in content personalization and digital media distribution is discussed by researchers like Brynjolfsson and McAfee (2014), who highlighted the importance of data-driven decision-making in the media industry. Authors like Floridi (2014) discussed ethical and societal challenges associated with the proliferation of virtual environments and digital technologies. Opportunities for innovation and collaboration in the metaverse and Industry 4.0 are highlighted by researchers like Westerman et al. (2014), who emphasized the importance of digital leadership and organizational agility.

The metaverse has gained increasing attention in recent years, with authors like Zuckerberg et al. (2021) discussing its potential to create immersive digital environments. Industry 4.0 has been a focus of research and industry reports, with authors such as Deloitte (2021) providing insights into its impact on manufacturing and supply chain management. Recent studies by scholars like Johnson et al. (2023) have explored theoretical frameworks for understanding the metaverse, drawing on concepts from media studies, sociology, and computer science. Similarly, researchers such as Lee et al. (2015) have developed theoretical models for analyzing the integration of Industry 4.0 technologies with existing business processes and organizational structures. Authors like Smith et al. (2019) explored the potential of virtual reality and AI-driven diagnostics in revolutionizing healthcare delivery and medical training. Studies by Brown et al. (2023) discussed the role of virtual environments in providing immersive learning experiences and enhancing skills development in the era of Industry 4.0. Recent studies by Li and Liu (2023) examined the use of digital twins and Building Information Modeling (BIM) in streamlining construction processes and enhancing building management practices. Research by Zhang and Wang (2024) investigated the use of augmented reality and personalized shopping experiences in transforming the retail industry and improving customer engagement. Authors such as Garcia and Martinez (2024) addressed challenges related to data privacy, cybersecurity, and digital inequality in the context of the metaverse and Industry 4.0 integration.

METAVERSE AND INDUSTRY 4.0 PAVING DISRUPTION ACROSS VARIED SECTORS

The blending of the metaverse and Industry 4.0 is a potentially disruptive phenomenon that can have an impact, on multiple sectors. Each concept carries qualities and their convergence has the potential to redefine how industries function, cooperate, and drive innovation. The intersection of Metaverse and Industry 4.0 represents a potential disruption across varied sectors like education, healthcare, travel, digital payments, digital currency, the IT sector, and many other business services.

A. **Manufacturing and Supply Chain:** The integration of augmented reality (AR), virtual reality (VR) and digital twins with Industry 4.0 technologies is transforming manufacturing processes. Factories equipped with sensors and connected devices can create digital twins in the metaverse, enabling real-time monitoring, predictive maintenance, and optimal utilization of production lines which leads to increased effectiveness, reduction in downtime, and improved quality control across the manufacturing and supply chain sectors.
B. **Healthcare:** In the healthcare industry, the metaverse combined with Industry 4.0 technologies is revolutionizing patient care, medical training, and telemedicine. Virtual reality simulations allow medical professionals to practice surgeries, conduct remote consultations, and train in immersive environments. IoT devices and AI-driven analytics enhance patient monitoring, diagnosis, and treatment, ultimately improving healthcare outcomes and accessibility.
C. **Education and Training:** The integration of the metaverse and Industry 4.0 technologies is reshaping education and training methods. Virtual classrooms, laboratories, and simulations provide immersive learning experiences for students and professionals. Adaptive learning algorithms powered by AI personalize educational content, while real-time data analysis tracks progress and identifies improvement areas. This enables more effective and scalable training programs across various sectors.
D. **Retail and E-commerce:** The metaverse offers new opportunities for retailers to engage with customers through immersive shopping experiences. Virtual stores allow consumers to browse products, try on virtual clothing, and interact with AI-powered assistants for personalized recommendations. Industry 4.0 technologies enable seamless logistics, inventory management, and supply chain optimization, ensuring efficient fulfillment and delivery of orders in the virtual and physical worlds.
E. **Entertainment and Media:** The entertainment industry is leveraging the metaverse and Industry 4.0 technologies to create interactive and immersive experiences for audiences. Virtual reality games, live events, and streaming platforms enable users to engage with content in unprecedented ways. Advanced algorithms analyze user behavior and preferences to tailor content recommendations and advertisements, enhancing user satisfaction and retention.

F. **Real Estate and Construction:** Virtual reality and digital twins are transforming the real estate and construction sectors by enabling virtual property tours, architectural visualization, and construction planning. Industry 4.0 technologies such as IoT sensors and building automation systems enhance building efficiency, sustainability, and safety. This integration streamlines the entire lifecycle of real estate development, from design and construction to operation and maintenance.
G. **Finance and Banking:** The metaverse and Industry 4.0 technologies are disrupting traditional financial services by enabling virtual banking, digital asset management, and decentralized finance (DeFi) applications. Virtual reality interfaces provide immersive banking experiences, while blockchain technology ensures secure and transparent transactions. AI-driven algorithms analyze financial data to offer personalized investment advice and risk management strategies.

Overall, the intersection of the metaverse and Industry 4.0 is driving innovation and disruption across a wide range of sectors, fundamentally transforming how businesses operate, interact with customers, and deliver value in the digital age.

Figure 1. Disruption in diverse sectors by blending of the metaverse and Industry 4.0

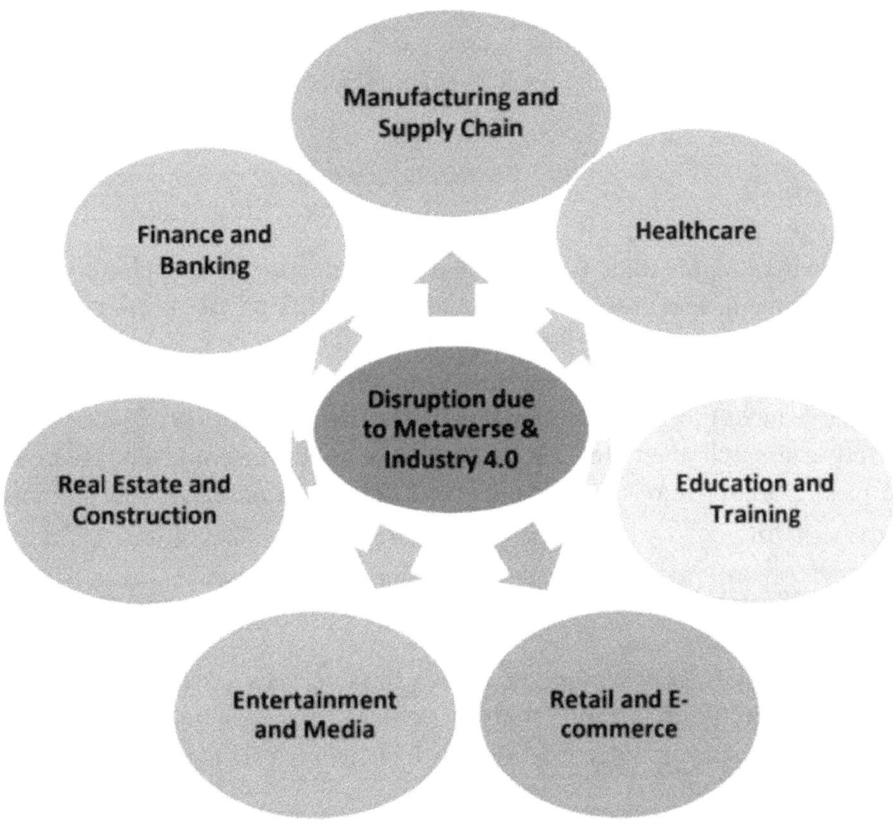

RESEARCH METHODOLOGY

Scope of the Study

This paper will research the varied perspectives of the metaverse, its advantages, and challenges. The intersection of Metaverse and Industry 4.0 represents a potential disruption across varied sectors like education, healthcare, travel, digital payments, digital currency, the IT sector, and many other business services. In this paper survey and study will be done on how metaverse and Industry 4.0 have disrupted these sectors and redefined their method to operate, innovate, collaborate, and flourish. Also, a study will be done on its challenges with respect to data security, privacy, and ethics in using advanced technologies.

Research Objectives

In the present study, following research objectives were considered-

1. To study how metaverse and Industry 4.0 have disrupted sectors like education, healthcare, travel, digital payments, digital currency, the IT sector, and many other business services.
2. To measure the impact of the integration of metaverse and Industry 4.0 on redefining the various sectors to operate, innovate, collaborate, and flourish.
3. To research the varied perspectives of the metaverse, its advantages, and challenges.
4. To identify challenges of Metaverse challenges with respect to data security, privacy, and ethics in using advanced technologies.
5. To propose a framework and model for enhanced implementation and integration of Metaverse and Industry 4.0.

Research Design

The research design used in this study is descriptive and exploratory. An exploratory study is done to identify problems, frame proper problem statement, and identify any issues to be addressed through enhanced research (Kinnear & Taylor, 1996). Here exploratory design is used for research because of very less work done in the area and few literature available. The objective is to prepare a framework and then a predictive model for effective implementation and integration of Metaverse and Industry 4.0. For descriptive research, the observational method is used as in this, the researcher can choose to be either a participant as an observer, complete observer, an observer as a participant, or a full participant (Bhat, 2018).

Data Collection Methods

For data collection and analysis, observation methods and interview sessions were conducted with IT experts. To find the research gap, literature study, periodicals, websites, books journals, magazines and organization records were studied as secondary data which mainly belonged between 1992-2024 at both national and global levels.

Sampling Design

Based on characteristics of the population and the objectives of the study, purposive sampling is selected. As it is a non-probability sample, only respondents using IT Analytics tools considered.

Sampling Universe-Delhi NCR

Sampling Unit-Executives, Analysts & Managers working in the IT domain using tools of virtual reality (VR), 3D virtual space, augmented reality (AR) and IoT.

Sample size-72 IT professionals were interviewed and their answers were compiled and analyzed further.

ANALYSIS AND FRAMEWORK OF THE PROPOSED MODEL

Proposed Model: The proposed model provides a framework for measuring the effect of the integration of metaverse and Industry 4.0 on redefining the various sectors like education, healthcare, travel, digital payments, digital currency, the IT sector, and many other business services to operate, innovate, collaborate, and flourish. It will help varied sectors understand varied perspectives of the metaverse, its advantages, and challenges. With respect to security and privacy of data and ethics in usage of advanced technologies.

The Framework Proposes the Following Steps

Creating a framework for the integration of the metaverse and Industry 4.0 involves outlining a structured approach to leveraging the capabilities of both concepts to drive innovation and transformation across various sectors. Here's a framework that outlines key steps and considerations:

Step 1: Assessment of Current State:

- Evaluate the current technological landscape and digital maturity level of the organization or sector.
- Identify existing Industry 4.0 initiatives, such as IoT deployments, AI applications, and digital twins, as well as any nascent efforts related to virtual reality or augmented reality.

Step 2: Define Objectives and Use Cases:

- Clearly define the objectives of integrating the metaverse and Industry 4.0 within the organization or sector.
- Identify specific use cases where the combination of virtual environments and advanced technologies can create value, improve processes, or enhance customer experiences.

Step 3: Technology Infrastructure:

- Assess the organization's existing IT infrastructure and capabilities to support the integration of the metaverse and Industry 4.0 technologies.

- Identify any gaps or areas for enhancement, such as network bandwidth, computing resources, or cybersecurity measures.

Step 4: Data Strategy:

- Develop a data strategy to ensure seamless integration and interoperability between virtual environments and Industry 4.0 systems.
- Define data standards, formats, and protocols for exchanging information between different technologies and platforms.

Step 5: Integration Architecture:

- Design an integration architecture that enables the seamless interaction between virtual environments and Industry 4.0 systems.
- Consider factors such as data synchronization, real-time communication, and scalability to support a wide range of use cases and applications.

Step 6: Human-Machine Interaction:

- Define the user interface and interaction design principles for virtual environments and Industry 4.0 systems.
- Ensure that the integration enhances user experience, usability, and productivity, taking into account factors such as user preferences, accessibility, and training needs.

Step 7: Security and Privacy:

- Implement robust, safe and secure measures to safeguard confidential data and assets in virtual environments and Industry 4.0 systems.
- Address privacy concerns related to the collection, storage, and processing of personal or confidential information in digital environments.

Step 8: Regulatory Compliance:

- Ensure compliance with relevant rules, standards and regulations leading to the use of virtual environments and Industry 4.0 technologies.
- Stay informed about emerging legal and ethical considerations related to the integration of these technologies, such as intellectual property rights and digital sovereignty.

Step 9: Pilot Projects and Iterative Development:

- Start with small-scale pilot projects to test the integration framework and validate its effectiveness in real-world scenarios.
- Iterate on the design and implementation based on feedback and lessons learned from pilot initiatives, gradually scaling up to larger deployments.

Step 10: Monitoring and Evaluation:

- Establish metrics and KPIs to measure the impact and performance of the integrated metaverse and Industry 4.0 solutions.
- Continuously monitor key indicators and assess the success of the integration in achieving its objectives, making adjustments as needed to optimize outcomes.

By following this framework, organizations can systematically integrate the metaverse and Industry 4.0 technologies to drive innovation, improve efficiency, and create value across various sectors and industries.

Challenges in Handling Metaverse with Industry 4.0 With Proposed Solutions

A number of challenges were identified in diverse sectors while handling Metaverse and Industry 4.0 integration and utilizing it further. In below Table1, the challenges are mentioned as specified by IT experts of interviewed sectors and then the solutions were proposed as per the model proposed.

Figure 2. Proposed framework and model for measuring the effect of Metaverse and Industry 4.0 integration

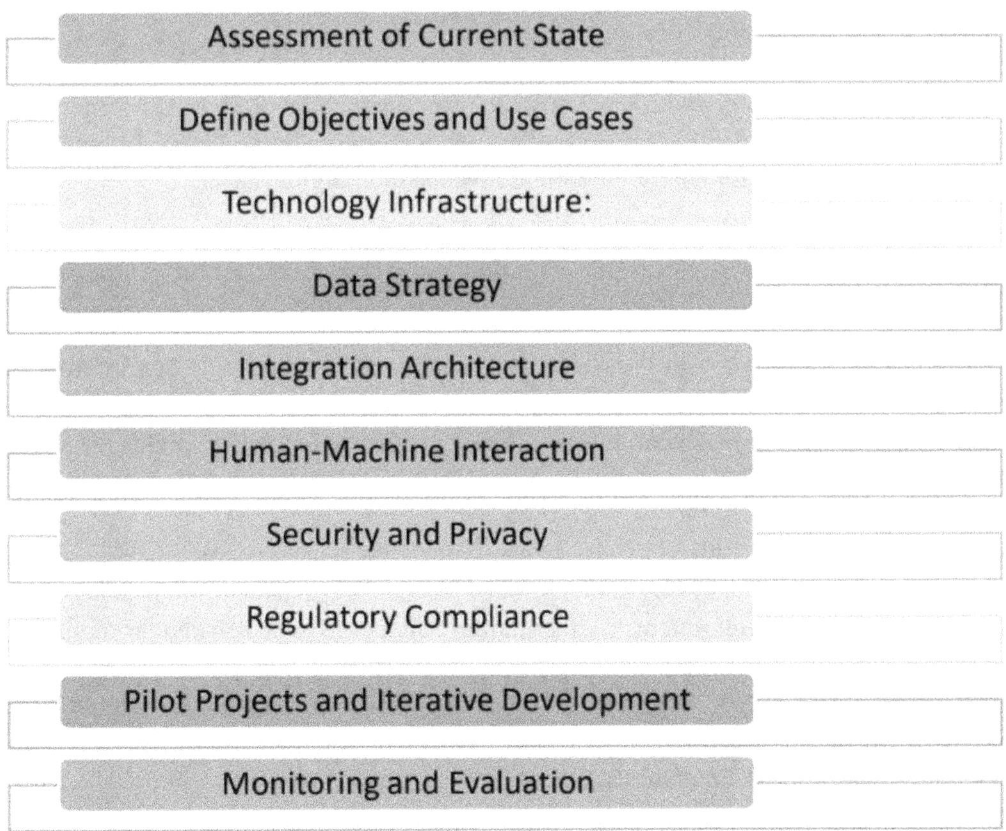

Table 1. Challenges identified in Metaverse 4.0 and solutions proposed

S. No.	Challenges Identified	Proposed Solutions to IT Managers, Analysts, and Executives
1	**Data Integration and Management:** Handling vast amounts of data generated from virtual environments and IoT devices in real-time.	Implement robust data integration platforms and AI-driven analytics to extract actionable insights and optimize processes.
2	**Skills Gap and Training:** Addressing the skills gap required to operate and maintain advanced technologies in both Industry 4.0 and the Metaverse.	Providing comprehensive upskilling programs and training workshops to skill/ reskill the workforce with the much needed IT advanced skills and capabilities.
3	**Security and Privacy Concerns:** Ensuring the security and privacy of sensitive data transmitted and stored within the Metaverse and interconnected Industry 4.0 systems.	Employing encryption, blockchain technology, and secure access controls to protect data integrity and privacy.
4	**Regulatory Compliance:** Navigating complex regulatory frameworks governing data protection, intellectual property rights, and virtual economies in the Metaverse and Industry 4.0.	Collaborating with policymakers to develop flexible regulations that promote innovation while safeguarding consumer rights and security.
5	**Infrastructure and Connectivity:** Ensuring reliable high-speed internet connectivity and infrastructure to support the seamless operation of Industry 4.0 technologies and immersive experiences in the Metaverse	Investing in broadband infrastructure and 5G networks to deliver fast and stable connectivity across urban and rural areas.
6	**Interoperability:** Ensuring seamless communication and compatibility between diverse Industry 4.0 technologies and virtual environments in the Metaverse.	Developing standardized protocols and APIs to facilitate interoperability and data exchange across platforms.
	Skill Gap: The convergence of virtual and physical technologies may require a new set of skills that are currently scarce in the workforce, leading to a skills gap.	Investing in training programs and educational initiatives to upskill the workforce in areas such as virtual reality, augmented reality, data analytics, and cybersecurity can help bridge the skills gap.

By addressing these challenges with innovative solutions and collaborative efforts between industry stakeholders, governments, and technology providers, the integration of the Metaverse with Industry 4.0 can unlock new opportunities for enhanced output, revenue, and digitalisation.

FINDINGS

The integration of the Metaverse and Industry 4.0 represents a transformative opportunity for various sectors and business services. By leveraging virtual environments, augmented reality, data analytics, and automation technologies, organizations can achieve disruptive innovation and achieve competitive edge in the digital era. The following Findings were identified from the model-

- **Enhanced Operational Efficiency**: By streamlining processes, optimizing resource utilization, and enabling real-time monitoring and control of physical systems within virtual environments.
- **Innovative Product Development**: By facilitating collaborative design and prototyping in virtual spaces, organizations can accelerate the innovation cycle and bring new products and services to market faster.
- **Improved Customer Experience**: Through immersive and personalized interactions, virtual showrooms, and product simulations, businesses can engage customers in novel ways and drive brand loyalty.

- **Empowered Workforce**: By providing immersive training experiences, remote collaboration tools, and digital twin technologies, organizations can empower their workforce with the skills and tools needed to excel in a rapidly evolving digital landscape.
- **Optimized Supply Chain Management**: By leveraging data analytics and predictive modeling in virtual supply chain simulations, businesses can optimize inventory management, logistics, and distribution networks.
- **Personalized Experiences**: Businesses can create personalized and immersive experiences for customers, driving engagement and loyalty through virtual showrooms, product simulations, and interactive marketing campaigns.
- **Expanded Market Reach**: The Metaverse provides businesses with new channels to reach global audiences, expand market reach, and create innovative revenue streams through virtual marketplaces and experiences.

CONCLUSION

Utilizing blockchain for data management can enhance security and transparency, ensuring the integrity of data shared between virtual and physical systems. By implementing innovative solutions, businesses can leverage the combined power of the Metaverse and Industry 4.0 to drive digital transformation, improve operational efficiency, and unlock new opportunities for growth and innovation. The convergence of the Metaverse and Industry 4.0 marks a transformative moment in the evolution of business and technology. This integration holds the promise of reshaping industries, revolutionizing processes, and redefining the way we interact with digital and physical worlds. By combining immersive virtual environments with advanced manufacturing and data-driven insights, businesses can unlock new levels of innovation, efficiency, and customer engagement. However, to understand and leverage the optimal potential of this integration requires addressing challenges such as data security, skill gaps, and regulatory complexities. With strategic investments in technology, education, and collaborative frameworks, businesses can harness the power of the Metaverse and Industry 4.0 to drive disruption, create value, and thrive in the digital age. Researchers, policymakers, and industry stakeholders can work together to unlock the full potential of the integration of the Metaverse and Industry 4.0, driving innovation, economic growth, and societal progress.

FUTURE DIRECTIONS AND RESEARCH AGENDA

Gaps in the literature and areas for future research include the long-term societal impacts of the metaverse, the scalability of virtual infrastructure, and the role of regulation in governing virtual environments. Researchers like Brynjolfsson and McAfee (2014) emphasized the need for interdisciplinary research and collaboration to handle challenges and unleash optimal potential of the metaverse and Industry 4.0. Future work will focus on developing and implementing interoperability standards to enable plug-and-play compatibility across platforms and devices. Further research will be on developing highly secure robust techniques, cryptography, and privacy-preserving methods for securing confidential and sensitive data and thereby ensure user safety in virtual environments.

REFERENCES

Bhat, A. (2018, August 23). *Descriptive Research: Characteristics, Methods + Examples*. QuestionPro. https://www.questionpro.com/blog/descriptive- research/#:~:text=In%20a%20descriptive%20research%20design

Brown, G., & Foster, C. (2023). The Use of Virtual Learning Environments in Higher Education—Content, Community and Connectivism—Learning from Student Users. In *AI, Blockchain and Self-Sovereign Identity in Higher Education* (pp. 125–142). Springer Nature Switzerland. doi:10.1007/978-3-031-33627-0_6

Brynjolfsson, E., & McAfee, A. (2014). *The Second Machine Age: Work, Progress, and Prosperity in a Time of Brilliant Technologies*. W. W. Norton & Company.

CastronovaE. (2005). Synthetic economies and the social question. *Available at* SSRN 782826.

Dede, C. (2009). Immersive interfaces for engagement and learning. *Science, 323*(5910), 66-69.

Floridi, L., & Taddeo, M. (Eds.). (2014). *The ethics of information warfare* (Vol. 14). Springer Science & Business Media. doi:10.1007/978-3-319-04135-3

García, Á., Bregon, A., & Martínez-Prieto, M. A. (2024). Digital Twin Learning Ecosystem: A cyber–physical framework to integrate human-machine knowledge in traditional manufacturing. *Internet of Things : Engineering Cyber Physical Human Systems*, *25*, 101094. doi:10.1016/j.iot.2024.101094

Gupta, P. (2023). HR Analytics: An Effective Tool for Performance Management and Business Development. In *HR Analytics in an Era of Rapid Automation* (pp. 112-126). IGI Global. https://www.worldcat.org/title/snow-crash/oclc/28102783/lists

Huang, K., Wang, K., Lee, P. K. C., & Yeung, A. C. L. (2023). The impact of industry 4.0 on supply chain capability and supply chain resilience: A dynamic resource-based view. *International Journal of Production Economics, 262*. doi:10.1016/j.ijpe.2023.108913

Lee, J., Azamfar, M., & Bagheri, B. (2021). A unified digital twin framework for shop floor design in industry 4.0 manufacturing systems. *Manufacturing Letters*, *27*, 87–91. doi:10.1016/j.mfglet.2021.01.005

Lee, J., Bagheri, B., & Kao, H. A. (2015). A cyber-physical systems architecture for industry 4.0-based manufacturing systems. *Manufacturing Letters*, *3*, 18–23. doi:10.1016/j.mfglet.2014.12.001

Li, Y., Gunasekeran, D. V., RaviChandran, N., Tan, T. F., Ong, J. C. L., Thirunavukarasu, A. J., Polascik, B. W., Habash, R., Khaderi, K., & Ting, D. S. W. (2023). The next generation of healthcare ecosystem in the metaverse. *Biomedical Journal*, 100679. doi:10.1016/j.bj.2023.100679 PMID:38048990

Liu, R., Li, H., & Lv, Z. (2023). Modeling methods of 3D model in digital twins. *Computer Modeling in Engineering & Sciences*, *136*(2), 985–1022. doi:10.32604/cmes.2023.023154

McLuhan, M. (1964). *Understanding media*. Mentor.

Porter, M. E., & Heppelmann, J. E. (2014). How smart, connected products are transforming competition. *Harvard Business Review*, *92*(11), 64–88.

Rizzo, A., & Koenig, S. T. (2017). Is clinical virtual reality ready for primetime? *Neuropsychology*, *31*(8), 877–899. doi:10.1037/neu0000405 PMID:29376669

Rizzo, A., Thomas Koenig, S., & Talbot, T. B. (2019). Clinical results using virtual reality. *Journal of Technology in Human Services*, *37*(1), 51–74. doi:10.1080/15228835.2019.1604292

Schumacher, A., Nemeth, T., & Sihn, W. (2019). Roadmapping towards industrial digitalization based on an Industry 4.0 maturity model for manufacturing enterprises. *Procedia CIRP*, *79*, 409–414. doi:10.1016/j.procir.2019.02.110

Schwab, K. (2017). *The fourth industrial revolution*. Currency.

Schwab, K., & Sala-i-Martín, X. (2016, April). *The global competitiveness report 2013–2014: Full data edition*. World Economic Forum.

Smith, S. A. (2019). Virtual reality in episodic memory research: A review. *Psychonomic Bulletin & Review*, *26*(4), 1213–1237. doi:10.3758/s13423-019-01605-w PMID:31037605

Stephenson, N. (1992). *Snow Crash*. Academic Press.

Sun, X., Lin, S., Sjöberg, V., & Jie, J. (2021). How to Exploit a DeFi Project. In Financial Cryptography and Data Security. FC 2021 International Workshops: CoDecFin, DeFi, VOTING, and WTSC, Virtual Event, March 5, 2021, Revised Selected Papers 25 (pp. 162-167). Springer Berlin Heidelberg. doi:10.1007/978-3-662-63958-0_14

Tapscott, D., & Tapscott, A. (2019). *Blockchain*. Rewolucja, Wydawnictwo PWN.

Wang, B., Liu, H., Liu, C., Yang, Z., Ren, Q., Zheng, H., & Lei, H. (2021, May). Blockeye: Hunting for defi attacks on blockchain. In *2021 IEEE/ACM 43rd International Conference on Software Engineering: Companion Proceedings (ICSE-Companion)* (pp. 17-20). IEEE.

Wang, M., Asian, S., Wood, L. C., & Wang, B. (2020). Logistics innovation capability and its impacts on the supply chain risks in the Industry 4.0 era. *Modern Supply Chain Research and Applications*, *2*(2), 83–98. doi:10.1108/MSCRA-07-2019-0015

Westerman, G., Bonnet, D., & McAfee, A. (2014). *Leading digital: Turning technology into business transformation*. Harvard Business Press.

Yoo, K., Welden, R., Hewett, K., & Haenlein, M. (2023). The merchants of meta: A research agenda to understand the future of retailing in the metaverse. *Journal of Retailing*, *99*(2), 173–192. doi:10.1016/j.jretai.2023.02.002

Zhang, K., Wang, J., Zhang, J., Wang, Y., & Zeng, Y. (2024). Exploring the impact of location-based augmented reality on tourists' spatial behavior, experience, and intention through a field experiment. *Tourism Management*, *102*, 104886. doi:10.1016/j.tourman.2024.104886

Zuckerberg, M. (2021). *Meta: founder's letter, 2021*. https://about.fb.com/news/2021/10/founders-letter/

Chapter 6
ArchiVerse:
A Symbiotic Relationship Between Architecture and Metaverse

Jashandeep Singh
https://orcid.org/0000-0003-0377-811X
Chitkara Business School, Chitkara University, India

ABSTRACT

Architecture, throughout history, has reflected humanity's progress and cultural values. This chapter explores the exciting new frontier of architectural design in the metaverse. The metaverse offers a boundless canvas for architects, free from physical constraints. Imagine towering, organic structures or underwater cities. This digital realm also holds immense potential for functionality, from virtual classrooms to interactive retail spaces. However, challenges exist. User experience, bridging the gap between virtual and real, and ethical considerations all require thoughtful navigation. As the metaverse evolves, architects stand poised to shape virtual landscapes and potentially the future of real-world design and human interaction. This chapter also proposes the term ArchiVerse, an amalgamation of architecture and metaverse.

INTRODUCTION

Architecture is a captivating blend of art and science, meticulously crafting spaces that are both functional and aesthetically pleasing. At its heart lies a commitment to fulfilling a purpose. A hospital is designed for efficient patient care, while a library prioritizes quiet areas for focused reading. Architects meticulously consider the activities that will take place within a structure, ensuring it facilitates those needs (Conway and Roenisch, 2005). Durability is equally important. Buildings are meant to endure, so architects select strong, weather-resistant materials and employ sound engineering principles. This is what allows a structure to stand the test of time. But architecture goes beyond mere practicality. It aspires to be a visual art form. Architects use elements like form, proportion, light, and texture to create a sense of harmony and evoke emotions in the users. This

DOI: 10.4018/979-8-3693-2422-6.ch006

is why a building can be both functional and breathtakingly beautiful (Moneta, 2020). The field of architecture extends beyond just buildings. It encompasses urban planning, ensuring efficient city layouts and access to resources. Landscape architecture weaves natural elements into our built environments, creating parks and green spaces that promote well-being. Interior design takes the science of space planning and applies it to craft functional and aesthetically pleasing interiors. As we move forward, sustainability becomes a growing focus for architects. The goal is to design buildings that are energy-efficient, utilize eco-friendly materials, and minimize their environmental impact. Technological advancements and virtual reality are creating exciting new possibilities for design and construction (Schumacher, 2022). In essence, architecture is a dynamic tapestry, forever shaping our world and leaving a lasting legacy for generations to come.

Architecture, much more than just the art of building, tells a story. It's a chronicle of human history, a reflection of cultural values, and a testament to our ever-evolving relationship with the world around us. From the simple shelters of our earliest ancestors to the soaring skylines of modern metropolises, the evolution of architecture reflects our journey as a species.

Evolution of Architecture

Early Beginnings: Functionality Takes Center Stage

The earliest examples of architecture date back to prehistoric times. Driven by basic needs for shelter and protection, early humans constructed rudimentary huts and caves. These structures were purely functional, using readily available materials like wood, mud, and animal skins (Benevolo, 1977). However, even in these simple forms, a sense of planning and organization can be observed, laying the groundwork for future advancements.

Ancient Civilizations: Monumental Achievements

The rise of ancient civilizations witnessed a significant leap in architectural sophistication. Egyptians mastered the art of stone masonry, constructing colossal pyramids that served as both tombs and testaments to their pharaohs' power. Mesopotamian ziggurats, towering stepped structures, reflected their beliefs about the connection between heaven and earth. The Greeks and Romans developed classical architecture, characterized by symmetry, proportion, and the use of columns (Moffett et al., 2003). The Parthenon, a temple dedicated to Athena, remains an iconic example of this style, showcasing the emphasis on harmony and beauty.

The Middle Ages: A Spiritual Dimension

The Middle Ages saw a shift in focus towards religious architecture. Gothic cathedrals soared skyward with pointed arches, stained glass windows, and intricate stonework. These awe-inspiring structures were designed to evoke a sense of spirituality and connection with the divine (Ching et al., 2017). Castles, with their thick walls and imposing presence, served both defensive and residential purposes for the nobility.

The Renaissance: A Rebirth of Classical Ideals

The Renaissance marked a revival of classical principles. Architects like Brunelleschi and Michelangelo drew inspiration from Greek and Roman architecture, emphasizing symmetry, proportion, and geometric forms. The dome of the Florence Cathedral and the façade of the Basilica di San Pietro are prime examples of this renewed interest in classical ideals (Shryock and Smail, 2011).

The Age of Exploration and Beyond: Global Influences

The Age of Exploration brought about an exchange of architectural styles between different cultures. European colonizers introduced Baroque and Rococo styles to their overseas territories, often blending them with local traditions. Islamic architecture, with its focus on geometry, domes, and intricate mosaics, continued to flourish around the world (Ching et al., 2017).

The Industrial Revolution: A New Era of Materials and Techniques

The Industrial Revolution ushered in a new era for architecture. The development of new materials like steel and concrete allowed for the construction of larger and taller structures. Skyscrapers began to dominate cityscapes, and technological advancements facilitated more efficient design and construction methods (Gaafar, 2021).

The 20th Century: A Tapestry of Styles

The 20th century witnessed a proliferation of architectural styles. Modernism, emphasizing functionality, clean lines, and open floor plans, gained widespread popularity. The Bauhaus movement, with its focus on merging art and industry, challenged traditional architectural notions. Art Deco, with its emphasis on geometric shapes and bold colors, added an element of glamour to urban landscapes (Ching et al., 2017). Postmodernism, a reaction to Modernism's perceived coldness, embraced eclecticism and historical references.

The 21st Century: Sustainability and Technological Advancements

Today, architects grapple with the challenges of the 21st century. Sustainability is paramount, with a focus on designing energy-efficient buildings that minimize environmental impact. Technological advancements like 3D printing are revolutionizing construction techniques, while virtual reality allows for immersive design visualization (Wu and Hao, 2023)..

Beyond Buildings: A Broader Scope

The field of architecture extends far beyond just buildings. Urban planning ensures efficient city layouts and access to resources. Landscape architecture incorporates natural elements into our built environments, creating parks and green spaces for well-being. Interior design applies the principles of space planning to create functional and aesthetically pleasing interiors (Sopher and Lescop, 2023).

The history and evolution of architecture is a captivating saga, intertwined with cultural narratives, technological advancements, and human ingenuity. Each era leaves its mark, not just in monumental structures, but also in the way we live, work, and interact with our surroundings. As we move forward, architecture will continue to evolve, reflecting our ever-changing world and shaping the future landscape for generations to come. The realm of architecture isn't confined to physical bricks and mortar anymore. The rise of the virtual world presents a new frontier for architectural design, offering exciting possibilities and blurring the lines between the physical and the digital.

ARCHITECTURAL DESIGNS AND VIRTUAL WORLD

A Canvas of Imagination

Virtual environments provide an unparalleled canvas for architects to unleash their creativity. Unbound by the limitations of material constraints and physical laws, they can design structures that defy gravity, push scale to unimaginable heights, and experiment with forms that would be impossible to build in the real world. Imagine towering, organic structures that seem to grow from the virtual ground, or cities suspended in mid-air, connected by intricate networks of walkways (Sopher and Lescop, 2023). The virtual world allows architects to explore these fantastical concepts, fostering innovation and pushing the boundaries of design.

Collaboration Redefined

The virtual space offers a transformative way for architects to collaborate. Teams spread across the globe can work together in real-time within a shared virtual environment. Imagine architects in different countries manipulating the same 3D model, instantly incorporating feedback and revisions (Fischer, 2022). This fosters better communication, streamlines the design process, and allows for a more collaborative approach to architecture.

Prototyping and Visualization

Virtual reality (VR) technology grants unparalleled visualization capabilities. Architects can create immersive walkthroughs of their designs, allowing clients to experience a building before it's even constructed (Gaafar, 2021). This allows for early identification of potential issues, facilitates better communication of design intent, and helps clients visualize the final product more effectively.

Building the Metaverse: Architectural Design in a Virtual Reality

The metaverse, a persistent virtual world, is rapidly evolving, and architecture is playing a crucial role in shaping its digital landscape (Nijjer et al., 2023). This convergence offers exciting possibilities for architects to create immersive experiences, redefine the way we interact with virtual spaces, and even influence real-world design (Al-Tabeeb and Al-Desouqi, 2023).

Designing for a New Reality

Unlike the limitations of the physical world, the metaverse allows architects to unleash their creativity. Here, defying gravity and exploring fantastical forms becomes possible. Imagine towering, organic structures that seem to teeter on the edge of virtual reality, or underwater cities shimmering with bio-luminescent light. This boundless canvas fosters innovation and pushes the boundaries of architectural design (Каширипур, 2023).

Beyond Aesthetics: Functional Spaces in the Metaverse

The metaverse isn't just about visually stunning landscapes. It demands functionality as well. Architects are designing spaces specifically for virtual experiences. Think virtual classrooms or concert halls where attendees can interact with each other and the environment. These virtual spaces can be optimized for specific activities, creating engaging experiences that transcend entertainment (Unali, 2023).

Reimagining Social Interaction

The metaverse allows architects to create virtual social spaces. Imagine bustling virtual piazzas, interactive art galleries, or even co-working spaces designed to foster collaboration and connection. These spaces can bridge geographic boundaries, allowing users to connect with others from across the globe in a rich, immersive environment (Ayiter, 2014).

Virtual Commerce and the Metaverse

The metaverse has the potential to revolutionize how we shop. Architects can design virtual stores, allowing brands to showcase their products in an interactive way. Imagine trying on clothes in a virtual dressing room or walking through a meticulously designed, 3D model of your dream furniture before purchasing it. This immersive experience can significantly influence real-world purchasing decisions (Shakeri and Ornek, 2023).

Building the Bridge: From Virtual to Reality

While some virtual designs might remain purely conceptual, others might inspire physical construction. Architects can leverage the metaverse as a testing ground. A virtual prototype can help identify potential flaws and refine the design before translating it into a real-world building. This can save time and resources during construction (Gomes et al., 2023).

Challenges and Considerations in Metaverse Architecture

The metaverse presents a captivating new frontier for architectural design, brimming with possibilities for creating immersive experiences and shaping virtual spaces. However, venturing into this digital realm comes with its own set of challenges and considerations that architects need to navigate skilfully (Forte et al., 2010).

Designing for User Experience

Unlike physical buildings with inherent limitations, the metaverse offers boundless freedom. This very freedom can be a double-edged sword (Bathla and Singh, 2022). Architects need to prioritize user experience to ensure virtual spaces are not just visually stunning but also comfortable and engaging. Vast virtual landscapes can be disorienting. Architects need to design intuitive navigation systems that allow users to move around seamlessly and find their way easily within virtual environments. The ability to defy gravity in the metaverse can be tempting, but it's crucial to maintain a sense of scale. Structures that are too large or too small can cause discomfort and disorientation for users (Chen, 2022). The physical world provides a constant stream of sensory feedback. In the metaverse, architects need to consider how to create a sense of touch, sound, and even smell to enhance user immersion and create a more realistic experience.

Bridging the Gap Between Virtual and Real

The metaverse isn't just about creating fantastical digital spaces. Some designs might inspire real-world construction projects. A breath-taking virtual structure might not be structurally sound in the real world. Architects need to consider the limitations of materials and engineering principles when translating virtual designs into physical buildings. The ability to experiment with fantastical forms in the metaverse can be liberating, but translating these designs into reality can be expensive and impractical (Frey et al., 2008). Architects need to find a balance between creativity and feasibility.

The Evolving Nature of Technology

The metaverse is a rapidly evolving landscape. The technology behind VR and AR is constantly changing, and architects need to adapt their designs accordingly. Not everyone has access to high-end VR headsets or powerful computers. Architects need to consider designing virtual experiences that are accessible to a broader audience, potentially with varying levels of fidelity. As the metaverse evolves, there's a need for standardization of design tools and platforms (Sopher and Lescop, 2023). This will allow architects to create virtual experiences that are interoperable across different metaverse platforms.

The Social and Ethical Impact

The metaverse has the potential to significantly impact how we interact with the world around us. Architects need to consider the social and ethical implications of their designs. While the metaverse offers opportunities for connection, it's crucial to design virtual spaces that encourage users to maintain a healthy balance between the virtual and real worlds. The metaverse will generate vast amounts of user data. Architects need to be mindful of data privacy concerns and design virtual spaces with robust security measures in place (Xu et al., 2023).

The intersection of architecture and the metaverse is a work in progress, brimming with both potential and challenges. By carefully considering user experience, the gap between virtual and real, the evolving nature of technology, and the social and ethical implications, architects can navigate this new frontier and create immersive virtual experiences that not only captivate users but also potentially influence and improve the way we design and interact with the physical world. As the metaverse continues to take shape, architects are poised to play a pivotal role in shaping its virtual landscapes and the future of human experience within them.

The Future of Architecture in the Metaverse

The metaverse, a persistent virtual world, is rapidly merging with architecture, birthing a future brimming with possibilities. This convergence holds the potential to revolutionize the way we design, experience, and interact with both virtual and physical spaces. Let's delve into the exciting prospects that lie ahead:

Beyond Reality: Unbound Creativity Takes Flight

The metaverse dismantles the limitations of the physical world. Architects can now explore unbridled creativity, designing structures that defy gravity, push scale to extraordinary heights, and experiment with forms that would be impossible to build in reality. Imagine towering, organic structures seamlessly integrated with the virtual landscape, or underwater cities pulsating with bioluminescent light (Lv et al., 2022). The metaverse becomes a canvas for limitless artistic expression, pushing the boundaries of architectural design and inspiring future real-world creations.

Evolving Functionality: Beyond Aesthetics in Virtual Spaces

While aesthetics are crucial, the future of architectural design in the metaverse extends beyond mere visuals. Architects will be pivotal in shaping the functionality of virtual spaces. Imagine meticulously designed virtual classrooms that optimize learning, or concert halls where attendees can interact with the environment and each other in real-time (Hua, 2022). These virtual spaces will be purpose-built, catering to specific activities and virtual interaction, creating immersive experiences that transcend simple entertainment.

The Rise of Virtual Commerce and Experiential Retail

The metaverse presents a transformative platform for commerce. Architects can design virtual stores that allow brands to showcase their products in an interactive way. Imagine trying on clothes in a virtual fitting room with realistic avatars, or customizing furniture in a meticulously designed 3D model of your dream living space before making a purchase. This immersive, personalized experience can significantly influence real-world purchasing decisions and redefine the retail landscape (Scheer, 2023).

Redefining Social Interaction: From Piazzas to Galleries

The metaverse has the potential to revolutionize how we connect and interact. Architects can design virtual spaces that foster a sense of community, like bustling virtual piazzas where users from across the globe can gather, play games, or simply socialize. They can create interactive art galleries showcasing digital artworks in 3D, allowing visitors to immerse themselves in the pieces in ways impossible in physical galleries. These virtual spaces can bridge geographic distances and forge deeper social connections (Bernasconi and Blume, 2023).

Blurring the Lines: From Virtual Design to Real-World Construction

While some virtual designs might remain purely conceptual, others may inspire physical construction projects. The metaverse can serve as a testing ground for architects. A virtual prototype can help identify potential flaws in a design before breaking ground in the real world. This allows for early refinement and optimization, potentially leading to more efficient and sustainable construction practices (Al-Tabeeb and Al-Desouqi, 2023).

Collaboration Reimagined: Global Teams and Client Co-Creation

The metaverse fosters a new era of collaboration in architecture. Teams from across the globe can work together in real-time within a shared virtual environment, manipulating the same 3D model and incorporating feedback seamlessly. This streamlines the design process, facilitates better communication, and allows for richer collaboration (Singh and Nijjer, 2024). Additionally, clients can actively participate in the design process, stepping into a virtual model of their future home and providing feedback in real-time. This co-creation approach can lead to more successful projects that better meet the needs and desires of the end-user (Kaur and Singh, 2023).

Preserving the Past and Shaping the Future: Education and Cultural Heritage

The metaverse presents a unique opportunity to preserve cultural heritage and historical landmarks. Architects can create meticulously detailed virtual recreations of these sites, allowing people from all over the world to experience them in an immersive way. This can be a valuable educational tool, fostering a deeper understanding of history and culture. Furthermore, lessons learned from designing these virtual spaces can be applied to real-world urban planning and infrastructure development, shaping the future of our cities (Scavuzzo, 2022).

Challenges and Considerations: Navigating the New Frontier

Despite the exciting possibilities, venturing into the metaverse also presents challenges that architects need to address:

User Experience (UX) Design

Creating intuitive navigation systems, maintaining a sense of scale, and incorporating realistic sensory feedback are crucial for user comfort and engagement in virtual spaces (Shalender and Singla, 2024).

Bridging the Gap Between Virtual and Real

Translating fantastical virtual designs into structurally sound and feasible physical buildings requires careful consideration of materials, engineering principles, and cost constraints.

Standardization and Accessibility

Ensuring interoperability between different metaverse platforms and designing virtual experiences accessible to a wider audience with varying levels of technology access will be crucial for widespread adoption (Singh et al., 2022).

CONCLUSION

Architecture, far more than just bricks and mortar, is a chronicle of human history. From rudimentary shelters to soaring skyscrapers, it reflects our cultural values and relationship with the world. Now, on the precipice of a new era, architecture is poised to take a giant leap into the virtual realm of the metaverse. This convergence presents a landscape brimming with possibilities. The metaverse offers architects an unfettered canvas, unbound by the limitations of the physical world. Imagine gravity-defying structures, fantastical forms, and cities suspended in mid-air. This unleashes boundless creativity, pushing the boundaries of design and potentially inspiring future real-world innovations. Beyond aesthetics, architects will play a crucial role in shaping the functionality of these virtual spaces. They can design immersive learning environments, interactive art galleries, or even virtual concert halls that foster social interaction. This extends to the realm of commerce, where architects can create virtual stores with interactive features, revolutionizing retail and influencing real-world purchasing decisions.

However, venturing into the metaverse isn't without its challenges. User experience is paramount. Architects need to design intuitive navigation, maintain a sense of scale, and consider sensory feedback to create comfortable and engaging virtual spaces. Additionally, translating fantastical virtual designs into real-world structures requires careful consideration of feasibility and cost.

Despite these challenges, the future of ArchiVerse (Architecture + Metaverse) holds immense promise. The metaverse fosters a new era of collaboration, allowing geographically dispersed teams to work together in real-time within a shared virtual environment. Clients can co-create their dream homes, leading to more successful projects. Furthermore, the metaverse presents a unique opportunity to preserve cultural heritage and historical landmarks through meticulously detailed virtual recreations.

REFERENCES

Al-Tabeeb, A. K., & Al-Desouqi, A. A. (2023). Metaverse in Architecture: An Approach to Documenting and Exploring the Egyptian Heritage Through Metaverse. *Green Building & Construction Economics*, 276-295.

Ayiter, E. (2014). (Re) Building proun# 5A in the metaverse. In *2014 International Conference on Cyberworlds*(pp. 403-406). IEEE. 10.1109/CW.2014.63

Bathla, D., & Singh, A. (Eds.). (2022). *Applying Metalytics to Measure Customer Experience in the Metaverse*. IGI Global. doi:10.4018/978-1-6684-6133-4

Benevolo, L. (1977). *History of modern architecture* (Vol. 2). Mit Press.

Bernasconi, C., & Blume, L. B. (2023). Theorizing architectural research and practice in the metaverse: The meta-context of virtual community engagement. *Archnet-IJAR: International Journal of Architectural Research*. Advance online publication. doi:10.1108/ARCH-08-2023-0203

Chen, T., Zhou, H., Yang, H., & Liu, S. (2022). A review of research on metaverse defining taxonomy and adaptive architecture. In *2022 5th International Conference on Pattern Recognition and Artificial Intelligence (PRAI)* (pp. 960-965). IEEE. 10.1109/PRAI55851.2022.9904076

Ching, F. D., Jarzombek, M. M., & Prakash, V. (2017). *A global history of architecture*. John Wiley & Sons.

Conway, H., & Roenisch, R. (2005). *Understanding architecture: an introduction to architecture and architectural history*. Routledge. doi:10.4324/9780203973196

Fischer, A. (2022). *Architecture as art in metaverse.* University of Zurich.

Forte, M., Lercari, N., Galeazzi, F., & Borra, D. (2010). Metaverse communities and archaeology: The case of Teramo. *Proceedings of EuroMed*, 79-84.

Frey, D., Royan, J., Piegay, R., Kermarrec, A. M., Anceaume, E., & Le Fessant, F. (2008). Solipsis: A decentralized architecture for virtual environments. *1st International Workshop on Massively Multiuser Virtual Environments*.

Gaafar, A. A. (2021). Metaverse in architectural heritage documentation & education. *Advances in Ecological and Environmental Research*, *6*(10), 66–86.

Gomes, E., Rebelo, F., Vilas Boas, N., Noriega, P., & Vilar, E. (2023). Virtual Reality in the Teaching of History of Architecture and Urbanism: A Literature Review. In *International Conference on Human-Computer Interaction* (pp. 437-453). Cham: Springer Nature Switzerland. 10.1007/978-3-031-35696-4_32

Hua, J. (2022). On the Architechural Design from the view of the Future Metaverse. In Диалог культур-диалог о мире и во имя мира (pp. 565-569). Academic Press.

Каширипур, M. M. (2023). Metaverse city: definition and direction development for urban planning and architecture. *Вестник Брестского государственного технического университета*, *3*(132), 2-10.

Kaur, A., & Singh, J. (2023). Brand Building in Metaverse. In *Applications of Neuromarketing in the Metaverse* (pp. 78–87). IGI Global. doi:10.4018/978-1-6684-8150-9.ch006

Lv, Z., Shang, W. L., & Guizani, M. (2022). Impact of digital twins and metaverse on cities: History, current situation, and application perspectives. *Applied Sciences (Basel, Switzerland)*, *12*(24), 12820. doi:10.3390/app122412820

Moffett, M., Fazio, M. W., & Wodehouse, L. (2003). *A world history of architecture*. Laurence King Publishing.

Moneta, A. (2020). Architecture, heritage, and the metaverse. *Traditional Dwellings and Settlements Review*, *32*(1), 37–49.

Nijjer, S., Singh, J., Sharma, P., Malhotra, M., & Verma, R. (2023). Unraveling a New Age of Travel in Blockchain Based Metaverse. In *Mobile Radio Communications and 5G Networks: Proceedings of Third MRCN 2022* (pp. 555-570). Singapore: Springer Nature Singapore. 10.1007/978-981-19-7982-8_47

Scavuzzo, S. T. (2022). *Immersive Experience of Ancient Architectural Heritage and Related Historical Events* (Doctoral dissertation, TU Wien).

Scheer, A. W. (2023). From Process and Enterprise Architecture to Digital Enterprise Twin in the Metaverse. In *The Composable Enterprise: Agile, Flexible, Innovative: A Gamechanger for Organisations, Digitisation and Business Software* (pp. 29–49). Springer Fachmedien Wiesbaden. doi:10.1007/978-3-658-42483-1_3

Schumacher, P. (2022). The metaverse as opportunity for architecture and society: Design drivers, core competencies. *Architectural Intelligence, 1*(1), 11. doi:10.1007/s44223-022-00010-z PMID:35993030

Shakeri, S., & Ornek, M. A. (2023). How metaverse evolves the architectural design. *Architecture and Planning Journal, 28*(3), 35. doi:10.54729/2789-8547.1230

Shalender, K., & Singla, B. (2024). Creator Economy in Metaverse Space: Use Cases, Adoption Challenges, and Integration Roadmap. In Creator's Economy in Metaverse Platforms: Empowering Stakeholders Through Omnichannel Approach (pp. 1-11). IGI Global.

Shryock, A., & Smail, D. L. (2011). *Deep history: The architecture of past and present.* Univ of California Press. doi:10.1525/9780520949669

Singh, J., Malhotra, M., & Sharma, N. (2022). Metaverse in education: An overview. *Applying metalytics to measure customer experience in the metaverse*, 135-142.

Singh, J., & Nijjer, S. (2024). Metaverse in Psychological Treatments: Is MEDverse the Next Normal? In Entrepreneurship and Creativity in the Metaverse (pp. 20-25). IGI Global.

Sopher, H., & Lescop, L. (2023). Learning in metaverse: The immersive atelier model of the architecture studio. *Archnet-IJAR: International Journal of Architectural Research, 17*(3), 536–553. doi:10.1108/ARCH-10-2022-0213

Unali, M., Caffio, G., & Zollo, F. (2023). Towards a Virtual Museum of Ephemeral Architecture: Methods, Techniques and Semantic Models for a Post-digital Metaverse. In *Beyond Digital Representation: Advanced Experiences in AR and AI for Cultural Heritage and Innovative Design* (pp. 191–207). Springer Nature Switzerland.

Wu, T., & Hao, F. (2023). Edu-Metaverse: Concept, architecture, and applications. *Interactive Learning Environments*, 1–28.

Xu, M., Guo, Y., Hu, Q., Xiong, Z., Yu, D., & Cheng, X. (2023). A trustless architecture of blockchain-enabled metaverse. *High-Confidence Computing, 3*(1), 100088.

Chapter 7
Metaverse and Brand:
A Futuristic Approach of Digital Marketing Strategy for Luxury Brand – India's Hidesign

Supriya Lamba Sahdev
ISBR Business School, India

Chitra Krishnan
https://orcid.org/0000-0003-1135-8852
Symbiosis Centre for Management Studies, Symbiosis International University (Deemed), Noida, India

ABSTRACT

By offering customers a satisfying shopping experience, Hidesign has effectively expanded its market and taken the lead in the Indian luxury market within the framework of the experience economy. Some luxury brands are venturing into the metaverse platform to broaden their brand influence and distribution channels, with the goal of attracting a younger demographic and so gaining a larger market share. In light of the widespread use of the metaverse concept, this study examines and discusses luxury firms' scene marketing communication strategies using Hidesign as an example. Ultimately, it offers workable recommendations for luxury brand metaverse marketing.

INTRODUCTION

In the realm of the Internet, the term "metaverse" is certain to become one of the buzzwords of the year 2021. Brand marketing has been revitalized by the rise of the meta poetic idea. To enhance the presentation of scene marketing communication, the diversification of scene presentation involves the implementation of digital avatars, Non-Fungible Tokens (NFT), virtual entertainment, and augmented reality (Xiang et al., 2021). Second, the vividness of the scene experience is enhanced by the three metaverse core technologies (blockchain, extended reality, and artificial intelligence), which allow for a more integrated use

DOI: 10.4018/979-8-3693-2422-6.ch007

of time, space, and other environmental factors. This gives the scene life and enhances the customers' inner feelings and visual stimulation (Xue, 2021). Third, consumers are able to fully engage their bodies and minds in the scene, fully mobilizing their sensory-motor systems to interact with the surrounding environment and become fully immersed in the created scene. This is made possible by the integration of mind and body in the scene, the metaverse support, and the empowerment of the scene experience (Liu et al., 2021). The fourth scene interactivity involves the integration of interactive technologies into the metaverse. This allows scene marketing communication to create interactive scenes with realistic emotions using the three core technologies of augmented reality, virtual reality, and extended reality. This allows customers to engage in immersive interactions with other customers and consumer scenes. This research discusses the characteristics of meta verse and its evolution trend, the significance of metaverse to brand scene marketing, the theoretical basis of marketing communication under the concept of meta verse, the problems of meta verse in the process of scene marketing communication and their solutions, pertinent case studies, and suggests references for the new direction of luxury brand meta verse marketing communication based on the background of metaverse. It does this by integrating literature related to digital marketing, scene marketing, and the metaverse concept, as well as using Hidesign's metaverse marketing as an example.

DIGITAL MARKETING FOR LUXURY BRANDS

Luxury Brand

Luxury brands are known for their exclusivity, high-quality craftsmanship, and the aura of prestige they bring to consumers. They often employ meticulous attention to detail and the use of premium materials to create products that are not only functional but also symbolize a certain lifestyle or social status (Vigneron & Johnson, 2004). Luxury brand consumers are not only purchasing products; they are buying into a world of elegance and sophistication that these brands represent (Kapferer, 2012). The appeal of luxury brands lies in their ability to evoke emotions and desires beyond the utilitarian nature of their offerings, making them a powerful force in the global consumer market. Generally speaking, luxury is an economic good with a particular socio-political meaning and moral connotation because, in the past, luxury goods were only available to members of the upper classes and royalty. In The Wealth of Nations, Ada M. Smith defined luxury as "goods not belonging to necessity" (Smith, 1998). Luxury goods are, in a narrow sense, the best-quality and rare top-quality items in the same category (Liu et al., 2016). It is important to emphasize that luxury goods nowadays are evolving into the highest level and prestige brands, with a showier concept. In contrast, everyday luxury products place more emphasis on the intangible contextual utility, and the functional utility included in the price is essentially non-existent (Huang, 2018; Zhou, 2015).

Digital Marketing for Luxury Brands

Digital marketing has become a crucial component of the luxury brand landscape in the modern era. In response to the evolving consumer behaviour, luxury brands have harnessed the power of digital platforms to reach a wider, more diverse audience (Okonkwo, 2016). These brands employ various strategies, including social media marketing, influencer collaborations, and immersive online experiences to maintain and enhance their exclusivity while remaining relevant in the digital age (Kapferer & Bastien, 2009). Digital marketing allows luxury brands to engage with consumers on a more personal level, creating a sense of community and belonging that resonates with the target audience. As luxury consumers increasingly spend time online, luxury brands must adapt to the digital landscape to maintain their allure and competitiveness (Okonkwo, 2016).

In order to effectively mobilize corporate resources to carry out marketing activities through contemporary electronic tools and communication network technology in order to achieve effective sales of corporate products and services, Wang and Lu detailed the definition of digital marketing, which is a series of business activities process based on computer information network technology (Wang & Lu, 2003). In order to achieve the management activities and management methods of planning, organization, coordination, service, innovation, and other functions of marketing management, Odden further emphasizes that digital marketing typically requires the use of computers, communications, networks, artificial intelligence, and other technologies to quantify marketing objects and marketing behaviours (Odden, 2015).

Metaverse

The concept of the metaverse, originally popularized by science fiction, has rapidly transformed into a tangible digital reality. The metaverse represents a convergence of virtual and physical worlds through immersive digital environments where individuals can interact, socialize, work, and create. It is a vast, interconnected network of virtual spaces, each with its unique characteristics and purposes (Castronova, 2005). Recent advances in technology, particularly in virtual reality (VR) and augmented reality (AR), have accelerated the development of the metaverse, making it a multidimensional, shared digital universe (Kermlin, 2021). The metaverse transcends traditional limitations and is not confined to a single platform; rather, it encompasses a plethora of interconnected platforms, applications, and experiences. Users can navigate this digital realm, build avatars, engage in commerce, and experience a wide range of activities, effectively reshaping the way we interact with the digital world (Smith, 2020). As it continues to evolve, the metaverse holds vast potential for various industries, from entertainment and gaming to education, healthcare, and beyond, presenting both opportunities and challenges as society adapts to this paradigm shift (Kermlin, 2021). The term "meta verse" is currently defined differently, and no agreement has been reached to bring it all together. Neal Stephenson first developed the idea of the meta verse in his science fiction book Snow Crash from 1992. In this book, Stephenson created a virtual three-dimensional world that is parallel to real life and where people work, play, and live in digital bodies that are connected to terminals that can interact and communicate with one another. In the film Avatar, the lead character wears a helmet and uses a digital doppelganger to live in a different reality (Takahashi, 2021). As a result, a number of digital firms and massive conglomerates have established the metaverse. For instance, the parent company of Facebook declared that it would rebrand the company as Meta and that it would transform Facebook into a metaverse business within five years. The CEO and founder of Facebook, Mark Zuckerberg, claims that the metaverse is a concept that encompasses numerous businesses and even the entire technology sector, and that it is the mobile Internet's replacement (Ball, 2022). According to Yu et al., the metaverse is the ultimate digital medium that unites all digital technologies from the past, present, and future into one. This will transform the relationship between the virtual and physical worlds and create a new, higher-dimensional world that exists outside of reality (Yu & Geng, 2021). Chen and Dong contend that the metaverse is a digital living place including a novel social structure, and that it is a virtual world that has been mapped and interacts with the actual world by technological means (Chen & Dong, 2021). In their most recent study, Pu and Xiang also demonstrate how the metaverse is a virtual world connected to the real world via intelligent devices and information and communication technology. It is created and recreated based on human subjective imagination and functions as a mirror projection of the real world overlaid on the future that people expect and desire (Pu & Xiang, 2022). In summary, the metaverse concept's fundamental components include building an intelligent digital realm outside of the real world on the basis of new information technology and including novel elements like the blending of reality and reality. Without a doubt, the metaverse offers fantastic chances for scene realization, scene immersion, and scene engagement. As a result, the idea of scene-based marketing communication is evolving within the framework of metaverse poetry, with the goal of disseminating messages through the creation of real-life or made-up scenarios that impact users' wants or beliefs (Kapferer, 2012). The scenario platform will undoubtedly become well-known as a new communication tool if the idea of meta verse is incorporated, offering users an engaging and dynamic experience (Okonkwo, 2016).

Metaverse Marketing for Indian Luxury Brands: Strategies and Insights

The metaverse represents a digital universe where individuals can interact, socialize, work, and engage with brands in immersive digital environments. While Indian luxury brands were gradually exploring the metaverse, several global luxury brands had started venturing into this evolving landscape. Some key strategies and insights include:

Creating Virtual Flagship Stores: Indian luxury brands can establish a virtual presence within the metaverse, creating digital flagship stores that replicate their physical boutiques. These virtual spaces enable consumers to explore and interact with products in a visually immersive environment.

Virtual Events and Fashion Shows: Luxury brands can host exclusive virtual events and fashion shows to engage with their audience. For instance, in 2020, Gucci organized a virtual fashion show in Roblox, allowing users to explore the brand's virtual garden and purchase digital items.

Digital Collaborations and Partnerships: Indian luxury brands can partner with metaverse influencers, artists, or content creators to generate interest and credibility. Collaborations can include limited-edition virtual products, creating unique selling points.

NFTs and Digital Collectibles: Exploring the sale of NFTs (Non-Fungible Tokens) and digital collectibles can create new revenue streams for luxury brands. Examples like Prada's NFT collection and virtual sneakers by RTFKT Studios demonstrate this trend.

Virtual Customer Service and Concierge: Providing top-notch customer service within the metaverse is essential. Brands can offer virtual customer representatives and personalized shopping assistance to enhance the customer experience.

Metaverse Loyalty Programs: Indian luxury brands can introduce metaverse-specific loyalty programs, offering incentives for engagement and purchases in the digital space.

Augmented Reality (AR) and Virtual Try-Ons: Brands can incorporate AR technology for virtual try-ons and product visualization. For example, Sephora allows customers to try on cosmetics virtually through its app.

Sustainability and Transparency: Leveraging blockchain technology to verify the authenticity and trace the origin of products can enhance transparency and trust. This resonates with consumer values and the growing importance of sustainability.

HIDESIGN METAVERSE MARKETING

Hidesign: Overview

Based in Pondicherry, India, Hidesign is a manufacturer of leather goods. The United States, the United Kingdom, Australia, Kenya, the United Arab Emirates, Spain, Portugal, New Zealand, and Sri Lanka were among the 24 nations in which the corporation operated in 2018. Hidesign's leather products division generates 160 crores in revenue.

Hidesign: Crafting Excellence in Leather Goods

Hidesign, a distinguished leather goods manufacturer based in Pondicherry, India, has been an emblem of fine craftsmanship and style for decades. Established in 1978 by Dilip Kapur, a former professor of international marketing, Hidesign has consistently set the standard for high-quality leather products that combine tradition, innovation, and contemporary fashion.

Heritage of Craftsmanship

Hidesign's journey is deeply rooted in a commitment to preserving the age-old craft of leather-making. The brand's artisans are known for their meticulous attention to detail, handcrafting every product with precision. The leather used in Hidesign products is carefully selected and tanned using eco-friendly methods, resulting in a distinctive, natural finish that only improves with age.

Product Range

Hidesign offers a wide range of leather goods, including handbags, wallets, belts, briefcases, travel bags, and accessories. Each piece reflects the brand's signature style, characterized by clean lines, elegant designs, and a touch of vintage appeal. Whether it's a classic leather handbag for everyday use or a stylish leather wallet, Hidesign products exude a sense of timeless luxury.

Global Presence

While Hidesign originated in India, it has expanded its presence to numerous countries worldwide. The brand's international boutiques and retail partnerships have allowed it to share its unique blend of Indian craftsmanship and contemporary aesthetics with a global audience. Hidesign's dedication to quality and design has garnered a loyal following not only in India but also in Europe, the United States, and beyond.

Sustainable Practices

Hidesign is committed to sustainability and ethical practices. The brand's emphasis on eco-friendly tanning methods, vegetable dyes, and environmentally responsible production processes aligns with a growing global awareness of the importance of sustainability in the fashion industry. Hidesign's dedication to ethical and sustainable practices is a testament to its responsibility as a global brand.

In a nutshell, Hidesign, with its roots in Pondicherry, India, is not just a leather goods manufacturer; it is a custodian of timeless craftsmanship and a symbol of sustainable luxury. Its dedication to quality, design, and responsible practices has positioned it as a global leader in the leather goods industry, admired by fashion-conscious individuals seeking sophistication, tradition, and environmental consciousness in their accessories.

Future Metaverse Strategies

Strategies that luxury brands like Hidesign could consider when venturing into the metaverse for marketing:

Virtual Flagship Stores: Hidesign can create virtual flagship stores in the metaverse, providing a digital space where customers can explore and interact with its products in a visually immersive way. This allows for brand promotion and a unique shopping experience.

Virtual Events: Hosting exclusive virtual events, such as fashion shows, product launches, or brand collaborations, can help Hidesign engage with its audience in the metaverse. This approach can generate excitement and drive interest in the brand.

Digital Product Personalization: Offering customization options for virtual products, such as digital skins, in the metaverse can be a unique selling point. Customers can personalize and express their style, reinforcing brand loyalty.

Collaborations with Metaverse Influencers: Partnering with influential figures within the metaverse can help Hidesign reach a broader audience and gain credibility within the virtual community.

Virtual Customer Service: Providing high-quality customer service through virtual representatives can enhance the customer experience in the metaverse, addressing inquiries and concerns promptly.

Metaverse Loyalty Programs: Creating loyalty programs specifically designed for metaverse customers can incentivize repeated engagement and purchases within the digital space.

Blockchain Technology: Consider integrating blockchain technology to authenticate and trace the origin of products, enhancing transparency and trust.

Adapting Metaverse Marketing strategies can offer several benefits to Hidesign, the renowned Indian leather goods manufacturer. Some potential advantages are appended below:

Global Reach and Expansion: Metaverse marketing can enable Hidesign to reach a global audience without the need for physical stores in various countries. It can expand its customer base and brand recognition far beyond its current geographical limitations

Immersive Brand Experience: The metaverse allows Hidesign to create immersive virtual environments that reflect the brand's heritage and values. Customers can engage with the brand in a unique and memorable way, enhancing brand loyalty and emotional connections.

Cost-Effective Marketing: Compared to traditional brick-and-mortar stores, setting up and maintaining a presence in the metaverse can be more cost-effective. This can result in cost savings that can be redirected into product development and other brand-enhancing initiatives.

New Revenue Streams: Hidesign can explore the creation of virtual products or digital skins that users can purchase for their avatars. This can generate new revenue streams in addition to physical product sales

Data Insights: Metaverse marketing can provide valuable data on customer behaviour and preferences. Hidesign can use this data to refine its marketing strategies, product offerings, and customer engagement.

Sustainability and Transparency: Utilizing blockchain technology within the metaverse can help Hidesign enhance transparency and authenticity, aligning with growing consumer expectations for sustainable and responsible brands

Enhanced Customer Engagement: Virtual events, immersive experiences, and personalized interactions can result in deeper customer engagement and stronger relationships with the brand.

Attracting a Tech-Savvy Audience: Adapting metaverse marketing can attract younger, tech-savvy consumers who are increasingly active in digital spaces and value innovative brand experiences.

Staying Competitive: By embracing metaverse marketing, Hidesign can stay competitive in the ever-evolving luxury goods market. Brands that adapt to new digital landscapes often gain a competitive edge.

Future-Proofing the Brand: As technology continues to advance, metaverse marketing positions Hidesign as a forward-thinking brand that is prepared for the future of marketing and commerce.

CONCLUSION

With an emphasis on the renowned Indian company Hidesign, we have explored the intriguing nexus between luxury brand marketing and the metaverse in this chapter. A futuristic approach to digital marketing has been presented by the metaverse, a growing digital space, and it offers great potential for luxury businesses globally. As we've seen, Hidesign's use of metaverse marketing marks a trailblazing move into unexplored digital territory and ushers in a new era of connection and interaction between brands and consumers. Hidesign and other luxury businesses have a lot of prospects in the metaverse. Virtual events, digital flagship stores, and immersive virtual worlds allow marketers to create experiences that go beyond the confines of traditional retail. This change in commerce from transactional to experiential is representative of how consumers are becoming more diverse. In addition, metaverse marketing promotes diversity worldwide. With consumers spread across continents, Hidesign's reach is no longer limited by geography and can convey the brand's ethos of quality and workmanship to a wide range of people globally. Hidesign and other high-end brands are well-positioned to successfully traverse the unknown seas of the metaverse as we move forward. The adoption of digital skins, transparent blockchain technology, and sustainable metaverse practices are all in line with the expectations and values of the contemporary luxury customer. The metaverse's digital domain offers opportunities for distinctive branding, but it also poses issues including data security, customer privacy, and the requirement for constantly improving digital skills. But these obstacles also present chances for development and creativity, and Hidesign's foray into the metaverse demonstrates its commitment to addressing issues head-on. The metaverse invites Hidesign and luxury brands worldwide to adjust, change, and rethink the art of luxury brand marketing as the digital era progresses. Although metaverse marketing is a futuristic strategy, its real power comes from its capacity to influence the course of events. Hidesign can rewrite the story of luxury on this platform by creating fresh narratives, fresh experiences, and a revitalized relationship with its audience. To sum up, Hidesign's entry into the metaverse is a thrilling move towards the future. Like a skilled craftsman, Hidesign continues to influence the direction of luxury brand marketing in the digital era as the metaverse develops and its opportunities increase. The story is still being written, the canvas is enormous, and the tools are futuristic.

It is trending for brands to take advantage of the metaverse because young consumers, who make up the majority of the consumer market, are gradually becoming familiar with the concept of Metaverse. Since they are also the ones who will shape the future of the industry, their opinions of brands and the purchases they make will have an impact on those brands' future growth and success. Users enter the metaverse, a virtual realm where reality and virtuality collide. Consequently, brands must contend with both real-world consumers and their virtual incarnations in the metaverse. To do this, brands leverage the metaverse to generate momentum and effectively cater to the social needs of users in the virtual realm while also advancing the digitalization and revitalization of the brand. This study lays down the foundation for a macro-level analysis of luxury firms' digital marketing tactics by integrating the metaverse. The microscopic analysis is insufficient since the particular pertinent data is insufficient. Future studies can integrate several businesses to thoroughly examine the existing state of affairs with presence of big data. Viewed through the prism of the metaverse, Hidesign and the industry as a whole have enormous potential for the future of luxury branding.

REFERENCES

Ball, M. (2022). *Framework for the Metaverse—MatthewBall.vc*. Available at: https://www.matthewball.vc/all/forwardtothemetaverseprimer

Castronova, E. (2005). *Synthetic Worlds: The Business and Culture of Online Games*. University of Chicago Press.

Chen, G., & Dong, H. (2021). *Peking University Scholars Release START Map of Metaverse Features and Properties*. Available at: https://share.gmw.cn/ it/2021-11/19/content_35323118.html

Huang, Y. (2018). *Research on the Marketing Strategy of Luxury Brands. Graduate*. Wuhan University.

Kapferer, J.-N. (2012). *The Luxury Strategy: Break the Rules of Marketing to Build Luxury Brands*. Kogan Page.

Kaplan, A. M., & Haenlein, M. (2010). Users of the world, unite! The challenges and opportunities of social media. *Business Horizons*, *53*(1), 59–68. doi:10.1016/j.bushor.2009.09.003

Kaplan, A. M., & Haenlein, M. (2019). The Metaverse as the final frontier: Implications for social media research. *Journal of Marketing Management*, *35*(15-16), 1422–1449.

Kermlin, J. (2021). The Metaverse: A New Digital Frontier? *Journal of Virtual Reality and Augmented Reality*, *3*(2), 87–103.

Liu, G., Wang, X., Gao, N., & Hu, H. (2021). From Virtual Reality to Metaverse: A New Direction for Online Education. *Modern Distance Education Research*, *33*, 14–16.

Liu, X., Xing, X., & Fu, B. (2016). *Luxury Studies*. Donghua University Press.

Odden, L. (2015). *21 Digital Marketing Trends & Predictions*. B2B Marketing Blog - Toprak. Available at: https://www.toprankblog.com/2014/05/digital-marketing-2015 /

Okonkwo, U. (2016). *Luxury Online: Styles, Systems, Strategies*. Palgrave Macmillan.

Pu, Q., & Xiang, W. (2022). *The Metaverse and Its Impact and Transformation on Human Society. Journal of Chongqing University: Social Science Edition, 19(21)*.

Smith, A. (1998). *An inquiry into the nature and causes of the wealth of nations*. Cofide.

Smith, A. (2020). *Navigating the Metaverse: A User's Guide to Virtual Reality*. Digital Publishers.

Takahashi, D. (2021). *Roblox CEO Dave Baszucki believes users will create the metaverse*. VentureBeat. Available at: https://venturebeat.com/2021/01/27/roblox-ceo-dav e -baszucki-believes-users-will-create-the-metaverse/

Vigneron, F., & Johnson, L. W. (2004). Measuring Perceptions of Brand Luxury. *Journal of Brand Management*, *11*(6), 484–506. doi:10.1057/palgrave.bm.2540194

Wang, T., & Lu, S. (2003). *Digital Marketing*. China Textile & Apparel Press.

Xiang, A., Gao, S., Peng, J., & Shen, Y. (2021). Knowledge Reorganization and Scene Re-configuration: A Meta-Universe for Digital Resource Management. *Library Information Knowledge*, *42*, 6–10.

Xue, J. (2021). *Exploration and Application of Metaverse in Broadcast Industry.* ABP.

Yu, G., & Geng, X. (2021). What is the "Metaverse": The Future Ecological Landscape of the Mediated Society. *Journal of Xinjiang Normal University: Philosophy and Social Science Edition, 2.*

Zhou, Y. (2015). *Luxury Brand Management*. University of International Business and Economics Press.

Chapter 8

Metaverse in Higher Education:
Reshaping Pedagogies and Entrepreneurial Ventures

Khalida Akbar
Durban University of Technology, South Africa

Vicent Mbonye
https://orcid.org/0000-0001-9890-614X
Partidos, South Africa

Trisha Govender
MANCOSA, South Africa

ABSTRACT

The integration of the Metaverse in higher education transforms pedagogies and fosters entrepreneurial prospects. This chapter explores the Metaverse's influence on education, emphasizing integration, challenges, opportunities, and ethics. Augmented and virtual reality immerse students, fostering critical thinking and creativity. The Metaverse spawns innovative educational tools, fostering collaborations between academia and entrepreneurship. Challenges include technological barriers, costs, and ethical concerns. Private institutions adapt policies, aligning with student expectations. The Metaverse enhances engagement, emphasizing personalized learning experiences. Ethical considerations are crucial in a transformative landscape. Collaborations between academia and industry drive innovation, contributing to the evolution of higher education. The Metaverse's integration signifies a profound shift, necessitating innovation, ethics, and collaboration. This chapter underscores its transformative potential in pedagogies, entrepreneurship, and ethical considerations in higher education.

INTRODUCTION TO THE METAVERSE IN HIGHER EDUCATION

Neal Stephenson introduced the term "metaverse" in his 1992 novel "Snow Crash" (Duan et al., 2021). providing a conceptual framework for a virtual reality space where users could interact with

DOI: 10.4018/979-8-3693-2422-6.ch008

each other and digital environments. The novel depicted an immersive online space that served as an extension of the physical world, exploring the implications of a digital universe intertwined with reality. This popularized the idea of a metaverse and stimulated discussions about the potential future of the internet, influencing subsequent works of fiction and contributing to the cultural imagination of virtual worlds.

Second Life was a virtual world and online game that was created by Linden Lab and launched in 2003. It was one of the first and most successful virtual world platforms, providing users with tools to create, trade, and interact in a shared 3D space. It emphasized user-generated content, allowing residents to build and script their virtual environments and creations. This aspect of user agency and creativity has influenced the idea that the metaverse should be a space where users can actively shape their experiences. Second Life has been described as an antecedent of the Metaverse (Gent, 2022; Ludlow & Wallace, 2007).

While neither "Snow Crash" nor Second Life directly predicted the current state of the metaverse, they laid the groundwork by introducing key concepts like virtual reality, shared digital spaces, and user agency. The evolving discussions around the metaverse draw inspiration from these early works, and their impact is evident in the ongoing development and exploration of virtual and augmented reality technologies, user-generated content platforms, and the integration of digital experiences into our daily lives.

As technology continued to advance, the metaverse as we know it today, is often associated with a broader and more interconnected digital universe that extends beyond virtual reality into augmented reality, mixed reality, and other immersive technologies. Additionally, the concept of the metaverse now includes elements of decentralization, blockchain technology, and persistent virtual worlds that can be experienced across different platforms and devices.

Within the context of higher education, the Metaverse holds immense relevance. It promises to revolutionize the way students engage with content, providing avenues for personalized learning, collaborative projects, and real-world applications of knowledge. The Metaverse is not just another digital tool to enhance education but can be a catalyst for pedagogical transformation.

The Metaverse also creates opportunities for entrepreneurial ventures in higher education. It allows for the creation of innovative educational platforms and collaborative research initiatives.

One of the central themes explored in this chapter is the Metaverse's direct influence on student engagement. By breaking down geographical barriers and offering a globally connected learning environment, it addresses challenges in keeping students actively involved in their educational journeys.

This introduction serves as a prelude to the comprehensive exploration that follows in the subsequent chapters. We delve into the Metaverse's potential to reshape pedagogies, unlock entrepreneurial opportunities, and redefine the landscape of higher education.

PEDAGOGICAL EVOLUTION THROUGH METAVERSE INTEGRATION

The COVID-19 pandemic disrupted traditional education by closing campuses and affecting student engagement, emphasizing the need for innovative curriculum delivery and a heightened focus on student well-being to navigate unforeseen disruptions effectively. In response, this led to the accelerated creation of virtual content and a significant shift towards the digitalization of higher education materials and e-learning (Onu et al., 2023), addressing both educational needs and overall well-being in the face of pandemic challenges (Ruz-Fuenzalida, 2021).

Beyond the influence of the COVID-19 pandemic, the increased popularity and accessibility of virtual and augmented learning have contributed to the growing interest in leveraging the Metaverse for educational applications (Lee et al., 2022; Tian, 2022; Onu et al., 2023). Metaverse technologies include virtual and augmented reality, mixed reality, 3D gaming, and holographic technology. Education in the Metaverse comprises virtual classrooms, training simulations and virtual labs (Kye et al., 2021; Onu et al., 2023). In this setting, students can engage in collaborative projects, exchange ideas through discussions, access global resources, and interact within a virtual environment (Akour et al., 2022).

Through immersive learning environments, the Metaverse offers students three-dimensional, experiential spaces that enhance engagement and memory retention. Collaborative opportunities in real-time, regardless of geographical locations, foster global connectivity and diverse perspectives. The integration of the Metaverse into education represents a significant pedagogical evolution, redefining traditional teaching and learning approaches (Onu et at., 2023). Realistic simulations and gamification elements within the Metaverse bring about hands-on, enjoyable learning experiences that prepare students for real-world applications of knowledge. Additionally, the metaverse contributes to accessible and inclusive education, breaking down physical and geographical barriers. Educators can dynamically adapt teaching methods, leveraging continuous professional development opportunities within the Metaverse. Data analytics provide insights into student interactions, aiding educators in tailoring instruction to individual learning styles. In essence, Metaverse integration revolutionizes pedagogy, creating a dynamic and transformative educational landscape that goes beyond the limitations of traditional educational paradigms.

It is recommended that educational institutions create frameworks to ensure responsible and ethical use of the Metaverse and implement mechanisms that protect the safety, privacy, and wellbeing of students, staff, and other stakeholders involved in metaverse-based learning environments (Onu et al., 2023).

Impact on Student Engagement and Learning Outcomes

Student engagement is a multi-faceted and complex aspect, no singular definition can adequately capture its entirety. This intricate phenomenon involves a dynamic interplay of various behavioral, cognitive, and affective indicators, making it challenging to encapsulate in a single, comprehensive definition. The nuanced nature of student engagement encompasses diverse elements such as relationships, learning activities, and the learning environment. Recognizing its complexity is crucial to appreciating the broad spectrum of ways in which students actively participate and invest in their educational experiences (Bond 2020).

The Metaverse offers solutions to challenges related to student engagement by leveraging technologies like virtual and augmented reality, mixed reality, 3D gaming, and holographic technology. It creates an immersive environment for students, allowing, for instance, those studying planets to explore the galaxy through the Metaverse with zoom capabilities. This functionality enables students to closely observe the texture and features of the cosmos (Kaddoura and Husseiny, 2023). This form of immersion serves as a powerful motivator, actively engaging and inspiring students (Nashville, 2021).

The Metaverse dismantles geographical barriers, fostering improved collaboration by exposing students to diverse cultures and a rich exchange of ideas (Onu et al., 2023). This exposure promotes a broader perspective, leading to enhanced learning outcomes that go beyond physical boundaries (Onu et al. 2023). This transcendence of traditional classroom settings fosters a more inclusive and globally connected learning environment.

The landscape of educational methodologies is ever-evolving, with each approach tailored to foster different aspects of learning and cognitive development. Among these, the Metaverse stands out for its innovative approach to education. The Metaverse's capacity for creating tailored and adaptive learning experiences significantly enhances student engagement by catering to the unique needs and preferences of each learner. This immersive digital environment allows educators to dynamically customize content and interactions, offering students a highly personalized educational journey that transcends traditional learning models and maximizes knowledge and skill acquisition (Frost et al., 2020; Kounlaxay & Kim, 2020; Onu et al., 2023). In the realm of active learning of the following applies to pedagogies.

Problem-Based Learning

Problem based learning is characterised by the active acquisition and synthesis of knowledge through group work and self-directed learning (Savery, 2015). Learners engage in problem-solving through self-directed or collaborative research to investigate and resolve diverse problems requiring solutions. Regular provision of detailed feedback, opportunities for learner reflection, and the design of learning settings aimed at fostering intrinsic motivation are crucial components of this process (Hmelo-Silver, Duncan, & Chinn, 2007).

Discovery-Based Learning

Discovery-Based Learning emphasises learner autonomy and intrinsic motivation, fostering a love for learning beyond formal schooling. This approach, rooted in active exploration, experimentation, and problem-solving, aims to empower students to take ownership of their learning journey. Unlike traditional education models focused on extrinsic motivation, Discovery-Based Learning prioritises learner interest and engagement, crucial for long-term knowledge retention (Mayer, 2004). Additionally, (Willis, 2006) suggests learner interest and engagement is paramount for long-term knowledge retention . Thus, the essence of discovery-based learning lies in students' exploration of their surroundings through hands-on experimentation and grappling with thought-provoking issues(Ormrod, 1995), within an environment that acknowledges the constraints of prior knowledge and encourages inquiry (Schmidt et al., 2007).

Inquiry-Based Learning

Inquiry-Based Learning (IBL) involves activities that start with a question, leading to investigating solutions, creating new knowledge, discussing discoveries, and reflecting on newfound knowledge(Savery, 2015). Effective IBL encourages student curiosity, makes inquiry visible, and integrates technology to facilitate information gathering and presentation(Owens, Hester, & Teale, 2002). Students propose their own questions, complete an investigation, identify and present previously unknown results or answers with minimal traditional teacher guidance and support. Owens et al. (2002) report that effective inquiry-based learning encourages student curiosity, makes inquiry visible, emphasises the importance of topics and questions, facilitates the process of gathering and presenting information, and integrates technology. IBL is highly focused on the process of learning, but also ensures that students are directing their learning and teachers are available to scaffold student capacities to move from a confirmation to an open inquiry skill stage (Bianchi & Bell, 2008; Bishop et al., 2006; Owens et al., 2002).

Project-Based Learning

Project-Based Learning (PjBL) involves students in undertaking tasks that yield tangible products or presentations mirroring real-world scenarios. It enhances problem-solving skills and encourages creativity, enabling students to address issues and challenges relevant to them and their communities. This approach is explored through an interdisciplinary approach, facilitating knowledge transferability and often involves students working collaboratively in small groups (Barron & Darling-Hammond, 2008).

The aforementioned pedagogical approaches predominantly center around student-centered or learner-centered learning paradigms. This signifies that students take on an active role in their educational journey, with educators serving as facilitators of learning rather than traditional

In recent research, active learning pedagogies have been highlighted as key in teaching aspects of AI. For instance, these methods aim to actively involve students in the learning process, tailor instruction to individual needs and emphasise the practical application of machine learning principles. For instance, Huang and Ma (2018)conducted a study introducing machine learning to first-year undergraduate engineering students using an authentic and active learning platform. This approach helped students understand the importance of machine learning in addressing real-world problems through data-driven approaches.

Chenoweth and Linos (2018)reported positive outcomes from teaching machine learning using personalised learning in predominantly online courses at two universities. They found a significant interest in machine learning among students, regardless of their majors, indicating the effectiveness of personalised learning. Likewise, Sulmont, Patitsas, and Cooperstock (2019) explored effective teaching strategies for machine learning among non-major undergraduate students. Their research highlighted the efficacy of visualization, real-world applications, and customization to students' domains in addressing learning barriers.

Koshelev, and Ustalov (2019) adopted the project based learning approach to teach machine learning to students. The results showed that there was a high acquisition of theoretical knowledge and practical problem-solving skills with positive implications for employment.

ENTREPRENEURIAL PROSPECTS IN THE METAVERSE

Open Education has exerted a substantial influence on the landscape of online distance education. Following the 1960s, the Open Education movement played a pivotal role in establishing Open Universities on a global scale (Jeong, 2019). Online learning is progressively gaining prominence, particularly in higher education and continuous adult education. The COVID-19 pandemic acted as a catalyst, speeding up this trend by disrupting traditional, attendance-based activities across all levels of education. Worldwide, remote emergency teaching became imperative as a response to health-related physical distancing measures (Boltz et al., 2021). From its inception, online education has predominantly leaned on asynchronous and synchronous e-learning(Amiti, 2020). These rely on software or web applications within two-dimensional digital environments, characterised by in-plane digital windows with width and height but lacking depth. Standard asynchronous online learning tools encompass learning management systems (e.g., Moodle, Blackboard), occasionally supplemented by collaborative web applications and social networks. Asynchronous tools are designed to facilitate flexible, anytime, anywhere communication and interaction among educators, students, and content (Amiti, 2020; Stöhr et al., 2020). Synchronous e-learning facilitate simultaneous online interactions between educators and students within a digital, virtual space(Amiti, 2020). The implementation of synchronous online learning is achieved through the utilisation of web conferencing platforms such as Zoom, WebEx, Microsoft Teams, Adobe Connect, and Skype (Gegenfurtner & Ebner, 2019; Puspitasari, 2021)

Nevertheless, applications functioning in 2D, web-based environments are characterised by well-documented limitations and inefficiencies. Prolonged daily usage of synchronous online platforms gives rise to phenomena like Zoom fatigue (Bailenson, 2021; Riedl, 2022). Asynchronous platforms, on the other hand, frequently grapple with emotional isolation, which proves to be a detrimental factor affecting participation motivation. Therefore, e-learning courses on these platforms experience elevated drop-out rates (Anderson & Rivera Vargas, 2020). While the utilisation of social media and collaborative applications, such as blogs and wikis, can enhance active engagement, it does not necessarily address natural communication and the emotional stress experienced by users (Dunn & Kennedy, 2019). 2D platforms exhibit limitations that adversely affect education. One notable constraint is low self-perception, where users encounter a significantly restricted understanding of themselves within these environments. They are often portrayed as disembodied entities, represented solely through a photo or a live webcam headshot feed, lacking personalisation options (Mystakidis, 2022). Moreover, the absence of presence is notable in web conferencing sessions on 2D platforms, where these sessions are perceived merely as video calls to join rather than virtual collective meeting places. In extended meetings, participants often disengage and become distracted. Additionally, inactivity is prevalent on 2D platforms, as they provide limited interaction opportunities among participants. Unless instructors initiate learning activities, students are confined to passive participation, with few chances to actively engage (Mystakidis, 2022) Furthermore, there is a limitation in crude emotional expression on 2D platforms, as users have very restricted options to convey their feelings, often limited to smileys and emojis. All these constraints can be effectively addressed by transitioning to 3D immersive spatial environments (Mystakidis, 2022). Leveraging the Metaverse in education presents numerous potential advantages over traditional models. It enables students with learning difficulties to partake in immersive experiences, such as exploring historical sites or conducting potentially hazardous experiments, all within a secure virtual setting alongside their classmates (Harris et al., 2022).

The Metaverse facilitates real-time, dynamic communication with digital elements. It enables diverse interactions with virtual environments, digital objects and human participants through various technologies like Virtual Reality (VR) and Augmented Reality (AR), AR. It comprises of interconnected social networks and immersive experiences on persistent multiuser platforms. Originating as a network of virtual realms, it initially permitted avatars to teleport, laying the groundwork for its subsequent development (Mystakidis, 2022). However, despite this enthusiasm, the Metaverse introduces various challenges that warrant careful consideration.

ADDRESSING CHALLENGES IN METAVERSE IMPLEMENTATION

Technological Challenges

The interactivity of online services within the Metaverse, while fostering user input, also presents opportunities for hackers to exploit vulnerable systems posing a significant risk to the security of personal data(Alja'afreh et al., 2023; Dwivedi et al., 2022; Koohang et al., 2023a).

Also, man-in-the-middle attacks represent a serious threat within the Metaverse, as they involve eavesdropping on or altering the communication between the user and the server(Y. Huang et al., 2023). In such attacks, there is a potential for interception or modification of data packets, leading to a compromise in the confidentiality, integrity, and availability of the system (Y. Huang et al., 2023). These attacks pose significant risks to the overall security and reliability of communications within the Metaverse, underscoring the need for robust security measures to mitigate such threats and ensure the protection of user data and system integrity.

The Metaverse, particularly those incorporating embedded web pages, is susceptible to Cross-Site Scripting (XSS) attacks (Y. Huang et al., 2023; Vondráček et al., 2023).. The integration of web pages within the Metaverse creates a vulnerability, allowing attackers to exploit this entry point for injecting malicious JavaScript code(Vondráček et al., 2023). In such attacks, perpetrators have the ability to inject harmful JavaScript code either directly into the client website or into a store location, which is subsequently requested by the client website. This method allows attackers to compromise the security of the website, potentially leading to unauthorised access, data manipulation, or other malicious activities.

Furthermore, the Metaverse expands upon the real-world building environment by introducing additional functionalities. Users can engage in "in-person" meetings within a Virtual Reality (VR) room, shop in a virtual mall, or even perform remote surgery(Koohang et al., 2023b). These diverse capabilities are integrated into the Metaverse system through a multitude of applications. Communication channels are established among these applications to create a unified, multi-functional Metaverse, akin to the arrangement seen in mobile devices. However, it's crucial to recognise that these communication channels, while enhancing interoperability, also introduce a potential security vulnerability. The interconnectedness of applications allows one app to access the status of system components and the outgoing information of another app (Y. Huang et al., 2023). This situation may inadvertently create a backdoor for third-party tracking or cross-app tracking. Consequently, there is a risk of users' privacy being compromised through third-party tracking and cross-app tracking (Y. Huang et al., 2023)

The immersive interaction within the Metaverse entails the use of various devices, including wearable devices, headsets, base stations, and controllers, involving extensive data exchange. Communication among these devices and remote/cloud services is pivotal in delivering a truly immersive experience for users. However, it's essential to note that these devices are embedded with numerous sensors capable of collecting highly sensitive information, including fingerprints, locations, and facial identities (C. Huang et al., 2022) The stakes are significantly higher in the event of a security breach concerning users of these devices, given that many biometrics, such as fingerprints and facial identity, are unique and remain unchanged throughout the lifespan of users. This distinctive characteristic makes these biometric identifiers particularly sensitive and valuable. Consequently, it becomes imperative to implement rigorous protection measures not only for individual devices but also for the communication channels among them (Cocioceanu et al., 2016; Zulfiqar et al., 2019).

Financial

Blockchain technology, cryptocurrency, and Non-Fungible Tokens (NFTs) assume a pivotal role in bolstering and securing the virtual economy within the Metaverse. They achieve this by certifying the unique identity of virtual assets, a record enshrined in the blockchain. This certification not only establishes ownership but also facilitates the trading of these virtual assets. The integration of these technologies contributes to the authenticity and security of the virtual economy in the Metaverse

(Peres et al., 2023). Cryptocurrency is a form of digital currency that operates on the foundation of blockchain technology (Fang et al., 2022). As a result, cryptocurrency operates without dependency on any central platform. Users can enjoy an anonymised and secure payment experience facilitated by cryptocurrency. However, it's important to note that both cryptocurrency and NFTs come with their own set of drawbacks, including legal concerns and the potential for collusion among dominant entities. There is an expectation that these issues will be addressed and mitigated through ongoing technological advancements (Fang et al., 2022).

one significant obstacle lies in the creation of Metaverse learning environments, necessitating the acquisition of new resources and qualifications (Stanoevska-Slabeva, 2022). Additionally, there is a notable challenge associated with the required end devices essential for active participation in the Metaverse(Stanoevska-Slabeva, 2022). While not all schools in the Metaverse mandate the use of Virtual Reality (VR), as some Metaverses can be accessed solely through the web, it is acknowledged that sophisticated technology and tools, particularly VR, offer the best experience and sensation. However, the current high cost and limited availability of VR make it a rare and expensive item. Consequently, efforts are ongoing to explore and develop more affordable alternatives to VR. It is essential to recognise that if virtual world-based education heavily relies on VR and similar technologies, it may create a scenario where access is limited to a select few, excluding a broader spectrum of students. This emphasises the need for inclusivity and the development of cost-effective solutions to ensure equitable access to virtual education within the Metaverse (Tokarev et al., 2021)

Ethical

Students with disabilities, such as those with hearing or vision impairments, may necessitate specific accommodations (Akour et al., 2022) The potential for Metaverse addiction, particularly in the form of Virtual Reality (VR) addiction, is a significant concern. This is amplified by the prevalent addiction to electronic devices observed in many individuals. Recognizing and addressing this possibility is crucial to ensure a balanced and healthy engagement with immersive technologies within the Metaverse (MacCallum & Parsons, 2019).

In the world-building environment of the Metaverse, there is an emulation of the real world. Each user is endowed with character settings within this environment, providing comprehensive information encompassing hobbies, interests, friendships, and expertise. This wealth of information contributes to the construction of user profiles, revealing significant meta relations (Liu et al., 2022) These user profiles, often coupled with knowledge graphs, play a crucial role in powering recommendation systems (C. Huang et al., 2022). However, the extensive use of user profiling introduces a potential threat to users' privacy, prompting the necessity for implementing robust privacy protection mechanisms. Striking a balance between maintaining the immersive world-building environment and ensuring an accurate recommendation system while safeguarding users' privacy is of paramount importance.

The potential for imbalance arises when a student extensively uses their virtual reality headset for both educational and entertainment purposes. This can result in spending numerous hours each week in the digital world, potentially leading to neglect of their real-world life (MacCallum & Parsons, 2019). Such an imbalance may manifest in undesirable behaviors, including antisocial tendencies, extravagant habits, and health or mental health issues. It underscores the importance of promoting a healthy and balanced approach to the use of virtual reality tools, with a focus on well-being and responsible usage (MacCallum & Parsons, 2019).

PRIVATE HIGHER EDUCATION POLICIES IN THE METAVERSE ERA: EXAMINING ADAPTIVE STRATEGIES OF PRIVATE INSTITUTIONS ALIGNING WITH METAVERSE INTEGRATION

In the dynamic landscape of higher education, the integration of the Metaverse represents a transformative paradigm shift. Private higher education institutions are at the forefront of this change, adapting their policies, curricula, and teaching methodologies to align with the evolving technological landscape. This exploration delves into the adaptive strategies employed by private institutions as they embrace the Metaverse, aiming to remain competitive, meet student expectations, and address industry demands in the following ways:

Adapting to the Metaverse:Private higher education institutions recognize the imperative to integrate the Metaverse into their educational frameworks. This integration is not merely a technological upgrade but a strategic response to the changing educational ecosystem. As the Metaverse offers immersive and interactive learning experiences, institutions understand the need to redefine their policies to harness its potential fully.

Strategies for Pedagogical Transformation:The Metaverse's impact on pedagogies is profound, fostering critical thinking, creativity, and problem-solving skills through immersive experiences. Private institutions are redefining their teaching methodologies to leverage these benefits. Adaptive strategies include incorporating virtual simulations, experiments, and collaborative projects within virtual environments. This approach enhances student engagement, deepens comprehension, and ultimately improves learning outcomes.

Entrepreneurial Ventures in Education:The entrepreneurial spirit within private higher education institutions is thriving in the Metaverse era. These institutions recognize the opportunities to create innovative educational tools, content platforms, and startups focused on educational technology. Adaptive strategies involve fostering an environment conducive to entrepreneurial initiatives, supporting research and development, and forming collaborations with industry partners. Private institutions understand that embracing the entrepreneurial potential of the Metaverse is not only beneficial for their own growth but also contributes to the advancement of higher education practices.

Policy Redefinition for Technological Integration:The integration of the Metaverse comes with its set of challenges, including technological barriers and costs. Private institutions are strategically redefining their policies to address these challenges. Adaptive strategies involve investing in infrastructure, providing training for faculty, and ensuring equitable access to Metaverse technologies. Moreover, policies are being formulated to facilitate seamless integration, considering the diverse needs of students and faculty.

Ethical Considerations in the Metaverse:The transformative landscape of the Metaverse brings forth ethical considerations, including data privacy, content moderation, and ensuring a secure digital learning environment. Private institutions are proactively incorporating ethical guidelines into their policies. Strategies involve implementing robust data protection measures, establishing clear content moderation protocols, and prioritizing inclusivity and security. These measures are essential to build trust among stakeholders and maintain the integrity of the educational experience within the Metaverse.

Competitive Edge and Student Expectations: Private higher education institutions are acutely aware of the competitive edge offered by Metaverse integration. To meet evolving student expectations and industry demands, adaptive strategies include continuous monitoring of technological advancements, swift incorporation of emerging trends, and regular updates to curricula. This proactive approach ensures that private institutions not only keep pace with technological developments but also stay ahead in providing cutting-edge educational experiences.

Collaborative Initiatives with Industry: Recognizing the collaborative potential of the Metaverse, private institutions are actively engaging in partnerships with industry players. These collaborations drive innovation, research initiatives, and entrepreneurial opportunities. Adaptive strategies involve creating symbiotic relationships that benefit both academia and industry. This collaborative approach ensures that private institutions remain at the forefront of Metaverse developments and contribute meaningfully to its evolution.

Therefore private higher education institutions are navigating the Metaverse era with strategic adaptability. The integration of the Metaverse goes beyond technological implementation; it requires a holistic transformation of policies, pedagogies, and entrepreneurial initiatives. Private institutions that proactively redefine their approaches stand to gain a competitive advantage, ensuring that they not only meet but exceed the expectations of students and industry stakeholders in this transformative educational landscape. The Metaverse, with its immersive potential, is not just a tool; it is a catalyst for the reshaping of higher education, and private institutions are at the forefront of this transformative journey.

IMPACT ON STUDENT ENGAGEMENT AND LEARNING OUTCOMES

Within the dynamic sphere of higher education, the incorporation of the Metaverse arises as a crucial factor that is fundamentally altering the ways in which students are involved and how they achieve academic results. This investigation examines the profound effect that the Metaverse has on the manner in which students interact with academic material and the subsequent consequences for their academic achievements. In light of the increasing adoption of the Metaverse by private higher education institutions, it is imperative to comprehend its impact on student engagement in order to maximize the educational experience.

A Paradigm Shift in Student Engagement

By virtue of its interactive and immersive attributes, the Metaverse fundamentally transforms the conventional concept of student engagement. Students transcend geographical boundaries and enter a globally interconnected learning environment within the Metaverse. The interconnectedness of this space enables students to actively engage in collaborative projects, experiments, and simulations within virtual environments, thereby facilitating real-time collaboration. An increased degree of student engagement ensues, as they become profoundly invested in their academic trajectories.

Adaptive strategies implemented in private higher education institutions encompass the incorporation of interactive components and virtual simulations into the curricula. Institutions cultivate an atmosphere in which students actively participate in their learning experiences rather than simply receiving information by harnessing the potential of the Metaverse. The transformation in patterns of student involvement is propelled by the immersive characteristics of the Metaverse, which provide learners with a feeling of being present and having control over the digital environment.

Tailored Learning Experiences Encompass

An aspect of the Metaverse that significantly affects pupil engagement is the ability to deliver individualized learning experiences. Tailored content delivery, adaptive assessments, and individualized learning paths are all feasible within the Metaverse. By investigating adaptive learning technologies within the Metaverse, private institutions can ensure that students receive content that is specifically designed to suit their individual learning patterns and pacing. By catering to diverse student preferences and requirements, this customization increases student engagement and renders the learning experience more significant and applicable. The capacity of the Metaverse to accommodate a wide range of learning styles positively influences student motivation and satisfaction. Students demonstrate increased engagement in the learning process when the subject matter corresponds to their personal preferences. In light of the importance of personalized learning, private institutions are implementing adaptive strategies that utilize Metaverse technologies in order to customize educational experiences for each pupil.

Improving Comprehension and Critical Analysis

Through its immersive characteristics, the Metaverse surpasses conventional pedagogical approaches by providing students with experiences that cultivate more profound understanding and analytical reasoning. By encountering practical applications of theoretical concepts in virtual environments, students are able to establish connections between theory and practice. Adaptive strategies encompass the integration of problem-solving scenarios, simulations, and virtual laboratories within the Metaverse, thereby compelling learners to employ their acquired knowledge in real-world contexts. Institutions of private higher education are currently observing the profound and revolutionary effects that the Metaverse is having on the critical thinking and problem-solving skills of their students. The dynamic and interactive characteristics of virtual environments stimulate student participation and interaction with course materials, resulting in a heightened comprehension of abstract ideas. As a result of this transformation in learning dynamics, academic achievements are enhanced as pupils cultivate analytical abilities that transcend the limitations of conventional learning environments.

Conquering Geographical Obstacles

The impact of the Metaverse on student engagement transcends geographical limitations. Students hailing from various global locations are able to seamlessly collaborate in a digitally interconnected environment, thereby offering a wide range of perspectives that enrich discussions and projects. Private establishments are employing this facet of the Metaverse in a calculated manner in order to establish an internationalized educational setting. Collaborative assignments conducted in virtual environments provide students with valuable exposure to diverse cultural viewpoints, thereby enhancing their academic journeys. The elimination of geographical barriers additionally tackles obstacles related to tangible accessibility. The Metaverse facilitates the active engagement of students in educational endeavors, irrespective of their geographical location. Implementing adaptive strategies entails ensuring that all students have equal access to Metaverse technologies, thereby facilitating their ability to benefit from this interconnected global learning environment. Consequently, students are provided with an educational experience that is more inclusive and cultivates a sense of community, transcending geographical barriers.

Assessment of Learning Outcomes

As more and more private institutions of higher education adopt the Metaverse, it becomes crucial to quantify and evaluate its influence on academic achievements. Conventional evaluation approaches might not comprehensively measure the intricacies of learning in virtual environments. Adaptive strategies encompass the creation of novel evaluative instruments that are in harmony with the experiential and interactive characteristics of learning in the Metaverse. Academic organizations are investigating the implementation of real-time performance analytics, project-based evaluations, and virtual portfolios as means to track student development in the Metaverse. By implementing these adaptive assessment strategies, an all-encompassing comprehension of students' knowledge and skill development in ever-changing digital environments can be achieved. By adapting evaluation techniques to the immersive characteristics of the Metaverse, academic establishments can enhance the precision of their assessments regarding the efficacy of this paradigm-shifting pedagogical methodology.

In summary, the implications of the Metaverse for learning outcomes and student engagement in private institutions of higher education are significant. The Metaverse's capacity for transformation fundamentally alters conventional modes of engagement, facilitating individualized learning experiences, augmenting understanding, and transcending geographical limitations. With the strategic adaptation of approaches by institutions, students are increasingly engaged in their educational journeys, fostering the development of critical thinking abilities and immersing themselves in a globalized learning environment. The Metaverse serves as a catalyst for a paradigm transformation in higher education; it is not merely a technological instrument. Private educational establishments that successfully harness the immersive capabilities of the Metaverse are observing enhanced student engagement and superior academic achievements. The continuous investigation of the Metaverse's influence on education is of utmost importance in order to optimize learning experiences, refine adaptive strategies, and guarantee that students are adequately equipped to confront the ever-changing challenges of the digital era.

ETHICAL CONSIDERATIONS AND DATA PRIVACY IN THE METAVERSE

The Metaverse has ushered in a new era of collaboration between academia and industry, serving as a catalyst for innovation and research. This synergy between these two domains has proven instrumental in driving advancements within the Metaverse. To illustrate, Meta has joined forces with 15 universities throughout the United States, where a proactive adoption of immersive learning is underway. These universities are individually conducting virtual reality-based classroom sessions and activities, aiming to explore the potential contributions of immersive technologies to the evolution of education (Nick Clegg, 2023). Also Moreover, the company has introduced a diverse collection of education-focused apps accessible on Meta Quest, covering a wide array of subjects such as science, engineering, technology, and mathematics (STEM), history, language, and more (Nick Clegg, 2023).

Eduverse a tech company has created an online platform for teachers to engage students in the metaverse (Eduverse, 2023).

Microsoft has crafted an immersive experience for students through Every Windows Mixed Reality-ready PC. The introduction of Mixed Reality apps bring the content closer to the students in a highly engaging manner. This breakthrough technology in Mixed Reality transcends emotional barriers, enabling students to perceive life from fresh perspectives. By incorporating this immersive technology, an environment is established for learners to collaborate, offering access to experiences that were previously inaccessible. The outcomes thus far demonstrate their efficacy, with pre-test to post-test scores showing a notable improvement of one to two letter grades, and WCU-Los Angeles students experiencing a 10 percent enhancement in test scores compared to the previous year (Microsoft, 2023b) Also, the company has created Mesh for Microsoft Teams which is designed to infuse a personal and enjoyable element into collaboration within the metaverse (Microsoft, 2023a).

These partnerships underscore the dynamic potential of collaboration, enabling knowledge exchange, co-creation of educational content, and exploration of entrepreneurial opportunities within the Metaverse.

COLLABORATIVE VENTURES DRIVING INNOVATION

In the rapidly evolving landscape of higher education, collaborative ventures within the Metaverse stand as dynamic catalysts for innovation and research. Private higher education institutions strategically engage in partnerships with industry players, shaping the contours of educational practices within the immersive digital realm. Collaborative initiatives within the Metaverse go beyond traditional academic-industry relationships. These ventures leverage the transformative potential of virtual environments, where academia and industry converge to explore, innovate, and drive advancements in educational technologies. The unique characteristics of the Metaverse, including its immersive nature and interconnected spaces, provide a fertile ground for collaborative ventures that transcend traditional boundaries.

One aspect of these collaborative ventures involves knowledge exchange. Private institutions actively seek partnerships with industry leaders to gain insights into cutting-edge technologies and emerging trends within the Metaverse. These collaborations enable academia to stay abreast of industry advancements, ensuring that educational practices align with the latest developments. Industry partners, in turn, benefit from the academic expertise of private institutions, gaining access to research and theoretical insights that inform practical applications within the Metaverse. Entrepreneurial opportunities emerge as a natural outcome of collaborative ventures in the Metaverse. Private higher education institutions, in collaboration with industry, foster environments conducive to the development of innovative educational tools, content creation platforms, and startups focused on educational technology. The Metaverse becomes a testing ground for entrepreneurial initiatives, where academia and industry jointly explore the possibilities of creating groundbreaking educational solutions.

The synergy between academia and industry within the Metaverse extends to research initiatives. Collaborative ventures drive research efforts that explore the frontiers of Metaverse technologies, addressing challenges and uncovering new possibilities. These research endeavors often result in the development of frameworks, guidelines, and best practices that contribute to the overall understanding of the Metaverse's potential in higher education. Furthermore, collaborative ventures play a pivotal role in shaping the Metaverse into a dynamic space for multidisciplinary research. As private institutions collaborate with industry partners, expertise from diverse fields converges within virtual environments. This multidisciplinary approach fosters innovative research projects that explore the intersection of technology, education, and industry within the Metaverse.

The collaborative nature of these ventures extends beyond technological aspects, influencing policy development within private institutions. As academia and industry work together in the Metaverse, they contribute to the formulation of ethical guidelines, data privacy protocols, and content moderation standards. These collaborative efforts ensure that the Metaverse remains a secure and inclusive digital space for education, addressing ethical considerations that arise in the evolving digital landscape.

Case studies within private higher education institutions exemplify the impact of collaborative ventures in driving Metaverse innovation. Partnerships with tech giants, startups, and immersive technology developers lead to the creation of groundbreaking educational experiences. For example, joint projects may involve the development of virtual laboratories, interactive simulations, or collaborative learning environments that enhance student engagement and learning outcomes.The collaborative initiatives also facilitate the integration of real-world applications within virtual spaces. Industry partners bring practical insights and challenges to the educational landscape, allowing students to engage with authentic scenarios within the Metaverse. These real-world applications bridge the gap between theoretical knowledge and practical skills, preparing students for the dynamic demands of their future professions.

Therefore, collaborative ventures within the Metaverse represent a cornerstone of innovation and research within private higher education institutions. These partnerships transcend traditional boundaries, driving knowledge exchange, entrepreneurial opportunities, and multidisciplinary research. As academia and industry converge in virtual environments, they collectively shape the Metaverse into a transformative space that redefines higher education practices for the digital age. The collaborative spirit within the Metaverse propels private institutions to the forefront of innovation, ensuring that they remain adaptive and responsive to the evolving needs of students and the broader educational landscape.

CONCLUSION

The integration of the Metaverse within higher education marks a revolutionary epoch, demanding a paradigm shift in pedagogies, the establishment of ethical frameworks, and the cultivation of collaborative endeavors. This chapter undertakes the task of unraveling the transformative potential embedded in the Metaverse, shedding light on its profound impact on pedagogical evolution, the entrepreneurial landscape, and ethical considerations within the realm of higher education. This comprehensive exploration delves into the multifaceted influence of the Metaverse, encapsulating its capacity to reshape pedagogical approaches, foster entrepreneurial initiatives, and present both challenges and opportunities on the ethical frontier.The Metaverse, with its immersive digital landscapes comprising augmented and virtual reality elements, stands poised to redefine traditional educational practices. This transformative potential manifests in various dimensions, prominently altering the landscape of higher education pedagogies. Through the integration of Augmented Reality (AR) and Virtual Reality (VR) technologies, students are immersed in interactive learning experiences that transcend physical confines. The Metaverse, therefore, emerges as a catalyst for nurturing critical thinking, creativity, and problem-solving skills, offering students unparalleled and immersive educational journeys.

Simultaneously, the Metaverse serves as fertile ground for entrepreneurial ventures within higher education. It creates an environment conducive to developing innovative educational tools, content creation platforms, and startups focused on educational technology. Collaborative ventures between academia and industry within this digital domain pave the way for pioneering educational initiatives and technological advancements, fostering a synergy that propels innovation and research initiatives. However, amid the promising opportunities lie challenges and ethical considerations that demand meticulous attention. Technological barriers, implementation costs, and equitable access pose hurdles to widespread integration. Ethical concerns regarding data privacy, content moderation, and the creation of an inclusive and secure digital learning environment necessitate strategic solutions. This chapter emphasizes the paramount importance of addressing these challenges through the formulation of robust ethical guidelines, privacy protocols, and content moderation standards. As institutions adapt to the Metaverse, they strive to redefine their policies, curricula, and teaching methodologies, navigating the ethical landscape to ensure a secure and inclusive digital learning environment.

In essence, this expanded proposal provides a comprehensive overview of the Metaverse's influence on higher education pedagogies, entrepreneurial ventures, ethical challenges, and opportunities. The Metaverse is not merely a technological tool but a transformative force that requires institutions to innovate, establish ethical frameworks, and engage in collaborative efforts. As higher education embraces the Metaverse, the trajectory of pedagogical evolution, entrepreneurial landscapes, and ethical considerations is reshaped, setting the stage for an educational landscape that is dynamic, immersive, and responsive to the needs of a digital era.

REFERENCES

Akour, I. A., Al-Maroof, R. S., Alfaisal, R., & Salloum, S. A. (2022). A conceptual framework for determining metaverse adoption in higher institutions of gulf area: An empirical study using hybrid SEM-ANN approach. *Computers and Education: Artificial Intelligence*, *3*, 100052. doi:10.1016/j.caeai.2022.100052

Alja'afreh, M., Al Mallah, R., Karime, A., & El Saddik, A. (2023). Cybersecurity in the Metaverse: Challenges and Approaches. *2023 International Conference on Intelligent Metaverse Technologies & Applications (IMETA)*, 1–8. 10.1109/iMETA59369.2023.10294371

Amiti, F. (2020). Synchronous and asynchronous E-learning. *European Journal of Open Education and E-Learning Studies*, *5*(2). Advance online publication. doi:10.46827/ejoe.v5i2.3313

Anderson, T., & Rivera Vargas, P. (2020). A critical look at educational technology from a distance education perspective. *Digital Education Review*, *2020*(37), 208–229. doi:10.1344/der.2020.37.208-229

Bailenson, J. N. (2021). *Nonverbal overload: A theoretical argument for the causes of Zoom fatigue*. Academic Press.

Barron, B., & Darling-Hammond, L. (2008). *Teaching for Meaningful Learning: A Review of Research on Inquiry-Based and Cooperative Learning*. Book Excerpt. George Lucas Educational Foundation.

Boltz, L. O., Yadav, A., Dillman, B., & Robertson, C. (2021). Transitioning to remote learning: Lessons from supporting K-12 teachers through a MOOC. *British Journal of Educational Technology*, *52*(4), 1377–1393. doi:10.1111/bjet.13075

Bond, M., Buntins, K., Bedenlier, S., Zawacki-Richter, O., & Kerres, M. (2020). Mapping research in student engagement and educational technology in higher education: A systematic evidence map. *International Journal of Educational Technology in Higher Education*, *17*(1), 1–30. doi:10.1186/s41239-019-0176-8

Chenoweth, S., & Linos, P. K. (2018). *Qualitative Findings from an Online Course on Machine Learning.* Paper presented at the 2018 IEEE Frontiers in Education Conference (FIE). 10.1109/FIE.2018.8658554

Cocioceanu, A., Barbulescu, M., Ivanoaica, T., Raportaru, M., & Nicolin, A. I. (2016). Testing voice-based biometrics authentication platforms for Romanian utterances through infrequent consonant clusters. *2016 15th RoEduNet Conference: Networking in Education and Research*, 1–4.

Duan, H., Li, J., Fan, S., Lin, Z., Wu, X., & Cai, W. 2021, October. Metaverse for social good: A university campus prototype. In *Proceedings of the 29th ACM international conference on multimedia* (pp. 153-161). 10.1145/3474085.3479238

Dunn, T. J., & Kennedy, M. (2019). Technology Enhanced Learning in higher education; motivations, engagement and academic achievement. *Computers & Education*, *137*, 104–113. doi:10.1016/j.compedu.2019.04.004

Dwivedi, Y. K., Hughes, L., Baabdullah, A. M., Ribeiro-Navarrete, S., Giannakis, M., Al-Debei, M. M., Dennehy, D., Metri, B., Buhalis, D., Cheung, C. M. K., Conboy, K., Doyle, R., Dubey, R., Dutot, V., Felix, R., Goyal, D. P., Gustafsson, A., Hinsch, C., Jebabli, I., ... Wamba, S. F. (2022). Metaverse beyond the hype: Multidisciplinary perspectives on emerging challenges, opportunities, and agenda for research, practice and policy. *International Journal of Information Management*, *66*, 102542. doi:10.1016/j.ijinfomgt.2022.102542

Eduverse. (2023, December 16). *A Safe and Secure K-12 "Metaverse."* Author.

Fang, F., Ventre, C., Basios, M., Kanthan, L., Martinez-Rego, D., Wu, F., & Li, L. (2022). Cryptocurrency trading: A comprehensive survey. *Financial Innovation*, *8*(1), 1–59. doi:10.1186/s40854-021-00321-6

Gegenfurtner, A., & Ebner, C. (2019). Webinars in higher education and professional training: A meta-analysis and systematic review of randomized controlled trials. *Educational Research Review*, *28*, 100293. doi:10.1016/j.edurev.2019.100293

Gent, E. (2022). Lessons from a second life> before meta, Philip Rosedale created an online universe. *IEEE Spectrum*, *59*(1), 19–19. doi:10.1109/MSPEC.2022.9676346

Harris, M. C., Brown, D. J., Vyas, P., & Lewis, J. (2022). A methodology for the co-design of shared VR environments with people with intellectual disabilities: insights from the preparation phase. *International Conference on Human-Computer Interaction*, 217–230. 10.1007/978-3-031-05039-8_15

Hmelo-Silver, C. E., Duncan, R. G., & Chinn, C. A. (2007). Scaffolding and achievement in problem-based and inquiry learning: A response to Kirschner, Sweller, and. *Educational Psychologist*, *42*(2), 99–107. doi:10.1080/00461520701263368

Huang, C., Zhang, Q., Guo, D., Zhao, X., & Wang, X. (2022). Discovering association rules with graph patterns in temporal networks. *Tsinghua Science and Technology*, *28*(2), 344–359. doi:10.26599/TST.2021.9010090

Huang, L., & Ma, K.-S. (2018). *Introducing machine learning to first-year undergraduate engineering students through an authentic and active learning labware.* Paper presented at the 2018 IEEE Frontiers in Education Conference (FIE). 10.1109/FIE.2018.8659308

Huang, Y., Li, Y. J., & Cai, Z. (2023). Security and privacy in metaverse: A comprehensive survey. *Big Data Mining and Analytics*, *6*(2), 234–247. doi:10.26599/BDMA.2022.9020047

Jeong, H. (2019). Rethinking Open Universities: What makes them unique? *International Review of Research in Open and Distance Learning*, *20*(4), 152–166. doi:10.19173/irrodl.v20i4.4163

Kaddoura, S., & Al Husseiny, F. (2023). The rising trend of Metaverse in education: Challenges, opportunities, and ethical considerations. *PeerJ. Computer Science*, *9*, e1252. doi:10.7717/peerj-cs.1252 PMID:37346578

Koohang, A., Nord, J. H., Ooi, K.-B., Tan, G. W.-H., Al-Emran, M., Aw, E. C.-X., Baabdullah, A. M., Buhalis, D., Cham, T.-H., Dennis, C., Dutot, V., Dwivedi, Y. K., Hughes, L., Mogaji, E., Pandey, N., Phau, I., Raman, R., Sharma, A., Sigala, M., ... Wong, L.-W. (2023). Shaping the metaverse into reality: A holistic multidisciplinary understanding of opportunities, challenges, and avenues for future investigation. *Journal of Computer Information Systems*, *63*(3), 735–765. doi:10.1080/08874417.2023.2165197

Kye, B., Han, N., Kim, E., Park, Y., & Jo, S. (2021). Educational applications of metaverse: Possibilities and limitations. *Journal of Educational Evaluation for Health Professions*, *18*, 18. doi:10.3352/jeehp.2021.18.32 PMID:34897242

Liu, J., Chai, C., Luo, Y., Lou, Y., Feng, J., & Tang, N. (2022). Feature augmentation with reinforcement learning. *2022 IEEE 38th International Conference on Data Engineering (ICDE)*, 3360–3372.

Ludlow, P., & Wallace, M. (2007). *The Second Life Herald: The virtual tabloid that witnessed the dawn of the metaverse*. MIT Press.

MacCallum, K., & Parsons, D. (2019). Teacher perspectives on mobile augmented reality: The potential of metaverse for learning. *World Conference on Mobile and Contextual Learning*, 21–28.

Mayer, R. E. (2004). Should there be a three-strikes rule against pure discovery learning? *The American Psychologist*, *59*(1), 14–19. doi:10.1037/0003-066X.59.1.14 PMID:14736316

Microsoft. (2023a, December 16). *Mesh for Microsoft Teams aims to make collaboration in the 'metaverse' personal and fun*. https://news.microsoft.com/source/features/innovation/mesh-for-microsoft-teams/

Microsoft. (2023b, December 16). *Mixed Reality in your classroom*. https://www.microsoft.com/en-us/education/mixed-reality

Mystakidis, S. (2022). Metaverse. *Metaverse. Encyclopedia*, *2*(1), 486–497. doi:10.3390/encyclopedia2010031

Nick Clegg. (2023, December 16). *Metaverse Technologies Are Creating New Opportunities for Teachers to Inspire Students*. https://about.fb.com/news/2023/09/metaverse-technologies-education-opportunities/

Onu, P., Pradhan, A., & Mbohwa, C. (2023). Potential to use metaverse for future teaching and learning. *Education and Information Technologies*, 1–32. doi:10.1007/s10639-023-12167-9

Ormrod, J. E. (1995). *Educational psychology: Principles and applications*. Prentice-Hall.

Owens, R. F., Hester, J. L., & Teale, W. H. (2002). Where do you want to go today? Inquiry-based learning and technology integration. *The Reading Teacher*, *55*(7), 616–625.

Peres, R., Schreier, M., Schweidel, D. A., & Sorescu, A. (2023). Blockchain meets marketing: Opportunities, threats, and avenues for future research. [). Elsevier.]. *International Journal of Research in Marketing*, *40*(1), 1–11. doi:10.1016/j.ijresmar.2022.08.001

Puspitasari, I. N. N. (2021). Combination of synchronous and asynchronous models in online learning. *Jurnal Pendidikan Islam Indonesia*, *5*(2), 198–217. doi:10.35316/jpii.v5i2.301

Qiu, Y., Isusi-Fagoaga, R., & García-Aracil, A. 2023. Perceptions and use of metaverse in higher education: A descriptive study in China and Spain. Computers and Education: Artificial Intelligence.

Riedl, R. (2022). On the stress potential of videoconferencing: Definition and root causes of Zoom fatigue. *Electronic Markets*, *32*(1), 153–177. doi:10.1007/s12525-021-00501-3 PMID:35600914

Savery, J. R. (2015). Overview of problem-based learning: Definitions and distinctions. Essential readings in problem-based learning: Exploring and extending the legacy of Howard S. *Barrows*, *9*(2), 5–15.

Stanoevska-Slabeva, K. (2022). Opportunities and challenges of metaverse for education: a literature review. *EDULEARN22 Proceedings*, 10401–10410. 10.21125/edulearn.2022.2527

Stöhr, C., Demazière, C., & Adawi, T. (2020). The polarizing effect of the online flipped classroom. *Computers & Education*, *147*, 103789. doi:10.1016/j.compedu.2019.103789

Sulmont, E., Patitsas, E., & Cooperstock, J. R. (2019). What is hard about teaching machine learning to non-majors? Insights from classifying instructors' learning goals. *ACM Transactions on Computing Education*, *19*(4), 1–16. doi:10.1145/3336124

Tokarev, A., Skobelin, I., Tolstov, M., Tsyganov, A., & Pak, M. (2021). Development of VR educational instruments for school pre-professional education in a research university. *Procedia Computer Science*, *190*, 750–754. doi:10.1016/j.procs.2021.06.088

Vondráček, M., Baggili, I., Casey, P., & Mekni, M. (2023). Rise of the metaverse's immersive virtual reality malware and the man-in-the-room attack & defenses. *Computers & Security*, *127*, 102923. doi:10.1016/j.cose.2022.102923

Willis, J. (2006). *Based Strategies to Ignite Student Learning: Insights from a Neurologist and Classroom Teacher*. ASCD.

Zhang, X., Chen, Y., Hu, L., & Wang, Y. (2022). The metaverse in education: Definition, framework, features, potential applications, challenges, and future research topics. *Frontiers in Psychology*, *13*, 6063. doi:10.3389/fpsyg.2022.1016300 PMID:36304866

Zulfiqar, M., Syed, F., Khan, M. J., & Khurshid, K. (2019). Deep face recognition for biometric authentication. *2019 International Conference on Electrical, Communication, and Computer Engineering (ICECCE),* 1–6.

Chapter 9

Metaverse as the New Challenge of Tourism in the Phygital Age:
State of the Art and Research Agenda

Sawssen Ayadi
University of Sfax, Tunisia

Abir Zouari
https://orcid.org/0000-0002-1205-890X
University of Sfax, Tunisia

ABSTRACT

Firms have begun to use Phygital and Metaverse almost in all sectors, which makes these strategies important to gain competitive advantage in markets. Recently, tourism can be considered as one of these sectors as travel agencies and hotels have introduced these strategies gradually to improve the customer experience. Theoretically, research in tourism marketing is starting to give an interest in Phygital tourism and Metaverse that still insufficient. Thus, this chapter seeks to understand and provide insights to scholars on Phygital in general and Phygital tourism in particular. The review of marketing literature confirms that the Phygital phenomena is a new marketing strategy that is affecting more specifically the sector of tourism and offering new opportunities to managers and marketers of hotels and travel agencies. This is due to the change of tourists' behavior, and in response, tourism practitioners may introduce Metaverse to create a unique experience for their customers.

INTRODUCTION

Today, tourism is one of the most important sector in all economies that are affected by the rapid evolution of marketing and digital tools. So, deeper mutations are witnessed. Actually, tourists take into account the digital content, especially on social networks, as a reliable source of information. Castro et al. (2017) stated that they usually start with searching for other consumers' opinions and interacting with them. They, then, plan their trips online and finally share ideas about a destination. Therefore, managers

DOI: 10.4018/979-8-3693-2422-6.ch009

in hotels and travel agencies are always called to try to understand this behavioral transformation and tend to digitalize their services. They begin by offering interactive websites displaying popular tourism content (Munar, 2012) and from now on, they set up alerts for targeting potential consumers on social media (Berhanu and Raj, 2020). They tend to generate new opportunities by using new technologies in order to create tourism experiences (Buonincontri and Micera, 2016) that will be unique and personalized (Wang and Fesenmaier, 2013).

Digital tools evolve leading travelers and tourists change constantly their behavior. They are now looking for new experiences. They go beyond a purely physical behavior to be totally immerged in a parallel world with possibilities of virtual interaction (Neuberger *et al.* 2018). This new experience is referred to "phygital experience". This notion emerged as a trend topic and it is defined as "*the use of technology to bridge the digital with the physical world with the purpose of providing a unique interactive experience for the user*" (Del Vecchio et al. 2023). In a tourism context, the tourism experience is enhanced by personalization, contextual awareness, and real-time monitoring (Buhalis and Amaranggana, 2013; Gretzel et al. 2015a; Marchesani et al. 2024). Thus, individuals seem to be immerged in an hybrid experience allowing them to interact virtually while they are present in a physical world (Akmermer, 2022).

Still within the same vein of ideas, technologies continue to develop to reach the post-reality era or the Metaverse level (Putra et al. 2024). It is regarded as a disruptive technology within this industry (Gursoy et al. 2022), as it has the potential to transform the way customers and hospitality organizations of a tourist destination collaborate in the creation of tourism experiences, products, and services (George et al. 2021; Buhalis and Karatay 2022). Indeed, according to Doğan and Bayar (2024), today travelers costs to have a better travel experience from the moment they seek and need more control and flexibility over their journeys. Metaverse has the potential to revolutionize the tourism industry (Karaka and Baran, 2024), providing a new platform for immersive experiences and a shared virtual space for stakeholders. It becomes a prominent subject in tourism (Mihalic, 2024; Putra et al. 2024).

Theoretically, researchers like Gao et al. (2021), Mishra et al. (2021), Mele et al. (2023) or Pusceddu et al. (2023) claimed that phygital is quite recent notion and requires more investigations. However, according to Del Vecchio et al. (2023), this concept remain fragmented and its meaning and implications are far from a full understanding. Metaverse, also, is introduced and used lately in tourism service marketing, leading to little empirical understanding (Ghali et al. 2024; Mihalic, 2024; Putra et al. 2024). According to Prados-Castillo et al. (2024), this research area witness a growing interest since there is a notable increase in the literature production after 2018. Moreover, the tourist and hospitality industries may be significantly impacted by the metaverse, as evidence of its increasing awareness (Wei, 2024).

This paper's contribution is twofold. First, we extend literature in marketing and digital marketing by providing a review of phygital definitions and discussing the phygital experience. Second, we contribute by reviewing and discussing the existent literature on phygital tourism and invite future researchers to investigate the use of the metaverse. To ensure these contributions, this paper seeks to provide insights to scholars on phygital in general, phygital tourism and metaverse. Therefore, a documentation was used allowing us to provide a discussion of short literature review of articles from 2007 to 2024. The conclusion of this study proves that the phygital phenomena is a new marketing strategy applied in most sectors and affected their performance. This notion has a profound implications when it comes to tourism industry changing thus the tourists behavior and offering new opportunities to managers and marketers of hotels and travel agencies.

The reminder chapter is structured as follows: It began by presenting the phygital concept in general. After that, we explain tourism phygital. Finally, before concluding, we introduce metaverse in tourism as a new challenge for phygital tourism.

Phygital Concept

Although Nakazawa and Tokuda (2007) stated that the phygital concept uses the latest innovations in communication technologies implemented in the physical environment, the term "phygital" has appeared in 2013 (Courvoisier, 2020) and in retail sector in 2014 (Purcarea, 2018). However, not all the studies papers present a clear definition. The most of them use the term vaguely. In some cases, authors used the word phygital without explaining its meaning. They usually used it as an adjective (eg: Heljakka and Ihamäki, 2020; Klaus, 2021; Mele *et al.* 2023), and only few articles used it as a noun with the expression phygitality (eg: Heljakka and Ihamäki, 2020; Due and Toft, 2021; Särmäkari, 2023). Intuitively, researchers have agreed that this new form of marketing strategy is defined as the combination of the physical and the digital world (Neuhofer et al. 2015; Moravcikova and Kliestikova, 2017; Courvoisier, 2020; Johnson and Barlow, 2021; Yüce *et al.* 2021). Mele *et al.* (2023) established a review of literature of phygital definitions and classified them in a table indicating its research area. In line with their work, we take this table and we make the necessary changes.

Summarily, phygital can be defined as "*the concept of using technology in a way that aligns with the physical world, providing unique hybrid and interactive experiences for the user*" (Heljakka and Ihamäki, 2020). It aims to build an ecosystem, in marketing communication, (Švec and Madleňák, 2017) between brands and consumers, between the user and the product (Moravcikova and Kliestikova, 2017) and between retailers and customers (Mishra *et al.* 2021). In the same line, Reilly and Dawson (2021, p. 293) stated that "*Phygital is a neologism which refers to an increasingly apparent universe in which physical and digital artefacts intersect one another, holding out the promise of substantive new ways to (re)consider the materiality and ontology of objects*". In line with this perspective, other authors defined phygital as a concept that integrates digital technologies, including social presence and physical elements (Mele *et al.* 2021), and affecting social and personal behavior (Ballina *et al.* 2019).

Previously, research on the phygital concept in the tourism sector has focused on the case of heritage tourism (Abd Rahman *et al.* 2016; Antonczak and Papetti, 2017; Corne, 2017; Errichiello and Marasco, 2017). As phygital is always linked to the customer experience in retailing, we join Mishra *et al.* (2021) by saying that this phenomenon offers an engaging customer experience. Generally, the term combination of the physical and digital indicate that the condition in which an experience is not only physical or only digital, but it's an hybrid experience (Mieli, 2022). In a phygital experience, space or object, physical and digital do not replace each other; they reinforce each other and become deeply and seamlessly intertwined (Andrade and Dias, 2020; Turco and Giovannini, 2020; Nofal et al. 2017; Zurlo et al. 2018). Thus, phygital experience has been defined as "*a retail experience combining physical features and digital features in the same point of sale*" (Belghiti et al. 2017). It is often referred to an omnichannel customer experience that may strengthen the combination of digital experience and physical improvements and add value to products or services and (Moravcikova and Kliestikova, 2017; Purcărea, 2018). Consequently, customers may get the possibility of searching online, procure offline (Zaczkiewicz, 2019) and find information easily within-store (Mishra et al. 2021).

For the better knowledge and based on the work of Mele et al. (2023), we resume in table 1, the articles reviewed and we classified them according to the research area.

Table 1. Literature review of research area of phygital

Research Area	Authors
Branding	Moravcikova and Kliestikova (2017)
Gaming	Tyni et al. (2013), Tsekleves et al. (2014), Lupetti et al. (2015), Lupetti (2016), Heljakka and Ihamäki (2020)
Retailing	Armstrong and Rutter (2017), Purcarea (2018), Batat (2019), Due and Nielsen (2019), Banik (2021), Lawry (2021)
Fashion	Armstrong and Rutter (2017), Särmäkari (2023)
Tourism	Ballina et al. (2019), Stankov and Gretzel (2020), Liu et al. (2022)
Robotics	Hiraki et al. (2016)
Heritage communication	Nofal et al. (2017), Antoniou (2023)
Education	Schreibman et al. (2017)
Law and legal system	Švec and Madleňák (2017)
Cultural heritage	Andrade and Dias (2020), Çiftçi and Çizel (2024)
Customer experience	Rossi and Krey (2018), Mele et al. (2021), Batat (2022), Del Vecchio et al. (2023)
Arts and archaeology	Reilly and Dawson (2021), Zhukova et al. (2021)
banking	Acquaro (2017)

Adapted from Mele et al. (2023)

Phygital Tourism

The sector of tourism is considered as a significant contributor to many economies in the world. It encompasses a wide range of activities related to travel and leisure and it includes various industries and services that cater to tourists and travelers, such as transportation, accommodation, hospitality, entertainment, and recreation. These touristic activities generate employment, revenues, and cultural exchange opportunities. Moreover, the tourism sector may face few challenges that influence travel patterns. Among these challenges, we can state seasonality, environmental impacts, and geopolitical factors. The tourists' needs and behavior may also be seen as a challenge to tourism since they change constantly and follow marketing trends.

Generally, we argued that Phygital combines physical and digital aspects. In the context of tourism, this term refers to the integration of physical and digital elements to enhance the overall visitor experience. Today, the impact of the Phygital strategy is being felt throughout the tourism sector (Akmermer, 2022) mainly because it is very vulnerable to natural disasters, crises and sudden epidemics (Li et al. 2021). Indeed, Shin and Kang (2020) showed that technology plays a key role in the recovery of the hotel industry after the COVID-19 pandemic and is a key means of reducing risk. Kim et al. (2021) showed that consumers prove more positive attitudes towards hotels with robotic staff, during COVID-19 period. Consequently, the set up of a phygital technologies appears to be important to rebuild the destinations and their strategy (Akmermer, 2022). Since the development of new technologies in tourism and the emergence of the concept of "smart tourism", the exploration of phygital come back to the ground. Thus, researchers in tourism marketing are now giving it more attention and using it as an adjective in order to refer to the tourist experience.

Phygital tourism is described as "*an innovative way to connect with the environment in which physical and virtual locations are combined to complement and reinforce one another*" (Monaco and Sacchi,

2023). In this context, the visitor founds a new experience by intersecting digital data with physical objects and landscapes. In fact, the perception of the tourist space as well as the interaction with it has been altered by phygital arrivals and changing behaviors (Neuburger et al. 2018). It involves the automatic activation of information and communication technologies when contact occurs between the tourist's devices and the multiple sensors in the network (Buhalis and Amaranggana, 2013; Buonincontri and Micera, 2016). Thus, Gretzel et al. (2019) referred instead to tourists' information environments in the age of digitalization. In addition, while, Gaggioli (2017) proposed that phygital in tourism is a concept of space whose origin lies from the increasing convergence of the virtual dimension and the physical dimension, other researchers like Turco and Giovannini (2020) used the same term in reference to objects, places, environments and experiences.

On the other hand, Ballina et al. (2019) studied the phygital experience in smart tourism destinations. The smart concept is being widely used in tourism (Gretzel et al. 2015b; Marchesani et al. 2024). However, its theoretical foundations are not yet clear. According to Li et al. (2017), the term Smat Technology may be considered as similar to intelligence even though there is a big difference in the anticipation of the needs of the tourists. It includes three principles: smart information, smart exchange and smart processing (Gretzel *et al.* 2015b), which are developed under two related premises: technological omnipresence (wireless) and the generation of individual experiences in situ (Hojer and Wangel, 2015).

Smart technologies implies three main components (Gretzel *et al.* 2015b) that all of them are linked to information and communication technologies (ICT) (Sigala and Chalkati, 2014). The first is the smart destination, the key aspect insisting on the integration of ICTs in the tourist infrastructure. In fact, most researchers define the smart destination giving the primary emphasis on ICTs (Boes *et al.* 2015; Lamsfus *et al.* 2015; López de Avila, 2015; Xiang *et al.* 2015). The second component is the smart business (Gretzel *et al.* 2015b). It is understood as the generation of interactive platforms between all tourism stakeholders. Personalization is then encouraged and more significant experiences can be created (Binkhorst and Den Dekker, 2009). The third component is the social change caused by the merging of ICTs and the tourist experience (Hunter *et al.* 2015). ICTs produce changes in the models of tourists' behaviour (Li *et al.* 2017), given that smart technologies will allow the anticipation of their needs and enrichment of their experiences (Gretzel *et al.* 2015a). They have generated new opportunities to create tourist experiences (Buonincontri and Micera, 2016) especially through their potential for personalization (Wang and Fesenmaier, 2013). So, tourist experience improves knowledge of the context and monitorisation in real time through personalization (Marchesani et al. 2024).

Metaverse as a New Challenge of Phygital Tourism

In general, when travelling, tourists seek for a unique and unforgettable experience of entertainment. Indeed, the tourism sector comprises goods, services, experiences of traveling, hospitality, entertainment and the enjoyment of cultural, social, and environmental resources (Monaco and Sacchi, 2023). So, adopting a phygital strategy may not be sufficient, and implementing Metaverse solutions may represent an additional element that can improve tourism experience and affect consumers' decisions in the real tourism environment. The Metaverse technology provides a virtual environment where users can interact with others and explore destinations.

Metaverse and Marketing

Generally defined, the term "Metaverse" was used, historically, to represent one of the unrealistic ideas of alternative worlds (Volchek and Brysch, 2023). This term was invented in 1992 by Neal Stephenson and make its first appearance in his work "Snow Crash" (Bayram 2022). According to Sriram (2022), the term "meta" originates from the Greek word "meta" and the word "universe" (Choi and Kim 2017). Thus, Metaverse represents a virtual environment where people can engage socially by using digital avatars to create value and create experiences together (Doğan and Bayar, 2024).

This implies that it is a reality that extends beyond the one we currently inhabit, and that "*there is more to be constructed and experienced*" (Hollensen et al. 2022, p. 119). For those authors, the Metaverse is described as a parallel virtual world to the physical world. It is a three-dimensional (Doğan and Bayar, 2024) and open-source representation of the natural world, but it maintains a direct connection to it. Access to this digital world is facilitated through a computer and special glasses, resembling today's virtual realities headsets. The metaverse concept has immense potential in many sectors, including tourism and marketing. It refers to a collective virtual shared space that is created by the meeting of virtually enhanced physical reality and physically persistent virtual space.

Metaverse and Tourism Marketing

Metaverse offers a wide range of opportunities for touristic marketing, enabling marketers in travel agencies and hotels to create immersive experiences, engage with audiences in new ways, and ultimately drive interest and participation in travel experiences. The use of the Metaverse in tourism can provide several benefits. It has several advantages, including the ability to access virtual travel experiences from anywhere in the world. This can be especially helpful during limited travel, such as during a pandemic, or when individuals have limited mobility. Besides providing virtual travel experiences, the Metaverse can also offer opportunities for education and cultural exchange since tourists can visit historical sites and learn about new cultures from the comfort of their own homes.

In contrast to traditional "on-site tourism", metaverse tourism offers an immersive experience to travelers through technology (Mihalic, 2024; Putra et al. 2024). This concept is often referred to as "virtual tourism" and "metaversal tourism" (Buhalis et al., 2023; Go and Kang, 2022; Yang et al. 2023). According to Lee et al. (2021), Sigala et al. (2021), Gupta et al. (2022) or Gursoy et al. (2022), Metaverse offer to travelers the opportunity to experience tourism virtually without physically moving. It can be considered as one of the possibilities to practice stationary tourism (a form of tourism where individuals can enjoy their experience through technology and without physically moving) (Shafiee et al. 2021). Thus, this can be happen through virtual reality (VR) (Gursoy et al. 2022; Volchek and Brysch, 2023) and augmented reality (AR) (Dwivedi et al. 2022; Volchek and Brysch, 2023), mixed reality (MR) (Dwivedi et al. 2022), artificial intelligence (AI) (Bibri and Allam, 2022), ambient intelligence (AmI) (Buhalis and Karatay, 2022), Internet of Things (IoT) (Dwivedi et al. 2022), 5G–6G high speed connectivity (Bibri, 2022), Blockchain (Al-Ghaili et al. 2022), Digital Twins (Allam et al. 2022), Smart Contracts (Yang et al. 2022), Mirror Worlds (Park and Kim, 2022), Fog/ Edge computing (Al-Ghaili et al. 2022) and Life logging (Kye et al. 2021).

To illustrate the metaverse tourism, some travel and airlines companies uses VR and AR. For example, Emirates' launch a virtual in-flight hospitality experience to surpass physical boundaries in their ser-

Figure 1. An overview of QVerse

vices. Qatar airlines, also, introduce a VR platform to allow passengers to explore virtually the premium check-in area at Hamad International Airport (HIA). This platform is known as QVerse,

Benefits of Metaverse Tourism

Tourism marketing and the metaverse might interact in many ways. Tourists may benefit from virtual destination tours, immersive experiences, virtual events and festivals.

- Virtual destination of various locations: Travelers can virtually visit locations, taking in the sights and sounds without physically being there. This can aid in tantalizing prospective tourists and providing them with a preview of what to anticipate.
- Immersive experiences: Travel agencies and hotels can create virtual reality experiences where users can virtually participate in activities like hiking, diving, or exploring historical sites.
- Virtual Events and Festivals: Tourists may attend virtual events and festivals particularly during times when physical travel is restricted.

From travel agencies and hotels side, metaverse may help them to create more interactive Campaigns. They can design campaigns allowing customers to be engaged with the destination in creative ways. This could include treasure hunts, interactive storylines, or challenges that lead participants through various landmarks and attractions. They also may create Advertisement based on virtual Reality. These advertisements can be tailored to fit the virtual environment while providing valuable information about destinations and travel experiences.

As a result from the use of phygital technologies and metaverse, tourists may enjoy a responsible tourism experience or sustainable tourism experience. For this reason, Shin and Kang (2024) advocate that Metaverse tourism can be considered as a sustainable form of tourism. Thus, metaversal sustainable tourism paradigm emerges "*which assumes awareness of the metaverse's immersive character, becoming a new virtual space for living and exploration*" (Mihalic, 2024). This notion was introduced by Mihalic (2023) who offers a new perspective on what should metaverse be sustained and apply it lately on tourism field.

Metaverse Challenges and Tourism Future Research

It is true that metaverse is a great opportunity to make unique journeys; but authors state that it may endure some challenges for tourism stakeholders. Buhalis et al. (2023) resume these challenges into technological, economic, consumer experience and ethical and legal. The main encounters may concern tourists who may enjoy the new virtually journey without experiencing a high sensorial engagement. They will be engaged in a stationary tourism (Monaco and Sacchi, 2023) which refers to "*tourist experiences that people can enjoy through technology, without physically moving*". Consequently, they can also feel confused about what the reality is and what they see in metaverse. Even more, metaverse and tourism continue to develop over time and so technologies do. The technological environmental uncertainty emerged makes tourism stackholder face higher implementation prices.

To overlap these challenges, tourism infrastructure could rely on tourism future research. These latter are invited to understand the role of platforms like MySmart journey[1] in promoting phygital and metaverse tourism. They are called to respond to questions like: (1) how tourists and consumer organize their trip?, (2) in what extent they prefer immersive experience in spite of phygita tourism?, and (3) what motivates them to move from a phygital experience to a metaverse experience?. Travel agencies and tourism stackeholders are also at the center of future researchers since they are responsible to offer unforgettable journey to their client. So, they may focus on (1) how and what motivates them to change their strategies to prepare the metaverse trip, (2) what will hinder the move from phygital to metaverse, and (3) this change has will has a negative impact on their performance.

CONCLUSION

While the phygital is a quite recent concept, its application in all sectors and especially in tourism gains more and more importance. Some authors like Mele et al. (2023) have already review its literature identifying a number of definitions. This paper confirms that all these definitions are convergent even though they were relevant from different sectors. To the best of our knowledge, the phygital and the phygital tourism may be considered as a cure to maintain safety and sustainability. It allows individuals and tourists to live virtual experiences without really moving around. As these two concepts capture more attention, this study seems to be the first study providing a literature review for both phygital and phygital tourism. We suggest that phygital in general is new strategy that may enhance and create a unique customer experience and that phygital tourism is considered as a new trend essential to satisfy tourists. Marketing researchers may profit from this theoretical review to develop more these concepts and establish their conceptual models. Moreover, the table presented that resumes the phygital research area may give them general insights where phygital is applied and what. They may also try to figure out theoretically how to effectively use the potential of virtual tourism. Particularly, they are invited to discover potential tourists and understand their expectations and preferences as part of research.

On the other hand, our review may be benefit for marketing practitioners to the extent that it enhance them to follow a phygital strategy allowing the retention of more clients. That is to say, they should implement more immersive technology. Theoretically, researchers like Van Nuenen and Scarles (2021) stated that there is an increasing use of these new technologies in the travel industry. In nowadays, the rapid development of the tourism sector is dependent on the large spread of Internet and technologies (Stankov and Gretzel, 2020). Therefore, managers and marketers of hotels and travel agencies should be aware of this rapid growth and try to be up to date to be able to satisfy the constantly changing needs. According to Torres (2022), smart tourism (the use of information and communication technologies) may be a solution by using open data, cloud computing, geographic information systems, and artificial intelligence. Similarly, Metaverse can be an opportunity for engaging more tourists as it contribute to the creation of shared and perceived value in the tourism industry.

To conclude, the Metaverse can be used to create immersive and interactive experiences for tourists like virtual travel experiences (Gursoy et al. 2022). Metaverse tourism has the potential to elicit tourism enthusiasm. For instance, interactive virtual reality experiences can provide travelers with a precise understanding of the anticipated experiences upon visiting a specific destination. Metaverse in tourism is a rapidly growing market, as it offers innovative and immersive experiences to travelers (Fazio et al. 2023). The Metaverse technology provides a virtual environment where users can interact with others and explore destinations.

Interactive experiences are essential for tourists because they provide an immersive and engaging way to explore a destination. Through interactive experiences, tourists gain understanding of people, the history and the culture of the destination they are visiting. Interactive experiences allow them to be actively more involved in their journeys. This can strengthen the relationships with locals and leads to a greater appreciation for the destination. Interactive experiences have the potential to foster lasting memories that will endure long after the conclusion of a tourist's journey (Theodoropoulos et al. 2023). Furthermore, by generating digital replicas of tourist attractions, travel agents can provide virtual tours that enable visitors to explore the region from the comfort of their own residence (Buhalis et al. 2023).

Overall, the Metaverse has the potential to revolutionize the way people engage with tourism, offering new opportunities for exploration, interaction, and immersion in destinations around the world. However, as all studies, our work present some limitations. Firstly, this paper treats Metaverse as a new topic in marketing. It is still quite new and there is a relatively small number of published research on it. So, scholars are invited to build on this study and propose frameworks, analyze new studies as well as other future impacts of phygital and tourism phygital. Secondly, we proposed this study as a state of art and a discussion of phygital and metaverse in the sector of tourism. As tourism marketing literature evolves rapidly, researchers are called upon to update our literature review and explore further this field. Thirdly, it's important to consider potential challenges faced by tourism firms, such as digital inclusion, privacy concerns, and the need for infrastructure development to support widespread adoption of metaverse-based tourism experiences, and their impact on tourism sector. Finally, the metaverse continues to evolve. Thus, it will be important to see how it transforms the tourism industry and shapes the way people explore and experience destinations. Another future venue is to deep learning on metaversal sustainable tourism. This new stream of research corresponds with the growing consumer responsibility and the rise of corporate social responsibility (CSR) within businesses in general and travel agencies in particularly.

REFERENCES

Abd Rahman, N. H., Khalifah, Z., & Ismail, H. N. (2016). The role of sensory experiences in appreciating the cultural heritage attractions. *Tourism. Leisure and Global Change*, *3*, 117–128.

Akmermer, B. (2022). The Phygital Experiential Marketing Practices: The Conceptual Framework and Applications for Tourism Industry. In Handbook of Research on Interdisciplinary Reflections of Contemporary Experiential Marketing Practices (pp. 289-309). IGI Global.

Al-Ghaili, A. M., Kasim, H., Al-Hada, N. M., Hassan, Z. B., Othman, M., Tharik, J. H., Kasmani, R. M., & Shayea, I. (2022). A review of metaverse's definitions, architecture, applications, challenges, issues, solutions, and future trends. *IEEE Access : Practical Innovations, Open Solutions*, *10*, 125835–125866. doi:10.1109/ACCESS.2022.3225638

Allam, Z., Sharifi, A., Bibri, S. E., Jones, D. S., & Krogstie, J. (2022). The metaverse as a virtual form of smart cities: Opportunities and challenges for environmental, economic, and social sustainability in urban futures. *Smart Cities*, *5*(3), 771–801. doi:10.3390/smartcities5030040

Andrade, J. G., & Dias, P. (2020). A phygital approach to cultural heritage: Augmented reality at regaleira. *Virtual Archaeology Review*, *11*(22), 15–25. doi:10.4995/var.2020.11663

Antonczak, L., & Papetti, C. (2017). Towards a mobile enhancement of glocal heritage? Developing user experiences in relation to mobile technologies, geo-localisation and culture. In *ICWMC 2017–The Thirteenth International Conference on Wireless and Mobile Communications* (pp. 73-78). ThinkMind.

Armstrong, K., & Rutter, C. (2017). Exploring the enigma of the happiness construct in phygital fashion experiences. In *Advanced fashion technology and operations management* (pp. 220–233). IGI Global. doi:10.4018/978-1-5225-1865-5.ch009

Ballina, F.J., Valdes, L., & Del Valle, E. (2019). The Phygital experience in the smart tourism destination. *International Journal of Tourism Cities*.

Banik, S. (2021). Exploring the involvement-patronage link in the phygital retail experiences. *Journal of Retailing and Consumer Services*, *63*, 102739. doi:10.1016/j.jretconser.2021.102739

Batat, W. (2019). *Experiential marketing: Consumer behavior, customer experience and the 7Es*. Routledge. doi:10.4324/9781315232201

Batat, W. (2022). What does phygital really mean? A conceptual introduction to the phygital customer experience (PH-CX) framework. *Journal of Strategic Marketing*, 1–24. doi:10.1080/0965254X.2022.2059775

Bayram, A. (2022). Metaleisure: Leisure time habits to be changed with metaverse. *Journal of Metaverse*, *2*(1), 1–7.

Becker, L., & Jaakkola, E. (2020). Customer experience: Fundamental premises and implications for research. *Journal of the Academy of Marketing Science*, *48*(4), 630–648. doi:10.1007/s11747-019-00718-x

Belghiti, S., Ochs, A., Lemoine, J. F., & Badot, O. 2018. The phygital shopping experience: An attempt at conceptualization and empirical investigation. In *Marketing Transformation: Marketing Practice in an Ever Changing World: Proceedings of the 2017 Academy of Marketing Science (AMS) World Marketing Congress (WMC)* (pp. 61-74). Springer International Publishing.

Berhanu, K., & Raj, S. (2020). The trustworthiness of travel and tourism information sources of social media: Perspectives of international tourists visiting Ethiopia. *Heliyon*, *6*(3), e03439. doi:10.1016/j.heliyon.2020.e03439 PMID:32181382

Bibri, S. E. (2022). The social shaping of the metaverse as an alternative to the imaginaries of data-driven smart Cities: A study in science, technology, and society. *Smart Cities*, *5*(3), 832–874. doi:10.3390/smartcities5030043

Bibri, S. E., & Allam, Z. (2022). The Metaverse as a virtual form of data-driven smart urbanism: On post-pandemic governance through the prism of the logic of surveillance capitalism. *Smart Cities, 5*(2).

Binkhorst, E., & Den Dekker, T. (2009). Agenda for co-creation tourism experience research. *Journal of Hospitality Marketing & Management*, *18*(2-3), 311–327. doi:10.1080/19368620802594193

Boes, K., Buhalis, D., & Inversini, A. (2015). Conceptualising smart tourism destination dimensions. In *Information and Communication Technologies in Tourism 2015: Proceedings of the International Conference in Lugano, Switzerland, February 3-6, 2015* (pp. 391-403). Springer International Publishing.

Buhalis, D., & Amaranggana, A. (2013). Smart tourism destinations. In *Information and Communication Technologies in Tourism 2014: Proceedings of the International Conference in Dublin, Ireland, January 21-24, 2014* (pp. 553-564). Springer International Publishing.

Buhalis, D., Leung, D., & Lin, M. (2023). Metaverse as a disruptive technology revolutionising tourism management and marketing. *Tourism Management*, *97*, 104724. doi:10.1016/j.tourman.2023.104724

Buonincontri, P., & Micera, R. (2016). The experience co-creation in smart tourism destinations: A multiple case analysis of European destinations. *Information Technology & Tourism*, *16*(3), 285–315. doi:10.1007/s40558-016-0060-5

Castro, S. R., Silva, S. C., & Duarte, P. (2017). Does Digital Marketing really boost city tourism? Evidences from Porto's Experience. *European Journal of Applied Business & Management*, *3*(3), 84–100.

Choi, H. S., & Kim, S. H. (2017). A content service deployment plan for metaverse museum exhibitions—Centering on the combination of beacons and HMDs. *International Journal of Information Management*, *37*(1), 1519–1527. doi:10.1016/j.ijinfomgt.2016.04.017

Çiftçi, Ş. F., & Çizel, B. (2024). Exploring relations among authentic tourism experience, experience quality, and tourist behaviours in phygital heritage with experimental design. *Journal of Destination Marketing & Management*, *31*, 100848. doi:10.1016/j.jdmm.2023.100848

Corne, A. (2017). Destination performance: Decision-making tools for tourism sector. *European Journal of Tourism Research, 17*, 265-268.

Courvoisier, F. (2020). Le «phygital», une nouvelle approche centrée client pour l'horlogerie. Academic Press.

Cranmer, E. E., tom Dieck, M. C., & Jung, T. (2018). *How can tourist attractions profit from augmented reality? Augmented Reality and Virtual Reality: Empowering Human.*

Del Vecchio, P., Secundo, G., & Garzoni, A. (2023). Phygital technologies and environments for breakthrough innovation in customers' and citizens' journey. A critical literature review and future agenda. *Technological Forecasting and Social Change, 189*, 122342.

Due, B. L., & Nielsen, A. M. R. (2019). Prototyping the Omnichannel Solutions. *CIRCD Working Papers Soc. Interact., 5*(1), 1-29.

Due, B. L., & Toft, T. L. (2021). Phygital highlighting: Achieving joint visual attention when physically co-editing a digital text. *Journal of Pragmatics*, *177*, 1–17. doi:10.1016/j.pragma.2021.01.034

Errichiello, L., & Marasco, A. (2017). Tourism innovation-oriented public-private partnerships for smart destination development. In *Knowledge Transfer to and within Tourism*. Emerald Publishing Limited. doi:10.1108/S2042-144320170000008010

Fazio, G., Fricano, S., Iannolino, S., & Pirrone, C. (2023). Metaverse and tourism development: Issues and opportunities in stakeholders' perception. *Information Technology & Tourism*, *25*(4), 507–528. doi:10.1007/s40558-023-00268-7

Gaggioli, A. (2017). Phygital spaces: When atoms meet bits. *Cyberpsychology, Behavior, and Social Networking*, *20*(12), 774–774. doi:10.1089/cyber.2017.29093.csi

Gao, W., Li, W., Fan, H., & Jia, X. (2021). How customer experience incongruence affects omnichannel customer retention: The moderating role of channel characteristics. *Journal of Retailing and Consumer Services*, *60*, 102487. doi:10.1016/j.jretconser.2021.102487

Ghali, Z., Rather, R. A., & Khan, I. (2024). Investigating metaverse marketing-enabled consumers' social presence, attachment, engagement and (re) visit intentions. *Journal of Retailing and Consumer Services*, *77*, 103671. doi:10.1016/j.jretconser.2023.103671

Go, H., & Kang, M. (2022). Metaverse tourism for sustainable tourism development: Tourism Agenda 2020. *Tourism Review*, *78*(2), 1–16.

Gretzel, U. (2019). The role of social media in creating and addressing overtourism. *Overtourism: Issues, Realities and Solutions, 1*, 62-75.

Gretzel, U., Sigala, M., Xiang, Z., & Koo, C. (2015). Smart tourism: Foundations and developments. *Electronic Markets*, *25*(3), 179–188. doi:10.1007/s12525-015-0196-8

Gretzel, U., Werthner, H., Koo, C., & Lamsfus, C. (2015). Conceptual foundations for understanding smart tourism ecosystems. *Computers in Human Behavior*, *50*, 558–563. doi:10.1016/j.chb.2015.03.043

Gretzel, U., Zhong, L., & Koo, C. (2016). Application of smart tourism to cities. *International Journal of Tourism Cities*, *2*(2). Advance online publication. doi:10.1108/IJTC-04-2016-0007

Gupta, S., Nath Mishra, O., & Kumar, S. (2022). Tourist participation, well-being and satisfaction: The mediating roles of service experience and tourist empowerment. *Current Issues in Tourism*, 1–16.

Gursoy, D., Malodia, S., & Dhir, A. (2022). The metaverse in the hospitality and tourism industry: An overview of current trends and future research directions. *Journal of Hospitality Marketing & Management, 31*(5), 527–534. doi:10.1080/19368623.2022.2072504

Heljakka, K., & Ihamäki, P. 2020. Toys that mobilize: past, present and future of phygital playful technology. In *Proceedings of the Future Technologies Conference (FTC) 2019: Volume 2* (pp. 625-640). Springer International Publishing. 10.1007/978-3-030-32523-7_46

Hiraki, T., Fukushima, S., & Naemura, T. 2016. Phygital field: an integrated field with a swarm of physical robots and digital images. In SIGGRAPH ASIA 2016 Emerging Technologies (pp. 1-2). doi:10.1145/2988240.2988242

Höjer, M., & Wangel, J. (2015). Smart sustainable cities: definition and challenges. In *ICT innovations for sustainability* (pp. 333–349). Springer International Publishing. doi:10.1007/978-3-319-09228-7_20

Hollensen, S., Kotler, P., & Opresnik, M. O. (2022). Metaverse–the new marketing universe. *Journal of Business Strategy.*

Hunter, W. C., Chung, N., Gretzel, U., & Koo, C. (2015). Constructivist research in smart tourism. *Asia Pacific Journal of Information Systems, 25*(1), 105–120. doi:10.14329/apjis.2015.25.1.105

Johnson, M., & Barlow, R. (2021). Defining the phygital marketing advantage. *Journal of Theoretical and Applied Electronic Commerce Research, 16*(6), 2365–2385. doi:10.3390/jtaer16060130

Jung, T. H., & tom Dieck, M. C. (2017). Augmented reality, virtual reality and 3D printing for the co-creation of value for the visitor experience at cultural heritage places. *Journal of Place Management and Development, 10*(2), 140–151. doi:10.1108/JPMD-07-2016-0045

Karaca, S., & Baran, Z. (2024). Meta Evolution: Digital Marketing in Tourism. In Digital Business and Optimizing Operating Strategies (pp. 91-131). IGI Global.

Kim, J., Kang, S., & Lee, K. H. (2021). Evolution of digital marketing communication: Bibliometric analysis and network visualization from key articles. *Journal of Business Research, 130*, 552–563. doi:10.1016/j.jbusres.2019.09.043

Klaus, P. P. (2021). phygital–the emperor's new clothes? *Journal of Strategic Marketing*, 1–8. doi:10.1080/0965254X.2021.1976252

Kye, B., Han, N., Kim, E., Park, Y., & Jo, S. (2021). Educational applications of metaverse: Possibilities and limitations. *Journal of Educational Evaluation for Health Professions, 18*, 18. doi:10.3352/jeehp.2021.18.32 PMID:34897242

Lamsfus, C., Martin, D., Alzua-Sorzabal, A., & Torres-Manzanera, E. 2015. Smart tourism destinations: An extended conception of smart cities focusing on human mobility. In *Information and Communication Technologies in Tourism 2015: Proceedings of the International Conference in Lugano, Switzerland, February 3-6, 2015* (pp. 363-375). Springer International Publishing.

Lawry, C. A. (2022). Blurring luxury: The mediating role of self-gifting in consumer acceptance of phygital shopping experiences. *International Journal of Advertising, 41*(4), 796–822. doi:10.1080/02650487.2021.1903742

Lee, L. H., Braud, T., Zhou, P., Wang, L., Xu, D., Lin, Z., Kumar, A., Bermejo, C., & Hui, P. 2021. All one needs to know about metaverse: A complete survey on technological singularity, virtual ecosystem, and research agenda. *arXiv preprint arXiv:2110.05352.*

Li, X., Gong, J., Gao, B., & Yuan, P. (2021). Impacts of COVID-19 on tourists' destination preferences: Evidence from China. *Annals of Tourism Research*, *90*, 103258. doi:10.1016/j.annals.2021.103258 PMID:34924648

Li, Y., Hu, C., Huang, C., & Duan, L. (2017). The concept of smart tourism in the context of tourism information services. *Tourism Management*, *58*, 293–300. doi:10.1016/j.tourman.2016.03.014

Liu, X., Wang, D., & Gretzel, U. (2022). On-site decision-making in smartphone-mediated contexts. *Tourism Management*, *88*, 104424. doi:10.1016/j.tourman.2021.104424

Lopez de Avila, A. (2015, February). Smart destinations: XXI century tourism. In ENTER2015 conference on information and communication technologies in tourism, Lugano, Switzerland (pp. 4-6). Academic Press.

Lupetti, M. L. (2016, March). Designing playful HRI: Acceptability of robots in everyday life through play. In *2016 11th ACM/IEEE International Conference on Human-Robot Interaction (HRI)* (pp. 631-632). IEEE.

Lupetti, M. L., Piumatti, G., & Rossetto, F. (2015, June). Phygital play HRI in a new gaming scenario. In *2015 7th International Conference on Intelligent Technologies for Interactive Entertainment (INTETAIN)* (pp. 17-21). IEEE. 10.4108/icst.intetain.2015.259563

Marchesani, F., Masciarelli, F., & Ceci, F. (2024). Digital trajectories in contemporary cities: Exploring the interplay between digital technology implementation, the amplitude of social media platforms, and tourists inflow in cities. *Cities (London, England)*, *146*, 104749. doi:10.1016/j.cities.2023.104749

Mele, C., Russo-Spena, T., Tregua, M., & Amitrano, C. C. (2021). The millennial customer journey: A Phygital mapping of emotional, behavioural, and social experiences. *Journal of Consumer Marketing*, *38*(4), 420–433. doi:10.1108/JCM-03-2020-3701

Mele, C., Spena, T.R., Marzullo, M. & Di Bernardo, I. (2023). The phygital transformation: a systematic review and a research agenda. *Italian Journal of Marketing*, 1-27.

Mieli, M. (2022). Phygital. In *Encyclopedia of Tourism Management and Marketing* (pp. 487–489). Edward Elgar Publishing. doi:10.4337/9781800377486.phygital

Mihalic, T. (2023). *Metaversal sustainability. New understanding of what to sustain.* International conference BEM-23, Tokyo, Japan.

Mihalic, T. (2024). Metaversal sustainability: Conceptualisation within the sustainable tourism paradigm. *Tourism Review*. Advance online publication. doi:10.1108/TR-09-2023-0609

Mishra, S., Malhotra, G., Chatterjee, R., & Shukla, Y. (2021). Consumer retention through phygital experience in omnichannel retailing: Role of consumer empowerment and satisfaction. *Journal of Strategic Marketing*, 1–18. doi:10.1080/0965254X.2021.1892162

Monaco, S., & Sacchi, G. (2023). Travelling the Metaverse: Potential Benefits and Main Challenges for Tourism Sectors and Research Applications. *Sustainability (Basel)*, *15*(4), 3348. doi:10.3390/su15043348

Moravcikova, D., & Kliestikova, J. (2017). Brand building with using phygital marketing communication. *Journal of Economics. Business and Management*, *5*(3), 148–153.

Munar, A. M. (2012). Social media strategies and destination management. *Scandinavian Journal of Hospitality and Tourism*, *12*(2), 101–120. doi:10.1080/15022250.2012.679047

Nakazawa, J., & Tokuda, H. (2007, May). Phygital map: Accessing digital multimedia from physical map. In *21st International Conference on Advanced Information Networking and Applications Workshops (AINAW'07)* (Vol. 2, pp. 368-373). IEEE. 10.1109/AINAW.2007.288

Neuburger, L., Beck, J., & Egger, R. (2018). The 'Phygital'tourist experience: The use of augmented and virtual reality in destination marketing. In *Tourism planning and destination marketing* (pp. 183–202). Emerald Publishing Limited. doi:10.1108/978-1-78756-291-220181009

Neuhofer, B., Buhalis, D., & Ladkin, A. (2015). Smart technologies for personalized experiences: A case study in the hospitality domain. *Electronic Markets*, *25*(3), 243–254. doi:10.1007/s12525-015-0182-1

Nofal, E., Reffat, R. M., & Vande Moere, A. (2017, June). Phygital heritage: An approach for heritage communication. In *Proceedings of the 3rd Immersive Learning Research Network Conference (iLRN 2017), Coimbra, Portugal* (pp. 26-29). Academic Press.

Prados-Castillo, J. F., Torrecilla-García, J. A., & Liébana-Cabanillas, F. (2024). Metaverse as a booster of tourism transformation towards virtual management strategies. *Tourism Review*. Advance online publication. doi:10.1108/TR-10-2023-0750

Purcărea, T. (2018). The future of retail impacted by the smart Phygital era. *Erişim TArihi*, *11*, 2021.

Pusceddu, G., Moi, L., & Cabiddu, F. (2023). Do they see eye to eye? Managing customer experience in phygital high-tech retail. *Management Decision*. Advance online publication. doi:10.1108/MD-05-2022-0673

Putra, D. T., Mahmudin, T., Wiartha, N. G. M., Adnyana, I. M. S., & Septiviari, A. I. M. (2024). The Existence Of The Metaverse Tourism In Indonesia: Between Opportunities And Threats. *Reslaj: Religion Education Social Laa Roiba Journal*, *6*(3), 2291–2300. doi:10.47467/reslaj.v6i3.6162

Reilly, P., & Dawson, I. (2021). Track and Trace, and Other Collaborative Art/Archaeology Bubbles in the Phygital Pandemic. *Open Archaeology*, *7*(1), 291–313. doi:10.1515/opar-2020-0137

Särmäkari, N. (2023). Digital 3D fashion designers: Cases of atacac and The fabricant. *Fashion Theory*, *27*(1), 85–114. doi:10.1080/1362704X.2021.1981657

Schreibman, S., Papadopoulos, C., Hughes, B., Rooney, N., Brennan, C., Mac Caba, F., & Healy, H. (2017). Phygital Augmentations for Enhancing History Teaching and Learning at School. DH.

Shafiee, S., Rajabzadeh Ghatari, A., Hasanzadeh, A., & Jahanyan, S. (2021). Smart tourism destinations: A systematic review. *Tourism Review*, *76*(3), 505–528. doi:10.1108/TR-06-2019-0235

Shin, H., & Kang, J. (2020). Reducing perceived health risk to attract hotel customers in the COVID-19 pandemic era: Focused on technology innovation for social distancing and cleanliness. *International Journal of Hospitality Management*, *91*, 102664. doi:10.1016/j.ijhm.2020.102664 PMID:32921871

Shin, H., & Kang, J. (2024). How does the metaverse travel experience influence virtual and actual travel behaviors? Focusing on the role of telepresence and avatar identification. *Journal of Hospitality and Tourism Management*, *58*, 174–183. doi:10.1016/j.jhtm.2023.12.009

Sigala, M., Kumar, S., Donthu, N., Sureka, R., & Joshi, Y. (2021). A bibliometric overview of the Journal of Hospitality and Tourism Management: Research contributions and influence. *Journal of Hospitality and Tourism Management*, *47*, 273–288. doi:10.1016/j.jhtm.2021.04.005

Sriram, G. K. (2022). A comprehensive survey on metaverse. *International Research Journal of Modernization in Engineering Technology*, *4*(2), 772–775.

Stankov, U., & Gretzel, U. (2020). Tourism 4.0 technologies and tourist experiences: A human-centered design perspective. *Information Technology & Tourism*, *22*(3), 477–488. doi:10.1007/s40558-020-00186-y

Švec, M., & Madleňák, A. (2017). Legal frameworks for the phygital concept. *European Journal of Science and Theology*, *13*(6), 209–217.

Torres, G. C. (2022). *Phygital Approaches and Intangible Cultural Heritage as a Tourism Experience Enhancer. Tradition and Innovation for a 21st Century Academic Museum of the University of Coimbra* (Doctoral dissertation, Universidade de Coimbra).

Tsekleves, E., Gradinar, A., Darby, A., & Smith, M. (2014, October). Active Parks: 'Phygital' urban games for sedentary and older people. In *Games for Health 2014: Proceedings of the 4th conference on gaming and playful interaction in healthcare* (pp. 140-143). Wiesbaden: Springer Fachmedien Wiesbaden.

Turco, M. L., & Giovannini, E. C. (2020). Towards a phygital heritage approach for museum collection. *Journal of Archaeological Science, Reports*, *34*, 102639. doi:10.1016/j.jasrep.2020.102639

Tyni, H., Kultima, A., & Mäyrä, F. (2013, October). Dimensions of hybrid in playful products. In *Proceedings of International Conference on Making Sense of Converging Media* (pp. 237-244). 10.1145/2523429.2523489

Van Nuenen, T., & Scarles, C. (2021). Advancements in technology and digital media in tourism. *Tourist Studies*, *21*(1), 119–132. doi:10.1177/1468797621990410

Volchek, K., & Brysch, A. (2023, January). Metaverse and Tourism: From a New Niche to a Transformation. In *Information and Communication Technologies in Tourism 2023: Proceedings of the ENTER 2023 eTourism Conference, January 18-20, 2023* (pp. 300-311). Cham: Springer Nature Switzerland.

Wang, D., & Fesenmaier, D. R. (2013). Transforming the travel experience: The use of smartphones for travel. In *Information and Communication Technologies in Tourism 2013: Proceedings of the International Conference in Innsbruck, Austria, January 22-25, 2013* (pp. 58-69). Springer Berlin Heidelberg.

Wei, W. (2024). A buzzword, a phase or the next chapter for the Internet? The status and possibilities of the metaverse for tourism. *Journal of Hospitality and Tourism Insights*, *7*(1), 602–625. doi:10.1108/JHTI-11-2022-0568

Xiang, Z., Tussyadiah, I., & Buhalis, D. (2015). Smart destinations: Foundations, analytics, and applications. *Journal of Destination Marketing & Management*, *4*(3), 143–144. doi:10.1016/j.jdmm.2015.07.001

Yang, T. T., Ruan, W. Q., Li, Y. Q., & Zhang, S. N. (2023). Virtual tourist motivation: The differences between virtual tourism and on-site tourism. *Tourism Review*, *78*(5), 1280–1297. doi:10.1108/TR-07-2022-0331

Yüce, M., Filiztekin, E., & Özkaya, K. G. (2021). COVID-19 diagnosis—A review of current methods. *Biosensors & Bioelectronics*, *172*, 112752. doi:10.1016/j.bios.2020.112752 PMID:33126180

Zaczkiewicz, A. (2019). *Louis Vuitton and Banana Republic also scored high on an assessment conducted by NewStore*. Academic Press.

Zhukova, G., Ono, M., & Lavrova, S. (2021). Arts education ecosystem: Digital restrictions and phygital solutions. In *EDULEARN21 Proceedings* (pp. 9572-9578). IATED.

Zurlo, F., Arquilla, V., Carella, G., & Tamburello, M. C. (2018). Designing acculturated phygital experiences. In *Cumulus Conference Proceedings Wuxi 2018 Diffused Transition & Design Opportunities* (pp. 153-164). Academic Press.

ENDNOTE

1 https://mysmartjourney.com/en-ca/post/phygital-marketing-in-tourist-destinations

Chapter 10
Metaverse-Driven Advances in Immersive VR Experiences for Behaviour Analysis and Skill Development

Nidhi Gupta
Sharda University, India

Kirti Sharma
Sharda University, India

Shivam Kumar
Sharda University, India

Priyanshu Kumar
Sharda University, India

ABSTRACT

The concept of the metaverse and immersive virtual reality experiences has gained significant attention in recent years. Metaverse refers to a parallel digital universe that combines both the physical and digital worlds, allowing multiple users to interact and engage in various activities. Immersive virtual reality experiences, on the other hand, involve users interacting with the virtual world through avatars that replace physical existence. Metaverse applications are designed to provide immersive online experiences by leveraging technologies such as virtual reality and augmented reality. Behavioural analysis is crucial in various fields. It aims to analyse human behaviour patterns, motive and mental health disorders. The chapter proposed a SaaS platform in order to meet the growing demand for accurate behavioural analysis in the metaverse. This platform aims to provide comprehensive behavioural analysis and insights within the metaverse, enabling them to make data-driven decisions and optimize their interactions with users in virtual environments.

DOI: 10.4018/979-8-3693-2422-6.ch010

INTRODUCTION

The metaverse, described as a shared virtual space, is attracting considerable attention due to its potential applications across various domains, including behaviour analysis and skill development. It refers to a parallel digital universe that combines both the physical and digital worlds, allowing multiple users to interact and engage in various activities (Dimitriadou & Lanitis, 2023). Virtual Reality (VR) and Augmented Reality (AR) technologies are currently under exploration for their utility in training, education, and experiential learning within the metaverse (Mystakidis, 2022; Laine et al., 2022; Truong et al., 2023). These immersive technologies can establish realistic and interactive environments conducive to skill development and behaviour analysis, fostering heightened engagement and knowledge retention (Laine et al., 2022; Truong et al., 2023). The avatars enable users to go beyond the physical limits of reality and experience the metaverse in various ways (Jang & Kim, 2023). Moreover, the integration of VR and AR with the metaverse holds the potential to transform digital asset management and offer solutions for various challenges (Truong et al., 2023).

The adoption of immersive technologies in the metaverse, such as VR, AR, and mixed reality (MR), is crucial for creating fully immersive experiences in virtual environments (Teng et al., 2022).

These technologies enable the development of immersive VR learning environments with increasing fidelity, offering new opportunities for skill training and behaviour analysis (Laine et al., 2022). Furthermore, the potential of VR in delivering self-management programs for chronic conditions and its application in assessment and treatment within psychology have been recognized, highlighting the diverse applications of immersive VR experiences (Harvie, 2021; Kaiser et al., 2022)

Evolution of the Metaverse

The journey from virtual worlds to the metaverse has been marked by a series of technological advancements, paradigm shifts, and the convergence of immersive technologies. The concept of virtual worlds emerged in the late 20th century, with notable milestones in the 1980s and 1990s. Early examples included platforms like Habitat (1986) and Second Life (2003), where users could create and interact in virtual spaces. However, the true evolution towards the metaverse gained momentum in the 2010s. One pivotal moment was the introduction of VR headsets such as the Oculus Rift in 2012, which brought about a renewed interest in immersive experiences. Concurrently, the growth of online multiplayer games and social platforms like Fortnite and Roblox contributed to the development of shared virtual spaces. The term "metaverse" started gaining prominence during this period, emphasizing a collective, interconnected virtual space that extends beyond individual platforms. Further defining this evolution was the expansion of augmented reality (AR) technologies. Mobile AR applications, like Pokémon Go in 2016, demonstrated the potential for blending digital and physical realities. The introduction of spatial computing and mixed reality (MR) further blurred the lines between the physical and virtual, setting the stage for a more comprehensive metaverse experience. Fortnite and Roblox contributed to the development of shared virtual spaces. The term "metaverse" started gaining prominence during this period, emphasizing a collective, interconnected virtual space that extends beyond individual platforms. Further defining this evolution was the expansion of augmented reality (AR) technologies. Mobile AR applications, like Pokémon Go in 2016, demonstrated the potential for blending digital and physical realities. The introduction of spatial computing and mixed reality (MR) further blurred the lines between the physical and virtual, setting the stage for a more comprehensive metaverse experience.

Background on the Metaverse and Virtual Reality (VR) Experiences

The metaverse, an amalgamation of virtual reality (VR), augmented reality (AR), and immersive technologies, defines a shared virtual space. This collective environment enables user interaction with computer- settings and fellow users, fostering a profound sense of presence and engagement. VR experiences utilize computer technology to construct simulated environments, varying from replicas of reality to unique settings. Users actively engage with and immerse themselves in these environments, cultivating a heightened sense of presence and interaction.

The metaverse's prominence stems from its diverse applications, spanning education, training, entertainment, and social interaction. It serves as a platform for crafting immersive experiences that transcend conventional two-dimensional interfaces. Simultaneously, the evolution of VR experiences has witnessed notable advancements, presenting more lifelike and interactive environments applicable in training, education, and entertainment contexts. The integration of virtual reality (VR) and the metaverse holds significant importance in behaviour analysis across various domains. VR exposure therapy is effective in treating anxiety disorders (Powers & Emmelkamp, 2008; Opriş et al., 2011), and phobias (Botella et al., 2017), indicating the potential of VR in understanding and modifying human behaviour. Additionally, VR has been utilized in human behaviour recognition and understanding, with applications in intelligent surveillance, motion analysis, and virtual reality environments (Zhang & Ma), simulate and understand real-world behaviours, such as pedestrian behaviour and child pedestrian injury prevention, demonstrating the potential of VR in studying and preventing real-world behaviours (Schwebel et al., 2016; Schwebel et al., 2008). Moreover, the perception of avatars' nonverbal behaviours in virtual reality and the use of VR experiments in economics highlight the diverse applications of VR in understanding human behaviour and decision-making processes (Etienne, 2023; Innocenti, 2017). Additionally, the insertion of real agents' behaviours in autonomous driving simulators demonstrates the potential for VR to study and incorporate real-world behaviours into simulations, further emphasizing its relevance in behaviour analysis (Serrano et al., 2022). The application of VR technology in project management and its role in analyzing the movement behaviour and residential habits of users showcases its potential in studying and optimizing human behaviours in various contexts (Leng & Zhan, 2023). Furthermore, the concept of presence in VR applications and its impact on participants' behaviour underscores the significance of VR in creating realistic experimental situations and measuring human behaviour (Mestre, 2015). The use of VR-enabled simulation platforms to analyze driving patterns and behavioural inconsistencies between manual and autonomous modes further demonstrates the potential of VR in studying human behaviour in complex scenarios (Xu et al., 2022). Additionally, the study of cultural behaviours of virtual agents in augmented reality environments highlights the role of VR in understanding cultural influences on human behaviour and interactions (Obaid et al., 2012). In conclusion, the integration of VR and the metaverse holds immense importance in behaviour analysis, offering diverse applications in understanding, simulating, and modifying human behaviour across various domains.

Significance of Behaviour Analysis and Skill Development

Behaviour analysis is a field that focuses on understanding and modifying human behaviour. It involves the systematic application of principles derived from behavioural science to improve socially significant behaviour. Skill development, on the other hand, refers to the process of acquiring and honing specific abilities or competencies. Both behaviour analysis and skill development are crucial in various domains, including education, healthcare, sports, and professional training. Understanding behaviour and developing skills are essential for personal and professional growth. Behaviour analysis can help identify and address behavioural challenges, such as learning difficulties, social skills deficits, and maladaptive behaviours. Skill development, on the other hand, is essential for acquiring competencies that are necessary for success in various domains, such as academic achievement, job performance, and overall well-being.

This paper aims to explore the integration of Virtual Reality and the Metaverse in behavioural analysis, shedding light on how these technologies can be harnessed to study, understand, and predict human behaviour in virtual environments. Virtual Reality and the Metaverse have gained significant attention in recent years due to their potential for creating immersive experiences that have a profound impact on individuals' emotions, attitudes, and behaviours

CASE STUDIES: REAL-LIFE APPLICATION OF VR AND METAVERSE IN BEHAVIOUR ANALYSIS

There have been numerous studies that have explored the use of immersive VR experiences for personal growth and rehabilitation. These studies have demonstrated the effectiveness of virtual reality in improving social skills, reducing anxiety and phobias, enhancing self-esteem, and promoting overall well-being. This article aims to describe the theoretical understanding of VR and metaverse in Behavioural analysis.

Theoretical Understanding

Understanding the theoretical foundations of VR and the metaverse in behaviour analysis is crucial for maximizing their potential in behaviour analysis. One prominent framework is the Social Information Processing model, which posits that individuals' behaviour is influenced by their interpretation of social cues and their ability to generate appropriate responses. Behavioural analysis involves studying and interpreting human behaviour, with the goal of understanding the underlying factors and mechanisms that drive individuals' actions. A key aspect of behavioural analysis is the ability to observe and measure behaviours in a controlled and systematic manner. Virtual Reality and the Metaverse have emerged as innovative tools that can enhance traditional approaches to behavioural analysis. By creating virtual environments that closely mimic real-life scenarios, researchers can observe and analyze human behaviours in a more natural and immersive setting. These technologies offer numerous advantages in behavioural analysis, including the ability to manipulate and control variables, collect real-time data, and create standardized experimental conditions. Moreover, Virtual Reality and the Metaverse provide researchers with the opportunity to study behaviours that may be difficult or unethical to observe in real-world settings.

VR and the metaverse can provide a unique opportunity to analyze and intervene in these social information processing deficits. By creating virtual social situations and scenarios, individuals can practice interpreting social cues and forming appropriate responses in a controlled environment. This immersive experience allows forensic psychologists to observe and analyze the individual's behaviour in real-time, providing valuable insights into their cognitive processes and social interactions. One theoretical foundation is social learning theory, which suggests that individuals learn by observing and imitating others. In immersive VR experiences, users have the opportunity to observe and interact with virtual avatars and environments, allowing for the examination of social learning processes in a controlled and realistic setting. Another theoretical foundation is cognitive behavioural theory, which highlights the role of thoughts, emotions, and behaviours in shaping human experience. In immersive VR experiences, cognitive-behavioural principles can be applied to identify and modify maladaptive thoughts and behaviours in a safe and controlled environment. Another relevant theoretical framework is the Theory of Mind. This theory suggests that individuals with certain psychological disorders may have difficulty understanding and empathizing with others' thoughts and emotions. VR and the metaverse can be utilized to enhance the Theory of Mind.

Sherman & Craig (2003) provide a comprehensive understanding of VR, covering its interface, application, and design, which forms the theoretical basis for the development and utilization of VR technology. Furthermore, (Sherrill et al.,2019) delve into the theoretical foundations and existing research on virtual reality exposure therapy (VRE), particularly in the context of posttraumatic stress disorder (PTSD), offering insights into the psychological and therapeutic underpinnings of VR applications. Additionally, (Park & Kim, 2022) and (Cheng et al., 2022) contribute to the theoretical understanding of the metaverse, discussing its taxonomy, components, applications, and open challenges, thereby laying the foundation for research and development in this emerging virtual space. The theoretical underpinnings of VR and the metaverse extend to various disciplines, as evidenced by the works of (Martins et al., 2004), (Renshaw et al., 2016), and (Badrinarayanan & Arnett, 2008), which explore the theoretical considerations and integrated frameworks for virtual teams, the development of a Turing-type test for virtual reality, and effective virtual new product development teams, respectively. These contributions provide a theoretical framework for understanding the dynamics of virtual interactions, the assessment of virtual reality, and the functioning of virtual teams, thereby enriching the theoretical landscape of VR and the metaverse. Moreover, the theoretical foundations of VR and the metaverse are also explored in the context of education and social implications. (Rodriguez, 2016) discusses the teaching of VR with affordable technologies, emphasizing the theoretical principles and hands-on learning, while (Pot-Kolder et al., 2016) highlight the experiential aspect of VR exposure therapy and its impact on social participation in individuals with psychotic disorders. Additionally, (Dolata & Schwabe., 2023) map the social construction of the metaverse, shedding light on the diverse perspectives and stakeholders involved in defining this virtual space, thus contributing to the theoretical understanding of the metaverse from a sociotechnical standpoint.

Understanding Behaviour Analysis in the Context of Metaverse

Understanding Behaviour Analysis in the Context of the Metaverse involves leveraging virtual reality technology to create immersive experiences that facilitate behaviour assessment, intervention, and training. This can be done by designing virtual environments within the metaverse that replicate real-world situations and triggers relevant to the behaviour being analysed. By immersing individuals in these virtual environments, behaviour analysts can accurately observe and measure behaviour, make informed assessments, and develop targeted interventions. Furthermore, the interactive and customizable nature of virtual reality in the metaverse allows for personalized interventions and adaptive learning experiences. Integrating metaverse and VR technologies with behaviour analysis opens up new possibilities for creating engaging and effective interventions that can be tailored to each individual's specific needs and preferences. Metaverse & VR have the potential to revolutionize behaviour analysis by creating immersive, interactive, and realistic environments for assessment, intervention, and treatment. Metaverse & VR in Advancing Immersive Experiences for Behaviour Analysis involves utilizing virtual reality technology to simulate real-world scenarios and environments in order to observe and analyze behaviour.

This approach allows for a more controlled and precise measurement of behaviours, as well as the ability to create personalized and adaptive interventions. Ultimately, the use of metaverse and VR technologies in behaviour analysis enhances the accuracy and effectiveness of assessments, interventions, and training by providing a realistic and authentic context for behaviour analysis. The metaverse-driven advances in immersive VR experiences for behaviour analysis and skill development have the potential to redefine how we understand and improve human behaviour. The metaverse's evolution has exerted a profound impact on social interaction and behaviour. As the concept solidified, social platforms within the metaverse became more sophisticated, accommodating diverse forms of communication and interaction. Social VR experiences, exemplified by platforms like Alt Space VR and Facebook Horizon, emerged to facilitate real-time engagement with others in virtual environments. The integration of social features into online gaming platforms played a crucial role. Games like Fortnite became not only gaming spaces but also social hubs where users could attend virtual concerts, interact with friends, and even engage in collaborative projects. This shift from solitary gaming experiences to collaborative and social endeavours exemplifies the transformative impact of the metaverse on social dynamics. Furthermore, the metaverse has influenced behaviour by providing a digital context for self-expression and identity exploration. Avatars and digital personas allow individuals to transcend geographical limitations, fostering a more inclusive and diverse social landscape. The metaverse has also become a stage for social experiments and research, examining how individuals behave and interact in these digital spaces. In essence, the evolution of the metaverse from virtual worlds to its present state has been characterized by technological innovation, increased connectivity, and a growing emphasis on shared immersive experiences. This transformation has not only redefined how we engage with virtual environments but has also shaped new norms and behaviours in the digital realm.

Applications

Virtual reality (VR) has undergone significant milestones in its development, leading to its widespread applications in various fields. The integration of haptic technology and human-machine interfaces has contributed to immersive interactions, enabling high-resolution continuous finger motion tracking and superior performance in gesture/object recognition through artificial intelligence analysis (Sun et al., 2022). Additionally, VR has been compared with desktop-based 3D and 2D versions in a category learning experiment, showcasing its increasing application in cognitive psychology (Barrett et al., 2022). Furthermore, the feasibility of developing VR for individuals with dementia in nursing homes has been explored, highlighting the potential for addressing psychological needs in this population (Kim et al., 2021).

In the realm of psychology and behaviour studies, VR has been investigated for its impact on students' addiction to VR games, constructing an immersive context for entertainment and learning (Zhai et al., 2020). Moreover, VR has been utilized for consumers' evaluation of product packaging, revealing consistent consumer behaviour in VR compared to everyday life, with minor variations (Branca et al., 2022). However, a randomized trial testing the effectiveness of VR as a tool for pro-environmental dietary change showed no impact on intentions, self-efficacy, or psychological distance, indicating the need for further exploration in this area (Plechatá et al., 2022). Additionally, VR experiences have been studied in the context of spatial cognition among tourists, focusing on a behavioural geographic perspective, indicating the potential for understanding perception and behaviour in virtual spaces (Ji et al., 2022). Furthermore, the utilization of a voice-based VR advanced cardiac life support team leader refresher has been explored, highlighting the potential of VR in clinical competence and training (Katz et al., 2020). Moreover, VR has been reviewed in the context of training health professionals in dementia awareness, emphasizing the shared commonality of themes identified within qualitative research findings (Slater et al., 2022).

Virtual reality (VR) has emerged as a valuable method for behavioural analysis due to its ability to create realistic simulations and controlled environments, enabling researchers to study human behaviour in various contexts. VR has been utilized in diverse fields such as medicine, psychology, and education to understand and modify human behaviour. For instance, VR exposure therapy has been shown to generalize gains to real-life scenarios, making it an effective tool for treating phobic and anxiety disorders (Peeters et. al., 2019). Additionally, VR has been used to train individuals in nonverbal behaviours, allowing them to practice and improve their skills in a safe and controlled environment (Morina et al., 2015). Furthermore, VR has been employed in pain management, with studies demonstrating its effectiveness as a nonpharmacological pain reduction technique for burn patients during physical therapy (Etienne et. al., 2023). In the context of education, VR has been found to influence teachers' intention to adopt it, with attitude, social norms, and perceived behavioural control being predictors of behavioural intention to use VR, highlighting its potential for transforming educational practices (Hoffman et al., 2001). Moreover, in medical education, VR has been advocated for its ability to simulate difficult scenarios and standardize training, making it a valuable tool for training healthcare professionals (Breiki et al., 2022). Similarly, in the context of caregiving, a VR practice program has been developed to enhance the practical competency of caregivers taking care of dementia patients, demonstrating the potential of VR to improve practical skills and competencies (Fertleman et al., 2018). Furthermore, VR has been explored in the context of behavioural interventions for individuals with Down syndrome, with studies indicating that immersive and interactive technologies such as VR can be used to improve classroom behaviour and deliver rich visual experiences (Kim et. al., 2021). Additionally, VR has been proposed as a tool to improve adherence to weight loss behaviours, suggesting its potential to enhance the delivery, receipt, and enactment of interventions aimed at improving health-related behaviours (Michalski et al., 2022).

The current state of immersive VR in behaviour analysis encompasses a wide range of platforms and applications. Virtual reality exposure therapy (VRET) has been explored for anxiety disorders, demonstrating its potential as a therapeutic tool (Page & Coxon., 2016). Additionally, VR technology has been applied in various domains, including motor learning, training, and education, with a focus on optimizing performance through intrinsic motivation and attention for learning (Wulf & Lewthwaite, 2016). Furthermore, VR holds significant promise for maximizing the efficiency and effectiveness of skill learning in diverse settings, such as sports, medicine, and safety-critical industries (Harris et al., 2020). However, limitations in the efficacy of current interventions and the need for further research to address these limitations have been identified, particularly in the treatment of violence and aggression in at-risk populations such as schizophrenia (Dellazizzo et al., 2019).

The application of immersive VR in behaviour analysis includes its use in tourism, journalism, and sports psychology. Non-immersive VR experiences have attracted significant interest, and news organizations are producing new kinds of immersive stories using VR technology (Zhu et al., 2023; Shin & Biocca, 2017). Moreover, immersive VR has been shown to influence anxiety, behaviour, and oral health status in preschool children, demonstrating its potential in clinical applications (Aminabadi et al., 2022). However, limitations exist in the natural interaction capabilities typically associated with immersive VR, as well as the need to define the minimal requirements for experiencing VR in the context of tourism (Wyssenbach et al., 2021; Wu et al., 2019). Additionally, the impact of VR on individuals' immersion and its potential transfer to real environments have been explored, highlighting the need for further research to understand the broader implications of VR experiences (Winkler et al., 2020; Suda et al., 2022).

Virtual Reality Therapy and Behavioural Analysis are increasingly being integrated to enhance treatment strategies. VR therapy involves using immersive virtual environments to simulate therapeutic scenarios and allow for exposure-based interventions. This approach has shown promising results in various areas, such as phobia treatment, post-traumatic stress disorder therapy, and addiction treatment. The integration of Virtual Reality therapy and behavioural analysis allows for a more comprehensive understanding of human behaviour and the underlying factors influencing it. By using Virtual Reality and the Metaverse, researchers can track and analyze detailed behavioural data in real-time, providing valuable insights into patterns and triggers that may contribute to addictive behaviours or substance abuse. Furthermore, Virtual Reality and the Metaverse offer opportunities for personalized treatment strategies.

Additionally, virtual reality therapy can also be beneficial in the treatment of anxiety-related disorders. By exposing individuals to virtual environments that trigger their specific fears or anxieties, therapists can help patients gradually confront and overcome these challenges in a controlled and safe setting. This type of exposure therapy has shown positive results in treating fear of flying, fear of public speaking, and post-traumatic stress disorder symptoms for veterans. Furthermore, virtual reality therapy offers a practical solution to address the shortage of mental health professionals. With certain virtual reality simulations, patients can receive therapy remotely from distant locations, eliminating the need for in-person sessions. This not only increases accessibility to treatment for individuals in underserved areas but also reduces the cost and time associated with traditional therapy. In addition to its life scenarios and triggers, therapists can help patients develop healthier coping mechanisms and reduce their reliance on addictive substances or behaviours.

Additionally, virtual reality therapy offers a unique advantage in the treatment of eating disorders such as anorexia. By creating virtual environments that mimic real-world eating situations, individuals struggling with eating disorders can safely confront and challenge their fears and anxieties related to food. Therapists can guide patients through virtual scenarios that expose them to different food options, help them practice portion control, and address body image concerns. This immersive therapy can provide a controlled and supportive environment for individuals to develop a healthier relationship with food and their bodies, leading to improved outcomes in the treatment of eating disorders.

Furthermore, virtual reality has proven to be instrumental in the field of physical therapy and rehabilitation. Through the use of VR simulations, patients can engage in interactive exercises and activities that mimic real-world movements and tasks. This allows for a more engaging and motivating therapy experience, leading to increased patient compliance and better outcomes. Moreover, virtual reality can also be utilized in the field of behavioural analysis to enhance the ecological validity of studies.

By creating realistic, immersive, and interactive scenarios, researchers can better observe and understand human behaviour in a controlled yet lifelike environment. This can lead to more accurate and reliable data on behavioural responses, as individuals are more likely to respond authentically in a virtual reality setting compared to traditional laboratory settings. Overall, virtual reality and the metaverse offer exciting opportunities in the field of behavioural analysis. Virtual reality and the metaverse have proven to be valuable tools in the assessment, understanding, and treatment of mental health disorders and behavioural addictions. Virtual reality therapy provides a unique platform for the assessment and treatment of substance use disorders. By immersing individuals in virtual environments that simulate real-life situations, therapists can assess and modify problematic behaviours associated with substance use disorders. Additionally, the integration of virtual reality and artificial intelligence using machine learning techniques has opened up new possibilities for optimizing individual psychological treatment strategies. With the ability to obtain "digital biomarkers" data, therapists can tailor treatment plans to individual needs and monitor progress more effectively. Furthermore, virtual reality has the potential to revolutionize basic cognitive research. By creating immersive and interactive virtual environments, researchers can study cognitive processes in a more ecologically valid manner. This allows for a better understanding of how individuals navigate and interact with their surroundings, providing valuable insights into cognitive functioning. Ultimately, the integration of virtual reality and the metaverse in behavioural analysis holds great promise for improving the assessment, understanding, and treatment of mental health disorders and behavioural addictions. In conclusion, virtual reality and the metaverse have shown significant potential in enhancing the ecological validity of studies in behavioural analysis.

These technologies provide a realistic and immersive environment that allows researchers to observe and analyze human behaviour more authentically. They have proven to be effective in treating various mental health disorders such as anxiety disorders, eating disorders, and gaming disorders. Through virtual reality therapy, individuals can be exposed to controlled and safe environments that simulate real-life situations, allowing for the assessment and modification of problematic behaviours. Additionally, the use of virtual reality in conjunction with cognitive behavioural therapy and visual-motor therapy, known as VEBIM, has shown promise in combatting these disorders (Applications of Virtual Reality in Mental Health, 2019). Overall, virtual reality and the metaverse offer exciting opportunities in the field of behavioural analysis. These technologies provide a virtual environment that allows individuals to experience various situations that may be difficult or even impossible to deal with in reality; as such, they are more effective and safer than traditional treatments (Goharinejad, S. et al.,2022).

LITERATURE SURVEY ON BEHAVIOUR ANALYSIS USING VR AND METAVERSE

The literature review on virtual reality (VR) and immersive technologies spans various domains, including mental health, consumer behaviour, e-participation, environmental change, and education. Studies have highlighted the potential of VR in mental health assessment, understanding, and treatment, particularly in addressing conditions such as anxiety disorders, stress-related disorders, obesity, eating disorders, addiction, and schizophrenia (Freeman et al., 2017; Riva & Serino, 2020). Additionally, VR has been explored as an adjunctive treatment for alcohol use disorder, showing promise in craving assessment and cue-induced therapy (Lebiecka et al., 2021). However, gaps exist in meaningful applications to mental health, indicating the need for further research in this area (Freeman et al., 2017). In the realm of consumer behaviour, immersive technologies such as VR have been the subject of systematic reviews, focusing on their influence across various sectors and industries (Ambika et al., 2023). Furthermore, VR has been investigated for its potential in pro-environmental dietary change, indicating a growing interest in leveraging immersive technologies for societal and behavioural interventions (Plechatá et al., 2022). However, gaps in research related to immersive technologies and consumer behaviour have been identified, emphasizing the need for holistic analyses and comparisons across different immersive technologies and sectors (Ambika et al., 2023). Moreover, the use of VR in e-participation research and as a tool for evaluating product packaging and sensory cues has been explored, highlighting the potential of VR in enhancing research methodologies and consumer evaluations (Porwol & Dumas, 2022; Branca et al., 2022). Additionally, VR has been studied in the context of spatial cognition among tourists, indicating its potential for understanding perception and behaviour in virtual spaces (Ji et al., 2022). However, gaps in research related to economic performance and spatial cognition in the context of VR experiences have been identified, suggesting opportunities for further exploration (Ji et al., 2022; Soowook & Oh, 2016). Furthermore, the literature has also delved into the development of VR-based training curricula for behavioural health anticipatory guidance, indicating the potential of VR in medical education and training (Herbst et al., 2021). Additionally, studies have explored the use of VR in deep learning for omnidirectional vision, highlighting the potential of VR in advancing technological capabilities (Ai et al., 2022). However, research gaps related to the usability and effectiveness of VR-based training curricula have been identified, emphasizing the need for further investigation (Herbst et al., 2021). 4. Literature Survey on Behaviour Analysis Using VR & Metaverse Virtual reality has also been found to be effective in destigmatizing mental disorders by providing individuals with first-hand experiences of the perceptions and experiences of those affected by schizophrenia. These immersive virtual reality experiences can enhance empathy and positive attitudes towards individuals with mental disorders. Additionally, virtual reality has been successfully used in the treatment of specific phobias, PTSD, anxiety disorders, depression, schizophrenia, eating disorders, and pain management (Haeyen et al., 2021). Overall, the use of virtual reality in forensic psychology and personal growth settings holds great potential for enhancing behaviour analysis, skill development, and treatment interventions (Tuente et al., 2018). In the context of forensic mental health care, interactive virtual reality interventions have shown promise as a way for patients to actively engage in practising behavioural skills (Kip et al., 2020).

ADVANCEMENTS IN IMMERSIVE TECHNOLOGIES FOR BEHAVIOUR ANALYSIS

The use of metaverse and virtual reality in behaviour analysis has allowed researchers to create realistic and controlled environments that can elicit authentic reactions from individuals. These technologies enable researchers to study behaviour in a way that is more natural and ecologically valid than in traditional laboratory settings. Virtual reality technology, with its good immersion and interactivity, has broad application prospects in the field of behaviour analysis. By creating virtual environments that closely mimic real-world situations, researchers can observe and analyze behaviour more accurately and comprehensively. For example, virtual reality simulations can be used to study social interactions, phobias, and even risky behaviours in a safe and controlled environment. Additionally, virtual reality technology can also be used for behaviour skills training, particularly in educational settings. The integration of metaverse and virtual reality technology in healthcare and clinical settings holds great promise for behaviour analysis and treatment. The combination of advanced technologies, such as augmented reality, artificial intelligence, and digital twins, within the metaverse can provide clinicians with powerful tools for assessing and treating various mental health disorders. For example, virtual reality environments can be used to simulate exposure therapy for individuals with anxiety disorders, allowing them to gradually confront and overcome their fears in a safe and controlled manner. Furthermore, virtual reality technology can be used to create virtual social environments for individuals with autism spectrum disorder, helping them develop and practice social skills in a comfortable and supportive setting. Overall, metaverse and virtual reality technologies have the potential to revolutionize behaviour analysis by providing immersive and realistic experiences that can enhance assessment, treatment, and intervention strategies for various behavioural and mental health conditions. The metaverse and virtual reality have the potential to revolutionize behaviour analysis by providing immersive and realistic experiences that can enhance assessment, treatment, and intervention strategies for various behavioural and mental health conditions.

ROLE OF VR IN ADVANCING IMMERSIVE EXPERIENCES

Virtual Reality plays a pivotal role in advancing immersive experiences for behaviour analysis. By creating virtual environments that simulate real-world scenarios and interactions, VR technology allows researchers to observe and analyze behaviour in a controlled and customizable setting. This can lead to more accurate and detailed data collection, as well as a deeper understanding of how individuals behave in specific situations. Additionally, VR technology can be used to create immersive training programs and interventions for behaviour analysis. These programs can provide individuals with the opportunity to practice and develop targeted skills in a safe and supportive environment. Furthermore, virtual reality technology can enhance the sense of presence and immersion, enabling individuals to truly experience and engage with the virtual environment. Through the integration of virtual reality with artificial intelligence and machine learning, personalized treatment strategies and adaptive interventions can be developed. These technologies can dynamically analyze individual responses and adjust the virtual environment or interventions accordingly, maximizing effectiveness and personalization.

Furthermore, virtual reality technology has a profound impact on our bodies and brains. When we engage in immersive experiences through virtual reality, our brains are tricked into perceiving the virtual environment as real. This triggers various sensory inputs, including visual, auditory, and tactile sensations, which stimulate our neural pathways and activate different regions of the brain. As a result, our brain processes and reacts to the virtual stimuli as if they were happening in the physical world. This phenomenon, known as presence, is what makes virtual reality such a powerful tool in behaviour analysis. By creating a sense of presence, virtual reality can elicit authentic behavioural responses and allow researchers to gain valuable insights into how individuals interact with their surroundings.

Moreover, virtual reality technology can transport individuals to different places and situations that may not be easily accessible in real life. This opens up countless possibilities for behaviour analysis research and interventions. For example, virtual reality can be used to simulate challenging social situations, such as public speaking or job interviews, allowing individuals to practice and develop their skills in a controlled and supportive environment.

In addition, the integration of artificial intelligence and machine learning techniques with virtual reality can optimize individual treatment strategies (Rahayu, S, F. et al., 2020). This integration enables the collection and analysis of "digital biomarkers" data, which can provide valuable insights into an individual's psychological state and treatment progress. Furthermore, the use of wearables and other sensor technologies in conjunction with virtual reality allows for the collection and analysis of physiological data associated with aggressive behaviour or emotional states (Kip, H. et al., 2020). Virtual Reality and the Metaverse offer the opportunity to study behaviours in a more ecologically valid manner, as they allow for realistic interactions with digital avatars and virtual objects. Moreover, advanced technologies such as virtual reality, augmented reality, and remote rendering have been integrated into the Metaverse to enhance the real-time and seamless interaction between individuals and virtual objects, further enriching the potential for behavioural analysis. These technologies also enable researchers to collect objective and quantitative data on participants' behaviours, such as their movements, gestures, and physiological responses, providing a more comprehensive understanding of human behaviour. Additionally, Virtual Reality and the Metaverse offer a unique opportunity for studying social interactions and group dynamics. This combination of technologies enables a more comprehensive and objective assessment of behavioural patterns, allowing for tailored treatment plans that address the specific needs of each individual. Furthermore, the use of virtual reality and the metaverse in behavioural analysis can extend beyond individual therapy settings. immersive environments allow for accurate behaviour analysis and skill development in various fields such as healthcare, education, sports training, and therapy. The metaverse can provide learners with the skills to build virtual environments and overcome barriers in education, healthcare, and other fields (Chen et al., 2023) The metaverse-driven advances in immersive VR experiences for behaviour analysis and skill development have the potential to transform multiple industries, including healthcare, education, marketing, and entertainment. By combining technologies such as virtual reality, augmented reality, artificial intelligence, and digital twins, the metaverse offers a unique platform for creating immersive virtual environments that accurately replicate real-world scenarios (Wheeler & Natarajan, 2023).

PROPOSED METHODOLOGY: CONSTRUCTING A MULTIDISCIPLINARY PLATFORM

We have a problem when it comes to understanding and improving how people behave and learn new skills. The usual methods we use, like observing them or asking questions, aren't always good enough, especially for complex situations. Traditional methods of behaviour analysis and skill development, such as observation and self-report, often fall short in capturing the complexities of human behaviour. Metaverse-driven immersive VR experiences offer a promising solution by providing a controlled and interactive environment where individuals can be observed and assessed in real time. This multidisciplinary platform seamlessly merges behaviour analysis principles with immersive VR technology, creating a powerful tool for understanding and improving human behaviour. We now have come up with the solution with a multidisciplinary platform with immersive virtual reality (VR) that seamlessly merges behaviour analysis and immersive virtual reality (VR) experiences. With applications spanning from forensic psychology to personal growth, this platform bridges the gap between two seemingly disparate domains, creating a unified solution that caters to the needs of forensics It creates very real and interactive pretend worlds. People can learn and act in these pretend worlds, and we can watch and study their behaviour there. However, we need to figure out how to make these VR experiences just right and how to use the data we collect from them in a good way The metaverse-driven advances in immersive VR experiences offer a multi-disciplinary platform that can revolutionize behaviour analysis and skill development. By utilizing a SAAS-based platform for the metaverse, the benefits of VR can be more effectively harnessed for behaviour analysis and skill development. A SAAS solution allows users to access and use VR applications through the internet, eliminating the need for extensive hardware setups and technical expertise. With a SAAS-based platform, researchers and educators can easily create, customize, and deploy immersive VR experiences that are tailored to specific behaviour analysis goals and skill development objectives. This platform provides a user-friendly interface where users can design virtual environments, insert interactive elements, and define behavioural metrics for data collection.

THE PROCESS: FROM SCENARIO SELECTION TO SOLUTION SUGGESTION

To implement the application of VR and the Metaverse in behaviour analysis, a multidisciplinary platform can be developed using the following steps as shown in Fig 1

1. Selecting the desired VR scenario or experience that aligns with the behaviour being analysed.
2. Creating a virtual environment or simulation that accurately represents the desired scenario, using advanced graphics and immersive technology.
3. Incorporating AI models that can react and analyze user actions in real-time within the virtual environment.
4. Enabling user-AI interaction to create a dynamic and responsive experience for the user.
5. Analyzing and capturing user data and actions during the VR experience to gather relevant behavioural insights.
6. Providing the user with a virtual debriefing session immediately after the VR experience, in which they can discuss and reflect on their actions and behaviours with the AI, allowing for a deeper understanding of their behaviour.
7. Generating a comprehensive report that includes different parameters and suggested solutions based on the analysis conducted during the VR experience.

The proposed platform has a wide range of potential applications across various disciplines, including:

Forensic psychology: Assess and understand criminal behaviour, evaluate risk factors, and develop treatment interventions for individuals with an antisocial personality disorder.

Clinical psychology: Treat anxiety disorders, phobias, and post-traumatic stress disorder (PTSD) through exposure therapy and cognitive-behavioural therapy (CBT) in immersive VR environments.

Education: Enhance skill development in areas such as language acquisition, social skills training, and vocational rehabilitation.

Sports psychology: Improve athletic performance by training athletes in virtual environments that replicate real-world sporting scenarios.

Personal growth: Promote self-awareness, emotional regulation, and stress management through guided VR experiences. A multi-disciplinary approach to VR-based behaviour analysis is crucial in fully utilizing the potential of the metaverse.

This platform involves collaboration between experts in fields such as psychology, computer science, data analysis, and user experience design. Through this interdisciplinary collaboration, researchers and practitioners can leverage the capabilities of the metaverse to analyze user behaviour and make informed decisions in areas such as consumer preferences and product design, training and performance evaluation, and behaviour modification interventions. By combining insights from different disciplines, researchers can develop more comprehensive and accurate models of human behaviour within virtual environments. This multi-disciplinary platform allows for the exploration of innovative techniques and methodologies in behaviour analysis, leading to a deeper understanding of human cognition, emotions, and this interdisciplinary approach, combined with the immersive nature of VR experiences in the metaverse, allows for a more holistic understanding of human behaviour and skill development. This can ultimately lead to the creation of more effective and tailored interventions for behaviour change and skill enhancement.

The integration of metaverse-driven advances in immersive VR experiences holds significant promise for behaviour analysis and skill development. The metaverse, facilitated by virtual reality (VR) and augmented reality (AR), is expected to revolutionize various fields, including psychology, neurorehabilitation, education, healthcare, and training. Mystakidis (2022) highlights the potential of the metaverse for educational innovation, particularly in laboratory simulations, procedural skills development, and STEM education, with remarkable results in training speed, performance, and retention.

Furthermore, Bansal et al. (2022) emphasize the universal and immersive nature of the metaverse, enabled by VR and AR technologies, indicating its potential for transformative applications in healthcare. Additionally, Usmani et al. (2022) underscore the metaverse as the future of Web 3.0, signifying its overarching impact on various domains, including mental health. The use of immersive VR experiences for behaviour analysis and skill development has been demonstrated in various studies. For instance, immersive VR has been employed in training dental students (LeBlanc et al., 2004), teaching pedestrian skills to children with autism spectrum disorder (Dixon et al., 2019), and enhancing creativity (Nanjappan, 2023). Furthermore, the potential of VR-based simulation in medical education to improve clinical skills and students' self-confidence has been recognized (Sukotjo et al., 2020). These findings collectively underscore the efficacy of immersive VR experiences in fostering skill development and behaviour analysis across diverse domains. Looking ahead, the metaverse is poised to reshape the landscape of immersive experiences, offering interactive and immersive environments for learning, training, and skill development. As highlighted by (Wilson & Soranzo, 2015), ongoing questions for researchers in the field of VR environments in psychological research underscore the evolving nature of this technology and the need for continued exploration. Moreover, the arrival of the metaverse in neurorehabilitation, as discussed by (Calabrò et al., 2022), presents a vision for the future of immersive experiences, indicating the potential for further advancements in behaviour analysis and skill development. In conclusion, the metaverse-driven advances in immersive VR experiences hold immense potential for behaviour analysis and skill development across various domains. As the metaverse continues to evolve, it is imperative for researchers and practitioners to harness its capabilities to create innovative and effective immersive experiences for learning, training, and behaviour analysis.

CONCLUSION AND FUTURE DIRECTIONS

The research paper presents a transformative approach to behaviour analysis and skill development. It emphasises on providing a controlled, interactive environment where individuals can be observed and assessed in real-time, VR experiences have the potential to revolutionize the way we understand and improve human behaviour. This multidisciplinary platform, powered by metaverse-driven immersive VR experiences, offers a promising solution to revolutionize behaviour analysis and skill development. By leveraging the power of VR technology and a SAAS-based delivery model, this platform has the potential to revolutionize the way we understand and improve human behaviour across a wide range of applications. As the metaverse continues to develop, we can expect to see even more innovative applications of

VR for behaviour analysis and skill development. Fast rendering of the virtual environment is crucial for providing an immersive VR experience that is realistic and engaging. Fast rendering allows users to interact with the environment seamlessly and without experiencing lag or latency. This is particularly important for behaviour analysis and skill development, as it enables users to focus on their behaviour and interactions with the environment without distractions caused by technical glitches. Future research should focus on developing new and innovative VR experiences, investigating the long-term effects of VR interventions, assessing the ethical considerations of using VR, and developing guidelines for VR use. Additionally, researchers should continue to develop fast rendering technologies to improve the realism and immersion of VR experiences. By addressing these challenges, we can harness the power of VR to revolutionize behaviour analysis and skill development.

REFERENCES

Ai, H., Cao, Z., & Zhu, J. (2022). *Deep learning for omnidirectional vision: a survey and new perspectives*. doi:10.36227/techrxiv.19807699

Ambika, A., Shin, H., & Jain, V. (2023). Immersive technologies and consumer behaviour: A systematic review of two decades of research. *Australian Journal of Management*. Advance online publication. doi:10.1177/03128962231181429

Aminabadi, N. A., Golsanamlou, O., Halimi, Z., & Jamali, Z. (2022). Assessing the different levels of virtual reality that influence anxiety, behaviour, and oral health status in preschool children: Randomized controlled clinical trial. *JMIR Perioperative Medicine*, *5*(1), e35415. doi:10.2196/35415 PMID:35436233

Badrinarayanan, V., & Arnett, D. B. (2008). Effective virtual new product development teams: An integrated framework. Journal of Business &Amp. *Journal of Business and Industrial Marketing*, *23*(4), 242–248. doi:10.1108/08858620810865816

Barrett, R., Poe, R., O'Camb, J. W., Woodruff, C., Harrison, S., Dolguikh, K., Chuong, C., Klassen, A. D., Zhang, R., Joseph, R. B., & Blair, M. R. (2022). Comparing virtual reality, desktop-based 3d, and 2d versions of a category learning experiment. *PLoS One*, *17*(10), e0275119. doi:10.1371/journal.pone.0275119 PMID:36201546

Barrett, R. C. A., Poe, R., O'Camb, J. W., Woodruff, C., Harrison, S. M., Dolguikh, K., Chuong, C., Klassen, A. D., Zhang, R., Joseph, R. B., & Blair, M. R. (2022). Comparing virtual reality, desktop-based 3D, and 2D versions of a category learning experiment. *PLoS One*, *17*(10), e0275119. doi:10.1371/journal.pone.0275119 PMID:36201546

Botella, C., Fernández-Álvarez, J., Guillén, V., García-Palacios, A., & Baños, R. (2017). Recent progress in virtual reality exposure therapy for phobias: A systematic review. *Current Psychiatry Reports*, *19*(7), 42. Advance online publication. doi:10.1007/s11920-017-0788-4 PMID:28540594

Branca, G., Resciniti, R., & Loureiro, S. M. C. (2022). Virtual is so real! consumers' evaluation of product packaging in virtual reality. Psychology &Amp. *Psychology and Marketing*, *40*(3), 596–609. doi:10.1002/mar.21743

Calabrò, R. S., Cerasa, A., Ciancarelli, I., Pignolo, L., Tonin, P., Iosa, M., & Morone, G. (2022). The arrival of the metaverse in neurorehabilitation: Fact, fake or vision? *Biomedicines*, *10*(10), 2602. doi:10.3390/biomedicines10102602 PMID:36289862

Chen, Y. J., Wang, C. J., & Chen, C. W. (2023). Effects of virtual reality on preoperative anxiety in children: A systematic review and meta-analysis of randomised controlled trials. *Journal of Clinical Nursing*, *32*(11-12), 2494–2504. doi:10.1111/jocn.16394 PMID:35672942

Cheng, X., Zhang, S., Fu, S., Liu, W., Guan, C., Mou, J., & Huang, C. (2022). Exploring the metaverse in the digital economy: An overview and research framework. Journal of Electronic Business &Amp. *Digital Economics*, *1*(1/2), 206–224. doi:10.1108/JEBDE-09-2022-0036

Cornet, L. J., & Van Gelder, J. L. (2020). Virtual reality: A use case for criminal justice practice. [Chicago]. *Psychology, Crime & Law*, *26*(7), 631–647. doi:10.1080/1068316X.2019.1708357

Dellazizzo, L., Potvin, S., Bahig, S., & Dumais, A. (2019). Comprehensive review on virtual reality for the treatment of violence: Implications for youth with schizophrenia. *NPJ Schizophrenia*, *5*(1), 11. Advance online publication. doi:10.1038/s41537-019-0079-7 PMID:31337763

Dimitriadou, E., & Lanitis, A. (2023). A critical evaluation, challenges, and future perspectives of using artificial intelligence and emerging technologies in smart classrooms. *Smart Learning Environments*, *10*(1), 12. Advance online publication. doi:10.1186/s40561-023-00231-3

Dolata, M., & Schwabe, G. (2023). What is the Metaverse and who seeks to define it? Mapping the site of social construction. *Journal of Information Technology*, *38*(3), 239–266. doi:10.1177/02683962231159927

Duinkharjav, B., Chen, K., Tyagi, A., He, J., Zhu, Y., & Sun, Q. (2022). Color-perception-guided display power reduction for virtual reality. *ACM Transactions on Graphics*, *41*(6), 1–16. doi:10.1145/3550454.3555473

Etienne, E., Leclercq, A.-L., Remacle, A., Dessart, L., & Schyns, M. (2023). Perception of avatars nonverbal behaviours in virtual reality. *Psychology and Marketing*, *40*(11), 2464–2481. doi:10.1002/mar.21871

Fernández-Álvarez, J., Guillén, V., García-Palacios, A., & Baños, R. (2017). Recent progress in virtual reality exposure therapy for phobias: A systematic review. *Current Psychiatry Reports*, *19*(7), 42. Advance online publication. doi:10.1007/s11920-017-0788-4 PMID:28540594

Fertleman, C., Aubugeau-Williams, P., Sher, C., Lim, A., Lumley, S., Delacroix, S., … Pan, X. (2018). *A discussion of virtual reality as a new tool for training healthcare professionals*. doi:10.3390/biomedicines10102602

Freeman, D., Reeve, S., Robinson, A., Ehlers, A., Clark, D. M., Spanlang, B., & Slater, M. (2017). Virtual reality in the assessment, understanding, and treatment of mental health disorders. *Psychological Medicine*, *47*(14), 2393–2400. doi:10.1017/S003329171700040X PMID:28325167

Harris, D., Bird, J. M., Smart, P., Wilson, M. R., & Vine, S. J. (2020). A framework for the testing and validation of simulated environments in experimentation and training. *Frontiers in Psychology*, *11*, 605. Advance online publication. doi:10.3389/fpsyg.2020.00605 PMID:32296379

Harris, D. J., Buckingham, G., Wilson, M. R., Brookes, J., Mushtaq, F., Mon-Williams, M., & Vine, S. J. (2020). The effect of a virtual reality environment on gaze behaviour and motor skill learning. *Psychology of Sport and Exercise*, *50*, 101721. doi:10.1016/j.psychsport.2020.101721

Harvie, D. (2021). Immersive education for chronic condition self-management. *Frontiers in Virtual Reality*, *2*, 657761. Advance online publication. doi:10.3389/frvir.2021.657761

Herbst, R. B., Rybak, T. M., Meisman, A., Whitehead, M., Rosen, B. L., Crosby, L. E., . . . Real, F. J. (2021). A virtual reality resident training curriculum on behavioural health anticipatory guidance: development and usability study (preprint) https://doi.org/ doi:10.2196/preprints.29518

Hoffman, H., Patterson, D., Carrougher, G., & Sharar, S. (2001). Effectiveness of virtual reality–based pain control with multiple treatments. *The Clinical Journal of Pain*, *17*(3), 229–235. doi:10.1097/00002508-200109000-00007 PMID:11587113

Ji, S., Hwang, H. J., Hwang, C., Koo, C., & Lee, E. (2022). The attributes of virtual reality(vr) experiences and spatial cognition among tourists: Focusing on a behavioural geographic perspective. *The Tourism Sciences Society of Korea*, *46*(4), 153–176. doi:10.17086/JTS.2022.46.4.153.176

Kim, J., Jang, H., Kim, D., & Lee, J. (2023). Exploration of the Virtual Reality Teleportation Methods Using Hand-Tracking, Eye-Tracking, and EEG. *International Journal of Human-Computer Interaction*, *39*(20), 4112–4125. doi:10.1080/10447318.2022.2109248

Kim, J., Park, S., & Lim, H. (2021). Developing a virtual reality for people with dementia in nursing homes based on their psychological needs: A feasibility study. *BMC Geriatrics*, *21*(1), 167. Advance online publication. doi:10.1186/s12877-021-02125-w PMID:33678160

Kip, H., Oberschmidt, K., & Bierbooms, J. J. (2020). eHealth technology in forensic mental healthcare: Recommendations for achieving benefits and overcoming barriers. *International Journal of Forensic Mental Health*, *20*(1), 31–47. doi:10.1080/14999013.2020.1808914

Laine, J., Lindqvist, T., Korhonen, T., & Hakkarainen, K. (2022). Systematic review of intelligent tutoring systems for hard skills training in virtual reality environments. *International Journal of Technology in Education and Science*, *6*(2), 178–203. doi:10.46328/ijtes.348

Lebiecka, Z., Skoneczny, T., Tyburski, E., Samochowiec, J., & Kucharska-Mazur, J. (2021). Is virtual reality cue exposure a promising adjunctive treatment for alcohol use disorder? *Journal of Clinical Medicine*, *10*(13), 2972. doi:10.3390/jcm10132972 PMID:34279455

Martins, L. D., Gilson, L. L., & Maynard, M. (2004). Virtual teams: What do we know and where do we go from here? *Journal of Management*, *30*(6), 805–835. doi:10.1016/j.jm.2004.05.002

Mestre, D. (2015). *On the usefulness of the concept of presence in virtual reality applications*. doi:10.1117/12.2075798

Michalski, S. C., Szpak, A., Ellison, C., Cornish, R., & Loetscher, T. (2022). Using virtual reality to improve classroom behaviour in people with down syndrome: Within-subjects experimental design. *JMIR Serious Games*, *10*(2), e34373. doi:10.2196/34373 PMID:35124567

Morina, N., Ijntema, H., Meyerbröker, K., & Emmelkamp, P. M. G. (2015). Can virtual reality exposure therapy gains be generalized to real-life? a meta-analysis of studies applying behavioural assessments. *Behaviour Research and Therapy*, *74*, 18–24. doi:10.1016/j.brat.2015.08.010 PMID:26355646

Mystakidis, S. (2022). Metaverse. *Metaverse. Encyclopaedia*, *2*(1), 486–497. doi:10.3390/encyclopedia2010031

Page, S., & Coxon, M. (2016). Virtual reality exposure therapy for anxiety disorders: Small samples and no controls? *Frontiers in Psychology*, *7*. Advance online publication. doi:10.3389/fpsyg.2016.00326 PMID:27014137

Park, S. M., & Kim, Y. (2022). A metaverse: Taxonomy, components, applications, and open challenges. *IEEE Access : Practical Innovations, Open Solutions*, *10*, 4209–4251. doi:10.1109/ACCESS.2021.3140175

Peeters, D. (2019). Virtual reality: A game-changing method for the language sciences. Psychonomic Bulletin &Amp. *RE:view*, *26*(3), 894–900. doi:10.3758/s13423-019-01571-3 PMID:30734158

PlechatáA.HielkemaM.MerklL.MakranskyG.FrostM. (2023). Shifting from information- to experience-based climate change communication increases pro-environmental behaviour. doi:10.21203/rs.3.rs-2338078/v3

Plechatá, A., Morton, T. A., Pérez-Cueto, F. J., & Makransky, G. (2022). A randomized trial testing the effectiveness of virtual reality as a tool for pro-environmental dietary change. *Scientific Reports*, *12*(1), 14315. Advance online publication. doi:10.1038/s41598-022-18241-5 PMID:35995946

Porwol, L., & Dumas, C. (2022). Transforming eparticipation: vr-dialogue – building and evaluating an aisupported framework for next-gen vr-enabled e-participation research. Transforming Government: People. *Process and Policy*, *17*(2), 233–250. doi:10.1108/TG-12-2021-0205

Pot-Kolder, R., Veling, W., Geraets, C., & van der Gaag, M. (2016). Effect of virtual reality exposure therapy on social participation in people with a psychotic disorder (VRETp): Study protocol for a randomized controlled trial. *Trials*, *17*(1), 25. doi:10.1186/s13063-015-1140-0 PMID:26762123

Powers, M. B., & Emmelkamp, P. (2008). Virtual reality exposure therapy for anxiety disorders: A meta-analysis. *Journal of Anxiety Disorders*, *22*(3), 561–569. doi:10.1016/j.janxdis.2007.04.006 PMID:17544252

Queiroz, M., Wamba, S., Pereira, S., & Jabbour, C. (2023). The metaverse as a breakthrough for operations and supply chain management: Implications and call for action. *International Journal of Operations & Production Management*, *43*(10), 15391553. doi:10.1108/IJOPM-01-2023-0006

Renshaw, T., Sonnenfeld, N. A., & Meyers, M. (2016). Fundamentals for a turing test of virtual reality. *Proceedings of the Human Factors and Ergonomics Society Annual Meeting*, *60*(1), 2113–2117. doi:10.1177/1541931213601478

Riva, G., & Serino, S. (2020). Virtual reality in the assessment, understanding and treatment of mental health disorders. *Journal of Clinical Medicine*, *9*(11), 3434. doi:10.3390/jcm9113434 PMID:33114623

Rodriguez, N. (2016). Teaching virtual reality with affordable technologies. *Lecture Notes in Computer Science*, *9731*, 89–97. doi:10.1007/978-3-319-39510-4_9

Samala, A., Ambiyar, A., Bojić, L., Indarta, Y., Ipalakova, M., Denden, M., ... Dewi, I. (2023). Metaverse technologies in education: A systematic literature review using prisma. *International Journal of Emerging Technologies in Learning*, *18*(05), 231–252. doi:10.3991/ijet.v18i05.35501

Sari, R. N., Hayati, R. S., & Rahayu, S. L. (2020, October). Heuristic Evaluation In Mobile Augmented Reality Applications In Designing Houses. In *2020 8th International Conference on Cyber and IT Service Management (CITSM)* (pp. 1-5). IEEE.

Schwebel, D., Severson, J., & He, Y. (2016). Using smartphone technology to deliver a virtual pedestrian environment: Usability and validation. *Virtual Reality (Waltham Cross)*, *21*(3), 145–152. doi:10.1007/s10055-016-0304-x PMID:29531502

Serrano, S., Llorca, D., Daza, I., & Sotelo, M. (2022). Insertion of real agents behaviours in carla autonomous driving simulator doi:10.5220/0011352400003323

Sherman, W. R., & Craig, A. B. (2003). Understanding virtual reality—Interface, application, and design. *Presence (Cambridge, Mass.)*, *12*(4), 441–442. doi:10.1162/105474603322391668

Sherrill, A. M., Rothbaum, A. O., McSweeney, L. B., & Rothbaum, B. O. (2019). Virtual reality exposure therapy for posttraumatic stress disorder. *Psychiatric Annals*, *49*(8), 343–347. doi:10.3928/00485713-20190716-02

Shin, D., & Biocca, F. (2017). Exploring immersive experience in journalism. New Media &Amp. *New Media & Society*, *20*(8), 2800–2823. doi:10.1177/1461444817733133

Slater, M., Usoh, M., & Steed, A. (1994). Depth of presence in virtual environments. *Presence (Cambridge, Mass.)*, *3*(2), 130–144. doi:10.1162/pres.1994.3.2.130

Soowook, L. & Oh, Y. S. (2016). Study on virtual reality and e-commerce. *The International Journal of Advanced Culture Technology*, *4*(4), 70-74. doi:10.17703/IJACT.2016.4.4.70

Suda, Y., Fukuhara, K., Sato, K., & Higuchi, T. (2022). Improved walking through an aperture in a virtual environment transfer to a real environment: Introduction of enriched feedback and gradual increase in task difficulty. *Frontiers in Sports and Active Living*, *4*, 844436. Advance online publication. doi:10.3389/fspor.2022.844436 PMID:35308597

Sun, Z., Zhu, M., Shan, X., & Lee, C. (2022). Augmented tactileperception and haptic-feedback rings as human-machine interfaces aiming for immersive interactions. *Nature Communications*, *13*(1), 5224. Advance online publication. doi:10.1038/s41467-022-32745-8 PMID:36064838

Teng, Z., Cai, Y., Zhang, X., & Li, X. (2022). Factors affecting learners' adoption of an educational metaverse platform: An empirical study based on an extended utaut model. *Mobile Information Systems*, *15*, 1–15. Advance online publication. doi:10.1155/2022/5479215

Truong, V., Le, L., & Niyato, D. (2023). Blockchain meets metaverse and digital asset management: A comprehensive survey. *IEEE Access : Practical Innovations, Open Solutions*, *11*, 26258–26288. doi:10.1109/ACCESS.2023.3257029

Tuente, S K., Bogaerts, S., IJzendoorn, S V., & Veling, W. (2018, August 6). *Effect of virtual reality aggression prevention training for forensic psychiatric patients (VRAPT): study protocol of a multi-center RCT*. Academic Press.

Usmani, S., Sharath, M., & Mehendale, M. (2022). Future of mental health in the metaverse. *General Psychiatry*, *35*(4), e100825. doi:10.1136/gpsych-2022-100825 PMID:36189180

Wheeler, D., & Natarajan, B. (2023). Engineering semantic communication: A survey. *IEEE Access : Practical Innovations, Open Solutions*, *11*, 13965–13995. doi:10.1109/ACCESS.2023.3243065

Wilson, C., & Soranzo, A. (2015). The use of virtual reality in psychology: A case study in visual perception. *Computational and Mathematical Methods in Medicine*, *2015*, 1–7. doi:10.1155/2015/151702 PMID:26339281

Winkler, N., Roethke, K., Siegfried, N., & Benlian, A. (2020). Lose yourself in vr: exploring the effects of virtual reality on individuals' immersion. *Proceedings of the Annual Hawaii International Conference on System Sciences.* 10.24251/HICSS.2020.186

Wu, H., Ai, C., & Cheng, C. (2019). Virtual reality experiences, attachment and experiential outcomes in tourism. *Tourism Review*, *75*(3), 481–495. doi:10.1108/TR-06-2019-0205

Wulf, G., & Lewthwaite, R. (2016). Optimizing performance through intrinsic motivation and attention for learning: The optimal theory of motor learning. Psychonomic Bulletin &Amp. *RE:view*, *23*(5), 1382–1414. doi:10.3758/s13423-015-0999-9 PMID:26833314

Wulf, G., & Lewthwaite, R. (2016). Optimizing performance through intrinsic motivation and attention for learning: The optimal theory of motor learning. Psychonomic Bulletin &Amp. *RE:view*, *23*(5), 1382–1414. PMID:26833314

Wyssenbach, T., Zeballos, M., Loosli, S., & Schwaninger, A. (2021). Nonverbal behaviour of interviewers influences the competence ratings of observers in recruitment interviews: A study investigating social influence using 360-degree videos with virtual reality and 2d screen displays. *Virtual Reality (Waltham Cross)*, *26*(2), 669–686. doi:10.1007/s10055-021-00540-3

Zhai, Asmi, Zhou, Ahmad, Anwar, Saneinia, & Li. (2020). Investigating the Mediation and Moderation Effect of Students' Addiction to Virtual Reality Games: A Perspective of Structural Equation Modeling. Discrete Dynamics in Nature and Society. doi:10.1155/2020/5714546

Zhai, X., Asmi, F., Zhou, R., Ahmad, I., Anwar, M. A., Saneinia, S., & Li, M. (2020). Investigating the mediation and moderation effect of students' addiction to virtual reality games: A perspective of structural equation modeling. *Discrete Dynamics in Nature and Society*, *2020*, 1–13. doi:10.1155/2020/5714546

Zhu, C., Wu, D. C. W., Hall, C. M., Fong, L. H. N., Koupaei, S. N., & Lin, F. (2023). Exploring non-immersive virtual reality experiences in tourism: Empirical evidence from a world heritage site. *International Journal of Tourism Research*, *25*(3), 372–383. doi:10.1002/jtr.2574

Chapter 11
Challenges of a Metaverse Shaping the Future of Entrepreneurship

Muhammad Usman Tariq
https://orcid.org/0000-0002-7605-3040
Abu Dhabi University, UAE & University of Glasgow, Glasgow, UK

ABSTRACT

The chapter thoroughly examines the various barriers that affect how entrepreneurial endeavours develop in the ever-changing metaverse. Entrepreneurs face never-before-seen obstacles as the metaverse, defined by virtual surroundings and cutting-edge technology like augmented reality and virtual reality, develops as a revolutionary platform for business. The chapter thoroughly explores these issues, which include social and cultural factors, economic complexity, ethical problems, and technical limitations. The last section of the chapter offers a forward-looking outlook on potential developments and breakthroughs in the metaverse, highlighting the need for ongoing collaboration and adaptation between engineers, entrepreneurs, legislators, and legal experts to traverse this rapidly changing digital landscape successfully. It emphasizes how critical it is to resolve these issues to fully realize the metaverse's potential for creative and prosperous enterprise.

OVERVIEW

The emergence of the metaverse has brought about a profound paradigm change in entrepreneurship. This section critically examines the many obstacles that influence entrepreneurial activities in the metaverse. The metaverse, defined by virtual environments, augmented reality (AR), and virtual reality (VR) technology, poses new challenges to entrepreneurs closely related to the imagination, creation, and management of businesses.

DOI: 10.4018/979-8-3693-2422-6.ch011

Barriers Associated With Technology

Technological obstacles are at the forefront of the metaverse's difficulties. The dynamic nature of virtual environments is an ongoing challenge for businesses, calling for constant innovation and adaptability. Because AR and VR technologies are developing quickly, entrepreneurs must be very tech-savvy to remain current on the most recent developments (Johnson, 2022). Creating apps that work well with the metaverse adds another level of complexity, necessitating a sophisticated grasp of immersive technologies and spatial computing (Smith et al., 2021).

Furthermore, a significant obstacle is the compatibility of various metaverse platforms. Diverse technical standards and protocols might present compatibility challenges for entrepreneurs, which they must overcome (Brown & White, 2023). This calls for a cautious approach to implementing new technologies and a sharp understanding of the possible drawbacks of developing software tailored to a single platform.

Moral Conundrums

Entrepreneurs encounter a maze of moral conundrums as they traverse the metaverse. Beyond the traditional bounds of corporate ethics, ethical issues are raised by the production and distribution of virtual content. In the metaverse, permission, privacy, and digital rights concerns become crucial (Jones & Williams, 2023). Careful consideration is necessary to address the ethical issues raised by who owns and governs the virtual areas inside the metaverse.

Furthermore, the metaverse creates additional ethical difficulties by obfuscating the distinctions between the real and virtual worlds. Concerns about responsible technology usage and the possible effects of immersive experiences are brought up by virtual worlds replicating real-world events (Lee & Kim, 2022). Entrepreneurs must balance the influence on consumers' well-being and social conventions with the ethical ramifications of building virtual environments that mimic reality.

Consequences for Upcoming Business Initiatives

To picture the future of entrepreneurial endeavours, it is essential to comprehend the problems that exist inside the metaverse. The entrepreneurial environment of the metaverse is shaped by the interaction of ethical quandaries and technical obstacles, which affects corporate executives' tactics and choices. According to Chen et al. (2023), entrepreneurs must have a forward-thinking mentality and include flexibility and adaptability in their company strategies. The metaverse is complicated, and navigating it requires a multifaceted strategy that considers ethical issues and technical developments.

Unmatched chances for creativity and invention exist in the metaverse, but realising its full potential will need a thorough grasp of its difficulties. To tackle the challenges the metaverse poses, entrepreneurs need to collaborate and learn continuously (García & Rodríguez, 2023). Working together, industry players, legislators, and academics may help create moral guidelines and technological specifications that support a responsible and long-lasting metaverse ecology.

To sum up, entrepreneurs in the metaverse confront various difficulties, including ethical conundrums and technological impediments. This complicated world demands a smart and progressive strategy to navigate. Entrepreneurs need to be on the lookout for changes in the metaverse and embrace innovation while maintaining moral principles. Ethics and technology will shape future entrepreneurial endeavours in the metaverse, opening the door to a vibrant and long-lasting corporate environment.

INTRODUCTION TO THE METAVERSE AND ENTREPRENEURSHIP

The idea of the metaverse has become a powerful force in recent years, transforming our understanding of reality and bringing civilization closer to a place where virtual worlds, augmented reality, and virtual reality all come together. This introduction aims to clarify the metaverse by outlining its essential traits and underlying technology. It also lays the groundwork for comprehending the metaverse as a groundbreaking entrepreneurship platform and examining the hitherto untapped potential for creativity and company formation in this ever-evolving digital environment.

What the Metaverse Is Not

The phrase "metaverse," first used by science fiction author Neal Stephenson in his 1992 book "Snow Crash," describes a shared virtual environment that combines the entirety of the internet, augmented reality, and virtual worlds (Stephenson, 1992). It is a digital world where the real and virtual worlds collide, enabling real-time user interaction with computer-generated surroundings and other users.

One of the metaverse's primary features is its immersiveness, allowing users to interact with the digital world via various sensory modalities. In contrast to conventional online environments, the metaverse establishes a parallel reality that people may explore and engage with both artificial and real aspects (Castronova, 2005). The metaverse is dynamic and always changing, thanks to user contributions, content development, and technology breakthroughs.

Bases of Technology for the Metaverse

The technologies of advanced computing, artificial intelligence (AI), augmented reality (AR), and virtual reality (VR) form the backbone of the metaverse. A crucial element that enables the metaverse to comprehend and react to the actual space users inhabit is spatial computing, which enables a smooth merging of the digital and physical realities (Milgram & Kishino, 1994). This makes it possible for users to feel as though they are physically present in the virtual environment, obfuscating the distinction between the real and virtual worlds.

Technologies like AR and VR are essential in forming the immersive experiences seen in the metaverse. Augmented reality (AR) improves users' perception of and engagement with their environment by superimposing digital information over the physical world (Azuma, 1997). Conversely, virtual reality (VR) transports viewers to fully artificial surroundings, offering a simulated reality that may be explored and interacted with (Steuer, 1992). These technologies work together to create the metaverse's framework, which makes it easier to create a variety of dynamic digital settings.

Creating the Conditions for Metaverse Entrepreneurship

The rise of the metaverse as a unique digital environment has significant business ramifications. Entrepreneurs are in the front of a fresh wave of opportunities within the metaverse as technology advances. The combination of AR, VR, and spatial computing opens up new possibilities for company creation and operation.

The metaverse presents a challenging environment for entrepreneurs who do not need a strong background in technology. It is critical to keep up with the most recent developments in AR and VR since the metaverse's dynamics are shaped by the quick progress of these technologies (Johnson, 2022). Furthermore, to construct smooth and engrossing experiences in virtual worlds, knowledge of spatial computing and its applications becomes crucial (Smith et al., 2021).

The metaverse brings about how organizations engage with customers. The immersive and participatory aspect of the metaverse surpasses conventional marketing and engagement strategies. According to Gartner (2023), entrepreneurs can produce captivating virtual encounters, facilitating closer relationships with their target audience. The metaverse is a blank canvas for creative product launches, customer service, and marketing campaigns.

Entrepreneurs need to address the ethical implications of the metaverse in addition to technological ones. Digital rights, privacy, and consent are issues brought up by virtual material production and distribution (Jones & Williams, 2023).In this new digital frontier, entrepreneurs must responsibly and respectfully connect with consumers while navigating the ethical terrain of the metaverse.

An Overview of the Upcoming Wave of Metaverse Entrepreneurship

Entrepreneurs are positioned at the nexus of technology, creativity, and commercial acumen as they take advantage of this new wave of opportunity within the metaverse. The metaverse gives entrepreneurs a blank canvas to rethink industries and customer experiences, opening up previously unheard-of possibilities for innovation and company development.

Entrepreneurs are able to develop virtual settings that surpass the constraints of the real world due to the immersive nature of the metaverse. Entrepreneurs may now access a worldwide audience in previously unthinkable ways with the help of virtual shops, interactive experiences, and digital ecosystems—all extensions of established business paradigms (Chen et al., 2023). This change in the business environment necessitates a strategic way of thinking that welcomes and navigates the intricacies of the metaverse's possibilities.

Innovation in the metaverse goes well beyond offers of goods and services; it permeates every aspect of corporate structures. Entrepreneurs can investigate novel sources of income, including blockchain-based transactions, digital assets, and virtual real estate (Swan, 2015). Because the metaverse is decent and decentralized, it provides opportunities for economic models that place a premium on user involvement and contribution, which redefines conventional ideas of value generation.

In addition, the metaverse promotes global connectedness and cooperation. Entrepreneurs can participate in interdisciplinary collaborations by using the many expertise and viewpoints in the metaverse community (García & Rodríguez, 2023). As entrepreneurs collaborate beyond geographic borders to create in the digital sphere, collaborative innovation becomes a driving force.

In summary, the metaverse's distinctive features and technological underpinnings make it an innovative platform for business. Entrepreneurs must embrace technology knowledge, ethical considerations, and a forward-thinking perspective as they navigate this ever-changing digital ecosystem. In addition to providing unmatched chances for creativity and company development, the metaverse pushes innovators to rethink conventional wisdom and advance the development of a digital frontier.

TECHNOLOGICAL CHALLENGES IN THE METAVERSE

Entrepreneurs face several technological obstacles when they go into the metaverse, which holds the potential to create immersive and linked digital places. These challenges—which include creating immersive environments, scaling, interoperability, and integrating cutting-edge technologies like blockchain, artificial intelligence (AI), and the Internet of Things (IoT)—are examined in this section.

Creation of Immersive Environments

One of the main features that makes the metaverse so appealing is the development of immersive surroundings. However, creating settings that smoothly meld the real and virtual worlds is a big challenge for companies. A sophisticated grasp of spatial computing and user experience design is necessary to create realistic and interactive virtual environments (Smith et al., 2021). The difficulty is maintaining graphical accuracy and simulating the intricacy and variety of interactions in the actual world.

Immersion settings come with an additional element of complexity due to their dynamic nature. Entrepreneurs have to deal with how customer expectations are always changing, which forces them to be on the cutting edge of AR and VR technology developments (Johnson, 2022). Moreover, entrepreneurs must master the complexities of cross-platform development to guarantee a seamless and immersive experience across all devices and platforms.

Scalability Issues

Scalability is a crucial factor for business owners entering the metaverse to consider. The number of users may expand quickly. Thus, a reliable infrastructure that can handle more traffic without sacrificing efficiency is required. The scalability problem is not limited to server capacity; it includes metaverse interactions and content scalability.

Complex solutions are needed to ensure immersive environments stay responsive and captivating as the number of users increases. To address scalability concerns, entrepreneurs should investigate content delivery networks, load-balancing techniques, and distributed computer architectures (Brown & White, 2023). Furthermore, as entrepreneurs want to offer a flawless experience to people everywhere, the problem of scalability is intricately linked to latency and bandwidth problems.

Barriers to Interoperability

The metaverse is a network of connected virtual places rather than a single platform. For entrepreneurs, interoperability—the capacity of several platforms and technologies to function seamlessly—becomes critical. Different ecosystems, each with technological standards and protocols, comprise the metaverse (Chen et al., 2023). Connecting these disparate technologies is a formidable obstacle for businesses building seamless, integrated experiences.

The absence of common data exchange and communication protocols hampers the smooth movement of assets and data between various metaverse platforms. To ensure their companies can overcome platform-specific limits, entrepreneurs must address compatibility difficulties (García & Rodríguez, 2023). The difficulties of reaching audiences across various metaverse ecosystems impact business strategies as much as the technical parts of development due to interoperability issues.

Including Cutting-Edge Technologies

The metaverse is a confluence of many cutting-edge technologies rather than just a visual experience. The challenge for entrepreneurs is to improve functionality and user engagement by seamlessly integrating blockchain, IoT, and AI into their projects. According to Lee and Kim (2022), artificial intelligence (AI) is essential for developing intelligent virtual creatures, improving user interactions, and customizing experiences inside the metaverse. However, there are issues with algorithmic transparency, data privacy, and ethical considerations when incorporating AI.

Blockchain technology presents benefits and difficulties because it promises to enable safe and transparent transactions. While maintaining the security and integrity of virtual assets, entrepreneurs must manage the complexity of decentralized ledgers, smart contracts, and tokenization (Swan, 2015). Blockchain integration complicates development and forces business owners to reconsider conventional ownership and transaction structures.

In addition, integrating Internet of Things devices in the metaverse poses difficulties with data security, administration, and the smooth transition between real and virtual worlds. Entrepreneurs have to deal with problems including device interoperability, real-time data synchronization, and possible security breaches brought on by the interconnectedness of IoT devices in the metaverse.

Effects on User Experience, Functionality, and Design

Technological obstacles significantly influence the layout, operation, and user experience of entrepreneurial endeavours inside the metaverse. Creating immersive environments that are smooth and engaging for users requires solving scalability and interoperability issues (Castronova, 2005). The restrictions imposed by these difficulties may impact the metaverse apps' overall attractiveness, responsiveness, and visual richness.

Scalability difficulties directly impact the functioning of metaverse ventures. To guarantee that scalability difficulties do not impair performance, entrepreneurs must make smart decisions regarding the distribution of information, user interactions, and the overall scope of their operations. This might entail creating dynamic content delivery techniques, optimizing assets for various devices, and embracing modular development approaches.

Difficulties with interoperability affect the technical architecture and the user experience in general. Entrepreneurs must traverse the dispersed terrain of several platforms and ecosystems to build a coherent metaverse experience. Cross-platform interactions, the transfer of virtual assets, and seamless transitions between virtual worlds become challenging tasks that need careful planning and specialized technological knowledge.

The incorporation of cutting-edge technology forms the foundation of metaverse endeavours. Blockchain presents new ownership and transaction paradigms, while AI integration affects user interactions and content customization. To ensure that the integration improves rather than worsens the user experience, entrepreneurs must carefully weigh the advantages of these technologies against any potential drawbacks.

In conclusion, entrepreneurs face major obstacles due to technological limitations in the metaverse. Through the creation of immersive experiences, scalability, interoperability, and sophisticated technology integration, this dynamic terrain demands a creative and deliberate strategy to be navigated. These difficulties affect more than just technical matters; they also affect the functioning, design, and user experience of entrepreneurial endeavours in the metaverse.

ECONOMIC AND BUSINESS MODEL CHALLENGES IN THE METAVERSE

The metaverse presents new economic and business model hurdles for entrepreneurs since it is a complex and linked digital realm. This section explores these issues in more detail, including digital asset management, monetization tactics, and building long-term business models in the virtual economy. It also covers the challenges of managing the metaverse's digital economy, including non-fungible tokens (NFTs), virtual real estate, and digital commodities and services.

Strategies for Making Money in the Metaverse

Businesses operating in the metaverse must stray from conventional business methods to be profitable. Entrepreneurs must manoeuvre through a market where experiences and customer engagement are as important as physical goods or services. Finding successful monetization techniques that mesh with the immersive and dynamic character of the metaverse is one of the main problems.

Virtual currencies, such as in-game tokens or platfcommercializationtocurrencies, have become a popular commercialization method (Chen et al., 2023). Users may use these virtual currencies to transact and buy virtual products and services inside the metaverse. The difficulty for entrepreneurs, however, is in creating and maintaining the value of these virtual currencies since user demand and market movements have the potential to affect their exchange rates.

Furthermore, distinguishing between accessibility and profitability is more difficult with subscription models and freemium strategies, which give fundamental services for free while charging for premium features (Gartner, 2023). In order to create a profitable and engaging user experience, entrepreneurs need to consider how to monetize their ideas carefully.

Difficulties With Digital Asset Management

Digital assets, which include anything from virtual real estate to digital commodities and services, are the main focus of the metaverse. For entrepreneurs, managing these assets is a complex problem. For instance, strategic approaches are needed to develop, acquire, and monetize virmonetizationtate (Brown & White, 2023). Entrepreneurs must negotiate the complexities of virtual property rights, land development, and user involvement within these digital areas.

There are new issues with intellectual property rights, licencing, and content control when digital products and services are created and managed. In addition to creating an atmosphere that supports user-generated material, entrepreneurs need to implement reliable procedures for monitoring and safeguarding digital assets (Castronova, 2005). A thriving and safe digital marketplace requires balancing user freedom and content management.

Digital asset management has become more difficult due to the introduction of NFTs to indicate ownership of unique digital assets (Swan, 2015). The integration of NFTs into business models, authenticity, and provenance are challenges that entrepreneurs face. Concerns regarding the carbon footprint of NFTs have been raised by their production and trading. Therefore, the difficulty goes beyond technical implementation to environmental sustainability.

Development of Long-Term Business Plans

In the metaverse, sustainability extends beyond environmental concerns and includes creating economic models that can persist and change with the quickly changing digital ecosystem. Due to the metaverse's dynamic nature, company owners must create adaptable and agile business models that endure changes in consumer behaviour, technology advancements, and industry trends.

For a company concept to be robust, sustainable monetization is essential to stay ahead of changes in customer tastes and developing technology; entrepreneurs need to constantly innovate and diversify their revenue streams (García & Rodríguez, 2023). Creating long-term plans that strike a balance between the need for constant innovation and adaptability and short-term profitability is the difficult part.

Entrepreneurs must also consider sustainability's ethical and social aspects in the metaverse. Sustainable business strategies must include developing digital literacy, community-building, and inclusive and accessible virtual places (Jones & Williams, 2023). Developing sustainable practices is made more difficult by navigating the ethical issues of data privacy, digital rights, and user well-being.

Difficulties of Manipulating the Economy of the Metaverse

The economy of the metaverse is a complex environment that includes using cryptocurrencies and NFTs, digital products and services, and virtual real estate. To prosper in the dynamic economic environment of the metaverse, entrepreneurs must successfully negotiate these intricacies.

Challenges in Virtual Real Estate

Within the metaverse, virtual real estate poses a distinct economic difficulty. Land development, user involvement, and property rights are concerns that entrepreneurs have to deal with. As entrepreneurs seek methods to commercialize these commercializees, they must exercise strategic thinking in purchasing and administrating virtual land (Brown & White, 2023). Considering elements like location, accessibility, and user traffic, creating a sense of scarcity and value in virtual real estate might be difficult.

Digital Products and Services

The metaverse has a huge market for virtual apparel and accessories, digital entertainment, and digital art. The complexities of user-generated material, licencing agreements, and intellectual property rights must be negotiated by entrepreneurs. It is extremely difficult to promote creativity and innovation while maintaining a safe and active digital marketplace (Castronova, 2005). The rise of NFTs adds to the complexity of this environment as business owners need help with sustainability, ownership, and authenticity issues.

Cryptocurrencies and NFTs

By providing new avenues for ownership and transaction, cryptocurrencies and NFTs have become essential parts of the metaverse economy. Nonetheless, the legal environment around these digital assets and the erratic nature of bitcoin valuations make businesses difficult (Swan, 2015). Using NFTs raises questions about ethical digital asset creation, trade, and environmental sustainability. In order to properly utilize cryptocurrencies in their business models, entrepreneurs need to traverse these hurdles carefully.

Effects on Business Initiatives

The problems above to business models and the economy significantly affect entrepreneurial endeavours in the metaverse. Monetization tactics directly impact revenue generation and user engagement. Entrepreneurs need to continually modify and iterate their techniques in order to maintain a balance between customer satisfaction and revenue (Chen et al., 2023).

Metaverse enterprises' design and functioning are influenced by digital asset management. Entrepreneurs must design user-friendly and safe platforms for customers to engage with digital goods and services, virtual real estate, and other digital products. Entrepreneurs must implement efficient content moderation and asset protection procedures to address the issues of intellectual property rights and NFT integration issues, which impact the user experience as a whole.

Developing enduring business models is essential to the resilience and endurance of entrepreneurial endeavours inside the metaverse. Entrepreneurs must foresee and adapt to changes in consumer behaviour, technical progress, and market conditions. The entrepreneurial journey incorporates sustainability issues, such as ethical practices and environmental effects (García & Rodríguez, 2023). Understanding the interconnectedness of digital products and services, virtual real estate, and the usage of cryptocurrencies and NFTs is essential to navigating the metaverse economy. To drive the success and resilience of their initiatives, entrepreneurs need to have a comprehensive awareness of these economic factors.

To conclude, businesses face complex obstacles due to economic and business model issues in the metaverse. It takes creativity, agility, and a thorough grasp of the metaverse's economic ecology to navigate this dynamic terrain, including developing successful monetization methods, assets, and long-term business models. The intricacies of digital products and services, virtual real estate, and the amalgamation of cryptocurrencies and NFTs imbue many levels of complexity that impact the configuration, operation, and user experience of entrepreneurial endeavours operating in the metaverse.

ETHICAL AND LEGAL ISSUES IN THE METAVERSE

Although the metaverse presents unheard-of chances for enterprise, it poses many moral and legal difficulties. An extensive examination of the moral and legal dilemmas that entrepreneurs encounter in the metaverse is given in this part. These dilemmas include data security, intellectual property rights, privacy, and virtual space governance. It also examines the need for regulatory frameworks and ethical standards to guarantee ethical company conduct and user protection in this rapidly changing digital environment.

Issues With Privacy in the Metaverse

Since virtual environments gather much user data to personalise interactions and improve experiences, privacy is a major problem in the metaverse. Entrepreneurs must consider the ethical ramifications of data gathering, storage, and use. Because users are frequently engaged in intimate and highly interactive virtual settings, it is possible for them to unintentionally reveal sensitive information, which raises questions about data ownership and permission (Jones & Williams, 2023).

The difficulty is striking a balance between the need to preserve user privacy and the need for personalised experiences. To build user trust, entrepreneurs must establish strong privacy rules, educate consent procedures, and practise open data (Lee & Kim, 2022). Traditional privacy ideas must be reevaluated in light of the metaverse, forcing businesspeople to walk a tightrope between customisation and intrusion.

Challenges in Data Security

Entrepreneurs have more data security issues due to the metaverse's interconnectedness. Cyber dangers, from identity theft to unauthorised access to sensitive information, target virtual places. Entrepreneurs are accountable for implementing strong cybersecurity measures like encryption, secure authentication, and frequent security audits (Johnson, 2022).

In addition to being morally and legally required, protecting the confidentiality and integrity of user data is also required. Metaverse data breaches can have far-reaching effects on user confidence and could result in legal ramifications (García & Rodríguez, 2023). In order to protect their users' digital identities and information, entrepreneurs need to be on the lookout and use industry best practices.

Challenges to Intellectual Property Rights

The metaverse blurs the boundaries between the real and virtual worlds, creating complex issues with intellectual property rights. Entrepreneurs have to deal with ownership, licencing, and infringement difficulties in the digital sphere. The relevance of existing intellectual property rules is questioned by virtual assets such as digital art, user-generated material, and virtual real estate (Castronova, 2005).

The metaverse's intellectual property rights are made more difficult by producing and exchanging non-fungible tokens (NFTs). The legal recognition of digital ownership, provenance, and authenticity are issues that entrepreneurs need to overcome. Due to the lack of existing legal precedents and frameworks about virtual assets, businesses must exercise caution, ensuring that ownership arrangements are transparent and that established intellectual property rights are respected (Swan, 2015).

Control Over Digital Environments

Entrepreneurs face governance issues because of the metaverse's decentralised and heterogeneous character. The absence of well-defined legal frameworks in virtual environments can give rise to problems with user behaviour, content control, and conflict resolution. Entrepreneurs must set up efficient governance systems to keep everything in order and provide a satisfying user experience (Brown & White, 2023).

A problem is finding a balance between maintaining user autonomy and ensuring virtual places are used responsibly is a problem. Entrepreneurs may need to work with industry stakeholders, legislators, and user groups to create moral standards and governance frameworks that consider the metaverse's dynamic character (Gartner, 2023). The lack of widely accepted models for governance highlights the necessity for entrepreneurs to lead the way in developing ethical and inclusive practices.

Legal Frameworks and Ethical Guidelines Are Essential

Because the metaverse is dynamic and always changing, it is necessary to create legal frameworks and ethical standards to safeguard user rights and promote ethical corporate practices. Entrepreneurs are instrumental in forming these frameworks through their partnerships with user groups, legal professionals, and other industry colleagues.

Ensuring Responsible Business Practises: Ethical standards are crucial to guarantee responsible business practices in the metaverse. Entrepreneurs must set explicit ethical guidelines about data gathering, user interaction, and content production. This entails implementing privacy-by-design principles, encouraging a culture of responsible innovation, and being clear with consumers about how their data will be used (Lee & Kim, 2022).

Ethical standards should also cover inclusion, equity, and diversity in virtual environments. According to García and Rodríguez (2023), entrepreneurs have a responsibility to tackle prejudices in AI algorithms proactively, advance accessibility, and establish virtual environments that are hospitable and inclusive for users with varying backgrounds and abilities.

Legal frameworks protect user rights and hold business owners responsible for unethical behaviour. They also provide user protection. Policymakers and legislators are essential in creating thorough legal frameworks that tackle the particular difficulties posed by the metaverse. Data security, consumer rights, intellectual property rights, and user safety should all be included in these frameworks.

Clearly defining policies and procedures reduces the likelihood of fraud, data abuse, and privacy violations in the metaverse. According to Jones and Williams (2023), legal frameworks must progress with technology improvements, furnishing entrepreneurs with a sturdy base to construct and manage their enterprises with due diligence.

Partnership for Industry Standards

Industry groups, regulatory agencies, and business owners must work together to create moral standards and legislative frameworks. According to Gartner (2023), entrepreneurs are responsible for actively participating in industry-wide conversations to establish ethical norms and regulatory standards that promote a reliable and safe metaverse environment. Proactive interaction with user communities is also crucial. One way to foster a feeling of ownership and accountability in the metaverse is to ask users for comments, respond to their concerns, and include users in the process of co-creating ethical rules (Brown & White, 2023).

In conclusion, entrepreneurs must take a proactive and cooperative strategy to address the metaverse's complex ethical and legal challenges. Laws and ethical standards must be developed to address intellectual property rights, privacy, data security, and virtual space governance difficulties. In an ever-changing digital ecosystem, entrepreneurs need to lead the way in promoting ethical business practices, giving user safety a top priority, and actively participating in creating industry standards that preserve moral principles.

SOCIAL AND CULTURAL CHALLENGES IN THE METAVERSE

As a digital frontier that cuts beyond geographical borders, the metaverse presents a variety of social and cultural difficulties for business owners. The concerns about user diversity, inclusion, and the cultural ramifications of virtual communities and interactions are examined in this section. It also looks at how these difficulties could affect user participation, market penetration, and the general prosperity of metaverse business endeavours.

Challenges of User Diversity and Inclusivity

The diversity and inclusion of users in the metaverse is one of the main issues. Virtual spaces should be hospitable and open to people with different origins, skills, and viewpoints. According to García and Rodríguez (2023), entrepreneurs have challenges designing environments that accommodate a worldwide user base while honouring cultural quirks and individual distinctions.

Concerns like accessibility, cultural conventions, and language obstacles make it difficult to create an inclusive metaverse. Entrepreneurs must create user interfaces, information, and interactions adaptable to people with diverse language and cultural backgrounds. Overcoming these obstacles is strategically necessary and morally required to draw in and keep a diverse user base (Jones & Williams, 2023).

Virtual Communities and Their Cultural Consequences

The metaverse redefines community dynamics and social interactions. Entrepreneurs need to be cognizant of the cultural ramifications of virtual spaces, considering how people from diverse backgrounds view and interact with digital platforms. Cultural subtleties impact social conventions, communication techniques, and the development of virtual communities in the metaverse (Castronova, 2005).

Finding the right balance between avoiding cultural appropriation or distortion and producing culturally relevant material may be difficult. In order to co-create virtual experiences that connect with various cultural backgrounds, entrepreneurs must be culturally competent, recognise the diversity of their user base and actively seek out user input (Gartner, 2023).

Effects on Market Reach and User Engagement

User involvement and the market reach of entrepreneurial endeavours are directly impacted by the social and cultural issues present in the metaverse. Ignoring these issues can lead to exclusive online environments, which reduces the attraction of goods and services to particular consumer demographics. However, overcoming these obstacles might result in a wider market reach and higher levels of user engagement.

User Involvement

Virtual places' social and cultural dynamics are closely linked to user participation inside the metaverse. Entrepreneurs need to design spaces where people from different backgrounds may engage and form meaningful connections. Users gravitate towards platforms that connect with their cultural values and preferences. Hence, issues linked to inclusion and cultural sensitivity directly impact the depth of user involvement (Chen et al., 2023).

Events in the metaverse that are virtual, such as social meetings and community-driven projects, must be planned with cultural sensitivity in mind. To build immersive and relevant experiences that capture a broad range of people, entrepreneurs must use cultural knowledge. If this is done, users could continue participating, reducing the chance of fostering a sense of community and brand loyalty.

Market Reach

The metaverse's cultural environment directly impacts market reach. The varied cultural expectations and tastes of potential customers must be navigated by entrepreneurs looking to break into international markets. Because it increases the appeal of metaverse businesses overall and offers doors to undiscovered markets, cultural inclusion becomes a strategic objective (García & Rodríguez, 2023).

Attempts to expand the market may be hampered by issues with recognising the cultural implications and variety of users. Entrepreneurs must perform in-depth market research and have a solid grasp of the cultural quirks that affect users' choices and behaviour in the metaverse. In addition to increasing market reach, a cultural diversity strategy makes entrepreneurial endeavours more resilient and sustainable.

The Overall Effectiveness of Business Endeavours

The success of business endeavours in the metaverse is largely impacted by the social and cultural issues that have been highlighted. Success is determined by profits and the capacity to provide people worldwide with inclusive and meaningful digital experiences.

Entrepreneurial Ventures That Are Inclusive

In the metaverse, inclusivity plays a major role in determining success. Entrepreneurs who take the initiative to handle cultural ramifications and user diversity foster settings where users feel heard, recognised, and appreciated. Within different communities, inclusive initiatives boost customer loyalty and good word-of-mouth marketing by fostering a sense of belonging (Jones & Williams, 2023).

When making decisions, entrepreneurs have to consider various viewpoints and ensure that their virtual spaces and products appeal to a wide spectrum of cultural backgrounds. Businesses prioritising inclusivity are better equipped to overcome obstacles and adjust to the metaverse's changing cultural environment.

Adaptability and Cultural Competency

In the metaverse, cultural competency is a key strategic advantage for successful entrepreneurship. Entrepreneurs who exhibit cultural sensitivity and adaptation can successfully navigate cultural subtleties and preferences by customising their goods to various markets. This flexibility encompasses user engagement programmes, community management, marketing tactics, and content production (Castronova, 2005).

An essential component of entrepreneurial endeavours' long-term viability and success is the capacity to adjust and refine plans in response to cultural insights. The maintenance of metaverse initiatives' relevance, attractiveness, and responsiveness to the dynamically shifting virtual community is ensured by cultural competency.

In conclusion, businesses need to consider the social and cultural issues in the metaverse. User engagement, market reach, and the general success of entrepreneurial endeavours are strongly impacted by user diversity, inclusion, and the cultural ramifications of virtual interactions and communities. Successfully navigating these obstacles calls for a deep comprehension of cultural dynamics, a dedication to inclusion, and strategic flexibility in order to establish profitable and long-lasting endeavours inside the ever-changing metaverse.

FUTURE DIRECTIONS AND INNOVATIONS IN THE METAVERSE

The metaverse, an expansive digital domain that consists of virtual and interactive places, is about to undergo revolutionary changes that will alter the face of entrepreneurship. Future developments in several trends and technology will shape the metaverse's course and affect how businesspeople interact with this ever-evolving digital environment.

New Technologies and Trends

Extended Reality (XR) technology development is one important area of metaverse progression. It is anticipated that both virtual reality (VR) and augmented reality (AR) will advance significantly, increasing the immersiveness of virtual encounters (Smith et al., 2021). Incorporating increasingly advanced XR technology will provide entrepreneurs new channels for artistic expression and user interaction, stimulating inventive ways for business ideation and development.

Another interesting direction is the meeting point of blockchain technology with the metaverse. Blockchain technology and decentralized finance (DeFi) might revolutionize digital ownership, safe transactions, and decentralized apps. By examining these connections, businesspeople can find novel approaches to commercialize digital assets and establish safe, open virtual marketplaces (Swan, 2015).

AI will be a major factor in determining how the metaverse develops in the future. The development of intelligent virtual creatures, customization, and user interactions will all be impacted by advances in AI technology. Using AI-driven solutions, entrepreneurs may improve customer support services and content recommendation systems and even create lifelike virtual characters, contributing to more dynamic and captivating virtual experiences (Lee & Kim, 2022).

It is also predicted that efforts will be made to create standards for metaverse interoperability. How users navigate and engage with distinct virtual environments may be redefined by collaborative projects to establish seamless linkages across different metaverse platforms. According to Chen et al. (2023), standardization initiatives have the potential to promote a more unified and integrated metaverse economy, giving entrepreneurs more freedom to establish and grow their virtual businesses.

Increased integration of spatial computing—which includes technologies that see and engage with the physical world—within the metaverse is anticipated. By utilizing spatial computing, entrepreneurs may create virtual experiences that are more contextually aware and lifelike, making it harder to distinguish between the actual world and the virtual world. According to Johnson (2022), there is a possibility that this integration may provide consumers with an enhanced sensation of presence in virtual worlds.

The Metaverse Redefinition of Entrepreneurship

There is a great deal of opportunity for the metaverse to reinvent entrepreneurship. Beyond traditional ideas about how businesses are founded and run, the metaverse offers a paradigm shift that makes innovation more accessible and presents novel business models.

The metaverse offers accessible tools and platforms for generating virtual experiences, which might enable a wide spectrum of people to participate in its growth. According to García and Rodríguez (2023), inclusion can transform the entrepreneurial scene by promoting a collaborative innovation culture in which people with different backgrounds and skill sets actively contribute to creating the metaverse.

It is also conceivable that entrepreneurs in the metaverse will investigate novel monetization techniques and business structures. Incorporating virtual currencies, blockchain-based transactions, and creative subscription models might revolutionize conventional income streams. Because of the metaverse's versatility, entrepreneurs may experiment with different strategies for creating and capturing value, challenging accepted conventions in digital business (Gartner, 2023).

Co-creation and user-generated content are anticipated to be crucial elements of metaverse entrepreneurship. Entrepreneurs can actively engage people in creating virtual environments and experiences, as well as assist in the creation of metaverse platforms. By working together, the metaverse community may feel more united in its ownership, increase user engagement, and cultivate brand loyalty (Castronova, 2005).

Constant Innovation and Adjustment

Because the metaverse is dynamic, entrepreneurs must constantly innovate and adapt. Entrepreneurs must adopt agile business practices that enable quick iteration and responsiveness to new trends to stay competitive and relevant. Sustained success in the metaverse requires the capacity to change course in response to customer preferences, market factors, and technology improvements (García & Rodríguez, 2023).

Using user-centric design concepts is essential to guaranteeing that virtual experiences are engaging for many users. To iteratively improve their virtual services, entrepreneurs should prioritize ongoing user input, usability testing, and maintaining a thorough grasp of user behaviours. Success in the competitive and dynamic metaverse landscape requires remaining attentive to user demands and preferences (Chen et al., 2023).

In the metaverse, ethical issues should be central to every commercial endeavour. Ethical concerns in AI algorithms, transparent data practices, and responsible business practices facilitate building trust among users and stakeholders. According to Jones and Williams (2023), developing a safe, inclusive, and reliable metaverse environment depends heavily on the moral leadership of entrepreneurs.

In conclusion, entrepreneurs adept at navigating new trends and technology have great potential for the metaverse's future. There are chances for innovation and company development at the nexus of XR, blockchain, AI, interoperability standards, and spatial computing. In the metaverse, entrepreneurship is being redefined with a focus on user-centric practices, new business models, and democratization. Entrepreneurs must possess moral leadership and a constant state of creativity and adaptability to prosper in the quickly changing digital landscape.

CONCLUSION: NAVIGATING THE COMPLEX LANDSCAPE OF METAVERSE ENTREPRENEURSHIP

The vast digital space known as the metaverse, which crosses all conventional borders, has the potential to foster innovative entrepreneurship. Entrepreneurs must overcome several complex hurdles that are intimately woven within this promise to fully realise the potential of this dynamic and ever-evolving digital universe. When we consider the possibilities of the metaverse, it is clear that solving these issues is important and necessary to support creative and profitable business endeavours in this revolutionary domain.

Diverse Difficulties in the Metaverse

There are many different types of hurdles that entrepreneurs in the metaverse must overcome. Complex technological challenges include developing immersive environments, scaling, and integrating cutting-edge technology like blockchain and artificial intelligence. In a virtual economy where cryptocurrencies and NFTs are essential, economic and business model difficulties, including monetisation methods and the administration of digital assets, necessitate strategic navigation.

A further degree of complexity is introduced by ethical and legal quandaries, which address issues related to data security, intellectual property rights, privacy, and virtual space governance. Issues with user diversity, inclusion, and the cultural ramifications of virtual interactions are brought about by social and cultural forces. These difficulties create a tapestry that business owners must carefully weave through to prosper in the cutthroat metaverse.

Taking on Obstacles in Metaverse Entrepreneurship

In order to fully utilise the metaverse, a proactive and calculated strategy is needed to deal with these complex issues.

Innovation and flexibility: A culture of ongoing innovation and flexibility is essential for entrepreneurs to adopt. Agility is a need in the ever-changing metaverse, where it is not a luxury. To be relevant, one must be dedicated to keeping up with technology breakthroughs, comprehending changing customer preferences and iterating quickly.

Inclusiveness and User-Centric Design: Giving inclusiveness and user-centric design a top priority is critical. Entrepreneurs need to make sure various audiences find value in virtual experiences. Incorporating users actively into the co-creation of virtual spaces not only promotes a sense of ownership but also guarantees that digital environments are engaging, inclusive, and culturally sensitive.

Ethical Leadership: In the metaverse, where borders between the virtual and physical worlds are blurred, ethical issues should be the priority for business endeavours. Building user trust and fostering a safe and moral metaverse environment is made possible by ethical business practices, open data management, and ethical AI algorithms.

Collaborative Approach: Working together is essential for navigating the metaverse's complicated terrain. Entrepreneurs, technologists, legislators, and legal experts must collaborate to create industrial standards, moral guidelines, and legislative frameworks. By working together, we can ensure the metaverse develops into a responsible, inventive, and welcoming digital environment.

The Ethos of Collaboration

In addition to tackling problems, a collaborative approach cultivates an ecosystem where many stakeholders actively participate in the metaverse's advancement. Technologists and entrepreneurs work together to progress technology and create new business models. The development of regulatory frameworks that strike a balance between innovation, user protection, and ethical concerns is aided by policymakers and legal professionals.

Stakeholders and user groups are essential in forming the metaverse and ensuring user expectations are satisfied by virtual experiences. Collaboration is facilitated by industry groups and standards organisations that provide interoperability standards, best practices, and ethical principles.

Gazing Forward

The difficulties we confront now present chances for development and innovation when we consider the future of entrepreneurship in the metaverse. Together, we can overcome these obstacles and create a metaverse that redefines entrepreneurship and develops into a worldwide digital ecosystem that fosters innovation, diversity, and ethical concerns.

To sum up, the metaverse presents a frontier full of business opportunities. Working together is essential to navigate this digital world effectively. By adopting this cooperative mindset, we can surmount obstacles, unleash creativity, and jointly establish a metaverse that enhances the quality of life for users everywhere. Together, engineers, businesspeople, legislators, and legal specialists can turn the metaverse from a confusing terrain into a blank canvas for innovative projects, ushering in a new era of digital enterprise.

REFERENCES

Allam, Z., Sharifi, A., Bibri, S. E., Jones, D. S., & Krogstie, J. (2022). The metaverse as a virtual form of smart cities: Opportunities and challenges for environmental, economic, and social sustainability in urban futures. *Smart Cities*, *5*(3), 771–801. doi:10.3390/smartcities5030040

Bibri, S. E., & Allam, Z. (2022). The Metaverse as a virtual form of data-driven smart urbanism: On post-pandemic governance through the prism of the logic of surveillance capitalism. *Smart Cities, 5*(2).

Brown, A., & White, B. (2023). Metaverse Platforms: Navigating Compatibility Challenges. *Journal of Virtual Business*, *15*(2), 45–62.

Castronova, E. (2005). *Synthetic Worlds: The Business and Culture of Online Games*. University of Chicago Press.

Chakraborty, D., Patre, S., & Tiwari, D. (2023). Metaverse mingle: Discovering dating intentions in metaverse. *Journal of Retailing and Consumer Services*, *75*, 103509. doi:10.1016/j.jretconser.2023.103509

Chen, S., & ... . (2023). Entrepreneurship in the Metaverse: Navigating Opportunities and Challenges. *Journal of Business Innovation*, *30*(1), 78–95.

Chen, Z., Wu, J., Gan, W., & Qi, Z. (2022, December). Metaverse security and privacy: An overview. In *2022 IEEE International Conference on Big Data (Big Data)* (pp. 2950-2959). IEEE. 10.1109/BigData55660.2022.10021112

Damar, M. (2021). Metaverse shape of your life for future: A bibliometric snapshot. *Journal of Metaverse*, *1*(1), 1–8.

Dwivedi, Y. K., Hughes, L., Baabdullah, A. M., Ribeiro-Navarrete, S., Giannakis, M., Al-Debei, M. M., Dennehy, D., Metri, B., Buhalis, D., Cheung, C. M. K., Conboy, K., Doyle, R., Dubey, R., Dutot, V., Felix, R., Goyal, D. P., Gustafsson, A., Hinsch, C., Jebabli, I., ... Wamba, S. F. (2022). Metaverse beyond the hype: Multidisciplinary perspectives on emerging challenges, opportunities, and agenda for research, practice and policy. *International Journal of Information Management*, *66*, 102542. doi:10.1016/j.ijinfomgt.2022.102542

Gao, H., Chong, A. Y. L., & Bao, H. (2023). Metaverse: Literature Review, Synthesis and Future Research Agenda. *Journal of Computer Information Systems*, 1–21. doi:10.1080/08874417.2023.2233455

García, M., & Rodríguez, P. (2023). Collaborative Innovation in the Metaverse: Stakeholder Approach. *Journal of Metaverse Studies*, *10*(1), 102–120.

Gartner. (2023). *Metaverse Marketing Trends: Shaping the Future of Engagement*. Author.

Grupac, M., Machcinik, S., & Negoianu, A. E. (2023). Immersive engagement and geospatial mapping technologies, deep learning and neural network algorithms, and visual perception and data mining tools in metaverse interactive and extended reality environments. *Linguistic and Philosophical Investigations*, *22*(0), 196–212. doi:10.22381/lpi22202312

Hong, Y., Sawang, S., & Yang, H. P. (2023). How is entrepreneurial marketing shaped by E-commerce technology: A case study of Chinese pure-play e-retailers. *International Journal of Entrepreneurial Behaviour & Research.*

Ioannidis, S., & Kontis, A. P. (2023). Metaverse for tourists and tourism destinations. *Information Technology & Tourism*, 1–24.

Johnson, R. (2022). Technological Literacy in the Metaverse: A Critical Analysis. *Journal of Emerging Technologies*, *18*(4), 221–238.

Jones, L., & Williams, K. (2023). Ethical Considerations in the Metaverse: Navigating Digital Rights and Privacy. *Journal of Business Ethics*, *40*(2), 203–220.

Koohang, A., Nord, J., Ooi, K., Tan, G., Al-Emran, M., Aw, E., ... Wong, L. (2023). Shaping the metaverse into reality: Multidisciplinary perspectives on opportunities, challenges, and future research. *Journal of Computer Information Systems*. Advance online publication. doi:10.1080/08874417.2023.2165197

Lee, H., & Kim, J. (2022). Responsible Use of Technology in the Metaverse: A Framework for Entrepreneurs. *Technology and Society Journal*, *25*(1), 56–73.

Mancuso, I., Petruzzelli, A. M., & Panniello, U. (2023). Digital business model innovation in metaverse: How to approach virtual economy opportunities. *Information Processing & Management*, *60*(5), 103457. doi:10.1016/j.ipm.2023.103457

Papagiannidis, S., Bourlakis, M., & Li, F. (2008). Making real money in virtual worlds: MMORPGs and emerging business opportunities, challenges and ethical implications in metaverses. *Technological Forecasting and Social Change*, *75*(5), 610–622. doi:10.1016/j.techfore.2007.04.007

Smith, M., & ... . (2021). Spatial Computing and Immersive Technologies: A Comprehensive Guide for Entrepreneurs. *Journal of Virtual Innovation*, *12*(3), 134–150.

Sun, J., Gan, W., Chao, H. C., & Yu, P. S. (2022). Metaverse: Survey, applications, security, and opportunities. *arXiv preprint arXiv:2210.07990.*

Swan, M. (2015). *Blockchain: Blueprint for a New Economy*. O'Reilly Media.

Weking, J., Desouza, K. C., Fielt, E., & Kowalkiewicz, M. (2023). Metaverse-enabled entrepreneurship. *Journal of Business Venturing Insights*, *19*, e00375. doi:10.1016/j.jbvi.2023.e00375

Westerveld, P., Fielt, E., Desouza, K. C., & Gable, G. G. (2023). The business model portfolio as a strategic tool for value creation and business performance. *The Journal of Strategic Information Systems*, *32*(1), 101758. doi:10.1016/j.jsis.2023.101758

Xu, Y., Liu, W., He, T., & Tsai, S. B. (2023). Buzzword or fuzzword: An event study of the metaverse in the Chinese stock market. *Internet Research*.

Yaqoob, I., Salah, K., Jayaraman, R., & Omar, M. (2023). Metaverse applications in smart cities: Enabling technologies, opportunities, challenges, and future directions. *Internet of Things : Engineering Cyber Physical Human Systems*, *23*, 100884. doi:10.1016/j.iot.2023.100884

Yawised, K., Apasrawirote, D., & Boonparn, C. (2022). From traditional business shifted towards transformation: The emerging business opportunities and challenges in 'Metaverse' era. *Incbaa*, *2022*, 162–175.

Yemenici, A. D. (2022). Entrepreneurship in the world of metaverse: Virtual or real? *Journal of Metaverse*, *2*(2), 71–82. doi:10.57019/jmv.1126135

Chapter 12
Role of Blockchain Technology for User Data Security in Metaverse

Babita Jha
https://orcid.org/0000-0001-8586-0250
Christ University, India

Sushant Garg
Christ University, India

Tushar Singhal
Christ University, India

ABSTRACT

The metaverse is generating widespread interest among organizations of various scales, as companies acknowledge its capacity for profound transformation. Prominent organizations are actively adopting the metaverse concept to improve their operations and interact with clients in innovative and captivating manners. This chapter examines the vital function that blockchain plays in bolstering user data security as it explores the urgent problem of data breaches in the metaverse sector. The authors also carefully examine recent data breach cases in the metaverse sector, such as sandbox incursions, deepfake attacks, and digital avatar assaults. By outlining these practical difficulties, they make clear how urgent it is to come up with reliable ways to safeguard user data in the metaverse. The study findings have emphasized the dynamic and evolving nature of the metaverse industry, which is now undergoing substantial development and continuous exploration. They have also focused on significant blockchain technologies that demonstrate potential in ensuring data security.

INTRODUCTION

The advancements in computer science have significantly impacted our daily lives by revolutionising human communication and interaction. Three notable waves of technological progress have been ob-

DOI: 10.4018/979-8-3693-2422-6.ch012

served from the standpoint of end users, with each wave focusing on the advent of personal computers, the Internet, and mobile devices, respectively. The current wave of computer innovation, known as the fourth wave, is centred around spatial and immersive technologies, including Virtual Reality and Augmented Reality. This wave is expected to bring about the next paradigm shift in ubiquitous computing, with the potential to completely transform online work, enterprise, leisure, and education. The term used to describe this concept is Metaverse (Mystakidis et al.,2022).

Rise of the Metaverse

Neal Stevenson introduced the phrase "metaverse" in his science fiction novel Snow Crash, published in 1992 (Stevenson et al., 2003). It denoted a secondary virtual reality realm generated by computers that individuals worldwide might connect to and enter via headphones and goggles. The "The Street" protocol, which serves as an analogue of the

information superhighway, connects many virtual locales and communities to support the Metaverse. Within the Metaverse, individuals assume the appearance of alterable digital entities referred to as Avatars (Mystakidis et al.,2022).

The Metaverse is a multiuser environment where physical reality and digital virtuality exist simultaneously and persistently. This cosmos is referred to as post-reality. This phenomenon relies on the convergence of many technologies, such as augmented reality and virtual reality, that facilitate interactions involving multiple senses between individuals, virtual surroundings, and digital objects. As a result, the Metaverse has become a lasting platform that connects multiple users and immersive worlds through social engagement and networking. It enables seamless, immediate communication between users through dynamic interactions with digital objects. Initially, avatars have the ability to navigate between different virtual realms.

Radoff identifies seven layers of metaverse architecture: experience, discovery, creator economy, spatial computing, decentralisation, human interface, and infrastructure. Dionisio delineated four fundamental domains crucial for the advancement of the metaverse: scalability, interoperability, ubiquitous access and identification, and immersive realism.

The Emergence of Blockchain as a Groundbreaking Technology

The blockchain framework, encompassing the hash algorithm employed for block timestamping, was introduced in a white paper released in 2008 by an individual or collective of engineers operating under the alias 'Satoshi Nakamoto' (S. Nakamoto, 2008). The objective of developing blockchain technology was to create a decentralised ecosystem that eliminates the need for third-party involvement in data and operations. For example, monetary trades between individuals or businesses are typically consolidated and supervised by a third-party entity. In order to complete an online payment or currency transfer, a bank or credit card issuer must act as an intermediary. Additionally, a transaction incurs a fee from a financial institution or credit card firm. In lieu of the two primary entities engaged in the transaction, a third-party company assumes responsibility for managing and preserving all data and information within a centralised transaction system.

This was the primary driving force behind the creation of the decentralised ecosystem that blockchain technology was supposed to establish. Blockchain is a decentralised database system that stores a growing list of authenticated data entries across all participating nodes. The information of each completed transaction is consistently updated in a publicly accessible ledger that contains the data. Blockchain, being a decentralised solution, obviates the necessity for other organisations to be engaged. All transactions conducted on a blockchain are universally shared and accessible to every node. The system's transparency gets better when comparing this aspect to centralised transactions that involve a third party. Furthermore, because to the anonymity of each Blockchain node, other nodes can verify transactions with enhanced security. Bitcoin was the pioneering application of Blockchain technology. Bitcoin established a decentralised cryptocurrency environment, enabling users to engage in transactions involving virtual currency for the purchase and sale of products.

The Function of Blockchain in the Metaverse

The concept of the metaverse might elicit a range of thrilling experiences or enjoyable activities in our thoughts. The circumstance that is most relevant to us, however, is simply a different world where economic ecology is inevitable. Moreover, a key feature offered by the blockchain is the facilitation of digital assets, like the standardised token. Blockchain technology is essential for the efficient functioning of the metaverse, as it enables seamless economic operations. Blockchain technology allows metaverse users to engage in the wider crypto-economy by facilitating the conversion of virtual commodities into real currency. The advent of blockchain technology has facilitated the utilisation of cryptocurrencies such as Bitcoin for the purpose of purchasing and selling virtual assets within the metaverse. Financial resources and other valuable possessions can be transferred and employed throughout all virtual realms inside the Metaverse. Within the crypto-enabled metaverse, individuals have the ability to embark on virtual journeys, acquire virtual clothing, and attend virtual performances. Blockchain facilitates the development of applications and digital trade within the metaverse, establishing it as a publicly accessible platform with a decentralised and opensource ecosystem. The metaverse, a blockchain with an open-source architecture, will provide decentralised wallets and exchanges with a user interface that is intuitive and user-friendly.

How May Blockchain Safeguard Data Privacy and Security

Transactions are documented within a sequence of interconnected blocks known as a blockchain. Every block is equipped with hyperlinks to both the preceding and succeeding blocks. Consequently, it is exceedingly difficult for an individual to modify a solitary record.

This arises from the necessity for an attacker to modify a sequence of blocks in order to evade detection. Despite their seemingly insignificant nature, blockchains possess various other attributes that contribute to heightened security. Cryptography is commonly used to ensure the security of record-keeping on the blockchain. Each network participant possesses their private key concurrently as a result of the transactions that have been executed. Each individual can utilise these keys as unique electronic signature. If any document is altered, the peer network will recognise the discrepancy and render the digital signature invalid. Blockchains are increasingly becoming more decentralised. The security of the system is significantly strengthened by one of the primary characteristics of blockchain. For example, it is distributed throughout peer-to-peer networks. They remain current due to regular updates. As there is no connectivity to a centralised place, there is neither a single source of failure nor a single point of access. Due to the concentration of control over 51% of the blockchain, any modifications to the blockchain will necessitate a substantial level of computational capacity. Even the most resolute hackers and attackers found this task impossible to accomplish. Blockchain technology has a high level of resilience against fraudulent activities and manipulative actions.

LITERATURE REVIEW

A metaverse is a virtual universe that serves as a foundation and can connect and sustain various applications. As a result, the variety of activities that users can engage in within the metaverse corresponds to the wide range of applications that are included into it. To achieve this ambitious aim, the early metaverse instances will utilise several recent technology advancements. Virtual reality (VR) has the capacity to generate fully immersive three-dimensional environments, while augmented reality (AR) enables a seamless fusion of the virtual and physical domains (Pietro et al., 2022). The Metaverse is quite effective in creating a strong sensation of virtual identity substitution. Furthermore, individuals can enhance their self-perception by participating in digital endeavours within the Metaverse. A personalised avatar can evoke a sense of uniqueness and enhance the sense of being fully engaged in the Metaverse, wherein the virtual persona remains consistent across the entire virtual world. The Metaverse disregards the physical separation between individuals, enabling the provision of dynamic online social environments. Due to their robust sensation of identity and immersive experiences, individuals are no longer confined to conventional social activities. Individuals now have the opportunity to engage in a diverse array of innovative pursuits, and individuals residing in distant nations can participate in these communal endeavours irrespective of their geographical proximity. Although the Metaverse's design is aesthetically pleasing, it is certain that other challenges will emerge due to the rapid advancement of Metaverse-related technologies. The primary issues at hand pertain to the safeguarding of individuals' assets and the preservation of their future privacy: ensuring security and privacy within the Metaverse. The Metaverse Security Governance Shanghai Initiative (Chen et al., 2022) has put forth eight guiding principles and goals. These include achieving progress in both virtual and real contexts, ensuring order is maintained, promoting strong development, establishing institutional standards, respecting privacy, safeguarding the future, embracing rationality and pragmatism, and fostering openness and collaboration. In order to ensure the longevity of the metaverse, it is imperative that its structure is decentralised to mitigate the dangers associated with centralization, such as the vulnerability of one point of failure, the absence of transparency, and the dominance of a limited number of entities. Moreover, the metaverse encompasses two essential components: the virtual economy and value system facilitated by the blockchain. Blockchain technology offer a decentralised and transparent alternative for establishing a sustainable virtual economy and generating value. Blockchain is a decentralised ledger that combines hash-chained chunks of organised data and provides attributes like auditability, transparency, immutability, and decentralisation. The blockchain can be categorised into three distinct groups: That is to say. Consensus protocols play a crucial role in blockchain by ensuring the consistency of the ledger and the scalability of the system. They can be categorised as public, consortium, or private, according on the level of decentralisation. In addition, smart contracts can be deployed on the blockchain to provide automated execution of predefined functions between mutually suspicious parties. NFTs, in the context of blockchain, refer to tokens that are indivisible and irreplaceable. They serve the purpose of facilitating asset identification and establishing ownership provenance. The term De-Fi stands for decentralised finance, aiming to offer complex, transparent, and secure financial services. The exchange of stocks and currencies within the metaverse (Wang et al., 2022). The distributed ledger technology (DLT) network is specifically engineered to guarantee the origin and consistency of data, enable auditing, prevent tampering, provide pseudonymization, withstand majority attacks, assure security, and maintain privacy and secrecy. The blockchain network is distinguished by three characteristics: it is transparent, secure, and well-suited for conducting online transactions. The subsequent passage delineates the security attributes of the systems based on blockchain technology. Data Consistency: Within a blockchain network, the concept of maintaining identical copies of data on every node at all times is known as data consistency. The data consistency of Bitcoin is a subject of contention, with different studies asserting that it is both feeble and robust. The Eventual Consistency Model is suggested for distributed networks to guarantee data consistency. This model achieves a harmonious equilibrium between the uniformity and accessibility of the data, implementing updates in a delayed way, while granting readers the possibility to retrieve the most up-to-date values. It is crucial to understand that eventual consistency does not ensure immediate data consistency. Instead, it ensures data consistency throughout time, without any time-related limitations. However, if the reader accesses the node prior to the data update, the model may provide outdated information. In order to address such situations, a consistency model must ensure that no reading may occur until all nodes have been updated. However, this poses a difficulty in terms of cost (Idrees et al., 2021). The requirements of industries pertaining to the technological foundations and progress of Industry 4.0 are still in need of further refinement, as past iterations of blockchain technology have not yet adequately met the objectives of the industrial sector. To achieve the required level of industrial automation, it is essential to employ advanced blockchain technology. One of the main demands of Industry 4.0 is the incorporation of advanced technologies like as supply chain management, artificial intelligence (AI), and the Internet of Things (IoT) alongside cybersecurity. To enhance privacy, security, transparency, and data integrity for enterprises, it is necessary to establish a new era of blockchain technology called “Blockchain4.0” in alignment with technological breakthroughs. Consequently, InterValue has been utilised in the creation of a Blockchain 4.0 platform. The main objective of InterValue with Blockchain 4.0 is to create a Directed Acyclic Graph (DAG) that offers improved scalability, usability, and dependability. Multiple publications have highlighted the implementation of blockchain 4.0 and its benefits in numerous industrial sectors due to its advancements in scalability, interoperability, and transaction rate compared to prior generations. Software-defined networking (SDN) and blockchain are emerging technologies that can be utilised to guarantee safe network connectivity and construct secure systems. Enhancements in domains such as scalability, security, and TR will consequently be implemented in the upcoming future (Mourtzis et al., 2023).

METHODOLOGY

This research has adopted a Systematic Literature Review approach to address the following objective-

1) Understanding the role of Blockchain in Metaverse
2) Security and privacy concerns in Metaverse
3) Threat to the user Information
4) How Blockchain ensures Data security in the metaverse.

The review consists of the following process: (1) identify the need of review, (2) specify the research question, (3) develop review protocol, (4) identify and select paper, (5) assess the paper quality, (6) extract and synthesize the data.

The need of the review is stated at the starting of the Methods section and based on the objective the following research questions are proposed which are:-

Data security threats in Metaverse?

How Blockchain and Metaverse work together? Role of Blockchain in Metaverse?

How Blockchain ensures data security in Metaverse?

To gather the relevant paper the initial search was conducted on the following online databases:- IEEE Xplorer, Elsiver. Majority of the papers were obtained from IEEE Xplorer reason being majority of the research paper in the field of Blockchain and Metaverse were published in IEEE Xplorer only. Not only the relevant research papers the content was also extracted from the necessary blogs of IBM also in the field of Blockchain.

Search results from the initial search were aggregated. Then the papers were examined against the inclusion and exclusion criteria on the basis of abstract, introduction and conclusion. After that full text screening was applied to all papers against the eligibility criteria.

The inclusion and exclusion criteria guarantee that search results are accessible and relevant. Particularly the search result should be relevant to the Blockchain and Metaverse.

Inclusion criteria

1) The full text PDF of the paper is available.
2) Paper is written in English.
3) Paper is about Data Security, Blockchain and Metaverse.

Exclusion criteria

1) Paper is not written in English
2) The full text PDF of the paper is not available.
3) The paper is not about Data Security, Blockchain, Metaverse.

Eligibility criteria

1) Address a research topic related to Data Security, Blockchain, Metaverse.
2) It's a complete research paper presenting the research problem, process and result.

Relatedness criteria

1) Answers any one of the questions from Q1, Q2, Q3, and Q4

BLOCKCHAIN FOR METAVERSE

Examining the technical aspects of implementing blockchain technology in the metaverse. This section examines state-of-the-art metaverse solutions based on blockchain technology, focusing on the technical aspects of data collection, storage, sharing, interoperability, and privacy protection, as seen in Figure 1.

Data Collection

Data collecting is an essential stage in the metaverse ecosystem. During the payment process, individuals provide sensitive information, including their bank or credit card details. Moreover, in the metaverse, it is necessary to acquire users' sensitive data, like biometric information and gestures, in order to construct digital avatars. Data collecting facilitates the training of machine learning and artificial intelligence algorithms, which can assist in decision-making, creating digital products, developing recommendation systems, and marketing in the metaverse. Collecting data in the metaverse will help applications in generating more advanced insights that can evolve and adjust to new situations. As depicted in the illustration, the metaverse is envisioned as a digital platform where users can engage in digital commerce, entertainment, communication, and professional activities using a range of electronic devices. Consequently, large quantities of diverse data will be generated. Here are several data collecting techniques that can be utilised in the metaverse. Web forms will serve as a data acquisition method within the metaverse, enabling the collection of information from users. Customers have the option to efficiently and quickly complete online forms prior to gaining accessibility to the metaverse functionalities. Bots have the ability to gather users' personal information and crucial authentication components, such as their social security numbers. Within the metaverse, a state-of-the-art camera is employed to collect data on the user's physical characteristics. The user's physical characteristics are employed to generate a digital depiction of the individual in the virtual realm. This is illustrated in Figure 1, which showcases the technological function of blockchain in the metaverse. The world. Customers will derive benefits from employing AR/VR equipment to navigate the metaverse. These gadgets will be utilised to gather data regarding the users' behaviour.

Challenges in Data Collection in Metaverse

Data generated within the metaverse through decentralised applications (Dapps) like WeiFund, Etheria, 4G Capital, and Ampliative Art will be extensive, lacking a specific organisation, and constantly updated. The task of collecting the vast quantities of data being generated is a significant challenge.

Figure 1. Demonstrating the role of blockchain in metaverse from technical standpoint

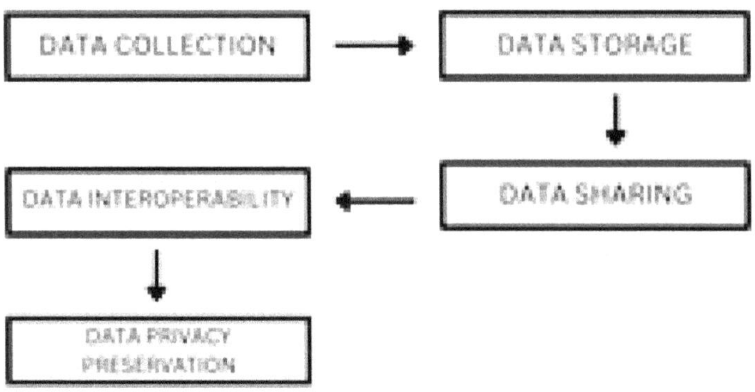

Data assurance or integrity will be crucial in the metaverse for the development of applications like recommender systems. Obtaining data from sources of uncertain origin will adversely affect the reliability of these systems. The data volume of the metaverse will significantly increase as it provides top-notch digital

services, such as the Horizon Worlds and Horizon Venues applications, through virtual reality headsets. The surge in streaming for entertainment and other purposes will exert pressure on data collection infrastructure. Obtaining duplicate and erroneous data can result in a decrease in data quality.

How Blockchain Can Help

Utilising blockchain technology will streamline the acquisition of authentic data for applications like social networking within the metaverse. The utilisation of a distributed ledger in blockchain technology will facilitate the implementation as shown in Fig. 2, which pertains to the technical features of blockchain for the metaverse, verification of transaction records and monitoring of data in the metaverse. Consequently, the process of collecting data is resistant to attacks since most of the nodes in the ledger must approve any changes made to the metaverse data. The data collected in the metaverse undergoes validation using a specialised technique that relies on blockchain-specific validation and consensus procedures. Every action within a blockchain is documented as a transaction, with each

Figure 2. Blockchain for metaverse technical aspects
Source: Gadekallu et al. (2022)

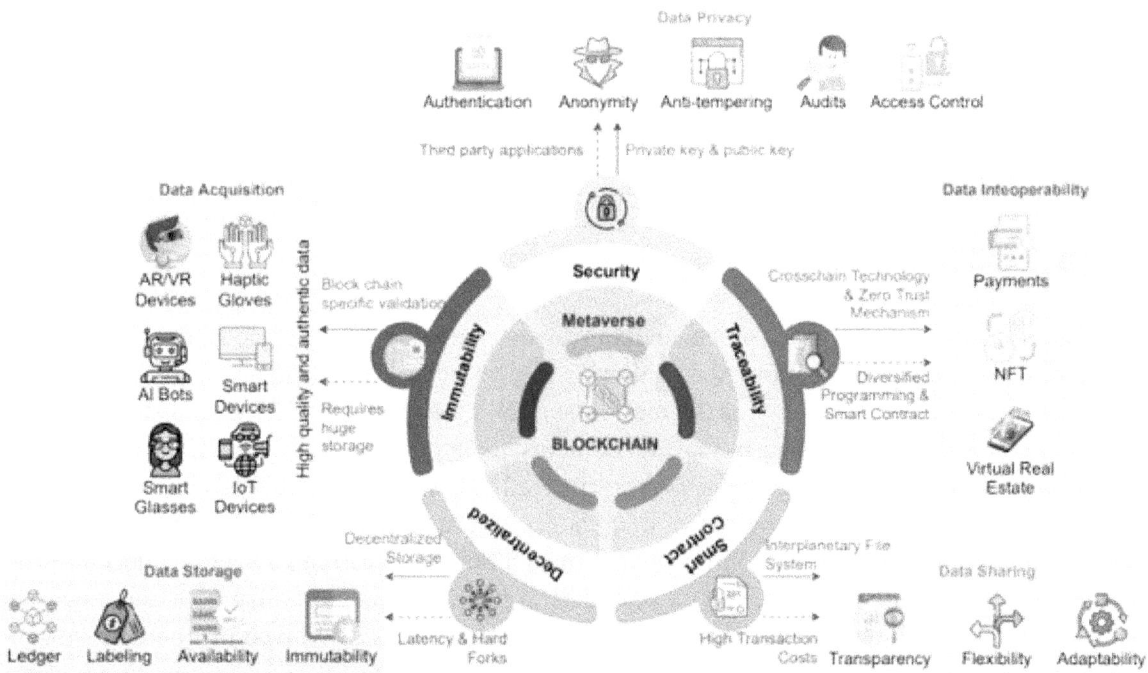

Source - Blockchain for the Metaverse: A Review.
Gadekallu, T. R., Huynh-The, T., Wang, W., Yenduri, G., Ranaweera, P., Pham, Q. V., ... & Liyanage, M. (2022). Blockchain for the metaverse: A review. *arXiv preprint arXiv:2203.09738*.

block including a cryptographic hash of the previous block, along with a timestamp and metadata (Luo et al., 2021). Consequently, altering data within a block will have an impact on the remaining blocks. The data obtained from any block is not immune to tampering. The likelihood of producing a replicated block is extremely low, guaranteeing the absence of any duplication during the process of data collection.

Data Storage

The metaverse is a virtual realm governed by humans that coexists with the physical world. The metaverse will consist of online-accessible events, locations, and objects. The metaverse necessitates extensive data storage capacity. Each person who enters the metaverse generates a data file that expands through social interactions. Upon the development and implementation of the metaverse, a substantial amount of data will be produced, hence exerting significant strain on the real world's capacity to analyse said information. In order to effectively utilise the metaverse, prioritising data storage is essential.

Challenges in Data Storage in Metaverse

The metaverse encompasses both the physical world and a digital reality that exist simultaneously. With the increasing number of people entering the digital realm, there is a significant rise in the production of data files. Consequently, the metaverse will generate an enormous quantity of data. Once the metaverse is fully operational, the storage capacity of the physical world will be under significant strain. Consequently, the storage of data will be a substantial obstacle to the implementation of metaverse applications, including gaming, entertainment, real estate, healthcare, and other domains (Wang et al., 2021). Should the metaverse depend on a centralised storage system, there exists a risk of data leakage, manipulation, or loss. The high probability of data loss and corruption in centralized applications poses a threat to the metaverse's ability to provide sensitive data, such as biometric data, speech inflections, and vital signs. The abundance of data generated by metaverse applications poses a significant challenge in terms of data labelling and categorization.

How Blockchain Can Help

Each transaction produces a fresh block, making metaverse storage impervious to manipulation. Consequently, data is preserved along the chain as a replica of the initial blocks, thereby improving the data transparency and reliability of the metaverse. The breach of centralised data storage would jeopardise metaverse applications across several domains, including real estate and digital assets (Yang et al., 2022). The use of blockchain technology will lead to a significant increase in the number of blocks that contribute to the distribution of data, hence improving the availability of data in metaverse applications, such as crucial monitoring and life support notifications. Due to its decentralised nature, blockchain technology enables data scientists in the metaverse to collaborate and engage in data purification. This process significantly reduces the time and costs involved in labelling data and preparing datasets for analysis.

Data Sharing

Data sharing has the potential to provide significant advantages to a diverse group of individuals and organisations involved in the metaverse. Enhanced synergy between individuals and applications can be achieved through the utilisation of a common platform. Data exchange within the metaverse will be advantageous for a wide range of individuals, including scientists and the general populace. Information collected from augmented reality/virtual reality (AR/VR) and Internet of Things (IoT) devices in the virtual world will be used to create customised systems that are specifically designed to match the actions and habits of the users. This will enable a diverse array of applications to deliver an enhanced user experience. Through the utilisation of app integration, organisations can effectively conduct data analytics within the metaverse. Sharing data will facilitate the comprehension of clients, the assessment of advertising, the customisation of content, the formulation of content strategies, and the production of metaverse items (L. V. Kiong, 2022).

Challenges in Data Sharing in Metaverse

Utilising centralised data exchange platforms to share data in the metaverse could potentially jeopardise the security and confidentiality of data owners' sensitive information. In the traditional sharing environment, data exhibits significant variability, leading to increased latency and less data accessibility. Scaling mutable data has greater challenges compared to scaling immutable data (Yu et al,. 2021). A plethora of applications in the metaverse, including healthcare, traffic optimisation, media, and entertainment, will generate vast quantities of real-time data. As the need for immediate data increases in a common data sharing environment, the ability to adapt and modify data becomes a significant issue.

How Blockchain Can Help

Blockchain technology has the potential to enhance the clarity and accuracy of transactions in cryptocurrency trading, education, and various applications inside the metaverse. The governance and finance applications would provide a decentralised and unchangeable ledger of all transactions, allowing stakeholders to scrutinise them. Consequently, more data transparency will be advantageous for stakeholders in the metaverse. Blockchain technology will enable programmes and their users to have insight into the data management practices of third-party apps like Thunderbird, the Bat, and Pegasus. Additionally, it will eliminate illicit transactions in the grey market, thereby enhancing user trust and confidence. Moreover, the data owner will own complete authority over the data. Distributed ledger technology can also enhance the effectiveness of data audits. Consequently, blockchain reduces the duration and cost associated with data validation. Smart contracts will enhance the versatility of data sharing. They are frequently employed to automate the implementation of a contract, ensuring that all parties are immediately informed of the outcome, without the need for a middleman or unnecessary time consumption. Blockchain enables the programming of smart contracts using various methods. Consequently, the applications Nmusik, Ascribe, Tracr, UBS, and Applicature will experience advantages (Ali et al., 2021).

Data Interoperability

Data interoperability refers to the ability of different systems or software applications to exchange and interpret data in a seamless and efficient manner. Interoperability will drive the advancement of the metaverse. Within the metaverse, diverse applications, like banking and healthcare, will have the capability to communicate and share information. The metaverse will function as a platform for social and cultural interaction in virtual worlds. As virtual bridges are gradually constructed, users will have the ability to seamlessly transfer their avatars and possessions across different virtual worlds, ensuring their preservation. By implementing an identity standard, the user is provided with a distinct set of credentials that may be utilised across different virtual environments. This might perhaps refer to our genuine licence numbers, social security numbers, passport numbers, or other types of identification.

Challenges in Data Interoperability in the Metaverse

The metaverse will be created by integrating multiple digital domains. Conventional centralised digital platforms are currently available, but they lack integration and organisation. In order to participate in different virtual environments, individuals are required to establish accounts, create avatars, set up hardware, and establish payment infrastructure (Bian et al., 2021). The options for transferring a user's digital assets, such as non-fungible tokens (NFTs) and avatars, to a different digital platform are restricted. Migrating in virtual worlds is challenging due to a lack of interoperability. For instance, it is not possible to utilise

the same account across platforms like Decentraland and Roblox. The capacity to employ an application within the virtual realm will hinge upon the degree of connection among virtual worlds. Apps in the digital realm should possess the capability to exchange information without any restrictions, irrespective of their geographical location or the technology employed. Metaverse interoperability necessitates the capacity to regulate virtual world interactions in a satisfactory manner, which is a notable deficiency of the previous approach.

How Blockchain Can Help

A cross-chain protocol is an optimal method for guaranteeing compatibility between virtual worlds in the metaverse. This facilitates

the transfer of assets, including avatars, non-fungible tokens (NFTs), and currency, between virtual realms with the help of metaverse infrastructure, as depicted in Figure 3. This protocol will establish the foundation for widespread adoption of the metaverse. The adoption of cross-blockchain technology, as proposed (Jabbar et al,. 2020), will facilitate the seamless exchange of data and assets between different virtual worlds. This advancement will diminish the need for intermediaries in the metaverse. The metaverse infrastructure will facilitate seamless connectivity between individuals and software applications, owing to the implementation of blockchain technology.

Data Privacy Preservation

The metaverse will utilise advanced human-computer interface (HCI) technology, enabling users to interact with their virtual surroundings and engage in social activities. The centralization of Web 2.0 poses privacy concerns. With the expansion of the Internet of the Metaverse, or Web 3.0, the line

Figure 3. The metaverses underlying infrastructure

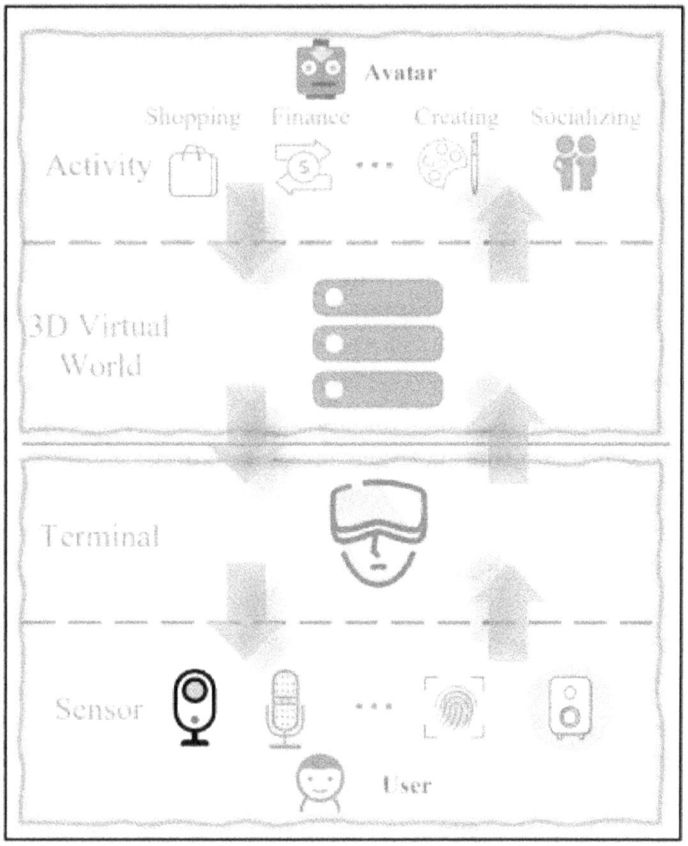

Source- Metaverse: Security and Privacy Concerns Ruoyu Zhao, Yushu Zhang, Youwen Zhu, Rushi Lan, and Zhongyun Hua

between the physical and virtual worlds will become increasingly blurred. The impact of Web 2.0 on the safeguarding of individual rights remains unattended to. Consequently, the matter of data privacy will pose more challenges in the upcoming Web 3.0. Insufficient application security procedures may heighten the risk of a data breach due to the significant expansion of data generated in the metaverse. The protection of privacy is a significant concern when it comes to safeguarding the confidentiality of personal data (Jovanovic et al., 2022).

Challenges in Data Privacy in Metaverse

Data privacy preservation in the metaverse poses significant challenges. During the initial phases, adapting to the metaverse ecosystem may provide challenges, since malicious actors could deceive users and illicitly acquire sensitive data. Utilising an artificial intelligence bot, like promobot, can result in the user being oblivious to the bot's identity and potentially perceiving it as a genuine individual, thereby fostering fraud. The concern over safeguarding the privacy of personal data mostly revolves around the disclosure of personally identifiable information (PII) (I. Hughes, 2022). Incorporating validity information into the metaverse will increase the complexity of simultaneously managing large volumes of data.

How Blockchain Can Help

Blockchain technology empowers metaverse users to exercise control over their data through the utilisation of private and public keys, so granting them full ownership of their data. Unauthorised use or acquisition of data from other entities inside the blockchain-enabled metaverse is prohibited for third-party intermediaries. Regarding personal data stored on the blockchain-enabled metaverse, individuals will have the ability to determine the specific conditions under which a third party can access their data (Kumar et al., 2021). The blockchain ledgers provide an audit trail as a basic feature to guarantee the completeness and consistency of transactions inside the metaverse. Implementing zero knowledge proof on the blockchain allows users to conveniently access crucial data in the metaverse, while also protecting their privacy and maintaining ownership over their assets. Zero Knowledge proofs are a cryptographic technique employed in blockchain systems, enabling users to demonstrate the truth of certain claims about themselves to programmes, while keeping the underlying information confidential.

Security and Privacy Concerns in Metaverse

Security and privacy issues inevitably accompany the evolution of all things, including the metaverse. More precisely, we have categorised these concerns into four distinct categories: User Information, Communication, Scenario, and Goods. The main objective of the article is to examine and address the security and privacy issues associated with User Information, while providing a brief overview of all four categories.

User Information

One of the defining features of the metaverse is the integration of several sensors, enabling the acquisition of a vast amount of user data. Undoubtedly, sensors play a crucial role as they aid users in enhancing their experience and fully engaging with the metaverse. Conversely, numerous users may lack awareness of the condition. The source cited is a publication (Falchuk et al,.2018). The user information collected by sensors, including physiological, physical, biometric, and social data, might be excessively personal. Exposing it will endanger the security and privacy of users (Liu et al., 2019). Therefore, it is crucial to ensure the protection of user information.

Communication

Transmission of information or exchange of messages between individuals or groups. The metaverse is characterised by its extensive interactivity and sociability, resulting in a significant amount of communication. Communication is essential for carrying out various activities in the metaverse, including sharing, cooperating, and fostering mutual trust and understanding. While it may not include the user information indicated before, many users are reluctant to notify individuals who do not engage in conversation because communication data is highly confidential and sensitive.

Hence, it is imperative to safeguard communication in a manner that prevents non-participants from comprehending and retrieving the communication's contents, while allowing authorised participants to do so.

Scenario

Given the surreal nature of the metaverse, it is conceivable that one may encounter similar security and privacy vulnerabilities as those found in the physical world. Two primary considerations are involved: the scenario itself and the avatars within the scenario. Regarding the first point, due to the high concentration of users on a metaverse platform and the limited availability of alternatives, it is inevitable that their understanding of civilizations, faiths, and other subjects will differ. Consequently, the situation will fail to meet the desires of all individuals and may potentially lead to perplexity for specific avatars. In the future, when more people join the metaverse, there will inevitably be individuals who engage in negative and unethical behaviour, such as criticising, monitoring, or sexually harassing other avatars. This has been observed in online games (Fox et al., 2018).

Goods

The metaverse exhibits ingenuity, exceptional innovation, extensive autonomy, and significant personalisation. Avatars have the ability to create a wide range of items, including character models, appearances, clothing, homes, and artwork, all tailored to human preferences. These items can be utilised or traded by creators, indicating that they are produced via exertion or at an expense (although they can also be freely bestowed by acquaintances), suggesting that they possess both metaphysical and monetary attributes. Avatars seek to protect the integrity of their value, ensuring that it is not unlawfully compromised. For instance, an avatar may create custom apparel for their own use and prefer not to encounter it being worn by others.

Concurrently, malicious users have the potential to interfere with commercial exchanges, while virtual representations of individuals may desire to conceal their identities during transactions. Therefore, ensuring the secure protection of items and transactions in the metaserve is of utmost importance.

Security and Privacy Issues Pertaining to User Information in the Metaverse

In contemporary society, the protection and confidentiality of user information have consistently been of utmost importance due to security and privacy concerns. Due to the immersive nature, seamless integration of virtual and real-world experiences, and the incorporation of multiple sensory inputs in the metaverse, a greater amount of user data will be collected compared to previous platforms like social networks. Consequently, illicit third parties develop a heightened interest in this data and may initiate an attack on the network, as seen in Figure 4. Consequently, once information is transmitted from the terminal, users no longer have direct physical control over it. This implies that there is a risk to the information once it leaves the terminal. In other words, it is crucial to protect user information at the terminal.

Figure 4. An illustration of the metaverse being attacked by the attacker

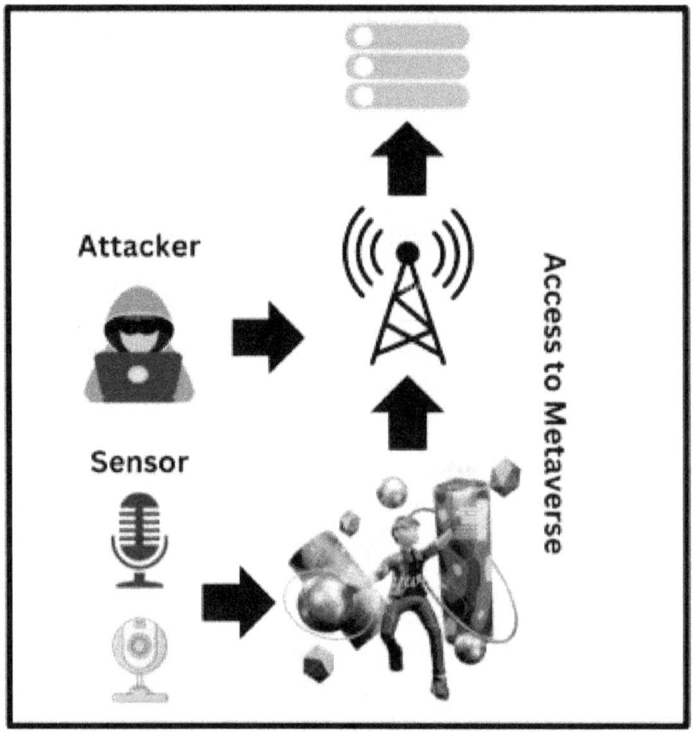

The Role of Blockchain in Ensuring the Data Security of User Data in the Metaverse

The Metaverse will profoundly influence human necessities. Hence, it is imperative to not disregard the security and privacy concerns of the Metaverse. “The Metaverse will revolutionise individuals’ lifestyles, social interactions, and commercial activities,” declared Henry Bagdasarian, the Founder of Identity Management Institute. “The evolving digital world will bring forth new security challenges.” Professionals in the field will be alarmed by the increasing security risks associated with the Metaverse. These risks will encompass novel forms of security breaches and data vulnerability, as well as the potential for identity theft and fraudulent activities. This concern arises as the emerging digital environment progresses towards a complete transition of our physical world into the digital realm.

Enhancing Security in Blockchain Technology

The utilisation of blockchain technology has the capacity to greatly enhance trust and security within the metaverse. Blockchain technology empowers users to exert greater authority over their personal data and privacy within the metaverse. Blockchain users have the ability to selectively share their data, granting explicit authorization for certain purposes. This empowers consumers to manage and safeguard their personal information, hence reducing the risk of unauthorised data collection and privacy violations. Blockchain technology employs point-to-point transmission, a consensus process, and encryption techniques to provide users with secure and reliable storage and movement of data.

Additionally, blockchain technology can be utilised to enhance trust and security in the realm of virtual reality through several means.

Immutable and Transparent Record-Keeping

The inherent immutability of blockchain ensures that any data saved on the blockchain is permanently fixed and cannot be altered or manipulated. It can be utilized in the metaverse to establish a clear and reliable system for recording various transactions, including the ownership of virtual assets, virtual land, and digital identities. Users can rely on the transparency of the blockchain to verify the authenticity and past records of these assets, hence reducing the risk of fraud or counterfeit products.

Decentralized Identity and Authentication

Blockchain-based identification systems in the metaverse empower users with decentralised control over their identities and authentication. The blockchain has the capability to store the distinct digital identity of each user, eliminating the requirement for centralised identity providers. The decentralised model reduces the risks associated with single points of failure and data breaches by giving users greater control over their personal information.

Consensus Mechanism

A consensus mechanism refers to a set of software protocols embedded in a blockchain's code that facilitates the synchronisation of a network's consensus on the status of a digital ledger. This is achieved by ensuring the existence of a unified dataset, which represents the universally accepted version of a blockchain's transaction history. This approach eliminates the need for each node, or computer inside the network, to individually retain a complete copy of the database.

The utilisation of blockchain-based consensus mechanisms in the metaverse ensures secure storage of user data, prevention of undesirable actions, and facilitates user participation without the need for mutual trust. Scalability solutions optimise networks, enabling the metaverse to handle increased numbers of users and transactions. Utilising consensus mechanisms based on blockchain technology has the potential to enhance the security, privacy, and scalability of the metaverse. Users will cultivate mutual trust, innovate novel applications, and exhibit heightened receptiveness towards this groundbreaking digital ecosystem.

The blockchain is an autonomous and distributed ledger, and the consensus mechanism ensures the uniformity and precision of data across several nodes. PBFT, PoW, PoS, and DPoS are well-known consensus mechanism algorithms (Du et al,.2017). Nevertheless, these algorithms have security weaknesses. The Proof of Work (PoW) consensus mechanism is susceptible to the double spend attack, wherein an attacker can gain control over the entire blockchain if their processing power exceeds 51% of the overall network.

Smart Contract

A smart contract is a programme that executes when specific conditions are met and is stored on a blockchain. They are frequently employed to mechanise the execution of a contract, ensuring that all parties can promptly and securely reach a resolution without the need for a middleman or any unnecessary delays. Blockchain transaction records are encrypted using smart contracts, rendering them more resistant to hacking attempts. In addition, due to the interconnectedness of each entry on a distributed ledger, hackers would need to alter the entire sequence in order to manipulate a single record.

Smart contracts are employed to enable users to exercise control over their own assets and to receive assets from external sources (Zheng et al, 2020). The contract is characterised by openness and transparency, which facilitates the promotion of transparency and the prevention of fraud. Nevertheless, there are individuals that do not desire the disclosure of the confidential contract information.

Moreover, once the protocol is published on the blockchain, it becomes immutable, meaning that developers are unable to modify it on the blockchain. Cybercriminals specifically aimed at exploiting the interconnection between the Ethereum and Solana blockchains, resulting in a financial loss of no less than 320 million dollars.

Cryptographic Algorithm

Cryptographic techniques aim to achieve complete or partial anonymity by using the concept of secrets in the field of cryptography. The primary objective of cryptography in the context of blockchain is to prevent the occurrence of double-spending, safeguard the security of participants, and prevent external authorities from exerting influence on users. Cryptography technologies utilise mathematical codes to protect the storage and transfer of data values. The precise comprehension of the implementation of cryptography is exemplified in figure 5. Cryptography is a method that ensures secure transmission of data or messages between a sender and a recipient. The sender uses encryption to secure the information being delivered, utilising a designated key and algorithm. Upon receiving the transmission, the recipient decrypts it in order to retrieve the original message. Encryption keys are utilized to execute the entire cryptographic process.

Cryptography methods are crucial for ensuring the security of digital ledgers, and the hashing process preserves root hashes for every transaction. If there is any modification, the hash is completely modified, indicating that the data has been compromised.

Figure 5. Application of cryptography in blockchain

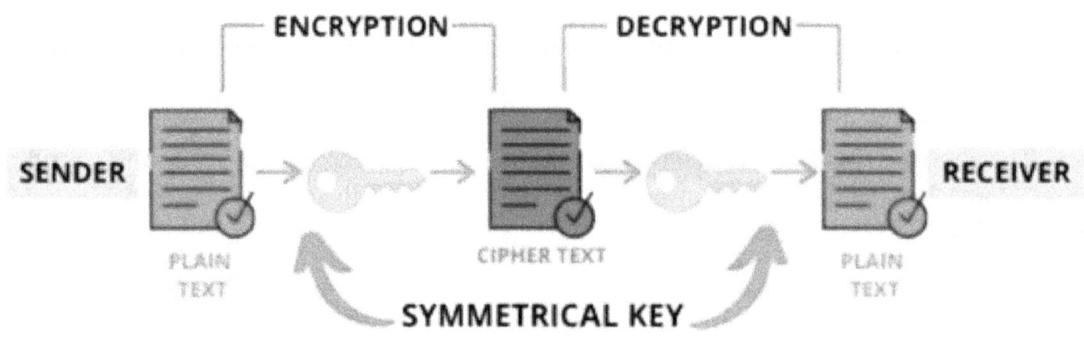

Source - *Everything you need to know about cryptography in Blockchain, LinkedIn.*
https://www.linkedin.com/pulse/everything-you-need-know-cryptography-blockchain-spydra/

Encryption guarantees the integrity of the blockchain by preventing any unauthorised modifications. Blockchain mostly employs elliptic curve encryption techniques, such as ECDSA, RSA, and DSA, to generate secure digital signatures for transactions (Zhao et al., 2019). Due to the progress of quantum computing, conventional methods can no longer provide reliable security. As a result, an increasing number of researchers are directing their attention towards developing strategies to survive quantum attacks (Dinh et al., 2011).

RECENT INSTANCES OF DATA BREACH IN THE METAVERSE

Sandbox

A recent incident involving the metaverse corporation Sandbox has revealed that an unauthorised third party gained access to an employee's computer and utilised the discovered data to initiate a phishing attempt. Sandbox is a metaverse corporation built on the Ethereum blockchain. It operates as a decentralised game ecosystem where creators may distribute and profit from voxel assets and gaming experiences.As per the Sandbox, an unauthorised individual obtained access to many email addresses and utilised them to send fraudulent emails that falsely claimed to be from the organisation. The phishing email contained a software that potentially enables the remote installation of malware on a user's computer, granting control over the machine and access to the user's personal information.The Sandbox indicated that if the recipient of the phishing email clicked on a hyperlink and their computer was infected with malware, it is possible that further personal information stored on the laptop may be accessed.

DeepFake

A recent paper from Europol looked at some potential crimes that might occur in the metaverse and how law enforcement should approach them. It also highlights how much more opportunity there will be for manipulation. In the age of computer-generated imagery, a thief just needs to replicate, or steal, the distinguishing characteristics of a specific identity to produce an impeccable DeepFake. A photographic likeness is not necessary. The false avatar's movements and facial expressions would be identical to the real one after it was taken. Because of this, it becomes difficult to trust who the 'people' in the metaverse are; you never know who you're talking to.

Criminal Possibilities

Already we have witnessed a case of deepfake last year where the deepface voice of company officials has been used to fool bank managers to transfer $35 Million to their account. Deepfakes might also be used to impersonate politicians or produce phony celebrity endorsements, which raises concerns about false information. Identity theft may be used to fabricate deep fake retaliation videos or to link individuals to dishonorable or unlawful actions. The potential for child abuse is the most concerning of all, though; for example, it might be even simpler for abusers to pose as children in order to deceive victims into believing they are safe.

Digital Avatar Assault

A digital avatar attack may or may not involve a compromise of sensitive data, although it almost always involves some sort of data. The attack's primary goal is to negatively impact the user's virtual experience rather than take their data. A digital avatar attack can inflict a great deal of mental pain, which may have real-world repercussions like anxiety or despair. Even in the unlikely event that no data is compromised, there may be harm from this psychological effect. User information such as chat logs, avatar movements, and even biometric data may be gathered in the metaverse, depending on the platform and how it functions. This information could be used to target more attacks or build a more complete picture of the victim if it is not properly secured or ends up in the wrong hands.

HOW CAN BLOCKCHAIN HELP IN PREVENTING DATA BREACHES?

The following are some ways that blockchain technology can improve metaverse security and reduce the cases related to sandbox, deepfake and digital avatar assault:

Decentralized Storage: Data can be distributed among a network of nodes using decentralized storage solutions made possible by blockchain technology. Preserving confidential data on a decentralized blockchain as opposed to one employee's PC can lower the possibility of data breaches and illegal access.

Immutable Record-Keeping: The immutability of blockchain technology guarantees that data contributed to the network cannot be removed or changed. Using this feature will make it more difficult for threat actors to alter or remove evidence of their actions by keeping an unchangeable record of user actions, transactions, and security-related events.

Identity Management: By offering a safe, decentralized identity management system, blockchain helps lower the possibility of identity theft and illegal access. Cryptographic keys kept on the blockchain allow users to regulate access permissions and maintain control over their digital identities.

Security Protocols with Smart Contracts: Smart contracts are self-executing agreements that have the conditions of the contract directly encoded into the code. Smart contracts minimize the need for centralized authorities by automatically enforcing security measures like requiring multi-factor authentication or confirming the legality of requests in the context of security standards.

Verification and Authentication: Blockchain technology can be utilized to create a verified and safe identity system. A blockchain can be used to store each user's identification, guaranteeing that only those with permission can view and change their personal data. By enforcing identity verification criteria, smart contracts on the blockchain can stop illegal deepfake impersonation. This can be especially helpful for prominent people like politicians and business executives.

Authenticity of Digital Content: A decentralized ledger for storing and authenticating digital content, such as pictures, movies, and audio files, can be made using blockchain technology. Every piece of content on the blockchain can have its time stamped and unique identifier connected to it. Users can examine a piece of content's blockchain record to confirm its legitimacy. The blockchain will display discrepancies in the data trail if the content has been altered or is a deepfake.

DRM, or digital rights management: Content providers' intellectual property can be safeguarded by implementing DRM solutions based on blockchain technology. This may deter people from producing and disseminating illicit deepfake content. In addition to guaranteeing that authors are paid for their labor, smart contracts have the ability to automatically pay royalties and stop illegal usage of their works.

Decentralized identification Management: By allowing a decentralized identification system, blockchain helps make sure that every user has a distinct and authenticated digital identity. This will lessen the possibility of harassment by making it more difficult for people to hide behind anonymous or fictitious profiles.

Immutable Records and Evidence: A safe and impenetrable record of interactions inside the metaverse can be kept thanks to the immutability of blockchain technology. Victims of harassment or assault may have a trustworthy and unchangeable record of the incident, which may be important for reporting to authorities or for legal purposes.

Consent and Boundaries with Smart Contracts: In virtual worlds, smart contracts can be used to create and enforce limits and consent. When users establish guidelines for appropriate conduct, smart contracts may automatically impose penalties—like alerting moderators or restricting the offender's access—when these guidelines are broken.

CONCLUSION

Users interact with real-time interactions with online environments and one another within the Metaverse, a virtual shared location. Metaverse is constantly changing and offers enormous possibilities but with significant risks. The Metaverse's user data is vulnerable, as evidenced by recent data breaches, which calls for strong security protocols. With its ability to improve security and safeguard user privacy through the use of decentralized networks, smart contracts, cryptographic algorithms, and decentralized identification and authentication protocols, blockchain technology presents a possible solution. These developments guarantee that users can interact safely and securely in this immersive virtual world as the Metaverse evolves.

REFERENCES

Ali, O., Jaradat, A., Kulakli, A., & Abuhalimeh, A. (2021). A comparative study: Blockchain technology utilization benefits, challenges and functionalities. *IEEE Access : Practical Innovations, Open Solutions*, *9*, 12730–12749. doi:10.1109/ACCESS.2021.3050241

Asaithambi, S., Ravi, L., Kotb, H., Milyani, A. H., Azhari, A. A., Nallusamy, S., Varadarajan, V., & Vairavasundaram, S. (2022). An Energy-Efficient and Blockchain-Integrated Software Defined Network for the Industrial Internet of Things. *Sensors (Basel)*, *22*(20), 7917. doi:10.3390/s22207917 PMID:36298266

Bian, Y., Leng, J., & Zhao, J. L. (2021, December). Demystifying metaverse as a new paradigm of enterprise digitization. In *International Conference on Big Data* (pp. 109-119). Cham: Springer International Publishing.

Casino, F., Dasaklis, T. K., & Patsakis, C. (2019). A systematic literature review of blockchain-based applications: Current status, classification and open issues. *Telematics and Informatics*, *36*, 55–81. doi:10.1016/j.tele.2018.11.006

Di Pietro, R., & Cresci, S. (2021, December). Metaverse: security and privacy issues. In *2021 Third IEEE International Conference on Trust, Privacy and Security in Intelligent Systems and Applications (TPS-ISA)* (pp. 281-288). IEEE.

Dincelli, E., & Yayla, A. (2022). Immersive virtual reality in the age of the Metaverse: A hybrid-narrative review based on the technology affordance perspective. *The Journal of Strategic Information Systems*, *31*(2), 101717. doi:10.1016/j.jsis.2022.101717

Dinh, H., Moore, C., & Russell, A. (2011). McEliece and Niederreiter cryptosystems that resist quantum Fourier sampling attacks. *Advances in Cryptology–CRYPTO 2011: 31st Annual Cryptology Conference, Santa Barbara, CA, USA, August 14-18, 2011 Proceedings*, *31*, 761–779.

Falchuk, B., Loeb, S., & Neff, R. (2018). The social metaverse: Battle for privacy. *IEEE Technology and Society Magazine*, *37*(2), 52–61. doi:10.1109/MTS.2018.2826060

Fox, J., Gilbert, M., & Tang, W. Y. (2018). Player experiences in a massively multiplayer online game: A diary study of performance, motivation, and social interaction. *New Media & Society*, *20*(11), 4056–4073. doi:10.1177/1461444818767102

Hassan, M. U., Rehmani, M. H., & Chen, J. (2019). Privacy preservation in blockchain based IoT systems: Integration issues, prospects, challenges, and future research directions. *Future Generation Computer Systems*, *97*, 512–529. doi:10.1016/j.future.2019.02.060

Hughes, I. (2022). The metaverse: Is it the future? *Itnow*, *64*(1), 22–23. doi:10.1093/itnow/bwac011

Jabbar, R., Fetais, N., Krichen, M., & Barkaoui, K. (2020, February). Blockchain technology for healthcare: Enhancing shared electronic health record interoperability and integrity. In 2020 IEEE International Conference on Informatics, IoT, and Enabling Technologies (ICIoT) (pp. 310-317). IEEE.

Jovanović, A., & Milosavljević, A. (2022). VoRtex Metaverse platform for gamified collaborative learning. *Electronics (Basel)*, *11*(3), 317. doi:10.3390/electronics11030317

Kiong, L. V. (2022). *Metaverse Made Easy: A Beginner's Guide to the Metaverse: Everything you need to know about Metaverse*. NFT and GameFi.

Ko, S. Y., Chung, H. K., Kim, J. I., & Shin, Y. (2021). A study on the typology and advancement of cultural leisure-based metaverse. *KIPS Transactions on Software and Data Engineering*, *10*(8), 331–338.

Kozinets, R. V. (2022). Immersive netnography: A novel method for service experience research in virtual reality, augmented reality and metaverse contexts. *Journal of Service Management*, *34*(1), 100–125. doi:10.1108/JOSM-12-2021-0481

Kumar, N. M., & Mallick, P. K. (2018). Blockchain technology for security issues and challenges in IoT. *Procedia Computer Science*, *132*, 1815–1823. doi:10.1016/j.procs.2018.05.140

Kumar, P., Kumar, R., Srivastava, G., Gupta, G. P., Tripathi, R., Gadekallu, T. R., & Xiong, N. N. (2021). PPSF: A privacy-preserving and secure framework using blockchain-based machine-learning for IoT-driven smart cities. *IEEE Transactions on Network Science and Engineering*, *8*(3), 2326–2341. doi:10.1109/TNSE.2021.3089435

Kye, B., Han, N., Kim, E., Park, Y., & Jo, S. (2021). Educational applications of metaverse: Possibilities and limitations. *Journal of Educational Evaluation for Health Professions*, *18*, 18. doi:10.3352/jeehp.2021.18.32 PMID:34897242

Lau, K. W. (2014). The gender differences in metaverse: a study of university art & design students. Open Journal of Art and Communication, 1(1), 14-19.

Liu, H., Yao, X., Yang, T., & Ning, H. (2018). Cooperative privacy preservation for wearable devices in hybrid computing-based smart health. *IEEE Internet of Things Journal*, *6*(2), 1352–1362. doi:10.1109/JIOT.2018.2843561

Luo, Y., Su, Z., Zheng, W., Chen, Z., Wang, F., Zhang, Z., & Chen, J. (2021). A novel memory-hard password hashing scheme for blockchain-based cyberphysical systems. *ACM Transactions on Internet Technology*, *21*(2), 1–21. doi:10.1145/3408310

Malik, S., Dedeoglu, V., Kanhere, S. S., & Jurdak, R. (2019, July). Trustchain: Trust management in blockchain and iot supported supply chains. In *2019 IEEE International Conference on Blockchain (Blockchain)* (pp. 184-193). IEEE. 10.1109/Blockchain.2019.00032

Mandal, A. (2023, May 17). The role of Blockchain in Building Trust and security in the metaverse. LinkedIn. https://www.linkedin.com/pulse/role-blockchainbuilding-trust-security-metaverse-ankit-mand al/

Mingxiao, D., Xiaofeng, M., Zhe, Z., Xiangwei, W., & Qijun, C. (2017, October). A review on consensus algorithm of blockchain. In 2017 IEEE international conference on systems, man, and cybernetics (SMC) (pp. 2567-2572). IEEE.

Mourtzis, D. (Ed.). (2021). *Design and operation of production networks for mass personalization in the era of cloud technology*. Elsevier.

Mystakidis, S. (2022). Metaverse. *Metaverse. Encyclopedia*, *2*(1), 486–497. doi:10.3390/encyclopedia2010031

Nakamoto, S. (2008). Bitcoin: A peer-to-peer electronic cash system. Decentralized business review.

Nguyen, C. T., Hoang, D. T., Nguyen, D. N., & Dutkiewicz, E. (2022, June). Metachain: A novel blockchain-based framework for metaverse applications. In 2022 IEEE 95th Vehicular Technology Conference:(VTC2022-Spring) (pp. 1-5). IEEE. 10.1109/VTC2022-Spring54318.2022.9860983

Rahman, M. S., Chamikara, M. A. P., Khalil, I., & Bouras, A. (2022). Blockchain-of-blockchains: An interoperable blockchain platform for ensuring IoT data integrity in smart city. *Journal of Industrial Information Integration*, *30*, 100408. doi:10.1016/j.jii.2022.100408

Rajawat, A. S., Goyal, S. B., Goyal, A., Rajawat, K., Raboaca, M. S., Verma, C., & Mihaltan, T. C. (2023, June). Enhancing Security and Scalability of Metaverse with Blockchain-based Consensus Mechanisms. In 2023 15th International Conference on Electronics, Computers and Artificial Intelligence (ECAI) (pp. 1-6). IEEE. 10.1109/ECAI58194.2023.10194035

Spydra. (2023) Everything you need to know about cryptography in Blockchain, LinkedIn. Available at: https://www.linkedin.com/pulse/everything-you-need-knowcryptography-blockchain-spydra/

Stephenson, N. (2003). *Snow Crash: A Novel.* Random House Publishing Group.

Vora, J., Italiya, P., Tanwar, S., Tyagi, S., Kumar, N., Obaidat, M. S., & Hsiao, K. F. (2018, July). Ensuring privacy and security in e-health records. In 2018 International conference on computer, information and telecommunication systems (CITS) (pp. 1-5). IEEE. 10.1109/CITS.2018.8440164

Wang, X., Liu, X., Cheng, C. T., Deng, L., Chen, X., & Xiao, F. (2021). A joint user scheduling and trajectory planning data collection strategy for the UAVassisted WSN. *IEEE Communications Letters, 25*(7), 2333–2337. doi:10.1109/LCOMM.2021.3067898

Wang, Y., Su, Z., Ni, J., Zhang, N., & Shen, X. (2021). Blockchain-empowered space-air-ground integrated networks: Opportunities, challenges, and solutions. *IEEE Communications Surveys and Tutorials, 24*(1), 160–209. doi:10.1109/COMST.2021.3131711

Wang, Y., Su, Z., Zhang, N., Xing, R., Liu, D., Luan, T. H., & Shen, X. (2022). A survey on metaverse: Fundamentals, security, and privacy. *IEEE Communications Surveys and Tutorials.*

What are smart contracts on Blockchain? IBM. (n.d.).https://www.ibm.com/topics/smart-contracts

Whitfield, B. (2023, March 23). What is a consensus mechanism? Built In. https://builtin.com/blockchain/consensus-mechanism

Xia, Q., Sifah, E. B., Smahi, A., Amofa, S., & Zhang, X. (2017). BBDS: Blockchain-based data sharing for electronic medical records in cloud environments. *Information (Basel), 8*(2), 44. doi:10.3390/info8020044

Yang, D., Zhou, J., Chen, R., Song, Y., Song, Z., Zhang, X., ... & Bai, C. (2022). Expert consensus on the metaverse in medicine. Clinical eHealth, 5, 1-9.

Yu, K., Tan, L., Aloqaily, M., Yang, H., & Jararweh, Y. (2021). Blockchainenhanced data sharing with traceable and direct revocation in IIoT. *IEEE Transactions on Industrial Informatics, 17*(11), 7669–7678. doi:10.1109/TII.2021.3049141

Zhang, Q., Jiang, X., & Zheng, Y. (2023). Blockchain adoption and gray markets in a global supply chain. *Omega, 115*, 102785. doi:10.1016/j.omega.2022.102785

Zhao, Y. (2019, July). Practical aggregate signature from general elliptic curves, and applications to blockchain. In *Proceedings of the 2019 ACM Asia Conference on Computer and Communications Security* (pp. 529-538). 10.1145/3321705.3329826

Zheng, Z., Xie, S., Dai, H. N., Chen, W., Chen, X., Weng, J., & Imran, M. (2020). An overview on smart contracts: Challenges, advances and platforms. *Future Generation Computer Systems, 105*, 475–491. doi:10.1016/j.future.2019.12.019

Chapter 13
The Metaverse Revolution:
Digital Strategies for Indian Industries in Post-COVID-19 Era

Kirti Sharma
https://orcid.org/0000-0001-5322-8998
Punjabi University, India

Sachin Dev
Baba Farid College of Management and Technology, India

Nomita Dey
https://orcid.org/0009-0004-7378-9687
Chandigarh University, India

ABSTRACT

The most important development in recent decades, according to many, is the digital transformation, which had a profound impact on our personal, social, and economic realms of existence and similarly accelerated the digital transformation of industries worldwide. The objective aimed to construct a solid knowledge base by connecting the Metaverse to digital strategies and demonstrating how they directly pertain to the complicated network of Indian businesses. Indian firms, after the COVID-19 paradigm change, have reached a critical point where the integration of digital strategies and the Metaverse offers a unique potential for transformation. As a lighthouse, this chapter provides stakeholders with a comprehensive strategy for navigating the intricate post-COVID-19 Indian industry landscape. It portrays the concept of the driving force underlying the development of a new business paradigm by emphasizing the ever-changing relationship that exists between the proactive adoption of Metaverse apps and the tactical use of digital strategies.

INTRODUCTION

The dynamic interplay between emerging technologies, innovative solutions, and the ever-evolving digital landscape defines the essence of this research. There is a significant global transformation taking

DOI: 10.4018/979-8-3693-2422-6.ch013

place within the ever-expanding digital world (Kiya.ai, 2023). This aspect is based on digital resources characterized by blockchain-enabled interrelated digital spaces. The metaverse will be the basis for this amazing shift. It has been recognized by many organizations adopting innovative strategies that Metaverse is where businesses are built between tradition and innovation (Metaverse Business Guide, 2022). An amazing fusion of statistics and facts results in an excellent digital cocktail mix (Sadiku et al., 2019). These are guidelines that have been highlighted as far as this wonderful growing field is concerned. They can access unlimited amounts of knowledge and expertise through strong business platforms and innovative technologies (Hinings et al., 2018). Digital transformation has always been fundamental to this shifting landscape. This article delves into the heart of India's economic growth, which has been greatly accelerated by rapid advancements in digital technology (Chung, 2020). Case studies reports, literature reviews, and some credible references are some of the sources of information for use in a research article.

Our research provides a glimpse at the way Indian firms evolved by utilizing the Metaverse's capabilities in order to control complications arose due to Covid. At the core of our discoveries lies an important realization—the adoption of the Metaverse requires more than embracing it; it calls for changes to infrastructure by enhancing interrelation, boosting possibilities and intelligently employing personnel. The transformation observed in how Indian companies operate, collaborate and innovate serves as evidence for the impact that the Metaverse can have. Recognizing both the limitations of existing sources and the rapid evolution of both strategies and the Metaverse itself, this study aims to provide guidance for entrepreneurs, policymakers and industry leaders. It reveals the real-world consequences, initial effects and unique chances urging companies to navigate and actively shape the emerging environment. As our journey through the digital Metaverse and India's economic landscape culminates, we stand at the precipice of an odyssey both profound and exhilarating. The Metaverse beckons as an uncharted realm ripe with opportunities and rife with challenges. It is becoming clearer that the Metaverse is not a result of progress; it has the power to bring together the physical and digital realms creating a significant impact. The main goal of this study is to conduct a thorough investigation of the revolutionary potential that the Metaverse holds for Indian enterprises in the complex post-COVID-19 environment. The Covid-19 has brought the world economy to a standstill, causing a complete upheaval in market trends (Jindal & Gambhir, 2022). This comprehensive study develops with a few interconnected goals, each of which adds to the overall comprehension of this transformative journey. This entails a thorough investigation of the difficulties and requirements that have motivated this important change. By examining how the Metaverse and digital strategies are changing business models, improving customer experiences, and affecting market dynamics, the research ultimately aims to shed light on the all-encompassing impact of these transformative forces on the complex fabric of top Indian industries and advance our understanding of how the Indian business landscape is evolving.

The results of the study highlight the Metaverse's revolutionary influence on the Indian industries by employing the large body of secondary data sources, particularly in the post-COVID period. It is understood that extensive infrastructure development is a critical requirement for fully using the business Metaverse's potential. After the pandemic, the need for dependable connection, powerful processing capacity, and a competent workforce increased as distant work and virtual collaboration became crucial. The way Indian companies function and interact with their customers is changing, virtual workspaces and data-driven solutions are at the forefront of this change. These developments, although encouraging, also highlight the critical need for strong data security measures, reinforcing the protection of private data and encouraging user confidence inside the Metaverse. The research findings highlight the significant market potential that the Metaverse offers for Indian companies, positioning early adopters as industry leaders and redefining the sector's future by bridging the gap between the physical and digital worlds through revolutionary technologies and innovative digital strategies. The final result is a valuable collection of revelations that serves as a source of light for aspiring entrepreneurs, researchers, policymakers, industry leaders, technology innovators, venture capitalists, educators and academics, start-up incubators, market analysts, futurists, social impact organizations, legal and regulatory authorities, media and journalists.

REVIEW OF LITERATURE

From economic shifts to cutting-edge technology, these insights shed light on how Metaverse integrates with digital strategies in the context of Indian industries in post-Covid era. However, it's worth noting that there is a scarcity of literature on this specific intersection. Below, we present a chronological overview of our literature review findings.

Parviainen et al. (2017) conducted an in-depth analysis of digitalization, focusing on the essential layers of process, organization, and business domain. This research highlighted that digitalization extends beyond the mere digitization of existing processes and outputs. It highlighted the importance to successfully monitor this transformational process in order to avail the benefits.

During the tumultuous times of the COVID-19 pandemic in 2020, a qualitative analysis examined how Small and Medium-sized Enterprises (SMEs) confronted challenges and leveraged digital transformation strategies. The research identified three primary approaches adopted by SMEs as they embarked on their digitalization journey: expediting digitalization, digitalizing sales functions, and forging strategic partnerships with digital entities to access new markets (Priyono et al., 2020).

Furthermore, another study provides a forward-looking assessment of the post-COVID-19 environment, anticipating a significant increase in internationally dispersed virtual teams. The report forecasts an unprecedented shift with the impending integration of augmented and virtual realities into collaborative workspaces through a thorough analysis of various technical options. The amalgamation of the research findings provides an in-depth understanding of the changing course toward sophisticated collaborative frameworks in the future. The research explores possible advantages and difficulties of implementing augmented and virtual reality in global cooperation as we navigate this ever-changing landscape. Higher connection improved operational. Among the expected improvements are efficiency and a paradigm shift towards immersive collaboration. These technological advancements present an opportunity to remove geographical constraints, improve real-time communication, and increase productivity in virtual teams as a whole. However, the report also underlines the importance of dealing with potential difficulties. For instance, these may range from variations in technology that impact accessibility to intricacies involved in adapting to a virtual work environment by individuals (Alon, 2020).

A literature review by the OECD tries to better understand the disruptive consequences aggravated by COVID-19 by examining how Artificial Intelligence (AI), Machine Learning (ML) and Big Data connect in the banking industry. It notes that the financial sector has been digitizing for some time but argues that the present pandemic has not only hastened but also exacerbated this trend. This study brings together various academic publications, industry papers, and empirical research that discuss how fintech is transforming finance. It explains the remarkable surge in AI, ML, and Big Data adoption in financial operations as a result of needing to overcome challenges posed by COVID-19 pandemic (2021). The literature synthesis is organized to show how these technology developments are causing a paradigm change in the financial industry rather than just being a reaction to the crisis.

In the same year, 2019, research focusing on Indian small and medium-sized enterprises (SMEs) revealed a clear negative relationship between accounts receivables and SME profitability while there was also an identifiable positive link between inventory levels and accounts payables.

Another study comprised an in-depth analysis of the literature having the objective of illuminating the processes for creating worth as well as how companies implemented AI technology in their operations. Using a determined procedure, this study review hopes to extract critical frameworks, examples, and insights from different reliable sources. Through this cautious examination, the survey looks to both expand how we could interpret the multifaceted collaboration between artificial intelligence (AI) and business and to be an essential asset for businesses addressing an evolving panorama of technological integration for long-term business benefit (Enholm et al., 2022).

Additionally, Rana et al. (2022) analyzed the techniques used by Indian B-schools in order to deal with the challenges ocurred by the covid-19 pandemic and the potential crises it can bring. It emphasized both short-term and long-term modifications, outlining their approaches. The report sheds light on the ground-breaking initiatives taking place, such as the financial investments in digital infrastructure and creative approaches to education.

This review of the literature extensively examines the well-established relationship between Digital Transformation (DT) and the propagation of technological innovation within the organizational structures. The study diligently explores the collection of literature demonstrating DT's vital function in stimulating innovation, starting with a wide range of scholarly articles, empirical research, and industry observations. An overview of the literature demonstrates a consistent trend wherein organizations executing digital transformation projects experience a substantial increase in technological advancements. It examines all aspects of the connection through an examination at how the adoption of transformative digital technology influences organizational structures, processes, and ideologies for encouraging innovation. Instances of how DT has acted as a stimulant to encourage businesses to come up with inventive and unique solutions are demonstrated via case studies and actual data (Ramos et al., 2022).

Various studies have investigated the fundamental impact caused by digitalization on organizations and the overall economy, highlighting important considerations for sustainable modification and advancement (Cheng et al., 2022).

Additionally, further studies highlighted the significance of a thorough comprehension of the metaverse and underlined several aspects associated with its theories, history, creation, and future prospects. The findings have indicated that, even though having a promising future, the metaverse is still in its initial stages of development owing to a lack of commercial knowledge, a lack of technological advances, and the expensive cost of software and hardware (Huang et al., 2022).

In conclusion, studies suggest that society is headed toward greater automation and technological development. A prime example of the transformative potential of virtual worlds is the Metaverse, which has been described to have a number of advantages, including ease of use, cost savings, productivity, innovation, and environmental friendliness. The reader is provided with current knowledge on the state of technology today by this comprehensive study, which also persuasively illustrates how technology has the potential to fundamentally change relationships between people.

In addition, a framework of concepts along with associated theories have been employed by Yawised et al. (2022) to evaluate the implications of business transformation and engagement with the world of Metaverse This research evaluated multiple facets of organizational efficiency, covering targets, objectives, methods of implementation, opportunities, and problems. By doing so, it revealed how companies can boost their adaptability by leveraging thematic qualitative evaluation as an effective method that can assist companies shift their organizational investments and competences to the digital environment - is referred to as the Metaverse.

Bushell (2022) undertook research that presented an understanding of the potential applications of Metaverse for people and corporations seeking to broaden their virtual reality reach and interact with others.

A survey delves deeply into the numerous applications of big data technology in important industries, such as transportation, e-health, business, finance, and the emerging Metaverse. This survey's comprehensive evaluation explores the emergence of virtual platforms, particularly the Metaverse, in addition to the application of big data technology. Artificial Intelligence (AI) stands out as a key field in the present technological landscape, influencing almost every facet of our modern existence. The evaluation underlines how essential technology is, especially when determining the direction for future augmented realities including the one called the Metaverse (Zhang et al., 2023).

RESEARCH GAP

While existing literature extensively examines the digital transformation's influence on businesses, there's a distinct scarcity of research focusing on the Metaverse's implications especially in emerging economies like India. This study endeavors to fill this void by investigating how Indian enterprises are adapting to the Metaverse. The research addresses the need for specific insights into the Metaverse's landscape and its applications in Indian Industries.

OBJECTIVES OF THE STUDY

The following are the research objectives (RO) of the study:

RO 1: To investigate the Metaverse landscape and understand its integration with digital strategies in the different industries.

RO 2: To examine Metaverse and its applications in top Indian Industries in Post-COVID era

RESEARCH METHODOLOGY

The research methodology encompasses a comprehensive literature review, secondary data analysis and expert insights. Our research approach is akin to embarking on an archaeological expedition, where we carefully extract precious insights from existing literature, industrial published reports, informative case studies, authentic websites and business magazines. These sources, like ancient artifacts, hold the keys to understanding the Metaverse and digital strategies and their relevance in the Indian context. While we did not engage in the collection of primary data, our role is that of a curator, assembling and showcasing existing knowledge to provide a holistic understanding.

FINDINGS AND DISCUSSION

In this section, we present key findings from this research and engage in a descriptive discussion regarding the Metaverse revolution.

Embarking on a Captivating Exploration of the Metaverse Concept

The findings from the study outline the Metaverse's substantial impact on India's businesses in the days following the COVID-19 pandemic, revealing a complex integration into digital strategy. The Metaverse is bringing immersive virtual shopping experiences and augmented reality (AR) apps to the retail and e-commerce businesses, reconsidering the traditional ways of consumer contact. As conventional education is replaced by dynamic virtual classrooms and collaborative platforms from the Metaverse, the educational environment changes considerably. In the healthcare sector, the Metaverse is a pathfinder because it provides virtual medical consultations and dynamic training simulations. Real estate embraces the Metaverse and gives potential buyers virtual options for property research to get over geographical restrictions. The entertainment and gaming industries are undergoing a massive upheaval due to virtual events and in-game economies that change user experiences totally. Combined together, the above findings demonstrate the crucial part the Metaverse performs in fostering innovative development as well as establishing unparalleled degrees of connections across various sectors, positioning India at the cutting edge of the global digital transformation.

Finally, the outcomes of the research illustrate how the metaphysical world is a promoter for groundbreaking innovation across a range of Indian businesses. With the potential to fundamentally change healthcare delivery, educational paradigms, real estate and entertainment, and even customer interactions in e-commerce, the world of the Metaverse is positioned as a cornerstone of India's digital growth. As companies continue to explore the constantly expanding Metaverse, India has established the benchmark for innovation, connection, and immersive experiences in the global technological revolution. It does this by using these breakthrough technologies.

India's Metaverse Aspirations: Fusing Real and Virtual Worlds in the Metaverse

Leading India's technical advancement is Kiya.ai, a pioneering company focused on artificial intelligence (AI) and new technologies. At the prestigious VivaTech conference in Paris in 2023, held within the India Pavilion, Bharatmeta (India's Innovative Leap into the Metaverse) made an enduring mark with its futuristic soar into the Metaverse (Kiya.ai, 2023).

Bharatmeta's audacious mission is to bridge the chasm between the physical and digital worlds, offering tangible banking, business, culture and teamwork within the Metaverse. Harnessing India's robust digital infrastructure encompassing digital payments, open commerce, identification systems, Bharatmeta is primed to be inclusive and accessible across a spectrum of devices, from XR headsets to mobile handsets and kiosks. This groundbreaking initiative underscores India's unwavering commitment to embracing transformative technological frontiers on a global scale.

Understanding Metaverse Integration With Digital Strategies in the Different Industries

Around $120 billion had been invested in the development of metaverse technological infrastructure in the first half of 2022, as investors continued to pour money into the platform's growth at an astounding rate.

As the Metaverse platform becomes prominent, big brand businesses are moving quickly to be the first to use it for promotional purposes. With the metaverse, some brands have already stepped forward which will be explicated further:

Facebook has rebranded itself and is actively building the metaverse. They are also promoting it by taking over some other widely used social media applications such as Instagram and WhatsApp. Facebook's Metaverse features virtual workrooms for digital professionals, virtual reality games, and providing a creative platform to individuals with magnificent skills. Facebook has also launched a variety of accessories (including a headgear and a pair of smart glasses) in collaboration with Ray-Ban.

Snapchat and TikTok have already started to provide AR experiences with various filters.

Samsung developed a treasure hunt on the platform where players could compete to win a Galaxy S22, while **Coca-Cola** introduced a special edition beverage inside the metaverse. To honour International Friendship Day, the business did this and held an online auction for virtual wearables within the "Friendship Box" on the decentraland platform along with a Friendship Card, a recognizable Bubble Jacket, and a sound visualizer.

Gucci is one of the most renowned and luxury brands which is also trying its hands on the metaverse's online marketplace. Formerly, Gucci launched the Gucci Virtual 25, an exclusive pair of digital sneakers. Later on, it designed the Roblox Gucci Garden, a virtual environment that replicates the Gucci Garden Archetypes in Florence, Italy.

Balenciaga, A designer pickaxe, accessories, a backpack, and a series of four Fortnite skins were all launched by this luxurious clothing brand. Also, the company created a Balenciaga Hub with a virtual shop in the Fortnite game.

Nike offers a virtual version of their Nike Dunk sneakers called Crypto kicks for sale. Fans of Nike from all around the world were invited to create an avatar and play sports games to win prizes in this metaverse.

Further industries navigating metaverse such as:

Retail and E-Commerce: Within the Metaverse's dynamic landscape, the retail and e-commerce sectors find themselves at the forefront of innovation, capitalizing on the immense potential of virtual stores and immersive shopping experience.

Gaming and Entertainment: In the constantly evolving Metaverse ecosystem, the gaming and entertainment industry takes center stage, harnessing the immersive capabilities of this digital realm.

Real Estate: Stepping into the Metaverse, real estate enterprises embark on a journey of virtual property investment—a realm offering boundless opportunities and challenges. These encompass the discerning pursuit of virtual land acquisition, the meticulous planning and execution of property development endeavors, and the adept management of rental income streams, all meticulously choreographed within the immersive tapestry of the virtual landscape.

Supply Chain: Across industries, supply chains extend their tendrils into the expansive canvas of the Metaverse—a domain of unparalleled digital intricacy.

Digital Marketing: The metaverse, an advancement in social technology, enables avatars—digital representations of people—to communicate with one another in a range of contexts. The metaverse offers a place for infinite, connected virtual communities using virtual reality (VR) equipment, augmented reality (AR) glasses, smartphone applications, or other devices, whether it be at work, in an office, attending concerts or sporting events, or even putting on clothing.

It is apparent about the virtual environment which takes place exclusively in artificial reality. In fact, there will be instances when the actual and virtual worlds intersect. This type of marketing will transform a way from bland media, such as text and video where natural and intuitive experiences are injected into a user's environment as customers can try out the company's product and services just like the way they would in reality.

Metaverse and Its Applications in Top Indian Industries in Post-COVID-19 Era

In particular in a post-COVID environment, the analysis reveals significant and important practical implications for the Indian industries. Businesses must prioritize infrastructure development at the top of their list of goals, which should include improved connectivity, more computational capacity, and strategic talent acquisition, in order to fully realize the Metaverse's potential for innovation and competition. Adaptation is essential as the environment changes, with a focus on integrating virtual workspaces and data-driven solutions to improve operational efficiency, particularly in light of the pandemic's profoundly transformational effects. Data security has grown crucial due to the rising reliance on virtual platforms, mandating the tight application of cyber security standards and raising user knowledge of online safety. Additionally, after the COVID-19 paradigm shift, Indian companies have a unique opportunity to distinguish themselves as market leaders by proactively embracing Metaverse applications. By doing so, they will be able to navigate and even shape the rapidly changing digital landscape while bridging the gap between the physical and digital worlds. Substantial modifications to business operations were brought about by the COVID-19 epidemic and the lockdowns that followed in many regions of the world. Enterprise executives convened, generated ideas, made choices, recruited, acquired, sold, and carried out numerous other facets of their business activities using digital channels. This sharp rise in virtual activity brought attention to the metaverse, a relatively new participant in the digital space with the potential to revolutionize industry.

In 2023, it is expected that the Metaverse Digital Media segment would generate US$16.99 million in revenue in India. A predicted market volume of US$40.44m by 2030 is the result of revenue growing at a projected annual rate of 13.19% (CAGR 2023-2030). The majority of revenue is produced in the United States, which is expected to have a market volume of US$188.10m in 2023. By 2030, there will likely be 1.61 million users in the Metaverse Digital Media category (statista, 2023). Businesses in India and throughout the world are moving toward the metaverse. Several Indian businesses, including technology, media and telecommunication (TMT), financial services (FS), pharmaceuticals and healthcare, retail and consumer goods, industrial products, government, automotive, and education technologies, are traversing the metaverse (PWC). The path to the digital future is being paved by Indian businesses like Tanishq, MakeMyTrip, and Mahindra & Mahindra, who have entered the metaverse such as:

HCL Technologies Ltd. (HCL) is an information technology company that specializes in creating robust mobile and immersive technology products and solutions. The idea started with the vision that offer every consumer access to a personal electronic gadget equipped with the newest technology. The corporation is currently using such technologies to evolve cell phones and connect them virtually by entering the metaverse age. The company's Viverse platform, which combines AI, AR, and VR to allow users to build their own virtual places and conduct NFT transactions, is the prominent feature.

Tata Consultancy Services (TCS) is an IT consulting company that provides business, technology, and engineering services with a cognitive-driven approach. The startup created a platform called Ava-presence, which combines the terms ``avatar” and “presence,” and uses blockchain, cloud computing, IoT, XR, and AI to assist customers.

Infosys Ltd (Infosys) is a technology-enabled business solution. Infosys offers a broad range of services, including business consulting, outsourcing, and technology-related services. Infosys has developed an augmented reality (AR)-based solution for the industrial sector that facilitates workers’ maintenance and repair of sophisticated machinery.

Wipro has developed a VR-based retail industry that allows customers to virtually try on clothing and accessories. Wipro has developed a manufacturing solution based on augmented reality (AR) that allows engineers to collaborate and troubleshoot complex machinery in real time.

Deloitte: With next-generation tactics, instruments, and technologies that can build and link virtual worlds for the industrial, corporate, and consumer settings, Deloitte assists customers in comprehending and capitalizing on the next big wave upending company and society. The most cutting-edge computational infrastructure is created for customers by Deloitte specialists using modern technologies like blockchain, IoT, AI, and metaverse.

Capgemini India Pvt Ltd (Capgemini) is an information technology consulting organization that focuses on engineering and technology professional services. The firm is moving toward the metaverse in order to give its clients a premium interface that will allow them to construct complex apps with blockchain-related features. To enhance the client experience and work on revolutionary technologies, Capgemini maintains a dedicated metaverse lab.

Maruti Suzuki: One of the leading automobiles companies in India, Maruti Suzuki, has revealed that its portfolio of vehicles will now have immersive experiences available in dealerships that are based on the metaverse. In January 2023, Maruti Suzuki revealed plans to unveil its own Metaverse, named ExpoVerse, in a massive pavilion at the Auto Expo. The virtual pavilion at Auto Expo 23 will offer a fully immersive experience for all product presentations and other experiential areas. Its strategy for launching its own Metaverse: Their initiative will link and make the Auto Expo available to everyone who chooses to attend, regardless of location.

Mahindra and Mahindra: Mahindra has unveiled XUV400verse, the metaverse platform for the all-electric XUV400. According to Mahindra, the platform will offer an immersive product experience while enabling users to interact, contribute, and socialize. XUV400verse includes a product and accessory zone, an LED wall with spatial sound interactive avatars, and a virtual showroom with guided and unguided options. Customers may create their own SUVs and avatars by using the 3D creation tool. The software will also provide virtual test drives with many camera angles and customization possibilities.

Hero MotoCorp Limited: formerly known as Hero Honda Motors is the world’s foremost manufacturer of two-wheelers. Hero MotoCorp was the first Indian two-wheeler company to establish a production facility in Latin America. In April 2021, Hero MotoCorp launched a “Virtual Showroom” function to give customers a more engaging online shopping experience. Thanks to augmented reality, Hero MotoCorp will be able to provide its customers with a 360-degree shopping experience. Customers will be able to learn about, interact with, and purchase Hero’s motorcycles and scooters through a seamless digital experience provided by the Virtual Showroom.

CONCLUSION, LIMITATIONS, AND RECOMMENDATIONS

As it continues to gain prominence, it presents businesses with a novel frontier where commerce, and assets management converge. India, a digital example, serves as a prime representation of the global shift towards a digital economy, with over 70% of its GDP driven by digital activities. Furthermore, the paper explored the transformative impact of digitalization of businesses and the broader economy and discussed how digitization extends beyond mere digitization and highlighted implications of technology. Although the primary data collection was not a part of our research, the information that is already available shows that organizations who have adopted digital strategies are in a good position. Improved online interactions and customized experiences lead to increased client engagement. Operations that have been streamlined are more effective and less expensive. Businesses are able to quickly shift course in reaction to market developments because of improved flexibility. Data security, however, continues to be a major obstacle, and the Metaverse's developing rules demand close monitoring.

Despite our in-depth analysis of the relevant secondary data, it is essential to understand that relying solely on these sources could be seen as a limitation. Additionally, because the Metaverse and digital tactics are evolving so quickly, our study may not be up to date with these fields' most recent advancements. Our research contributes value by illuminating how Indian companies have changed in the age of the Metaverse. This study adds fresh perspectives to the body of current literature in the field of the integration of the Metaverse and digital strategies in the context of Indian industries. The present study provides a distinctive viewpoint on how Indian industries are handling this rapidly changing world. A fresh perspective on how the Metaverse and digital strategies intersect in the context of Indian business is offered by the synthesis of current information.

REFERENCES

Alon, I. (2020). COVID-19 and International Business: A Viewpoint. *FIIB Business Review*, *9*(2), 75–77. doi:10.1177/2319714520923579

Belhaj, M., & Hachaıchi, Y. (2021). *Artificial Intelligence*. Machine Learning and Big Data in Finance Opportunities, Challenges, and Implications for Policy Makers.

BushellC. (2022). The Impact of Metaverse on Branding and Marketing. SSRN. doi:10.2139/ssrn.4144628

Castillo, M. J., & Taherdoost, H. (2023). The Impact of AI Technologies on E-Business. *Encyclopedia*, *3*(1), 107–121. doi:10.3390/encyclopedia3010009

Cheng, X., Zhang, S., Fu, S., Liu, W., Guan, C., Mou, J., Ye, Q., & Huang, C. (2022). Exploring the metaverse in the digital economy: An overview and research framework. *Journal of Electronic Business & Digital Economics*, *1*(1/2), 206–224. doi:10.1108/JEBDE-09-2022-0036

Enholm, I. M., Papagiannidis, E., Mikalef, P., & Krogstie, J. (2022). Artificial Intelligence and Business Value: A Literature Review. *Information Systems Frontiers*, *24*(5), 1709–1734. doi:10.1007/s10796-021-10186-w

Firmansyah, E. A., & Umar, U. H. (2023). Metaverse in business research: A systematic literature review. *Cogent Business & Management, 10*(2), 2. doi:10.1080/23311975.2023.2222499

Hinings, B., Gegenhuber, T., & Greenwood, R. (2018). Digital innovation and transformation: An institutional perspective. *Information and Organization, 28*(1), 52–61. doi:10.1016/j.infoandorg.2018.02.004

Huang, J., Sun, P., & Zhang, W. (2022). *Analysis of the Future Prospects for the Metaverse. Advances in Economics, Business and Management Research. 648*. Atlantis Press International B.V. Retrieved from https://creativecommons.org/licenses/by-nc/4.0/

Jindal, A., Jindal, P., & Chavan, L. (2023). Customer Engagement Through Emotional Branding. In *Promoting Consumer Engagement Through Emotional Branding and Sensory Marketing* (pp. 201–210). IGI Global.

Jindal, P., & Gambhir, R. (2022). Marketing in a Pandemic. In Developing Relationships, Personalization, and Data Herald in Marketing 5.0 (pp. 57-68). IGI Global. doi:10.4018/978-1-6684-4496-2.ch003

Kiya.ai. (2023). *Kiya.ai*. Retrieved from https://www.kiya.ai/bharatmeta-taking-india-forward-as-the-leading-force-in-the-area-of-metaverse/

Murugan, M., & Prabadevi, M. N. (2023). Impact of Industry 6.0 on Msme Entrepreneur's Performance and Entrepreneur's Emotional Intelligence in the Service Industry in India. *RGSA – Revista de Gestão Social e Ambiental, 17*(4). doi:10.24857/rgsa.v17n4-007

Panda, A. K., Nanda, S., & Panda, P. (2021). Working Capital Management, Macroeconomic Impacts, and Firm Profitability: Evidence from Indian SMEs. *Business Perspectives and Research, 9*(1), 144–158. doi:10.1177/2278533720923513

Parviainen, P., Kaariainen, J., Tihinen, M., & Teppola, S. (2017). Tackling the digitalization challenge: How to benefit from digitalization in practice. *International Journal of Information System and Project Management, 5*(1), 63–77. doi:10.12821/ijispm050104

Priyono, A., Moin, A., Aini, V. N., & Putri, O. (2020). Identifying Digital Transformation Paths in the Business Model of SMEs during the COVID-19 Pandemic. *Journal of Open Innovation, 6*(4), 104. Advance online publication. doi:10.3390/joitmc6040104

PWC. (n.d.). Retrieved from https://www.pwc.in/research-and-insights-hub/embracing-the-metaverse.html

Ramos, M. E., Azevedo, A., Meira, D., & Malta, M. C. (2022). Cooperatives and the Use of Artificial Intelligence: A Critical View. *Sustainability (Basel), 15*(1), 1–17. doi:10.3390/su15010329

Rana, S., Anand, A., Prashar, S., & Haque, M. M. (2022). A perspective on the positioning of Indian business schools post COVID-19 pandemic. *International Journal of Emerging Markets, 17*(2), 353–367. doi:10.1108/IJOEM-04-2020-0415

Sahoo, D., & Ray, S. (2023). Metaverse in Banking: An Initiative for Banking Transformation from Emerging Country Prospective. *Academy of Marketing Studies Journal, 27*(S4), 1–15.

Statista. (2023). Retrieved from https://www.statista.com/

Yawised, K., Apasrawirote, D., & Boonparn, C. (2022). From traditional business shifted towards transformation: The emerging business opportunities and challenges in 'Metaverse' era. *The International and National Conference on Business Administration and Accountancy 2022 (INCBAA 2022)*, 162-175.

Zhang, H., Lee, S., Lu, Y., Yu, X., & Lu, H. (2023). A Survey on Big Data Technologies and Their Applications to the Metaverse: Past, Current and Future. *Mathematics*, *11*(96), 1–28. doi:10.3390/math11010096

Chapter 14
Exploring the Metaverse:
Future Pathway for Digital Marketing

Puneet Sharma
https://orcid.org/0009-0005-5237-7031
Punjabi University, India

Bhavuk Mahindru
https://orcid.org/0000-0003-3505-620X
Multani Mal Modi College, India

ABSTRACT

In the limitless world of the digital universe, a revolutionary phenomenon is taking shape: metadata. The Metaverse is a virtual space that transcends the boundaries of the physical and digital worlds, aiming to change the way we interact with technology. A hyper-connected digital universe called the "metaverse" promises to fundamentally change how consumers, brands, and businesses will transact and interact in virtual realities. The potential of the metaverse is accelerated by the growing trend of (1) consumers participating and transacting in virtual spaces and (2) companies investing millions of dollars in developing related technologies regarding the metaverse. This chapter is about the synergy between the metaverse and digital marketing, exploring the huge opportunities present for brands and the important role it plays in shaping the future of digital marketing.

INTRODUCTION

The metaverse is a concept that's still under development, but it has the potential to revolutionize the way we interact with technology and each other. The term "metaverse" is a combination of the words "meta" (meaning "transcendent") and "universe". It refers to a virtual world that links our imaginations to reality. It uses many of the same technologies as virtual reality to create a new world where people can experience a new experience with their virtual character. A Metaverse is a hypothetical synthetic environment that is connected to the physical world. It can be accessed through a virtual reality headset or augmented reality goggle (Lee et al., 2021). It allows you to imagine a virtual environment and create

DOI: 10.4018/979-8-3693-2422-6.ch014

an immersive experience. In recent times, it has attracted a lot of attention around the world, with many brands adopting a new story to create their metaverse and offer their consumers an exciting experience. It's an exciting tool for ordinary people to transform their virtual relationships with their loved ones, as well as for companies and enterprises to provide an interactive service to their consumers. It redefines communication within the virtual world and creates an immersive experience allowing people to have conferences, games, travel, adventure, and so much more.

In today's world, digital marketing or internet marketing, in this mode of marketing, is used as the medium where companies present their products through hypertext (a mix of text, audio and video). The digitization of promotion and advertising has now become a fundamental part of marketing. Digital marketing is now an essential part of all major brands because of its interactive mode of communicating with stakeholders (Veleva & Tsvetanova, 2020). With broad exposure, it is easy to stimulate prospects. Digital marketing tools help to create effective marketing strategies. During COVID-19, companies, marketers and the public realized the benefits of digital marketing when many people used electronic marketing and electronic services when no other alternatives were available due to the lockdown; the utility and advantages of virtual reality became widely known; all this highlighted the need for virtual connection through the social media platform.

METAVERSE AND DIGITAL MARKETING

The metaverse, a burgeoning realm of interconnected virtual worlds, is poised to significantly impact the landscape of digital marketing. Marketing in the metaverse is a huge opportunity to promote brands and products in a 3D space (Bushell, 2022). Here's how:

- **Immersive experiences:** The metaverse transcends traditional marketing by offering captivating, interactive experiences. Imagine engaging potential customers in a virtual test drive of a car, attending a fashion show within a metaverse store, or attending a product launch event in a captivating virtual environment. Marketing in the Metaverse has its pros and cons. One of the biggest pros is that it expands your brand and allows you to reach a global audience (Molina, 2021).
- **Branded virtual spaces:** Businesses can establish a presence in the metaverse by creating unique virtual spaces, akin to digital showrooms or stores. These spaces allow customers to explore products in a 3D environment, fostering a more interactive and memorable shopping experience.
- **Virtual product placement:** Similar to product placement in movies or TV shows, brands can integrate their products seamlessly within the metaverse. This subtle form of advertising can raise brand awareness and familiarity within the virtual landscape.
- **Evolving influencer marketing:** Influencer marketing, a mainstay in digital marketing, takes on a new dimension in the metaverse. Influencers can create engaging content within virtual environments, promoting products or services to a highly targeted audience through their avatars.
- **Revolutionizing virtual commerce:** While online shopping is prevalent, the metaverse presents an opportunity to elevate the experience. Imagine trying on clothes virtually through your avatar, or personalizing a product in a real-time, interactive setting. These advancements can blur the lines between the physical and virtual, offering a more immersive and personalized shopping experience. This immersive revolution (Freepik, n.d.) would draw in more people who want to spend more time in a virtual world than they would in a physical one.

APPLICATIONS OF DIGITAL MARKETING IN THE METAVERSE

Businesses can leverage the unique potential of the metaverse to create engaging and interactive experiences that resonate with their target audience in this evolving digital landscape. Companies can strategically place marketing materials and ads at the appropriate time and in the right audience. To harness the power of marketing in the metaverse, marketers need to understand the technology edge; this necessitates a new breed of marketing professionals with creativity and design thinking (Shalender et al., 2023). Some specific applications of digital marketing in the metaverse:

1. Interactive and Immersive Advertising:

In the metaverse, real world advertising techniques can be taken to the next level. For example, billboards can be used to advertise on virtual highways, and even customers can be involved and interact with animated characters within an advertisement. If the promotion is through a contest, people will have the opportunity to participate in the contest virtually. In the coming years, people will enjoy new advertising experiences in an environment that is immersive (Bansal et al., 2023).

- **Virtual Billboards:** Place dynamic, eye-catching advertisements on high-traffic virtual locations like buildings or transportation hubs within the metaverse.
- **Branded AR experiences:** Develop interactive experiences that users can trigger through their avatars, like trying on virtual makeup or exploring a product's features in an augmented reality setting.
- **Gamified experiences:** Create engaging games or challenges that subtly promote your brand or product within the metaverse.

2. Building Virtual Brand Spaces:

Metaverse enables us to create an immersive experience for a brand, where customers can experience a virtual journey in the same way they feel and touch when shopping in the real world. All of this enables marketers to present their products in the metaverse. The immersive environment offered by metaverse provides a utilitarian and indulgent effect, as well as high levels of augmentation, to inspire customers, which can lead to a shift in customer behavior towards the brand (Rauschnabel et al., 2022).

- **Branded stores and showrooms:** Establish virtual storefronts where users can browse products, interact with virtual assistants, and even make purchases using their avatars.
- **Virtual event spaces:** Host product launches, workshops, or exclusive events within the metaverse to create a unique and memorable brand experience.
- **Interactive product demonstrations:** Showcase your products' functionalities and benefits through interactive demonstrations within your virtual space.

3. Leveraging NFTs and Virtual Assets:

If marketers want to be successful in this new environment, they need to consider what they can offer their audience. For some brands trying to market in the metaverse, this could mean branded apparel or accessories for client avatars. The metaverse is heavily reliant on cryptocurrencies, and some brands are offering coins or tokens in exchange for exclusive experiences within their communities or virtual worlds (Jeon et al., 2021).

- **NFT-gated experiences:** Offer exclusive content, discounts, or access to events within the metaverse to users who own your brand's NFTs.
- **Virtual product placement:** Partner with creators and events within the metaverse to strategically place your virtual products for brand exposure.
- **Develop and sell virtual merchandise:** Create unique digital items like clothing or accessories for avatars, fostering brand loyalty and generating revenue.

4. Community Building and Influencer Marketing:

Collaboration comes to the fore as a result of the metaverse's large-scale scalability. According to previous research, hyperconnected environments are known to facilitate faster dissemination of information, more control over brand messaging, enhanced firm-to-customer interactions, and brand co-creation opportunities. Collaborative virtual and mixed reality environments enable users to work together and create content as part of their discovery and personal expression (Swaminathan et al., 2020).

- **Run metaverse-based contests and giveaways:** Encourage user engagement and brand awareness through interactive challenges or raffles within the metaverse.
- **Partner with metaverse influencers:** Collaborate with influential figures within the metaverse to promote your brand or products to their established audience.
- **Build and engage with communities:** Foster a community around your brand by providing dedicated spaces for users to interact, socialize, and participate in discussions.

5. Data-Driven Personalization:

The metaverse has the potential to transform every aspect of marketing and advertising. It can open up new marketing possibilities because the platform allows companies to have virtual promotions without any physical or geographical limitations. It supports the notion that the metaverse is immersive and actively engages with interactive commercials and marketing campaigns (Abed & Rinkevic, 2022). It would allow businesses to deploy tools that monitor, measure, and count people's interactions with ads, potentially providing an additional source of customer behavior data.

- **Collect and analyze user data:** Leverage the vast amount of data generated within the metaverse to gain insights into user behavior, preferences, and interactions.
- **Personalize virtual experiences:** Tailor content, recommendations, and advertising within the metaverse based on individual user preferences and past interactions.

Figure 1. Metaverse Marketing framework: Sociometric configuration perspectives
https://doi.org/10.1002/mar.21767

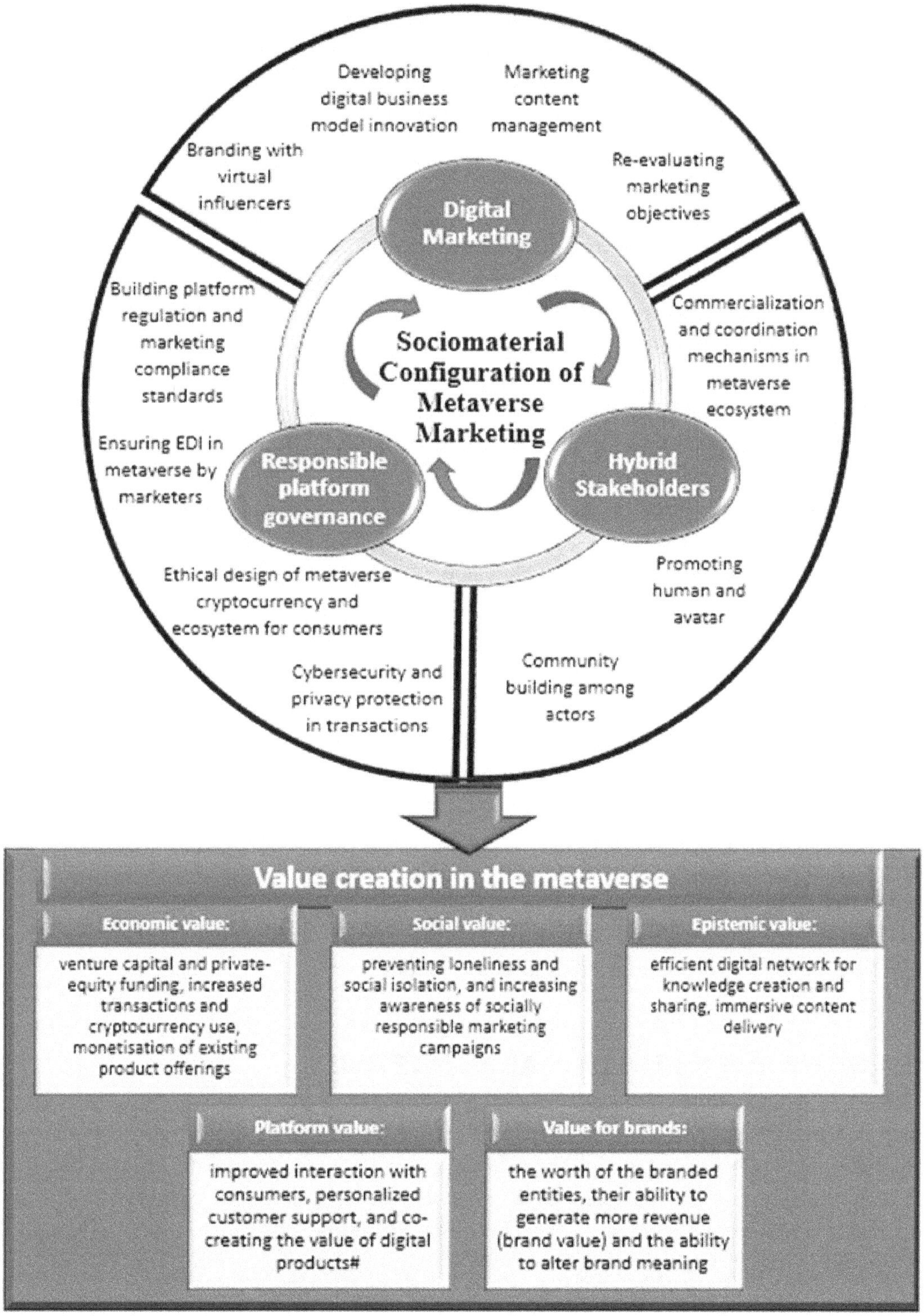

- **Optimize marketing strategies:** Use data-driven insights to continuously refine your metaverse marketing strategies and maximize their effectiveness.

The metaverse, a burgeoning realm of interconnected virtual worlds, undoubtedly presents a pathway for digital marketers to reimagine and revolutionize their strategies. Here's how:

Unveiling a Realm of Possibilities

- **Immersive Storytelling:** Transcend traditional narratives and craft captivating, 3D experiences that resonate deeply with audiences. Imagine showcasing products in interactive virtual showrooms, hosting virtual concerts, or offering test drives in simulated environments.
- **Targeted Engagement:** Leverage the metaverse's data-rich environment to create hyper-personalized marketing campaigns. Tailor content, recommendations, and advertising based on individual user preferences and interactions within the virtual world.
- **Community Cultivation:** Foster vibrant communities around your brand by providing dedicated spaces for users to interact, socialize, and participate in discussions. This fosters brand loyalty and creates a powerful network of advocates.
- **Revolutionized Commerce:** Bridge the gap between physical and virtual experiences. Imagine enabling virtual try-ons, offering real-time product customization, or hosting virtual shopping events. This streamlines the buying journey and enhances customer satisfaction.

Embracing the Evolving Landscape

- **Metaverse-Native Skill Sets:** Digital marketers need to equip themselves with new skill sets like understanding 3D design, VR/AR technologies, and blockchain applications.
- **Data Ethics and Transparency:** As the metaverse thrives on data, prioritizing user privacy and transparency is paramount. Building trust through ethical data practices will be crucial for sustainable marketing success.
- **Navigating the Regulatory Landscape:** The metaverse is in its nascent stages, and the legal and regulatory frameworks are constantly evolving. Staying updated on emerging regulations and adapting marketing strategies accordingly is essential.

IMPACT OF METAVERSE IN DIGITAL MARKETING

The metaverse presents a unique opportunity for digital marketing to become more immersive, interactive, and engaging. However, navigating the challenges and ethical considerations is crucial for brands to succeed in this new frontier. The metaverse, a network of interconnected virtual worlds, is expected to have a significant impact on various aspects of digital marketing, offering both exciting opportunities and challenges:

Opportunities

- **Immersive experiences:** The metaverse allows brands to create captivating and interactive experiences that go beyond traditional marketing methods. Imagine showcasing products in 3D showrooms, attending virtual concerts, or offering test drives within a virtual environment. This fosters deeper engagement and brand recall compared to static ads.
- **Enhanced brand storytelling:** Brands can leverage the immersive nature of the metaverse to tell their stories in a more impactful way. Virtual narratives, interactive games, and personalized experiences can create lasting connections with consumers.
- **Targeted advertising:** The metaverse offers the potential for highly targeted advertising based on user data and preferences within the virtual world. This allows brands to reach specific demographics and tailor their messaging for maximum impact.
- **Evolving influencer marketing:** Influencers can create engaging content and promote products within the metaverse, reaching a highly targeted audience through their avatars. This opens up new avenues for brand collaborations and marketing campaigns.
- **Revolutionizing virtual commerce:** The metaverse paves the way for a more immersive and personalized shopping experience. Imagine trying on clothes virtually, customizing products in real-time, or attending virtual shopping events. This can blur the lines between the physical and virtual, leading to increased sales and customer satisfaction.

Challenges

- **Privacy concerns:** The extensive data collection and user tracking potential within the metaverse raise significant privacy concerns. Brands need to be transparent about data usage and prioritize user privacy to build trust with consumers.
- **Accessibility and inclusivity:** Ensuring accessibility across diverse demographics is crucial. This includes factors like affordability of VR/AR equipment, representation within the metaverse, and catering to users with disabilities.
- **Evolving regulations:** As the metaverse is still evolving, legal and regulatory frameworks are still being developed. Brands need to stay updated on regulations and adapt their marketing strategies accordingly.
- **Technical limitations:** Current VR/AR technology may face limitations in terms of user experience, comfort, and compatibility. These limitations can hinder widespread adoption and hinder the effectiveness of metaverse marketing initiativesDigital marketers are adept at content and channel management, resulting in cost-effective acquisition per client (Pandey et al., 2020).
- **Developing New Metrics:** Traditional digital marketing metrics might not translate perfectly to the metaverse. Developing new metrics to gauge the effectiveness of marketing campaigns within this new environment is crucial.
- **Attribution Challenges:** Attributing conversions and sales to specific marketing efforts within the metaverse can be complex, making it difficult to measure ROI accurately.

CONCLUSION

The metaverse presents a paradigm shift for digital marketing, demanding a proactive and adaptable approach. By embracing innovation, prioritizing user experience, and navigating the evolving landscape, digital marketers can unlock the immense potential of the metaverse and forge a path to success in this new frontier. By embracing innovation, prioritizing user privacy, and adapting their strategies, brands can harness the potential of the metaverse to connect with audiences in a meaningful and impactful way. Marketing impacts from the metaverse's widespread adoption are transformative, providing new levels of consumer engagement and a tremendous opportunity to position brands within next-generation customer journeys (Dwivedi et al., 2020).

However, it's crucial to acknowledge that the metaverse is still under development, and its widespread adoption might take time. While the potential is undeniable, navigating the technical limitations and ethical considerations remains a challenge. Nevertheless, for those willing to embrace the change, the metaverse offers a thrilling pathway to redefine the future of digital marketing.

REFERENCES

Abed, A., & Rinkevic, K. (2022). *How do esports actors perceive the Metaverse as a servicescape for esports: An interpretative phenomenological analysis: An exploratory study about the business opportunities and challenges in the Metaverse*. Academic Press.

Bansal, A., Bansal, R., Bansal, A., Kumar, M., & Kumar, P. (2023). Normative Concerns in Neuromarketing. *Promoting Consumer Engagement Through Emotional Branding and Sensory Marketing*, 234-243.

BushellC. (2022). The Impact of Metaverse on Branding and Marketing SSRN. doi:10.2139/ssrn.4144628

Dwivedi, Y. K., Hughes, D. L., Coombs, C., Constantiou, I., Duan, Y., Edwards, J. S., Gupta, B., Lal, B., Misra, S., Prashant, P., Raman, R., Rana, N. P., Sharma, S. K., & Upadhyay, N. (2020). Impact of COVID-19 pandemic on information management research and practice: Transforming education, work and life. *International Journal of Information Management*, *55*, 102211. doi:10.1016/j.ijinfomgt.2020.102211

Freepik. (n.d.). https://www.freepik.com/free-vector/vr-sports-isometric-concept-with-virtual-reality-equipment-home-gym-martial-arts-games-isolated_7499008.htm#page=2&query=vr&position=1&from_view=author

Jeon, H., Youn, H., Ko, S., & Kim, T. (2021). Blockchain and AI Meet in the Metaverse. In T. M. Fern'andez-Caram'es & P. Fraga-Lamas (Eds.), *Advances in the Convergence of Blockchain and Artificial Intelligence*. IntechOpen. 10.5772/intechopen.99114

Lee, L.-H., Braud, T., & Zhou, P. (2021). All one needs to know about metaverse: A complete survey on technological singularity, virtual ecosystem, and research agenda. *Journal Of Latex Class Files*, *14*, 2021.

Molina, L. (2021). *Celebrity Avatars: A Technical Approach to Creating Digital Avatars for Social Marketing Strategies* [Doctoral dissertation]. Florida Atlantic University.

Pandey, N., Nayal, P., & Rathore, A. S. (2020). Digital marketing for B2B organizations: Structured literature review and future research directions. *Journal of Business and Industrial Marketing*, *35*(7), 1191–1204. doi:10.1108/JBIM-06-2019-0283

Rauschnabel, P. A., Babin, B. J., Tom Dieck, M. C., Krey, N., & Jung, T. (2022). What is augmented reality marketing? Its definition, complexity, and future. *Journal of Business Research*, *142*, 1140–1150. doi:10.1016/j.jbusres.2021.12.084

Shalender, K., Singla, B., & Sharma, S. (2023). Understanding the Logic and Science Behind the Emerging Field of Neuromarketing. *Promoting Consumer Engagement Through Emotional Branding and Sensory Marketing*, 44-51.

Swaminathan, V., Sorescu, A., Steenkamp, J. E. M., O'Guinn, T. C. G., & Schmitt, B. (2020). Branding in a Hyperconnected World: Refocusing Theories and Rethinking Boundaries. *Journal of Marketing*, *84*(2), 24–46. doi:10.1177/0022242919899905

Veleva, S. S., & Tsvetanova, A. I. (2020). Characteristics of the digital marketing advantages and disadvantages. *IOP Conference Series. Materials Science and Engineering*, *940*(1), 012065. doi:10.1088/1757-899X/940/1/012065

Chapter 15
Prospects and Difficulties for the Industry 4.0 Era in the Realm of the Metaverse

Ajit Bansal
Chitkara Business School, Chitkara University, India

Anu Bansal
Chitkara Business School, Chitkara University, India

ABSTRACT

When artificial and actual reality intersect, an interconnected digital shared environment known as the "Metaverse" is generated. In other words, it's a virtual world where clients can converse in current times with one more and computer-generated landscape. The idea has become more well-known in conversations concerning the future development of the web and online experiences. The metaverse is an online setting that eliminates all physical barriers from the actual world so users can interact with stuff or one another in real time through their avatars. Numerous fields have seen its use, including gaming, art, retail, medical care, educational institutions, manufacturing, social services, and a lot more. This study examines the possibilities and difficulties connected with the metaverse for Industry 4.0. It examines the metaverse potential from various angles, including social, instructive, scientific, and financial. The primary difficulties in the metaverse were also covered in this study, including administration of resources, decentralization, collaboration, and data integrity and confidentiality.

INTRODUCTION

In the last ten years, a number of developing technologies have made it possible to combine virtual and real-world settings. The most widely used one is the virtual world, which combines social forms with the upcoming wave of Internet-based apps. The idea of the metaverse is intriguing to the younger generation, but it might be frightening to certain conservatives. (Agarwal et al., 2022).

DOI: 10.4018/979-8-3693-2422-6.ch015

A “metaverse” is a virtual reality setting where persons can communicate in real time with other human beings and a digitally produced world. It expands on conventional notions of virtual reality by establishing a shared, permanent environment that works with a variety of devices and gadgets. A common conception of the metaverse is a completely absorbing, multifaceted environment that incorporates aspects of web browsing, additive reality, and augmented reality as well (Allam, Z et al., 2022).

The term “metaverse” refers to a relatively new and intriguing notion in technology which is expected to have a noteworthy impact on variety of activities, together with commerce, recreation, learning, and a variety of other fields of use of technology in everyday life. The name “metaverse” comes from the amalgamation of the two terms “verse” and “meta,” which respectively imply the “universe and transcend” or “the universe transcend.” A 3D implicit environment called as the “metaverse” incorporates elements of the authentic world and allows clients to experience a variety of scenarios.

Beyond AR and VR, there is the metaverse. It offers solutions for many different types of issues. Manufacturers, salespeople, traders, and advertising may all collaborate on an identical network while seated anywhere in the world. Optimizing marketing efforts in accordance with the needs of those engaged in the procedure of marketing constitutes one of the marketing tools offered by Metaverse. The metaverse encourages marketers to try out creative and novel approaches to product promotion. Marketing experts can share metaverse information and technological attributes; however all of this requires competent marketers who are conversant with contemporary IT technologies. There are benefits and drawbacks concerning advertising in the metaverse, but one of the main benefits is that it allows brands to access a global audience and expand their reach (Molina, 2021). The demographic that is ideal for The Metaverse is computer-savvy millennials and Generation Xers, as they have little trouble using and accessing this new digital age.

Because of its many features, Metaverse has a very broad range of uses. The gaming and leisure sectors employ Metaverse in some of its most common uses. Users can enjoy a vibrant and imaginative setting in Metaverse where they can play activities, watch films, go to concerts, and more.

The idea of virtual reality is hardly a unique notion; science fiction films and books continue to feature intriguing aspects of it. Avatar, Tron, Minority Report, and other films effectively employed virtual and augmented reality to their advantage. The best approach to leverage VR and AR for advertising is through digital marketing. As technology improves, people will accept innovative practices in their financial endeavors in a manner that is consistent with real-world adoption. One of the main elements of the metaverse that keeps the structure secure is the block chain (Yang et al., 2022). Founder of effective reality J Lanier characterizes Virtual reality as an innovation that “indicates you are genuine and highlights the existence of your sensory experience.” Through the use of a 3D eye display, virtual reality (VR) provides a fascinating environment where one can experience a virtual world.

Customers’ perceptions are altered via virtual reality through simulations (Cipresso, 2018). Users can engage in interactive experiences with augmented reality. Practical and computer-generated materials are combined in it. AR creates a virtual environment with items in it. Marketers can employ cues in an augmented reality (AR) environment to pique consumers’ desire for purchase in real-time engagement with their senses. The system may choose prospects who are in the correct mood by using neuromarketing.

The first is “5G, memory for the GPU and 3D; second is the formation of an understanding and conveying model that utilizes the computational power of the hardware; and third is the accessibility of content for individuals to involve in and engage in,” in the words of Park and Kim (2022). These are the three primary elements of the metaverse. It can communicate with both generated by computers items and “Avatar” personas in a three-dimensional environment. Silicon Valley’s giant corporations

Billions of millions have been invested by the likes of Google, Facebook, and Apple in the development of virtual reality technologies that users may access on their smartphones with Android (Faisal, 2017). Businesses can use virtual reality to showcase their goods by simulating the dimensions, form, and layout of a real, physical market. Consumers can explore both the interior and exterior ambiences to make sure the measurement, form and space meet their needs—especially in the real estate sector, where it can be challenging for marketers to showcase properties using conventional means.

Since it can offer educators and pupils a virtual environment wherein it is feasible to carry out training and experimentation that aren't possible in real life due to potential risks or expenses, the virtual world can have multiple uses and consequences in the field of education.

The metaverse will also benefit corporate development, employee cooperation and interaction, the creation of more realistic simulation frameworks for growth in cities, process optimization, and numerous other fields. However, there are drawbacks to the metaverse as well. These include dependency, impairment to the ability of the brain to discriminate between the real world and enhanced or simulated reality, security for privacy, safeguarding people's digital identities, data privacy, and the requirement for software technology infrastructure. Using cutting-edge hardware to transmit, receive, simulate, and analyze data in real-time, among other functions.

With regard to opportunities and problems, this article addresses the Metaverse for Industry 4.0 as a whole and goes beyond implementations.

It examines the prospects presented by the Metaverse in terms of various technical, commercial, educational, and societal facets. The primary issues are also covered, including interoperability, decentralization, and data assurance. The remaining paper is arranged as follows. The idea of comprehending the metaverse is covered in the next section. Section III delves into the topic by examining applications that go beyond Industry 4.0. The opportunities are outlined in section IV. After that, in section V we have discussed the probable solutions to address difficulties in navigating the Industry 4.0 era within the realm of the Metaverse. The final portion provides the conclusion.

The term "industry 4.0," also referred to as the "fourth economic revolution," refers to the imagined manufacturing system of the future. A team of individuals from a variety of fields, including business, government, and academia, developed the concept of Industry 4.0 as a component of an effort to connect every aspect of industry processes in order to attain sustainability. In order to encourage production automation and increase German competition in the manufacturing sector, the German government first formally approved and began implementing industry 4.0. In essence, Industry 4.0 will lead to more cost-effective and efficient operations and manufacturing. These are achieved by integrated control of industrial items and equipment, which operate simultaneously and smartly in connectivity, and the straightforward exchange of information. Nonetheless, some scholars hold diverse interpretations regarding the significance of industry 4.0.

Industry 4 makes use of cutting-edge technologies and communication equipment to propel the growth of the manufacturing sector. Three factors define the core elements of the industry 4.0 concept, according to Kagermann et al.: (1) horizontal integration, (2) vertical coupling, and (3) end-to-end technological interaction. Industry 4.0, according to Qin, Liu, and Grosvenor, promotes manufacturing efficiency through data collection and wise decision-making. Utilizing the latest cutting-edge technologies will simplify the processes. This is the ability to operate with interoperability in order to provide a stable production setting. Artificial intelligence functions are the most significant component of Industry 4.0, thanks to this collective awareness.

Because of increased interconnectedness and clever mechanization, the fourth manufacturing rebellion, also recognized as Industry 4.0, envisions fast change to sectors, technique, and societal habits and procedures in the twenty-first century. Arguably the most crucial ideas for the growth of international industry and the worldwide economy, according to Schwab, is "industry 4.0." He emphasizes that this concept is distinguished by a few new technological features, and that these developments are having a big impact on governments' plans for growth as well as the economies and industries. Industry 4.0 also refers to the transition that occurred in the community, supporting, and financial spheres from the information age of the 1990s and 2000s to an integrated connection period (e.g., metaverse) characterized by ubiquitous use of technology. That people have created and are inflowing an enhanced social reality as opposed to only using their natural senses and technological abilities.

The current, more advanced tools and machinery with advanced software and connected sensors that can be utilized to plan, anticipate, alter, and regulate operations and social outcomes are what Wang et al. described as the 4th industrial revolution. Industry 4.0 is, therefore a benefit for maintaining competitiveness in every sector. Industry 4.0 may be seen as an effective business plan. Its main objective is to optimize value chains as a result of dynamic, independent production. Additionally, industry 4.0 can be associated with four future-relevant concepts, including handling difficulty, invention capacity, and adaptability.

Based on the aforementioned notions, the majority of investigators classified subjects like Industrial the web, digital physical systems, and others as part of Industry 4.0. The impact of Industry 4.0 on the price and profitability of newly developed high-tech data and intelligent services has also been highlighted by several writers. Prior studies on Industry 4.0 indicate that the manufacturing industry received the majority of attention in the early stages. However, a wide range of industries, such as the automobiles technology, chemical, and electronic sectors, are now implementing Industry 4.0. In order to enhance the transformation of the entirety of goods life cycles and create novel goods in manufacturing, Industry 4.0 is combining obtainable thoughts into a new value chain. This involves connecting systems and objects that generate dynamic control and self-organization within the organization.

Industry 4.0 represents a hallucination or situation of a manufacturing procedure that will occur in the future. It will be characterized by the innovative levels of organizing, monitoring, and turning every aspect of the value chain along with the life cycle of goods through three kinds of combination processes: complete, vertical, and horizontal. These integrations will lead to improved efficiency and adaptability as well as cost optimization and reduction. Following that, the Internet of Things (IoT), computing via the cloud, manufacturing using additives, computerized physical systems (CPS), machine learning (AI), and other innovations are blended together to create dynamic, self-organized, real-time optimized cross-company value chains. Every one of these elements is essential to the future Industry 4.0 idea.

I. The Important Aspects of Metaverse

Important aspects of the metaverse consist of the following:

- **Perseverance:** Even after people log off, the metaverse is a permanent place that exists and changes. This contrasts with conventional online encounters, which are frequently associated with particular sessions.
- **Interchangeability:** Regardless of the platform or device they are using, individuals in the metaverse can engage with digital files and one another without difficulty. High levels of technology interoperability are necessary for this.

- **User-Created Material:** It is anticipated that people will be able to produce and contribute material in the metaverse. Digital goods such as art and property could fall under this category.
- **Economy:** Digital currencies and commodities with actual worth are probably part of the metaverse's economy. This might give rise to new kinds of virtual labour and business (Cali, U et al., 2022).
- **Social Interaction:** The concept of social interaction is fundamental to the metaverse. Socializing, collaborating, and communication are all possible in a virtual setting.

The metaverse is a concept that is currently being developed by a number of firms, and it has drawn a lot of interest from the tech, gaming, and media sectors. Nevertheless, the idea was still in its infancy as of my most recent knowledge upgrade in January 2022, and the creation of a fully working metaverse remains a continuous endeavour.

THE INTERACTION BETWEEN THE METAVERSE AND INDUSTRY 4.0

The communication between the Metaverse and Industry 4.0, along with relevance beyond, holds significant potential for transforming various sectors. Here are some key points of interaction:

1. **Digital Twin Integration:**
    - **Industry 4.0 Aspect:** Digital twins are essential representations of substantial objects or systems. In Industry 4.0, they are used to monitor and analyze real-world processes.
    - **Metaverse Interaction:** The Metaverse can enhance digital twins by providing immersive and interactive experiences. Engineers and workers can virtually explore and manipulate digital twins collaboratively and intuitively, improving decision-making processes.
2. **Collaborative Design and Simulation:**
    - **Industry 4.0 Aspect:** Collaborative design and simulation are crucial in manufacturing processes. VR and AR are already used in Industry 4.0 for design and training purposes.
    - **Metaverse Interaction:** The Metaverse can take collaborative design and simulation to the next level by enabling global teams to interact in a shared virtual space. This can enhance real-time collaboration, creativity, and problem-solving.
3. **Supply Chain Optimization:**
    - **Industry 4.0 Aspect:** Industry 4.0 emphasizes the integration of online technologies in supply chain administration for increased efficiency and transparency.
    - **Metaverse Interaction:** The Metaverse can offer an immersive way to visualize and optimize supply chain processes. Virtual representations of the entire supply chain can facilitate better decision-making and risk management.
4. **Remote Operations and Maintenance:**
    - **Industry 4.0 Aspect:** Remote monitoring and maintenance are critical components of Industry 4.0, allowing for predictive maintenance and minimizing downtime.
    - **Metaverse Interaction:** The Metaverse can enhance remote operations by providing a more immersive experience. Technicians can use AR or VR to troubleshoot issues in a virtual environment before addressing them in the physical world.
5. **Training and Skill Development:**

- ◦ **Industry 4.0 Aspect:** Industry 4.0 involves advanced technologies that require skilled workers. Training and up skilling are essential components.
- ◦ **Metaverse Interaction:** The Metaverse can provide realistic training simulations in a virtual environment. This can be particularly valuable for hands-on training in high-risk or complex scenarios.

6. **Decentralized and Secure Data Sharing:**
   - ◦ **Industry 4.0 Aspect:** Secure and decentralized data sharing is crucial for maintaining the integrity and privacy of sensitive industrial data.
   - ◦ **Metaverse Interaction:** Blockchain technology, often associated with the Metaverse, can enhance the security and transparency of data sharing in Industry 4.0 applications.
7. **Human-Machine Interaction:**
   - ◦ **Industry 4.0 Aspect:** Human-machine interaction is a central theme in Industry 4.0, with the aim of improving collaboration between humans and smart machines.
   - ◦ **Metaverse Interaction:** The Metaverse can provide new interfaces and experiences for human-machine interaction. This includes gesture-based controls, voice commands, and immersive interfaces that make interactions more natural and intuitive.

The convergence of the Metaverse and Industry 4.0 has the potential to revolutionize the way industries operate, collaborate, and innovate. It can lead to more efficient, connected, and intelligent systems across various domains.

CHALLENGES IN METAVERSE FOR INDUSTRY 4.0 AND BEYOND APPLICATIONS

The Metaverse idea presents a tremendous opportunity for Industry 4.0 as well as beyond, providing connected and immersive virtual environments that have the ability to transform a range of business and industry practises. But in order to successfully incorporate the Metaverse into Industry 4.0 as well as applications, a number of issues must be resolved:

1. **Interoperability:** Interoperability issues might arise when disparate technologies and platforms don't function together smoothly. Industry 4.0 needs protocols and guidelines to make sure that various virtual worlds as well as technologies may interact and work together in a fully productive Metaverse.
2. **Security and Privacy:** Valuable and private information is exchanged in large quantities within the Metaverse. It is imperative to provide strong security protocols and attend to privacy issues. Growing acceptance requires safeguarding users against cyber dangers, data breaches, and unauthorised access.
3. **Data Management**: Through interactions between people and virtual surroundings, the Metaverse produces a massive amount of data. Managing, storing, and analysing this data effectively present a number of difficulties. The development of governance of data and analytics skills is necessary in order to extract valuable insights from the massive amounts of data created.
4. **Ethical Issues:** As the Metaverse is incorporated more into day-to-day activities and corporate processes, ethical issues take on greater significance. To guarantee equitable and responsible prac-

tises, concerns like digital identification, virtual rights to ownership, and the moral application of AI in the Metaverse must be properly addressed.

5 **Digital Inclusion:** No location or demography should be excluded from accessing the Metaverse. To avoid developing a digital divide, it is imperative to ensure digital inclusion. This entails tackling problems with affordability, internet literacy, and connectivity.

6. **Difficulties with Immersive Technology:** Cutting-edge technologies like augmented reality, or AR, and virtual reality (VR) are needed to create accurate and realistic virtual worlds. Concerns that never go away involve tackling technical obstacles, advancing device abilities, and enhancing customer service.
7. **Regulatory systems:** Because the Metaverse crosses national boundaries, it is difficult to create uniform and efficient regulatory systems. To create regulations that guarantee user protection, legal clarity, and fair competitiveness in the Metaverse, states and regulating organisations must work together.
8. **Content Moderation and Administration:** Maintaining content created by users and other content within the realm of the Metaverse poses difficulties for governance and moderation, as well as for maintaining inclusive and secure virtual environments. It is essential to have rules and procedures for dealing with unacceptable behaviour.
9. **Education and Training:** As the Metaverse permeates more industries, educational and training initiatives are required to guarantee that people have the know-how to successfully traverse and utilise these virtual settings.
10. **Energy Consumption:** The Metaverse's enabling technologies, particularly those involved in creating lifelike virtual worlds, can consume a lot of energy. Finding sustainable solutions and addressing the effects on the environment are becoming more and more important.

In order to build a Metaverse that is safe, moral, open, and helpful for Industry 4.0 and beyond, companies, governments, and other stakeholders must work together to effectively overcome these obstacles.

A comprehensive strategy involving cooperation between technology developers, business executives, legislators, and regulatory agencies is needed to address these issues. Realizing the metaverse's potential in the setting of the Industry 4.0 paradigm and beyond uses will require continuous efforts to solve these challenges as it develop (Farshid, M. et al., 2018).

OPPORTUNITIES IN METAVERSE FOR INDUSTRY 4.0 AND BEYOND APPLICATIONS

Industries have a lot of chances to improve productivity, creativity, and teamwork as a result of the metaverse's integration with Industry 4.0 and other uses. Following are a few significant opportunities:

1. **Virtual Prototyping and Simulation:** The metaverse offers a framework for virtual prototypes and simulation, which enables industries to develop, test, and refine goods and procedures in a virtual setting prior to their actual deployment.

Benefits include a shorter time for market entry, fewer expenses for development, & the capacity to recognize and fix problems prior to the design process.

2. **Cooperative Design and Production:** Through virtual cooperation within the realm of the metaverse, physically separated groups can cooperate in the creation and production of goods. The associated benefits are enhanced teamwork, quicker decision-making, and more adaptability when putting together groups with a range of specialities.
3. **Possibility of Virtual Instruction and Development of Skills**: The Metaverse can be used by industries to create realistic and engaging online training programmes. It is especially useful for honing skills in dangerous situations or using sophisticated machinery, which lessens the requirement for actual training facilities.
4. **Remote Servicing and Procedures:** The Metaverse can improve remote operation and upkeep by giving technicians access to a simulated setting where they can troubleshoot, determine, and fix equipment. It can increase overall upkeep effectiveness and save downtime (Mishra, A., & Awasthi, S., 2022; Sood, K., et al., 2022).
5. **Visualization and Optimization of the Supply Chain:** Real-time visualization and optimization are made possible by the Metaverse's virtual depictions of the complete supply chain. Improved choices, higher resilience of the supply chain, and enhanced logistics can result from this.
6. **Digitized Twin Communication:** Using digital twins in conjunction with the Metaverse offers a more natural and engaging approach to engage with these digital depictions. This can improve decision-making and evaluation across a range of sectors.
7. **Secure and Decentralized Data Communication:** The Metaverse, which is frequently based on the technology of blockchain, can offer safe and decentralized platforms for exchanging data. In the background of Industry 4.0, this is necessary for preserving the confidentiality and integrity of critical data related to the industry.
8. **Enhancements in Human-Machine Communication:** The Metaverse may present novel opportunities and platforms for communication between humans and machines. In order to improve the general effectiveness of Industry 4.0 procedures, this incorporates gesture-based oversight, spoken orders, and holographic interfaces designed to render interactions seem simpler and fluid (Dwivedi, Y. K., et el., 2022).
9. **Accessible throughout Platforms:** Staff members can participate in Industry 4.0 activities from a variety of devices thanks to the Metaverse's cross-platform mobility. Because employees may communicate and collaborate regardless of where they are physically located, this adaptability fosters efficiency and cooperation.
10. **Integration of the Digital Economic Situation:** Novel company structures are made possible by the electronic economy of the Metaverse, which allows for the purchase, sale, and exchange of virtual products and services. Businesses might investigate monetizing digital assets in order to generate more income in the virtual world.
11. **Improved Integration of AI and Data Statistics:** Artificially intelligent and sophisticated data analytics apps can be developed on the Metaverse. Better insights, forecasts, and making choices in Industry 4.0 practices may result from this.
12. **Global Networking and Coordination:** Possibility: The Metaverse enables seamless connections between individuals across the globe, hence promoting global collaboration. It is especially advantageous for sectors of the economy that depend on cross-border cooperation for advancement, research, and issue resolution (Dawra, S. et al., 2022; Gupta, M., et al., 2023; Dhiman et el., 2018)).

Taking advantage of Industry 4.0 & the Metaverse can result in more inventive, linked, and effective industrial processes in a variety of industries. To remain competitive and prepare for the future, firms must investigate and strategically incorporate new technologies.

SOLUTIONS TO ADDRESS DIFFICULTIES IN NAVIGATING THE INDUSTRY 4.0 ERA WITHIN THE REALM OF THE METAVERSE

Businesses have advantages as well as disadvantages as Industry 4.0 and the Metaverse come together. The following are some possible fixes for issues encountered when traversing the Industry 4.0 period in the Metaverse:

1. Technology Integration: Response: Make sure that Industry 4.0 technologies are seamlessly integrated with Metaverse platforms. This entails creating standardized interfaces and protocols that enable efficient communication between various technologies. Compatibility and open norms are essential.
2. Data Protection and confidentiality: Response: Put strong security mechanisms in place to safeguard critical information both online and off. Make use of safe data-sharing protocols, decentralized identification systems, and encryption. Adherence to pertinent regulations is essential.
3. Training and Skill Creation: Fund training initiatives to equip laborers with Industry 4.0 and Metaverse skills. This includes training modules for amplified reality (AR) and effective reality (VR) that mimic real-world situations and improve practical abilities.
4. Cooperation and Communication: Remedy: Promote cooperation across teams scattered over real and virtual environments. To improve coordination and communication, make use of immersive communication technologies available in the Metaverse, like virtual meetings as well as collaboration policies.
5. Virtual Twins and The simulation: Response: Create precise digital replicas of tangible resources and procedures. Through simulation and forecasting, these electronic representations can enhance decision-making and streamline operations across the actual and virtual worlds.
6. Regulatory Adherence: Resolution: Keep up with the latest changes to laws pertaining to Industry 4.0 and the realm of the Metaverse. Take proactive steps to ensure compliance to steer clear of legal problems. Participate in the creation of pertinent policies by interacting with regulatory agencies.
7. Infrastructure and connectivity: Investing in a strong digital infrastructure will enable the Industry 4.0 and Metaverse systems to function flawlessly. To facilitate real-time data analysis and the transfer, make sure that networks are dependable, have minimal latency, and are high-speed connected.
8. Accessibility and Inclusivity: Remedy: Create Industry 4.0 systems and Metaverse experiences with inclusion in mind. Make sure that online settings are welcoming and open to a diverse and international workforce, and take into account accessibility considerations for people with different abilities.
9. Moral Aspects to Take into Account: The answer is to create and abide by moral standards for the application of Industry 4.0 technology in the Metaverse. Discuss issues pertaining to algorithmic prejudice, digital rights, and the moral consequences of immersive technology.

10. Constant Innovation: Remedy: Promote an innovative culture in order to adjust to the quickly changing environment of Industry 4.0 and the Metaverse. To remain ahead of novel obstacles and technology trends, foster innovation, research, and development.

By focusing on these crucial areas, companies can more successfully negotiate the intricacies of the Industry 4.0 age within the Metaverse, opening up new avenues for expansion and competition.

CONCLUSION

In summary, the metaverse is nonetheless in its early stages but has a lot of potential for the global community. Since the metaverse sector is still in its infancy, it is risky and not very sustainable.

Opportunities for various fields, including social, instructive, scientific, and economic, were examined in this article. Because of its consequences on our day-to-day lives and businesses, the COVID-19 pandemic has had the greatest consequence on society. Because it must work with both virtual and real surroundings as well as Metaverse developed by various companies, portability is the most difficult aspect of the problems. Investigators, designers, and anybody else who is concerned with Industry 4.0 along with uses utilizing Metaverse might find this study useful in understanding the challenges as well as the prospects.

REFERENCES

Agarwal, S., Bhardwaj, G., Saraswat, E., Singh, N., Aggarwal, R., & Bansal, A. (2022, February). Insurtech Fostering Automated Insurance Process Using Deep Learning Approach. In *2022 2nd International Conference on Innovative Practices in Technology and Management (ICIPTM)* (Vol. 2, pp. 386-392). IEEE. 10.1109/ICIPTM54933.2022.9753891

Allam, Z., Sharifi, A., Bibri, S. E., Jones, D. S., & Krogstie, J. (2022). The metaverse as a virtual form of smart cities: Opportunities and challenges for environmental, economic, and social sustainability in urban futures. *Smart Cities*, *5*(3), 771–801. doi:10.3390/smartcities5030040

Cali, U., Kuzlu, M., Karaarslan, E., & Jovanovic, V. (2022, November). Opportunities and Challenges in Metaverse for Industry 4.0 and Beyond Applications. In *2022 IEEE 1st Global Emerging Technology Blockchain Forum: Blockchain & Beyond (iGETblockchain)* (pp. 1-6). IEEE.

Dawra, S., Chand, P. K., & Aggarwal, A. (2022). Leader Member Exchange, Nepotism, and Employee Loyalty as the Determinants of Organizational Sustainability in Small and Medium Enterprises in India. *International Journal of Sociotechnology and Knowledge Development*, *14*(1), 1–21. doi:10.4018/IJSKD.297980

Dhiman, R., Chand, P. K., & Gupta, S. (2018). Behavioural aspects influencing decision to purchase apparels amongst young Indian consumers. *FIIB Business Review*, *7*(3), 188–200. doi:10.1177/2319714518790308

Dwivedi, Y. K., Hughes, L., Baabdullah, A. M., Ribeiro-Navarrete, S., Giannakis, M., Al-Debei, M. M., Dennehy, D., Metri, B., Buhalis, D., Cheung, C. M. K., Conboy, K., Doyle, R., Dubey, R., Dutot, V., Felix, R., Goyal, D. P., Gustafsson, A., Hinsch, C., Jebabli, I., ... Wamba, S. F. (2022). Metaverse beyond the hype: Multidisciplinary perspectives on emerging challenges, opportunities, and agenda for research, practice and policy. *International Journal of Information Management*, *66*, 102542. doi:10.1016/j.ijinfomgt.2022.102542

Farshid, M., Paschen, J., Eriksson, T., & Kietzmann, J. (2018). Go boldly! Explore augmented reality (AR), virtual reality (VR), and mixed reality (MR) for business. *Business Horizons, 61*(5), 657-663. / doi:10.1016/j.bushor.2018.05.009

Gupta, M., Taneja, S., Sharma, V., Singh, A., Rupeika-Apoga, R., & Jangir, K. (2023). Does Previous Experience with the Unified Payments Interface (UPI) Affect the Usage of Central Bank Digital Currency (CBDC)? *Journal of Risk and Financial Management, 16*(6), 286. doi:10.3390/jrfm16060286

Jaung, W. (2022). Digital forest recreation in the metaverse: Opportunities and challenges. *Technological Forecasting and Social Change*, *185*, 122090. doi:10.1016/j.techfore.2022.122090

Lin, H., Wan, S., Gan, W., Chen, J., & Chao, H. C. (2022, December). Metaverse in education: Vision, opportunities, and challenges. In *2022 IEEE International Conference on Big Data (Big Data)* (pp. 2857-2866). IEEE. 10.1109/BigData55660.2022.10021004

Mishra, A., & Awasthi, S. (2022). Metaverse: Opportunities and challenges for marketers. *Management Dynamics*, *22*(1), 10. doi:10.57198/2583-4932.1305

Nosalska, K., Piątek, Z. M., Mazurek, G., & Rządca, R. (2020). Industry 4.0: Coherent definition framework with technological and organizational interdependencies. *Journal of Manufacturing Technology Management*, *31*(5), 837–862. doi:10.1108/JMTM-08-2018-0238

Pereira, A. C., & Romero, F. (2017). A review of the meanings and the implications of the industry 4.0 concept. *Procedia Manufacturing*, *13*, 1206–1214. doi:10.1016/j.promfg.2017.09.032

Qin, J., Liu, Y., & Grosvenor, R. (2016). A categorical framework of manufacturing for industry 4.0 and beyond. *Procedia CIRP*, *52*, 173–178. doi:10.1016/j.procir.2016.08.005

Sandhu, N., & Saluja, S. (2023). *Fraud Triangle as an Audit Tool.* Management and Labour Studies., doi:10.1177/0258042X231160970

Sharma, A., & Bansal, A. (2023). Digital Marketing in the Metaverse: Beginning of a New Era in Product Promotion. In Applications of Neuromarketing in the Metaverse (pp. 163-175). IGI Global. doi:10.4018/978-1-6684-8150-9.ch012

Sood, K., Dhanaraj, R. K., Balusamy, B., Grima, S., & Uma Maheshwari, R. (Eds.). (2022). *Big Data: A game changer for insurance industry*. Emerald Publishing Limited. doi:10.1108/9781802626056

Wahlster, H., Helbig, J., Hellinger, A., & Wahlster, W. (2013). *Recommendations for implementing the strategic initiative INDUSTRIE 4.0. Securing the future of German manufacturing industry; final report of the Industrie 4.0.* Working Group. Forschungsunion. Retrieved from: http://forschungsunion.de/pdf/industrie_4_0_final_report.pdf

As we conclude our journey through the uncharted territories of the metaverse, we are reminded that this revolutionary digital frontier is redefining the fabric of business, society, and humanity at large. *New Business Frontiers in the Metaverse* has demystified the complexities of this emerging landscape, offering a comprehensive understanding of the dimensions that entrepreneurs will confront in the metaverse.

Through our exploration of integrated technologies like NFTs, Web 4.0, augmented reality, virtual reality, and mixed reality, we have seen how these innovations intertwine to shape the metaverse's entrepreneurial landscape. We have examined the metaverse's impact on diverse sectors, from business and services to education, healthcare, travel, tourism, hospitality, entertainment, digital payments, and digital currency.

As we navigate this digital paradigm shift, it is essential to address the myths and challenges head-on. This book has provided a detailed guide to navigate challenges and seize the opportunities embedded in this revolutionary digital paradigm shift. We have scrutinized the implications for public policy and unveiled opportunities for entrepreneurial ventures across various industries.

The metaverse is not just a technological revolution; it's a human revolution – a chance to redefine our relationships, our businesses, and our world. As entrepreneurs, policymakers, and individuals, we are faced with both unparalleled opportunities and unprecedented challenges. *New Business Frontiers in the Metaverse* invites scholars and visionaries to engage in a thought-provoking exploration, shaping the future of this digital frontier.

As we look to the future, we are reminded that the metaverse is a dynamic and evolving landscape. New technologies and innovations will continue to emerge, shaping the metaverse's entrepreneurial landscape. It is our responsibility to ensure that this digital frontier is harnessed for the greater good, promoting inclusivity, diversity, and ethical considerations.

New Business Frontiers in the Metaverse has provided a foundation for understanding the metaverse's complexities. However, this is just the beginning. We must continue to explore, innovate, and push the boundaries of what is possible in this digital frontier.

To the entrepreneurs, policymakers, and individuals who will shape the future of the metaverse, we offer a final thought: the metaverse is not just a destination; it's a journey. A journey that requires courage, creativity, and compassion. Let us embrace this journey together, shaping a future that is more connected, more innovative, and more transformative than ever before.

In conclusion, *New Business Frontiers in the Metaverse* has demystified the complexities of the metaverse, offering a comprehensive understanding of its transformative power. This book has provided a detailed guide to navigate challenges and seize the opportunities embedded in this revolutionary digital paradigm shift. Join the conversation, and let the exploration begin!

As we conclude this book, we are reminded that the metaverse is a collective effort. It requires collaboration, innovation, and creativity from individuals, organizations, and governments around the world. Let us work together to shape the future of the metaverse, ensuring that its transformative power benefits humanity at large.

The metaverse is not just a technological revolution; it's a human revolution – a chance to redefine our relationships, our businesses, and our world. Let us embrace this revolution with courage, creativity, and compassion, shaping a future that is more connected, more innovative, and more transformative than ever before. The future of the metaverse is in our hands; let us create a world that is truly limitless.

Compilation of References

Abbate, M. A., Aghdam, N. K., & Mirjalili, S. A. (2022). Systematic Review on Metaverse: And its Future Considerations. *Webology*, *19*(2), 10179.

Abd Rahman, N. H., Khalifah, Z., & Ismail, H. N. (2016). The role of sensory experiences in appreciating the cultural heritage attractions. *Tourism. Leisure and Global Change*, *3*, 117–128.

Abed, A., & Rinkevic, K. (2022). *How do esports actors perceive the Metaverse as a servicescape for esports: An interpretative phenomenological analysis: An exploratory study about the business opportunities and challenges in the Metaverse*. Academic Press.

Agarwal, S., Bhardwaj, G., Saraswat, E., Singh, N., Aggarwal, R., & Bansal, A. (2022, February). Insurtech fostering automated insurance process using deep learning approach. In *2022 2nd International conference on innovative practices in technology and management (ICIPTM)* (Vol. 2, pp. 386-392). IEEE. 10.1109/ICIPTM54933.2022.9753891

Aggarwal, A., Dhaliwal, R. S., & Nobi, K. (2018). Impact of structural empowerment on organizational commitment: The mediating role of women's psychological empowerment. *Vision (Basel)*, *22*(3), 284–294. doi:10.1177/0972262918786049

Ai, H., Cao, Z., & Zhu, J. (2022). *Deep learning for omnidirectional vision: a survey and new perspectives*. doi:10.36227/techrxiv.19807699

Aichner, T., & Gruber, B. (2017). Managing customer touchpoints and customer satisfaction in b2b mass customization: A case study. *International Journal of Industrial Engineering and Management*, *8*(3), 131–140. doi:10.24867/IJIEM-2017-3-114

Akkucuk, U., & Asugman, G. (2022). Metaverse marketing: Exploring the potential of metaverse for marketing. *Int. J. Mark. Stud.*, *14*, 52–63.

Akmermer, B. (2022). The Phygital Experiential Marketing Practices: The Conceptual Framework and Applications for Tourism Industry. In Handbook of Research on Interdisciplinary Reflections of Contemporary Experiential Marketing Practices (pp. 289-309). IGI Global.

Akour, I. A., Al-Maroof, R. S., Alfaisal, R., & Salloum, S. A. (2022). A conceptual framework for determining metaverse adoption in higher institutions of gulf area: An empirical study using hybrid SEM-ANN approach. *Computers and Education: Artificial Intelligence*, *3*, 100052. doi:10.1016/j.caeai.2022.100052

Alaimo, C., & Kallinikos, J. (2017). Computing the everyday: Social media as data platforms. *The Information Society*, *33*(4), 175–191. doi:10.1080/01972243.2017.1318327

Al-Ghaili, A. M., Kasim, H., Al-Hada, N. M., Hassan, Z. B., Othman, M., Tharik, J. H., Kasmani, R. M., & Shayea, I. (2022). A review of metaverse's definitions, architecture, applications, challenges, issues, solutions, and future trends. *IEEE Access : Practical Innovations, Open Solutions*, *10*, 125835–125866. doi:10.1109/ACCESS.2022.3225638

Ali, S. A. (2023). *Metaverse Marketing vs Digital Marketing*. Academic Press.

Ali, O., Jaradat, A., Kulakli, A., & Abuhalimeh, A. (2021). A comparative study: Blockchain technology utilization benefits, challenges and functionalities. *IEEE Access : Practical Innovations, Open Solutions*, *9*, 12730–12749. doi:10.1109/ACCESS.2021.3050241

Alja'afreh, M., Al Mallah, R., Karime, A., & El Saddik, A. (2023). Cybersecurity in the Metaverse: Challenges and Approaches. *2023 International Conference on Intelligent Metaverse Technologies & Applications (IMETA)*, 1–8. 10.1109/iMETA59369.2023.10294371

Allam, Z. (2022). The Metaverse as a Virtual Form of Smart Cities: Opportunities and Challenges for Environmental, Economic, and Social Sustainability in Urban Futures. *Sustainability*, *5*(3), 40. https://www.mdpi.com/2624-6511/5/3/40/htm

Allam, Z., Sharifi, A., Bibri, S. E., Jones, D. S., & Krogstie, J. (2022). The metaverse as a virtual form of smart cities: Opportunities and challenges for environmental, economic, and social sustainability in urban futures. *Smart Cities*, *5*(3), 771–801. doi:10.3390/smartcities5030040

Alon, I. (2020). COVID-19 and International Business: A Viewpoint. *FIIB Business Review*, *9*(2), 75–77. doi:10.1177/2319714520923579

Al-Tabeeb, A. K., & Al-Desouqi, A. A. (2023). Metaverse in Architecture: An Approach to Documenting and Exploring the Egyptian Heritage Through Metaverse. *Green Building & Construction Economics*, 276-295.

Ambika, A., Shin, H., & Jain, V. (2023). Immersive technologies and consumer behaviour: A systematic review of two decades of research. *Australian Journal of Management*. Advance online publication. doi:10.1177/03128962231181429

Aminabadi, N. A., Golsanamlou, O., Halimi, Z., & Jamali, Z. (2022). Assessing the different levels of virtual reality that influence anxiety, behaviour, and oral health status in preschool children: Randomized controlled clinical trial. *JMIR Perioperative Medicine*, *5*(1), e35415. doi:10.2196/35415 PMID:35436233

Amiti, F. (2020). Synchronous and asynchronous E-learning. *European Journal of Open Education and E-Learning Studies*, *5*(2). Advance online publication. doi:10.46827/ejoe.v5i2.3313

Amorim, T., Tapparo, L., Marranghello, N., Silva, A. C., & Pereira, A. S. (2014). A multiple intelligences theory-based 3D virtual lab environment for digital systems teaching. *Procedia Computer Science*, *29*, 1413–1422. doi:10.1016/j.procs.2014.05.128

Anderson, T., & Rivera Vargas, P. (2020). A critical look at educational technology from a distance education perspective. *Digital Education Review*, *2020*(37), 208–229. doi:10.1344/der.2020.37.208-229

Andrade, J. G., & Dias, P. (2020). A phygital approach to cultural heritage: Augmented reality at regaleira. *Virtual Archaeology Review*, *11*(22), 15–25. doi:10.4995/var.2020.11663

Ante, L. (2022). The non-fungible token (NFT) market and its relationship with Bitcoin and Ethereum. *FinTech*, *1*(3), 216–224. doi:10.3390/fintech1030017

Antonczak, L., & Papetti, C. (2017). Towards a mobile enhancement of glocal heritage? Developing user experiences in relation to mobile technologies, geo-localisation and culture. In *ICWMC 2017–The Thirteenth International Conference on Wireless and Mobile Communications* (pp. 73-78). ThinkMind.

Appel, G., Grewal, L., Hadi, R., & Stephen, A. T. (2020). The future of social media in marketing. *Journal of the Academy of Marketing Science*, *48*(1), 79–95. doi:10.1007/s11747-019-00695-1 PMID:32431463

Armstrong, K., & Rutter, C. (2017). Exploring the enigma of the happiness construct in phygital fashion experiences. In *Advanced fashion technology and operations management* (pp. 220–233). IGI Global. doi:10.4018/978-1-5225-1865-5.ch009

Asaithambi, S., Ravi, L., Kotb, H., Milyani, A. H., Azhari, A. A., Nallusamy, S., Varadarajan, V., & Vairavasundaram, S. (2022). An Energy-Efficient and Blockchain-Integrated Software Defined Network for the Industrial Internet of Things. *Sensors (Basel)*, *22*(20), 7917. doi:10.3390/s22207917 PMID:36298266

Austin, S. (2021). The New Wave of Web 3.0 Metaverse Innovations. *Entrepreneur*. https://www.entrepreneur.com/article/380250

Ayiter, E. (2014). (Re) Building proun# 5A in the metaverse. In *2014 International Conference on Cyberworlds*(pp. 403-406). IEEE. 10.1109/CW.2014.63

Badrinarayanan, V., & Arnett, D. B. (2008). Effective virtual new product development teams: An integrated framework. Journal of Business &Amp. *Journal of Business and Industrial Marketing*, *23*(4), 242–248. doi:10.1108/08858620810865816

Baeza-Yates, R. (2022). Ethical Challenges in AI. *ACM Transactions on Computing Logic, 1*(1), Article 1. . doi:10.1145/3488560.3498370

Bailenson, J. N. (2021). *Nonverbal overload: A theoretical argument for the causes of Zoom fatigue*. Academic Press.

Baker, E. W., Hubona, G. S., & Srite, M. (2019). Does "being there" matter? The impact of web-based and virtual world's shopping experiences on consumer purchase attitudes. *Information & Management*, *56*(7), 103153. doi:10.1016/j.im.2019.02.008

Ball, M. (2022). *Framework for the Metaverse — MatthewBall.vc*. Available at: https://www.matthewball.vc/all/forwardtothemetaverseprimer

Ballina, F.J., Valdes, L., & Del Valle, E. (2019). The Phygital experience in the smart tourism destination. *International Journal of Tourism Cities*.

Banik, S. (2021). Exploring the involvement-patronage link in the phygital retail experiences. *Journal of Retailing and Consumer Services*, *63*, 102739. doi:10.1016/j.jretconser.2021.102739

Bank of America. (2021, October 7). *Bank of America is First in Industry to Launch Virtual Reality Training Program in Nearly 4,300 Financial Centers*. Author.

Bansal, A., Bansal, R., Bansal, A., Kumar, M., & Kumar, P. (2023). Normative Concerns in Neuromarketing. *Promoting Consumer Engagement Through Emotional Branding and Sensory Marketing*, 234-243.

Barrett, R., Poe, R., O'Camb, J. W., Woodruff, C., Harrison, S., Dolguikh, K., Chuong, C., Klassen, A. D., Zhang, R., Joseph, R. B., & Blair, M. R. (2022). Comparing virtual reality, desktop-based 3d, and 2d versions of a category learning experiment. *PLoS One*, *17*(10), e0275119. doi:10.1371/journal.pone.0275119 PMID:36201546

Barron, B., & Darling-Hammond, L. (2008). *Teaching for Meaningful Learning: A Review of Research on Inquiry-Based and Cooperative Learning*. Book Excerpt. George Lucas Educational Foundation.

Barry, C. (2021). Gucci Digitally Outfits Gen-Z in Metaverse Foray with Roblox. *USA Today*. https://www.usatoday.com/ story/tech/gaming/2021/06/09/gucci-meets-roblox-designer-rolls-outdigital-only-collection/7616940002/

Batat, W. (2019). *Experiential marketing: Consumer behavior, customer experience and the 7Es*. Routledge. doi:10.4324/9781315232201

Batat, W. (2022). What does phygital really mean? A conceptual introduction to the phygital customer experience (PH-CX) framework. *Journal of Strategic Marketing*, 1–24. doi:10.1080/0965254X.2022.2059775

Bathla, D., & Singh, A. (Eds.). (2022). *Applying Metalytics to Measure Customer Experience in the Metaverse*. IGI Global. doi:10.4018/978-1-6684-6133-4

Bayram, A. (2022). Metaleisure: Leisure time habits to be changed with metaverse. *Journal of Metaverse*, *2*(1), 1–7.

Becker, L., & Jaakkola, E. (2020). Customer experience: Fundamental premises and implications for research. *Journal of the Academy of Marketing Science*, *48*(4), 630–648. doi:10.1007/s11747-019-00718-x

Beckmann, C., & Böhm, M. (2022). The Metaverse: A New Era of Human-Computer Interaction. *Computers in Human Behavior*, *126*, 107021.

Belghiti, S., Ochs, A., Lemoine, J. F., & Badot, O. 2018. The phygital shopping experience: An attempt at conceptualization and empirical investigation. In *Marketing Transformation: Marketing Practice in an Ever Changing World: Proceedings of the 2017 Academy of Marketing Science (AMS) World Marketing Congress (WMC)* (pp. 61-74). Springer International Publishing.

Belhaj, M., & Hachaıchi, Y. (2021). *Artificial Intelligence*. Machine Learning and Big Data in Finance Opportunities, Challenges, and Implications for Policy Makers.

Benevolo, L. (1977). *History of modern architecture* (Vol. 2). Mit Press.

Berhanu, K., & Raj, S. (2020). The trustworthiness of travel and tourism information sources of social media: Perspectives of international tourists visiting Ethiopia. *Heliyon*, *6*(3), e03439. doi:10.1016/j.heliyon.2020.e03439 PMID:32181382

Bernasconi, C., & Blume, L. B. (2023). Theorizing architectural research and practice in the metaverse: The meta-context of virtual community engagement. *Archnet-IJAR: International Journal of Architectural Research*. Advance online publication. doi:10.1108/ARCH-08-2023-0203

Bessière, K., Seay, A. F., & Kiesler, S. (2007). The ideal elf: Identity exploration in World of Warcraft. *Cyberpsychology & Behavior*, *10*(4), 530–535. doi:10.1089/cpb.2007.9994 PMID:17711361

Bhat, A. (2018, August 23). *Descriptive Research: Characteristics, Methods + Examples*. QuestionPro. https://www.questionpro.com/blog/descriptive- research/#:~:text=In%20a%20descriptive%20research%20design

Bian, Y., Leng, J., & Zhao, J. L. (2021, December). Demystifying metaverse as a new paradigm of enterprise digitization. In *International Conference on Big Data* (pp. 109-119). Cham: Springer International Publishing.

Bibri, S. E., & Allam, Z. (2022). The Metaverse as a virtual form of data-driven smart urbanism: On post-pandemic governance through the prism of the logic of surveillance capitalism. *Smart Cities, 5*(2).

Bibri, S. E. (2022). The social shaping of the metaverse as an alternative to the imaginaries of data-driven smart Cities: A study in science, technology, and society. *Smart Cities*, *5*(3), 832–874. doi:10.3390/smartcities5030043

Bibri, S. E., & Allam, Z. (2022). The Metaverse as a Virtual Form of Data-Driven Smart Urbanism: On Post-Pandemic Governance through the Prism of the Logic of Surveillance Capitalism. *Sustainability*, *5*(2), 37. https://www.mdpi.com/2624-6511/5/2/37

Bibri, S. E., Allam, Z., & Krogstie, J. (2022). The Metaverse as a virtual form of data-driven smart urbanism: Platformization and its underlying processes, institutional dimensions, and disruptive impacts. *Computational Urban Science*, *2*(1), 24. doi:10.1007/s43762-022-00051-0 PMID:35974838

Binkhorst, E., & Den Dekker, T. (2009). Agenda for co-creation tourism experience research. *Journal of Hospitality Marketing & Management*, *18*(2-3), 311–327. doi:10.1080/19368620802594193

Boes, K., Buhalis, D., & Inversini, A. (2015). Conceptualising smart tourism destination dimensions. In *Information and Communication Technologies in Tourism 2015: Proceedings of the International Conference in Lugano, Switzerland, February 3-6, 2015* (pp. 391-403). Springer International Publishing.

Boltz, L. O., Yadav, A., Dillman, B., & Robertson, C. (2021). Transitioning to remote learning: Lessons from supporting K-12 teachers through a MOOC. *British Journal of Educational Technology*, *52*(4), 1377–1393. doi:10.1111/bjet.13075

Bond, M., Buntins, K., Bedenlier, S., Zawacki-Richter, O., & Kerres, M. (2020). Mapping research in student engagement and educational technology in higher education: A systematic evidence map. *International Journal of Educational Technology in Higher Education*, *17*(1), 1–30. doi:10.1186/s41239-019-0176-8

Botella, C., Fernández-Álvarez, J., Guillén, V., García-Palacios, A., & Baños, R. (2017). Recent progress in virtual reality exposure therapy for phobias: A systematic review. *Current Psychiatry Reports*, *19*(7), 42. Advance online publication. doi:10.1007/s11920-017-0788-4 PMID:28540594

Branca, G., Resciniti, R., & Loureiro, S. M. C. (2022). Virtual is so real! consumers' evaluation of product packaging in virtual reality. Psychology &Amp. *Psychology and Marketing*, *40*(3), 596–609. doi:10.1002/mar.21743

Brown, A., & White, B. (2023). Metaverse Platforms: Navigating Compatibility Challenges. *Journal of Virtual Business*, *15*(2), 45–62.

Brown, G., & Foster, C. (2023). The Use of Virtual Learning Environments in Higher Education—Content, Community and Connectivism—Learning from Student Users. In *AI, Blockchain and Self-Sovereign Identity in Higher Education* (pp. 125–142). Springer Nature Switzerland. doi:10.1007/978-3-031-33627-0_6

Brynjolfsson, E., & McAfee, A. (2014). *The Second Machine Age: Work, Progress, and Prosperity in a Time of Brilliant Technologies*. W. W. Norton & Company.

Buhalis, D., & Amaranggana, A. (2013). Smart tourism destinations. In *Information and Communication Technologies in Tourism 2014: Proceedings of the International Conference in Dublin, Ireland, January 21-24, 2014* (pp. 553-564). Springer International Publishing.

Buhalis, D., Leung, D., & Lin, M. (2023). Metaverse as a disruptive technology revolutionising tourism management and marketing. *Tourism Management*, *97*, 104724. doi:10.1016/j.tourman.2023.104724

Buonincontri, P., & Micera, R. (2016). The experience co-creation in smart tourism destinations: A multiple case analysis of European destinations. *Information Technology & Tourism*, *16*(3), 285–315. doi:10.1007/s40558-016-0060-5

BushellC. (2022). The Impact of Metaverse on Branding and Marketing. SSRN. doi:10.2139/ssrn.4144628

Cacioli, J. P., & Mussap, A. J. (2014). Avatar body dimensions and men's body image. *Body Image*, *11*(2), 146–155. doi:10.1016/j.bodyim.2013.11.005 PMID:24394638

Calabrò, R. S., Cerasa, A., Ciancarelli, I., Pignolo, L., Tonin, P., Iosa, M., & Morone, G. (2022). The arrival of the metaverse in neurorehabilitation: Fact, fake or vision? *Biomedicines*, *10*(10), 2602. doi:10.3390/biomedicines10102602 PMID:36289862

Cali, U., Kuzlu, M., Karaarslan, E., & Jovanovic, V. (2022, November). Opportunities and Challenges in Metaverse for Industry 4.0 and Beyond Applications. In *2022 IEEE 1st Global Emerging Technology Blockchain Forum: Blockchain & Beyond (iGETblockchain)* (pp. 1-6). IEEE.

Casino, F., Dasaklis, T. K., & Patsakis, C. (2019). A systematic literature review of blockchain-based applications: Current status, classification and open issues. *Telematics and Informatics*, *36*, 55–81. doi:10.1016/j.tele.2018.11.006

Castillo, M. J., & Taherdoost, H. (2023). The Impact of AI Technologies on E-Business. *Encyclopedia*, *3*(1), 107–121. doi:10.3390/encyclopedia3010009

CastronovaE. (2005). Synthetic economies and the social question. *Available at* SSRN 782826.

Castronova, E. (2005). *Synthetic Worlds: The Business and Culture of Online Games*. University of Chicago Press.

Castro, S. R., Silva, S. C., & Duarte, P. (2017). Does Digital Marketing really boost city tourism? Evidences from Porto's Experience. *European Journal of Applied Business & Management*, *3*(3), 84–100.

Chakraborty, D., Patre, S., & Tiwari, D. (2023). Metaverse mingle: Discovering dating intentions in metaverse. *Journal of Retailing and Consumer Services*, *75*, 103509. doi:10.1016/j.jretconser.2023.103509

Chaston, I. (2001). e-Marketing Strategy. McGraw-Hill

Chen, G., & Dong, H. (2021). *Peking University Scholars Release START Map of Metaverse Features and Properties.* Available at: https://share.gmw.cn/ it/2021-11/19/content_35323118.html

Chen, T., Zhou, H., Yang, H., & Liu, S. (2022). A review of research on metaverse defining taxonomy and adaptive architecture. In *2022 5th International Conference on Pattern Recognition and Artificial Intelligence (PRAI)* (pp. 960-965). IEEE. 10.1109/PRAI55851.2022.9904076

Cheng, X., Zhang, S., Fu, S., Liu, W., Guan, C., Mou, J., & Huang, C. (2022). Exploring the metaverse in the digital economy: An overview and research framework. Journal of Electronic Business &Amp. *Digital Economics*, *1*(1/2), 206–224. doi:10.1108/JEBDE-09-2022-0036

Chen, L., & Zhou, C. (2022). The Metaverse: A New Frontier for Brands. *Journal of Business Research*, *144*, 113–121.

Chenoweth, S., & Linos, P. K. (2018). *Qualitative Findings from an Online Course on Machine Learning.* Paper presented at the 2018 IEEE Frontiers in Education Conference (FIE). 10.1109/FIE.2018.8658554

Chen, S., & … . (2023). Entrepreneurship in the Metaverse: Navigating Opportunities and Challenges. *Journal of Business Innovation*, *30*(1), 78–95.

Chen, Y. J., Wang, C. J., & Chen, C. W. (2023). Effects of virtual reality on preoperative anxiety in children: A systematic review and meta-analysis of randomised controlled trials. *Journal of Clinical Nursing*, *32*(11-12), 2494–2504. doi:10.1111/jocn.16394 PMID:35672942

Chen, Z., Wu, J., Gan, W., & Qi, Z. (2022, December). Metaverse security and privacy: An overview. In *2022 IEEE International Conference on Big Data (Big Data)* (pp. 2950-2959). IEEE. 10.1109/BigData55660.2022.10021112

Ching, F. D., Jarzombek, M. M., & Prakash, V. (2017). *A global history of architecture*. John Wiley & Sons.

Choi, H. S., & Kim, S. H. (2017). A content service deployment plan for metaverse museum exhibitions—Centering on the combination of beacons and HMDs. *International Journal of Information Management*, *37*(1), 1519–1527. doi:10.1016/j.ijinfomgt.2016.04.017

Çiftçi, Ş. F., & Çizel, B. (2024). Exploring relations among authentic tourism experience, experience quality, and tourist behaviours in phygital heritage with experimental design. *Journal of Destination Marketing & Management*, *31*, 100848. doi:10.1016/j.jdmm.2023.100848

Cocioceanu, A., Barbulescu, M., Ivanoaica, T., Raportaru, M., & Nicolin, A. I. (2016). Testing voice-based biometrics authentication platforms for Romanian utterances through infrequent consonant clusters. *2016 15th RoEduNet Conference: Networking in Education and Research*, 1–4.

Conway, H., & Roenisch, R. (2005). *Understanding architecture: an introduction to architecture and architectural history*. Routledge. doi:10.4324/9780203973196

Corne, A. (2017). Destination performance: Decision-making tools for tourism sector. *European Journal of Tourism Research, 17*, 265-268.

Cornet, L. J., & Van Gelder, J. L. (2020). Virtual reality: A use case for criminal justice practice. [Chicago]. *Psychology, Crime & Law, 26*(7), 631–647. doi:10.1080/1068316X.2019.1708357

Courvoisier, F. (2020). Le «phygital», une nouvelle approche centrée client pour l'horlogerie. Academic Press.

Cranmer, E. E., tom Dieck, M. C., & Jung, T. (2018). *How can tourist attractions profit from augmented reality? Augmented Reality and Virtual Reality: Empowering Human.*

Damar, E. (2021). The Metaverse: Concepts, challenges, and opportunities. *Technology in Society, 66*, 101649.

Damar, M. (2021). Metaverse shape of your life for future: A bibliometric snapshot. *Journal of Metaverse, 1*(1), 1–8.

Damer, B. (2008). Avatars, Explorations in Synthetic Consciousness and Cognition. In M. H. Schifreen (Ed.), Digital arts and culture 2009. Academic Press.

Davis, S. M., & Thorson, E. (2021). The metaverse: Promise, peril, and paradigm shift. *Journal of Advertising, 50*, 279–288.

Dawra, S., Chand, P. K., & Aggarwal, A. (2022). Leader Member Exchange, Nepotism, and Employee Loyalty as the Determinants of Organizational Sustainability in Small and Medium Enterprises in India. *International Journal of Sociotechnology and Knowledge Development, 14*(1), 1–21. doi:10.4018/IJSKD.297980

De Kare-Silver, M. (2001). e-shock: the new rules, e-strategies for retailers and manufacturers: Palgrave. *Developmental Review, 4*(3), 356–367.

Dede, C. (2009). Immersive interfaces for engagement and learning. *Science, 323*(5910), 66-69.

Del Vecchio, P., Secundo, G., & Garzoni, A. (2023). Phygital technologies and environments for breakthrough innovation in customers' and citizens' journey. A critical literature review and future agenda. *Technological Forecasting and Social Change, 189*, 122342.

Dellazizzo, L., Potvin, S., Bahig, S., & Dumais, A. (2019). Comprehensive review on virtual reality for the treatment of violence: Implications for youth with schizophrenia. *NPJ Schizophrenia, 5*(1), 11. Advance online publication. doi:10.1038/s41537-019-0079-7 PMID:31337763

Dhiman, R., Chand, P. K., & Gupta, S. (2018). Behavioural aspects influencing decision to purchase apparels amongst young Indian consumers. *FIIB Business Review, 7*(3), 188–200. doi:10.1177/2319714518790308

Di Pietro, R., & Cresci, S. (2021, December). Metaverse: security and privacy issues. In *2021 Third IEEE International Conference on Trust, Privacy and Security in Intelligent Systems and Applications (TPS-ISA)* (pp. 281-288). IEEE.

Dimitriadou, E., & Lanitis, A. (2023). A critical evaluation, challenges, and future perspectives of using artificial intelligence and emerging technologies in smart classrooms. *Smart Learning Environments, 10*(1), 12. Advance online publication. doi:10.1186/s40561-023-00231-3

Dincelli, E., & Yayla, A. (2022). Immersive virtual reality in the age of the Metaverse: A hybrid-narrative review based on the technology affordance perspective. *The Journal of Strategic Information Systems*, *31*(2), 101717. doi:10.1016/j.jsis.2022.101717

Dinh, H., Moore, C., & Russell, A. (2011). McEliece and Niederreiter cryptosystems that resist quantum Fourier sampling attacks. *Advances in Cryptology–CRYPTO 2011: 31st Annual Cryptology Conference, Santa Barbara, CA, USA, August 14-18, 2011 Proceedings*, *31*, 761–779.

Dionisio, J. D. N., Burns, W. G., & Gilbert, R. (2013). 3D virtual worlds and the metaverse: Current status and future possibilities. *ACM Computing Surveys*, *45*(3), 1–38. Advance online publication. doi:10.1145/2480741.2480751

Dogadkina, O. (2022). *Metaverse Shopping: Retailers' New Reality*. VentureBeat. https://venturebeat.com/datadecisionmakers/ metaverse-shopping-retailers-new-reality/

Dolata, M., & Schwabe, G. (2023). What is the Metaverse and who seeks to define it? Mapping the site of social construction. *Journal of Information Technology*, *38*(3), 239–266. doi:10.1177/02683962231159927

Donath, J. S. (1999). Identity and deception in the virtual community. *Communities in Cyberspace,* 29-59.

Duan, H., Li, J., Fan, S., Lin, Z., Wu, X., & Cai, W. (2021). Metaverse for Social Good: A University Campus Prototype. *MM 2021 - Proceedings of the 29th ACM International Conference on Multimedia*, 153–161. 10.1145/3474085.3479238

Ducheneaut, N., Wen, M. H., Yee, N., & Wadley, G. (2009, April). Body and mind: a study of avatar personalization in three virtual worlds. In *Proceedings of the SIGCHI conference on human factors in computing systems* (pp. 1151-1160). 10.1145/1518701.1518877

Due, B. L., & Nielsen, A. M. R. (2019). Prototyping the Omnichannel Solutions. *CIRCD Working Papers Soc. Interact.,* *5*(1), 1-29.

Due, B. L., & Toft, T. L. (2021). Phygital highlighting: Achieving joint visual attention when physically co-editing a digital text. *Journal of Pragmatics*, *177*, 1–17. doi:10.1016/j.pragma.2021.01.034

Duinkharjav, B., Chen, K., Tyagi, A., He, J., Zhu, Y., & Sun, Q. (2022). Color-perception-guided display power reduction for virtual reality. *ACM Transactions on Graphics*, *41*(6), 1–16. doi:10.1145/3550454.3555473

Dunn, T. J., & Kennedy, M. (2019). Technology Enhanced Learning in higher education; motivations, engagement and academic achievement. *Computers & Education*, *137*, 104–113. doi:10.1016/j.compedu.2019.04.004

Dwivedi, R. K., Singh, S., & Mahapatra, S. (2022). Metaversein Business Research: A Systematic Literature Review. *Journal of Global Information Technology Management*, *25*(4), 525–551.

Dwivedi, Y. K., Hughes, D. L., Coombs, C., Constantiou, I., Duan, Y., Edwards, J. S., Gupta, B., Lal, B., Misra, S., Prashant, P., Raman, R., Rana, N. P., Sharma, S. K., & Upadhyay, N. (2020). Impact of COVID-19 pandemic on information management research and practice: Transforming education, work and life. *International Journal of Information Management*, *55*, 102211. doi:10.1016/j.ijinfomgt.2020.102211

Dwivedi, Y. K., Hughes, L., Baabdullah, A. M., Ribeiro-Navarrete, S., Giannakis, M., Al-Debei, M. M., Dennehy, D., Metri, B., Buhalis, D., Cheung, C. M. K., Conboy, K., Doyle, R., Dubey, R., Dutot, V., Felix, R., Goyal, D. P., Gustafsson, A., Hinsch, C., Jebabli, I., ... Wamba, S. F. (2022). Metaverse beyond the hype: Multidisciplinary perspectives on emerging challenges, opportunities, and agenda for research, practice and policy. *International Journal of Information Management*, *66*, 102542. doi:10.1016/j.ijinfomgt.2022.102542

Dwivedi, Y. K., Hughes, L., Wang, Y., Alalwan, A. A., Ahn, S. J., Balakrishnan, J., Barta, S., Belk, R., Buhalis, D., Dutot, V., Felix, R., Filieri, R., Flavián, C., Gustafsson, A., Hinsch, C., Hollensen, S., Jain, V., Kim, J., Krishen, A. S., ... Wirtz, J. (2023). Metaverse marketing: How the metaverse will shape the future of consumer research and practice. *Psychology and Marketing*, *40*(4), 750–776. doi:10.1002/mar.21767

Eduverse. (2023, December 16). *A Safe and Secure K-12 "Metaverse."* Author.

Eladhari, M. (2007). The player's journey. *The players' realm: Studies on the culture of video games and gaming*, 171-87.

Enholm, I. M., Papagiannidis, E., Mikalef, P., & Krogstie, J. (2022). Artificial Intelligence and Business Value: A Literature Review. *Information Systems Frontiers*, *24*(5), 1709–1734. doi:10.1007/s10796-021-10186-w

Errichiello, L., & Marasco, A. (2017). Tourism innovation-oriented public-private partnerships for smart destination development. In *Knowledge Transfer to and within Tourism*. Emerald Publishing Limited. doi:10.1108/S2042-144320170000008010

Etienne, E., Leclercq, A.-L., Remacle, A., Dessart, L., & Schyns, M. (2023). Perception of avatars nonverbal behaviours in virtual reality. *Psychology and Marketing*, *40*(11), 2464–2481. doi:10.1002/mar.21871

Euromoney. (2022). *What is Blockchain?* https://www.euromoney.com/learning/blockchain-explained/whatis-blockchain

Falchuk, B., Loeb, S., & Neff, R. (2018). The social metaverse: Battle for privacy. *IEEE Technology*.

Falchuk, B., Loeb, S., & Neff, R. (2018). The social metaverse: Battle for privacy. *IEEE Technology and Society Magazine*, *37*(2), 52–61. doi:10.1109/MTS.2018.2826060

Fang, F., Ventre, C., Basios, M., Kanthan, L., Martinez-Rego, D., Wu, F., & Li, L. (2022). Cryptocurrency trading: A comprehensive survey. *Financial Innovation*, *8*(1), 1–59. doi:10.1186/s40854-021-00321-6

Farshid, M., Paschen, J., Eriksson, T., & Kietzmann, J. (2018). Go boldly! Explore augmented reality (AR), virtual reality (VR), and mixed reality (MR) for business. *Business Horizons, 61*(5), 657-663. / doi:10.1016/j.bushor.2018.05.009

Fazio, G., Fricano, S., Iannolino, S., & Pirrone, C. (2023). Metaverse and tourism development: Issues and opportunities in stakeholders' perception. *Information Technology & Tourism*, *25*(4), 507–528. doi:10.1007/s40558-023-00268-7

Firmansyah, E. A., & Umar, U. H. (2023). Metaverse in business research: A systematic literature review. *Cogent Business & Management*, *10*(2), 2. doi:10.1080/23311975.2023.2222499

Fischer, A. (2022). *Architecture as art in metaverse*. University of Zurich.

Floridi, L., & Taddeo, M. (Eds.). (2014). *The ethics of information warfare* (Vol. 14). Springer Science & Business Media. doi:10.1007/978-3-319-04135-3

Forte, M., Lercari, N., Galeazzi, F., & Borra, D. (2010). Metaverse communities and archaeology: The case of Teramo. *Proceedings of EuroMed*, 79-84.

Fox, J., Gilbert, M., & Tang, W. Y. (2018). Player experiences in a massively multiplayer online game: A diary study of performance, motivation, and social interaction. *New Media & Society*, *20*(11), 4056–4073. doi:10.1177/1461444818767102

Freeman, D., Reeve, S., Robinson, A., Ehlers, A., Clark, D. M., Spanlang, B., & Slater, M. (2017). Virtual reality in the assessment, understanding, and treatment of mental health disorders. *Psychological Medicine*, *47*(14), 2393–2400. doi:10.1017/S003329171700040X PMID:28325167

Freepik. (n.d.). https://www.freepik.com/free-vector/vr-sports-isometric-concept-with-virtual-reality-equipment-home-gym-martial-arts-games-isolated_7499008.htm#page=2&query=vr&position=1&from_view=author

Frey, D., Royan, J., Piegay, R., Kermarrec, A. M., Anceaume, E., & Le Fessant, F. (2008). Solipsis: A decentralized architecture for virtual environments. *1st International Workshop on Massively Multiuser Virtual Environments.*

Gaafar, A. A. (2021). Metaverse in architectural heritage documentation & education. *Advances in Ecological and Environmental Research*, *6*(10), 66–86.

Gaggioli, A. (2017). Phygital spaces: When atoms meet bits. *Cyberpsychology, Behavior, and Social Networking*, *20*(12), 774–774. doi:10.1089/cyber.2017.29093.csi

Gao, H., Chong, A. Y. L., & Bao, H. (2023). Metaverse: Literature Review, Synthesis and Future Research Agenda. *Journal of Computer Information Systems*, 1–21. doi:10.1080/08874417.2023.2233455

Gao, W., Li, W., Fan, H., & Jia, X. (2021). How customer experience incongruence affects omnichannel customer retention: The moderating role of channel characteristics. *Journal of Retailing and Consumer Services*, *60*, 102487. doi:10.1016/j.jretconser.2021.102487

García, Á., Bregon, A., & Martínez-Prieto, M. A. (2024). Digital Twin Learning Ecosystem: A cyber–physical framework to integrate human-machine knowledge in traditional manufacturing. *Internet of Things : Engineering Cyber Physical Human Systems*, *25*, 101094. doi:10.1016/j.iot.2024.101094

García, M., & Rodríguez, P. (2023). Collaborative Innovation in the Metaverse: Stakeholder Approach. *Journal of Metaverse Studies*, *10*(1), 102–120.

Gartner. (2023). *Metaverse Marketing Trends: Shaping the Future of Engagement.* Author.

Gegenfurtner, A., & Ebner, C. (2019). Webinars in higher education and professional training: A meta-analysis and systematic review of randomized controlled trials. *Educational Research Review*, *28*, 100293. doi:10.1016/j.edurev.2019.100293

Gent, E. (2022). Lessons from a second life> before meta, Philip Rosedale created an online universe. *IEEE Spectrum*, *59*(1), 19–19. doi:10.1109/MSPEC.2022.9676346

George-Parkin, H. (2022). *How The Metaverse & NFTs are Changing Fashion.* The Zoe Report. https://www.thezoereport.com/ fashion/metaverse-nft-fashion

Ghali, Z., Rather, R. A., & Khan, I. (2024). Investigating metaverse marketing-enabled consumers' social presence, attachment, engagement and (re) visit intentions. *Journal of Retailing and Consumer Services*, *77*, 103671. doi:10.1016/j.jretconser.2023.103671

Gilbert, N. (2022). *Number of Gamers Worldwide 2022/2023: Demographics, Statistics, and Predictions.* FinancesOnline. https://financesonline.com/number-of-gamersworldwide/

Gioia, D. A., Corley, K. G., & Hamilton, A. L. (2013). Seeking qualitative rigor in inductive research: Notes on the Gioia methodology. *Organizational Research Methods*, *16*(1), 15–31. doi:10.1177/1094428112452151

Go, H., & Kang, M. (2022). Metaverse tourism for sustainable tourism development: Tourism Agenda 2020. *Tourism Review*, *78*(2), 1–16.

Gomes, E., Rebelo, F., Vilas Boas, N., Noriega, P., & Vilar, E. (2023). Virtual Reality in the Teaching of History of Architecture and Urbanism: A Literature Review. In *International Conference on Human-Computer Interaction* (pp. 437-453). Cham: Springer Nature Switzerland. 10.1007/978-3-031-35696-4_32

Goyal, J., Singh, M., Singh, R., & Aggarwal, A. (2019). Efficiency and technology gaps in Indian banking sector: Application of meta-frontier directional distance function DEA approach. *The Journal of Finance and Data Science, 5*(3), 156-172.

Gretzel, U. (2019). The role of social media in creating and addressing overtourism. *Overtourism: Issues, Realities and Solutions, 1*, 62-75.

Gretzel, U., Sigala, M., Xiang, Z., & Koo, C. (2015). Smart tourism: Foundations and developments. *Electronic Markets, 25*(3), 179–188. doi:10.1007/s12525-015-0196-8

Gretzel, U., Werthner, H., Koo, C., & Lamsfus, C. (2015). Conceptual foundations for understanding smart tourism ecosystems. *Computers in Human Behavior, 50*, 558–563. doi:10.1016/j.chb.2015.03.043

Gretzel, U., Zhong, L., & Koo, C. (2016). Application of smart tourism to cities. *International Journal of Tourism Cities, 2*(2). Advance online publication. doi:10.1108/IJTC-04-2016-0007

Grupac, M., Machcinik, S., & Negoianu, A. E. (2023). Immersive engagement and geospatial mapping technologies, deep learning and neural network algorithms, and visual perception and data mining tools in metaverse interactive and extended reality environments. *Linguistic and Philosophical Investigations, 22*(0), 196–212. doi:10.22381/lpi22202312

Gupta, P. (2023). HR Analytics: An Effective Tool for Performance Management and Business Development. In *HR Analytics in an Era of Rapid Automation* (pp. 112-126). IGI Global. https://www.worldcat.org/title/snow-crash/oclc/28102783/lists

Gupta, V., Agarwal, S., & Bansal, A. (2024). Entrepreneurship in the World of Metaverse: Opportunities and Challenges. *Entrepreneurship and Creativity in the Metaverse*, 1-19. https://connect.comptia.org/blog/metaverse-statistics-facts-stats-market-size-and-future

Gupta, M., Taneja, S., Sharma, V., Singh, A., Rupeika-Apoga, R., & Jangir, K. (2023). Does Previous Experience with the Unified Payments Interface (UPI) Affect the Usage of Central Bank Digital Currency (CBDC)? *Journal of Risk and Financial Management, 16*(6), 286. doi:10.3390/jrfm16060286

Gupta, S., Nath Mishra, O., & Kumar, S. (2022). Tourist participation, well-being and satisfaction: The mediating roles of service experience and tourist empowerment. *Current Issues in Tourism*, 1–16.

Gursoy, D., Malodia, S., & Dhir, A. (2022). The metaverse in the hospitality and tourism industry: An overview of current trends and future research directions. *Journal of Hospitality Marketing & Management, 31*(5), 527–534. doi:10.1080/19368623.2022.2072504

Harris Poll, A. (2021). *Interest in NFTs from Certain Major Brands in the United States in March 2021, by Age and Gender* [Graph]. Available online: https://www.statista.com/statistics/1265870/us-nft-branding

Harris, D. J., Buckingham, G., Wilson, M. R., Brookes, J., Mushtaq, F., Mon-Williams, M., & Vine, S. J. (2020). The effect of a virtual reality environment on gaze behaviour and motor skill learning. *Psychology of Sport and Exercise, 50*, 101721. doi:10.1016/j.psychsport.2020.101721

Harris, D., Bird, J. M., Smart, P., Wilson, M. R., & Vine, S. J. (2020). A framework for the testing and validation of simulated environments in experimentation and training. *Frontiers in Psychology, 11*, 605. Advance online publication. doi:10.3389/fpsyg.2020.00605 PMID:32296379

Harris, M. C., Brown, D. J., Vyas, P., & Lewis, J. (2022). A methodology for the co-design of shared VR environments with people with intellectual disabilities: insights from the preparation phase. *International Conference on Human-Computer Interaction*, 217–230. 10.1007/978-3-031-05039-8_15

Harvie, D. (2021). Immersive education for chronic condition self-management. *Frontiers in Virtual Reality*, *2*, 657761. Advance online publication. doi:10.3389/frvir.2021.657761

Hassan, M. U., Rehmani, M. H., & Chen, J. (2019). Privacy preservation in blockchain based IoT systems: Integration issues, prospects, challenges, and future research directions. *Future Generation Computer Systems*, *97*, 512–529. doi:10.1016/j.future.2019.02.060

Heljakka, K., & Ihamäki, P. 2020. Toys that mobilize: past, present and future of phygital playful technology. In *Proceedings of the Future Technologies Conference (FTC) 2019: Volume 2* (pp. 625-640). Springer International Publishing. 10.1007/978-3-030-32523-7_46

Herbst, R. B., Rybak, T. M., Meisman, A., Whitehead, M., Rosen, B. L., Crosby, L. E., . . . Real, F. J. (2021). A virtual reality resident training curriculum on behavioural health anticipatory guidance: development and usability study (preprint) https://doi.org/ doi:10.2196/preprints.29518

Herrman, T. M., & Browning, S. (2021). *The Metaverse: A Primer*. Stanford University Press.

Hinings, B., Gegenhuber, T., & Greenwood, R. (2018). Digital innovation and transformation: An institutional perspective. *Information and Organization*, *28*(1), 52–61. doi:10.1016/j.infoandorg.2018.02.004

Hiraki, T., Fukushima, S., & Naemura, T. 2016. Phygital field: an integrated field with a swarm of physical robots and digital images. In SIGGRAPH ASIA 2016 Emerging Technologies (pp. 1-2). doi:10.1145/2988240.2988242

Hmelo-Silver, C. E., Duncan, R. G., & Chinn, C. A. (2007). Scaffolding and achievement in problem-based and inquiry learning: A response to Kirschner, Sweller, and. *Educational Psychologist*, *42*(2), 99–107. doi:10.1080/00461520701263368

Hoffman, H., Patterson, D., Carrougher, G., & Sharar, S. (2001). Effectiveness of virtual reality–based pain control with multiple treatments. *The Clinical Journal of Pain*, *17*(3), 229–235. doi:10.1097/00002508-200109000-00007 PMID:11587113

Höjer, M., & Wangel, J. (2015). Smart sustainable cities: definition and challenges. In *ICT innovations for sustainability* (pp. 333–349). Springer International Publishing. doi:10.1007/978-3-319-09228-7_20

Hollensen, S., Kotler, P., & Opresnik, M. O. (2022). Metaverse–the new marketing universe. *Journal of Business Strategy*.

Hong, Y., Sawang, S., & Yang, H. P. (2023). How is entrepreneurial marketing shaped by E-commerce technology: A case study of Chinese pure-play e-retailers. *International Journal of Entrepreneurial Behaviour & Research*.

Hua, J. (2022). On the Architechural Design from the view of the Future Metaverse. In Диалог культур-диалог о мире и во имя мира (pp. 565-569). Academic Press.

Huang, K., Wang, K., Lee, P. K. C., & Yeung, A. C. L. (2023). The impact of industry 4.0 on supply chain capability and supply chain resilience: A dynamic resource-based view. *International Journal of Production Economics, 262*. doi:10.1016/j.ijpe.2023.108913

Huang, L., & Ma, K.-S. (2018). *Introducing machine learning to first-year undergraduate engineering students through an authentic and active learning labware*. Paper presented at the 2018 IEEE Frontiers in Education Conference (FIE). 10.1109/FIE.2018.8659308

Huang, C., Zhang, Q., Guo, D., Zhao, X., & Wang, X. (2022). Discovering association rules with graph patterns in temporal networks. *Tsinghua Science and Technology*, *28*(2), 344–359. doi:10.26599/TST.2021.9010090

Huang, J., Sun, P., & Zhang, W. (2022). *Analysis of the Future Prospects for the Metaverse. Advances in Economics, Business and Management Research. 648*. Atlantis Press International B.V. Retrieved from https://creativecommons.org/licenses/by-nc/4.0/

Huang, L., & Dai, Q. (2022). The Metaverse: A New Paradigm for Social Interaction. *IEEE Transactions on Computational Social Systems*, *9*(2), 437–446.

Huang, Y. (2018). *Research on the Marketing Strategy of Luxury Brands. Graduate*. Wuhan University.

Huang, Y., Li, Y. J., & Cai, Z. (2023). Security and privacy in metaverse: A comprehensive survey. *Big Data Mining and Analytics*, *6*(2), 234–247. doi:10.26599/BDMA.2022.9020047

Hughes, I. (2022). The metaverse: Is it the future? *Itnow*, *64*(1), 22–23. doi:10.1093/itnow/bwac011

Hunter, W. C., Chung, N., Gretzel, U., & Koo, C. (2015). Constructivist research in smart tourism. *Asia Pacific Journal of Information Systems*, *25*(1), 105–120. doi:10.14329/apjis.2015.25.1.105

Intelligence, B. (2021). *Metaverse may be $800 Billion Market, Next Tech Platform*. Bloomberg Intelligence. https: // www.bloomberg.com/professional/blog/metaverse-may-be-800-billionmarket-next-tech-platform/

Ioannidis, S., & Kontis, A. P. (2023). Metaverse for tourists and tourism destinations. *Information Technology & Tourism*, 1–24.

Isaac, M. (2022). 6 reasons meta is in trouble. *The New York Times*. Retrieved from https://www.nytimes.com/2022/02/03/technology/facebook-meta-challenges.html

Jabbar, R., Fetais, N., Krichen, M., & Barkaoui, K. (2020, February). Blockchain technology for healthcare: Enhancing shared electronic health record interoperability and integrity. In 2020 IEEE International Conference on Informatics, IoT, and Enabling Technologies (ICIoT) (pp. 310-317). IEEE.

Jaung, W. (2022). Digital forest recreation in the metaverse: Opportunities and challenges. *Technological Forecasting and Social Change*, *185*, 122090. doi:10.1016/j.techfore.2022.122090

Jeon, H., Youn, H., Ko, S., & Kim, T. (2021). Blockchain and AI Meet in the Metaverse. In T. M. Fern'andez-Caram'es & P. Fraga-Lamas (Eds.), *Advances in the Convergence of Blockchain and Artificial Intelligence*. IntechOpen. 10.5772/intechopen.99114

Jeong, H. (2019). Rethinking Open Universities: What makes them unique? *International Review of Research in Open and Distance Learning*, *20*(4), 152–166. doi:10.19173/irrodl.v20i4.4163

Jindal, P., & Gambhir, R. (2022). Marketing in a Pandemic. In Developing Relationships, Personalization, and Data Herald in Marketing 5.0 (pp. 57-68). IGI Global. doi:10.4018/978-1-6684-4496-2.ch003

Jindal, A., Jindal, P., & Chavan, L. (2023). Customer Engagement Through Emotional Branding. In *Promoting Consumer Engagement Through Emotional Branding and Sensory Marketing* (pp. 201–210). IGI Global.

Ji, S., Hwang, H. J., Hwang, C., Koo, C., & Lee, E. (2022). The attributes of virtual reality(vr) experiences and spatial cognition among tourists: Focusing on a behavioural geographic perspective. *The Tourism Sciences Society of Korea*, *46*(4), 153–176. doi:10.17086/JTS.2022.46.4.153.176

Johnson, M., & Barlow, R. (2021). Defining the phygital marketing advantage. *Journal of Theoretical and Applied Electronic Commerce Research*, *16*(6), 2365–2385. doi:10.3390/jtaer16060130

Johnson, R. (2022). Technological Literacy in the Metaverse: A Critical Analysis. *Journal of Emerging Technologies*, *18*(4), 221–238.

Jones, L., & Williams, K. (2023). Ethical Considerations in the Metaverse: Navigating Digital Rights and Privacy. *Journal of Business Ethics*, *40*(2), 203–220.

Jovanović, A., & Milosavljević, A. (2022). VoRtex Metaverse platform for gamified collaborative learning. *Electronics (Basel)*, *11*(3), 317. doi:10.3390/electronics11030317

Jung, T. H., & tom Dieck, M. C. (2017). Augmented reality, virtual reality and 3D printing for the co-creation of value for the visitor experience at cultural heritage places. *Journal of Place Management and Development*, *10*(2), 140–151. doi:10.1108/JPMD-07-2016-0045

Kaddoura, S., & Al Husseiny, F. (2023). The rising trend of Metaverse in education: Challenges, opportunities, and ethical considerations. *PeerJ. Computer Science*, *9*, e1252. doi:10.7717/peerj-cs.1252 PMID:37346578

Kamenov, K. (n.d.). *Immersive Experience—The 4th Wave in Tech: Learning the Ropes*. Available online: https://www.accenture.com/ gb-en/blogs/blogs-immersive-experience-wave-learning-ropes

Kapferer, J.-N. (2012). *The Luxury Strategy: Break the Rules of Marketing to Build Luxury Brands*. Kogan Page.

Kaplan, A. M., & Haenlein, M. (2010). The Fairyland of Second Life: Virtual Social Worlds and How to Use Them. *Business Horizons*, *52*(6), 563–572. doi:10.1016/j.bushor.2009.07.002

Kaplan, A. M., & Haenlein, M. (2010). Users of the world, unite! The challenges and opportunities of social media. *Business Horizons*, *53*(1), 59–68. doi:10.1016/j.bushor.2009.09.003

Kaplan, A. M., & Haenlein, M. (2019). The Metaverse as the final frontier: Implications for social media research. *Journal of Marketing Management*, *35*(15-16), 1422–1449.

Karaca, S., & Baran, Z. (2024). Meta Evolution: Digital Marketing in Tourism. In Digital Business and Optimizing Operating Strategies (pp. 91-131). IGI Global.

Karampourniotis, P., & Fafaliou, I. (2022). The Metaverse: A Sustainable Way for Companies to Compete. In *Competitive Intelligence and Strategic Management* (pp. 169–184). Springer.

Kaur, A., & Singh, J. (2023). Brand Building in Metaverse. In *Applications of Neuromarketing in the Metaverse* (pp. 78–87). IGI Global. doi:10.4018/978-1-6684-8150-9.ch006

Kermlin, J. (2021). The Metaverse: A New Digital Frontier? *Journal of Virtual Reality and Augmented Reality*, *3*(2), 87–103.

Khandelwal, J. (2022). A Research Study of Businesses that are Thriving in the Virtual World of Metaverse. In PRIMA (Vol. 10, No. 2, p. 29). Publishing India Group.

Kim, J., Jang, H., Kim, D., & Lee, J. (2023). Exploration of the Virtual Reality Teleportation Methods Using Hand-Tracking, Eye-Tracking, and EEG. *International Journal of Human-Computer Interaction*, *39*(20), 4112–4125. doi:10.1080/10447318.2022.2109248

Kim, J., Kang, S., & Lee, K. H. (2021). Evolution of digital marketing communication: Bibliometric analysis and network visualization from key articles. *Journal of Business Research*, *130*, 552–563. doi:10.1016/j.jbusres.2019.09.043

Kim, J., Park, S., & Lim, H. (2021). Developing a virtual reality for people with dementia in nursing homes based on their psychological needs: A feasibility study. *BMC Geriatrics*, *21*(1), 167. Advance online publication. doi:10.1186/s12877-021-02125-w PMID:33678160

Kiong, L. V. (2022). *Metaverse Made Easy: A Beginner's Guide to the Metaverse: Everything you need to know about Metaverse*. NFT and GameFi.

Kip, H., Oberschmidt, K., & Bierbooms, J. J. (2020). eHealth technology in forensic mental healthcare: Recommendations for achieving benefits and overcoming barriers. *International Journal of Forensic Mental Health*, *20*(1), 31–47. doi:10.1080/14999013.2020.1808914

Kiya.ai. (2023). *Kiya.ai*. Retrieved from https://www.kiya.ai/bharatmeta-taking-india-forward-as-the-leading-force-in-the-area-of-metaverse/

Klaus, P. P. (2021). phygital–the emperor's new clothes? *Journal of Strategic Marketing*, 1–8. doi:10.1080/0965254X.2021.1976252

Koohang, A., Nord, J. H., Ooi, K.-B., Tan, G. W.-H., Al-Emran, M., Aw, E. C.-X., Baabdullah, A. M., Buhalis, D., Cham, T.-H., Dennis, C., Dutot, V., Dwivedi, Y. K., Hughes, L., Mogaji, E., Pandey, N., Phau, I., Raman, R., Sharma, A., Sigala, M., ... Wong, L.-W. (2023). Shaping the metaverse into reality: A holistic multidisciplinary understanding of opportunities, challenges, and avenues for future investigation. *Journal of Computer Information Systems*, *63*(3), 735–765. doi:10.1080/08874417.2023.2165197

Ko, S. Y., Chung, H. K., Kim, J. I., & Shin, Y. (2021). A study on the typology and advancement of cultural leisure-based metaverse. *KIPS Transactions on Software and Data Engineering*, *10*(8), 331–338.

Kozinets, R. V. (2022). Immersive netnography: A novel method for service experience research in virtual reality, augmented reality and metaverse contexts. *Journal of Service Management*, *34*(1), 100–125. doi:10.1108/JOSM-12-2021-0481

Kumar, N. M., & Mallick, P. K. (2018). Blockchain technology for security issues and challenges in IoT. *Procedia Computer Science*, *132*, 1815–1823. doi:10.1016/j.procs.2018.05.140

Kumar, P., Kumar, R., Srivastava, G., Gupta, G. P., Tripathi, R., Gadekallu, T. R., & Xiong, N. N. (2021). PPSF: A privacy-preserving and secure framework using blockchain-based machine-learning for IoT-driven smart cities. *IEEE Transactions on Network Science and Engineering*, *8*(3), 2326–2341. doi:10.1109/TNSE.2021.3089435

Kye, B., Han, N., Kim, E., Park, Y., & Jo, S. (2021). Educational applications of metaverse: Possibilities and limitations. *Journal of Educational Evaluation for Health Professions*, *18*, 18. doi:10.3352/jeehp.2021.18.32 PMID:34897242

Каширипур, М. М. (2023). Metaverse city: definition and direction development for urban planning and architecture. *Вестник Брестского государственного технического университета*, *3*(132), 2-10.

Laine, J., Lindqvist, T., Korhonen, T., & Hakkarainen, K. (2022). Systematic review of intelligent tutoring systems for hard skills training in virtual reality environments. *International Journal of Technology in Education and Science*, *6*(2), 178–203. doi:10.46328/ijtes.348

Lamsfus, C., Martin, D., Alzua-Sorzabal, A., & Torres-Manzanera, E. 2015. Smart tourism destinations: An extended conception of smart cities focusing on human mobility. In *Information and Communication Technologies in Tourism 2015: Proceedings of the International Conference in Lugano, Switzerland, February 3-6, 2015* (pp. 363-375). Springer International Publishing.

Lau, K. W. (2014). The gender differences in metaverse: a study of university art & design students. Open Journal of Art and Communication, 1(1), 14-19.

Lawry, C. A. (2022). Blurring luxury: The mediating role of self-gifting in consumer acceptance of phygital shopping experiences. *International Journal of Advertising*, *41*(4), 796–822. doi:10.1080/02650487.2021.1903742

Lebiecka, Z., Skoneczny, T., Tyburski, E., Samochowiec, J., & Kucharska-Mazur, J. (2021). Is virtual reality cue exposure a promising adjunctive treatment for alcohol use disorder? *Journal of Clinical Medicine*, *10*(13), 2972. doi:10.3390/jcm10132972 PMID:34279455

Lee, L. H., Braud, T., Zhou, P., Wang, L., Xu, D., Lin, Z., . . . Hui, P. (2021). All one needs to know about metaverse: A complete survey on technological singularity, virtual ecosystem, and research agenda. *arXiv preprint arXiv:2110.05352.*

Lee, L. H., Braud, T., Zhou, P., Wang, L., Xu, D., Lin, Z., Kumar, A., Bermejo, C., & Hui, P. 2021. All one needs to know about metaverse: A complete survey on technological singularity, virtual ecosystem, and research agenda. *arXiv preprint arXiv:2110.05352.*

Lee, H., & Kim, J. (2022). Responsible Use of Technology in the Metaverse: A Framework for Entrepreneurs. *Technology and Society Journal*, *25*(1), 56–73.

Lee, J., Azamfar, M., & Bagheri, B. (2021). A unified digital twin framework for shop floor design in industry 4.0 manufacturing systems. *Manufacturing Letters*, *27*, 87–91. doi:10.1016/j.mfglet.2021.01.005

Lee, J., Bagheri, B., & Kao, H. A. (2015). A cyber-physical systems architecture for industry 4.0-based manufacturing systems. *Manufacturing Letters*, *3*, 18–23. doi:10.1016/j.mfglet.2014.12.001

Lee, L.-H., Braud, T., & Zhou, P. (2021). All one needs to know about metaverse: A complete survey on technological singularity, virtual ecosystem, and research agenda. *Journal Of Latex Class Files*, *14*, 2021.

LeeL.-H.BraudT.ZhouP.WangL.XuD.LinZ.HuiP. (2021). *All One Needs to Know about Metaverse: A Complete Survey on Technological Singularity, Virtual Ecosystem, and Research Agenda*. Retrieved from http://arxiv.org/abs/2110.05352

Lessig, L. (1999). *Code and other laws of cyberspace*. Basic Books.

Liberman, N., Trope, Y., & Stephan, E. (2007). Psychological distance. Social psychology: Handbook of basic principles, 2(2), 353-383.

Li, F. (2007). *What is e-Business? How the Internet Transforms Organisations*. Blackwell.

Li, F., Whalley, J., & Williams, H. (2001). Between the Electronic and Physical Spaces: Implications for Organisations in the Networked Economy. *Environment & Planning A*, *33*, 699–716. doi:10.1068/a33161

Lin, H., Wan, S., Gan, W., Chen, J., & Chao, H. C. (2022, December). Metaverse in education: Vision, opportunities, and challenges. In *2022 IEEE International Conference on Big Data (Big Data)* (pp. 2857-2866). IEEE. 10.1109/BigData55660.2022.10021004

Liu, J., Chai, C., Luo, Y., Lou, Y., Feng, J., & Tang, N. (2022). Feature augmentation with reinforcement learning. *2022 IEEE 38th International Conference on Data Engineering (ICDE),* 3360–3372.

Liu, G., Wang, X., Gao, N., & Hu, H. (2021). From Virtual Reality to Metaverse: A New Direction for Online Education. *Modern Distance Education Research*, *33*, 14–16.

Liu, H., Yao, X., Yang, T., & Ning, H. (2018). Cooperative privacy preservation for wearable devices in hybrid computing-based smart health. *IEEE Internet of Things Journal*, *6*(2), 1352–1362. doi:10.1109/JIOT.2018.2843561

Liu, R., Li, H., & Lv, Z. (2023). Modeling methods of 3D model in digital twins. *Computer Modeling in Engineering & Sciences*, *136*(2), 985–1022. doi:10.32604/cmes.2023.023154

Liu, X., Wang, D., & Gretzel, U. (2022). On-site decision-making in smartphone-mediated contexts. *Tourism Management*, *88*, 104424. doi:10.1016/j.tourman.2021.104424

Liu, X., Xing, X., & Fu, B. (2016). *Luxury Studies*. Donghua University Press.

Li, X., Gong, J., Gao, B., & Yuan, P. (2021). Impacts of COVID-19 on tourists' destination preferences: Evidence from China. *Annals of Tourism Research*, *90*, 103258. doi:10.1016/j.annals.2021.103258 PMID:34924648

Li, Y., Gunasekeran, D. V., RaviChandran, N., Tan, T. F., Ong, J. C. L., Thirunavukarasu, A. J., Polascik, B. W., Habash, R., Khaderi, K., & Ting, D. S. W. (2023). The next generation of healthcare ecosystem in the metaverse. *Biomedical Journal*, 100679. doi:10.1016/j.bj.2023.100679 PMID:38048990

Li, Y., Hu, C., Huang, C., & Duan, L. (2017). The concept of smart tourism in the context of tourism information services. *Tourism Management*, *58*, 293–300. doi:10.1016/j.tourman.2016.03.014

Lopez de Avila, A. (2015, February). Smart destinations: XXI century tourism. In ENTER2015 conference on information and communication technologies in tourism, Lugano, Switzerland (pp. 4-6). Academic Press.

Ludlow, P., & Wallace, M. (2007). *The Second Life Herald: The virtual tabloid that witnessed the dawn of the metaverse*. MIT Press.

Luo, Y., Su, Z., Zheng, W., Chen, Z., Wang, F., Zhang, Z., & Chen, J. (2021). A novel memory-hard password hashing scheme for blockchain-based cyberphysical systems. *ACM Transactions on Internet Technology*, *21*(2), 1–21. doi:10.1145/3408310

Lupetti, M. L. (2016, March). Designing playful HRI: Acceptability of robots in everyday life through play. In *2016 11th ACM/IEEE International Conference on Human-Robot Interaction (HRI)* (pp. 631-632). IEEE.

Lupetti, M. L., Piumatti, G., & Rossetto, F. (2015, June). Phygital play HRI in a new gaming scenario. In *2015 7th International Conference on Intelligent Technologies for Interactive Entertainment (INTETAIN)* (pp. 17-21). IEEE. 10.4108/icst.intetain.2015.259563

Lv, Z., Shang, W. L., & Guizani, M. (2022). Impact of digital twins and metaverse on cities: History, current situation, and application perspectives. *Applied Sciences (Basel, Switzerland)*, *12*(24), 12820. doi:10.3390/app122412820

MacCallum, K., & Parsons, D. (2019). Teacher perspectives on mobile augmented reality: The potential of metaverse for learning. *World Conference on Mobile and Contextual Learning*, 21–28.

Malaby, T. (2006, April). Parlaying Value: Capital in and beyond Virtual Worlds. *Games and Culture*, *1*(2), 141–162. doi:10.1177/1555412006286688

Maleki Vishkaei, B. (2022). Metaverse: A New Platform for Circular Smart Cities. In *Cases on Circular Economy in Practice* (pp. 51–69). IGI Global. doi:10.4018/978-1-6684-5001-7.ch003

Malik, S., Dedeoglu, V., Kanhere, S. S., & Jurdak, R. (2019, July). Trustchain: Trust management in blockchain and iot supported supply chains. In *2019 IEEE International Conference on Blockchain (Blockchain)* (pp. 184-193). IEEE. 10.1109/Blockchain.2019.00032

Mancuso, I., Petruzzelli, A. M., & Panniello, U. (2023). Digital business model innovation in metaverse: How to approach virtual economy opportunities. *Information Processing & Management*, *60*(5), 103457. doi:10.1016/j.ipm.2023.103457

Mandal, A. (2023, May 17). The role of Blockchain in Building Trust and security in the metaverse. LinkedIn. https://www.linkedin.com/pulse/role-blockchainbuilding-trust-security-metaverse-ankit-mand al/

Marabelli, M., & Newell, S. (2022). Everything you always wanted to know about the metaverse* (*but were afraid to ask). *Proceedings of the Academy of Management Annual Meeting*. 10.5465/AMBPP.2022.11559abstract

Marchesani, F., Masciarelli, F., & Ceci, F. (2024). Digital trajectories in contemporary cities: Exploring the interplay between digital technology implementation, the amplitude of social media platforms, and tourists inflow in cities. *Cities (London, England)*, *146*, 104749. doi:10.1016/j.cities.2023.104749

Martins, L. D., Gilson, L. L., & Maynard, M. (2004). Virtual teams: What do we know and where do we go from here? *Journal of Management*, *30*(6), 805–835. doi:10.1016/j.jm.2004.05.002

Mayer, R. E. (2004). Should there be a three-strikes rule against pure discovery learning? *The American Psychologist*, *59*(1), 14–19. doi:10.1037/0003-066X.59.1.14 PMID:14736316

McDowell, M. (2022). What Teen Brands can Teach Us About Fashion in the Metaverse. *Vogue Business*. https://www.voguebusiness.com/technology/what-teen-brands-can-teach-us-about-fashionin-the-metaverse

McKinsey Digital. (2022, March 29). *What is the metaverse—and what does it mean for business?* McKinsey. https://www. mckinsey.com/capabilities/growth-marketing-and-sales/our-insights/value-creation-in-the-metaverse

McLuhan, M. (1964). *Understanding media*. Mentor.

Medium. (2022, March 16). *HSBC to become the first global financial services provider to enter The Sandbox*. Author.

Mele, C., Spena, T.R., Marzullo, M. & Di Bernardo, I. (2023). The phygital transformation: a systematic review and a research agenda. *Italian Journal of Marketing*, 1-27.

Mele, C., Russo-Spena, T., Tregua, M., & Amitrano, C. C. (2021). The millennial customer journey: A Phygital mapping of emotional, behavioural, and social experiences. *Journal of Consumer Marketing*, *38*(4), 420–433. doi:10.1108/JCM-03-2020-3701

Messinger, P. R., Ge, X., Stroulia, E., Lyons, K., Smirnov, K., & Bone, M. (2008). On the relationship between my avatar and myself. *Journal of Virtual Worlds Research*, *1*(2). Advance online publication. doi:10.4101/jvwr.v1i2.352

Mestre, D. (2015). *On the usefulness of the concept of presence in virtual reality applications*. doi:10.1117/12.2075798

Meta. (2022b). *This is Meta Quest Pro*. https://www.meta.com/quest/quest-pro/tech-specs/#tech-specs

Michalski, S. C., Szpak, A., Ellison, C., Cornish, R., & Loetscher, T. (2022). Using virtual reality to improve classroom behaviour in people with down syndrome: Within-subjects experimental design. *JMIR Serious Games*, *10*(2), e34373. doi:10.2196/34373 PMID:35124567

Microsoft. (2023a, December 16). *Mesh for Microsoft Teams aims to make collaboration in the 'metaverse' personal and fun*. https://news.microsoft.com/source/features/innovation/mesh-for-microsoft-teams/

Microsoft. (2023b, December 16). *Mixed Reality in your classroom*. https://www.microsoft.com/en-us/education/mixed-reality

Mieli, M. (2022). Phygital. In *Encyclopedia of Tourism Management and Marketing* (pp. 487–489). Edward Elgar Publishing. doi:10.4337/9781800377486.phygital

Mihalic, T. (2023). *Metaversal sustainability. New understanding of what to sustain*. International conference BEM-23, Tokyo, Japan.

Mihalic, T. (2024). Metaversal sustainability: Conceptualisation within the sustainable tourism paradigm. *Tourism Review*. Advance online publication. doi:10.1108/TR-09-2023-0609

Mileva, G. (2022). *The Ultimate Guide to Metaverse Virtual Real Estate*. Influencer Marketing Hub. https://influencermarketinghub. com/metaverse-virtual-real-estate/

Milgram, P., & Kishino, F. (1994). A taxonomy of mixed reality visual displays. *IEICE Transactions on Information and Systems*, *77*(12), 1321–1329.

Mingxiao, D., Xiaofeng, M., Zhe, Z., Xiangwei, W., & Qijun, C. (2017, October). A review on consensus algorithm of blockchain. In 2017 IEEE international conference on systems, man, and cybernetics (SMC) (pp. 2567-2572). IEEE.

Mishra, A., & Awasthi, S. (2022). Metaverse: Opportunities and challenges for marketers. *Management Dynamics*, *22*(1), 10. doi:10.57198/2583-4932.1305

Mishra, S., Malhotra, G., Chatterjee, R., & Shukla, Y. (2021). Consumer retention through phygital experience in omnichannel retailing: Role of consumer empowerment and satisfaction. *Journal of Strategic Marketing*, 1–18. doi:10.1080/0965254X.2021.1892162

Moffett, M., Fazio, M. W., & Wodehouse, L. (2003). *A world history of architecture*. Laurence King Publishing.

Molina, L. (2021). *Celebrity Avatars: A Technical Approach to Creating Digital Avatars for Social Marketing Strategies* [Doctoral dissertation]. Florida Atlantic University.

Monaco, S., & Sacchi, G. (2023). Travelling the Metaverse: Potential Benefits and Main Challenges for Tourism Sectors and Research Applications. *Sustainability (Basel)*, *15*(4), 3348. doi:10.3390/su15043348

Moneta, A. (2020). Architecture, heritage, and the metaverse. *Traditional Dwellings and Settlements Review*, *32*(1), 37–49.

Moravcikova, D., & Kliestikova, J. (2017). Brand building with using phygital marketing communication. *Journal of Economics. Business and Management*, *5*(3), 148–153.

Morina, N., Ijntema, H., Meyerbröker, K., & Emmelkamp, P. M. G. (2015). Can virtual reality exposure therapy gains be generalized to real-life? a meta-analysis of studies applying behavioural assessments. *Behaviour Research and Therapy*, *74*, 18–24. doi:10.1016/j.brat.2015.08.010 PMID:26355646

Mourtzis, D. (Ed.). (2021). *Design and operation of production networks for mass personalization in the era of cloud technology*. Elsevier.

Moy, C., & Gadgil, A. (2022). *Opportunities in the metaverse: How businesses can explore the metaverse*. Academic Press.

Munar, A. M. (2012). Social media strategies and destination management. *Scandinavian Journal of Hospitality and Tourism*, *12*(2), 101–120. doi:10.1080/15022250.2012.679047

Murugan, M., & Prabadevi, M. N. (2023). Impact of Industry 6.0 on Msme Entrepreneur's Performance and Entrepreneur's Emotional Intelligence in the Service Industry in India. *RGSA – Revista de Gestão Social e Ambiental, 17*(4). doi:10.24857/rgsa.v17n4-007

Mystakidis, S. (2022). Metaverse. *Metaverse. Encyclopedia*, *2*(1), 486–497. doi:10.3390/encyclopedia2010031

Mystakidis, S. (2022). The Metaversebetween Utopia and Dystopia: Towards A Critical Understanding of the Emerging Virtual World. *Futures*, *138*, 102965.

Nadini, M., Alessandretti, L., Di Giacinto, F., Martino, M., Aiello, L. M., & Baronchelli, A. (2021). Mapping the NFT revolution: Market trends, trade networks, and visual features. *Scientific Reports*, *11*(1), 20902. doi:10.1038/s41598-021-00053-8 PMID:34686678

Nakamoto, S. (2008). Bitcoin: A peer-to-peer electronic cash system. Decentralized business review.

Nakazawa, J., & Tokuda, H. (2007, May). Phygital map: Accessing digital multimedia from physical map. In *21st International Conference on Advanced Information Networking and Applications Workshops (AINAW'07)* (Vol. 2, pp. 368-373). IEEE. 10.1109/AINAW.2007.288

Narin, N. G. (2021). A Content Analysis of the AIDS Media. *Journal of Metaverse*, *1*(1), 17–24. https://lens.org/132-852-388-772-732

Narin, O. (2021). The Metaverse: An Overview of the Future of the Internet. *Journal of Technology Management & Innovation*, *16*(2), 1–15.

Navarro, J., Peña, J., Cebolla, A., & Baños, R. (2022). Can avatar appearance influence physical activity? User-avatar similarity and Proteus effects on cardiac frequency and step counts. *Health Communication*, *37*(2), 222–229. doi:10.1080/10410236.2020.1834194 PMID:33054371

Neuburger, L., Beck, J., & Egger, R. (2018). The 'Phygital'tourist experience: The use of augmented and virtual reality in destination marketing. In *Tourism planning and destination marketing* (pp. 183–202). Emerald Publishing Limited. doi:10.1108/978-1-78756-291-220181009

Neuhofer, B., Buhalis, D., & Ladkin, A. (2015). Smart technologies for personalized experiences: A case study in the hospitality domain. *Electronic Markets*, *25*(3), 243–254. doi:10.1007/s12525-015-0182-1

Nguyen, C. T., Hoang, D. T., Nguyen, D. N., & Dutkiewicz, E. (2022, June). Metachain: A novel blockchain-based framework for metaverse applications. In 2022 IEEE 95th Vehicular Technology Conference:(VTC2022-Spring) (pp. 1-5). IEEE. 10.1109/VTC2022-Spring54318.2022.9860983

Nick Clegg. (2023, December 16). *Metaverse Technologies Are Creating New Opportunities for Teachers to Inspire Students*. https://about.fb.com/news/2023/09/metaverse-technologies-education-opportunities/

Nijjer, S., Singh, J., Sharma, P., Malhotra, M., & Verma, R. (2023). Unraveling a New Age of Travel in Blockchain Based Metaverse. In *Mobile Radio Communications and 5G Networks: Proceedings of Third MRCN 2022* (pp. 555-570). Singapore: Springer Nature Singapore. 10.1007/978-981-19-7982-8_47

NingH.WangH.LinY.WangW.DhelimS.FarhaF.DaneshmandM. (2021). A Survey on Metaverse: the State-of-the-art, Technologies, Applications, and Challenges. Retrieved from http://arxiv.org/abs/2111.09673

Nofal, E., Reffat, R. M., & Vande Moere, A. (2017, June). Phygital heritage: An approach for heritage communication. In *Proceedings of the 3rd Immersive Learning Research Network Conference (iLRN 2017), Coimbra, Portugal* (pp. 26-29). Academic Press.

Nosalska, K., Piątek, Z. M., Mazurek, G., & Rządca, R. (2020). Industry 4.0: Coherent definition framework with technological and organizational interdependencies. *Journal of Manufacturing Technology Management*, *31*(5), 837–862. doi:10.1108/JMTM-08-2018-0238

Nowak, K. L., Fox, J., & Ralston, R. A. (2020). *Imagined Futures in Digital Media: Navigating the Unknown through Technology*. Routledge.

Odden, L. (2015). *21 Digital Marketing Trends & Predictions*. B2B Marketing Blog - Toprak. Available at: https://www.toprankblog.com/2014/05/digital-marketing-2015 /

Okonkwo, U. (2016). *Luxury Online: Styles, Systems, Strategies*. Palgrave Macmillan.

Onu, P., Pradhan, A., & Mbohwa, C. (2023). Potential to use metaverse for future teaching and learning. *Education and Information Technologies*, 1–32. doi:10.1007/s10639-023-12167-9

Ormrod, J. E. (1995). *Educational psychology: Principles and applications*. Prentice-Hall.

Owens, R. F., Hester, J. L., & Teale, W. H. (2002). Where do you want to go today? Inquiry-based learning and technology integration. *The Reading Teacher*, *55*(7), 616–625.

Page, S., & Coxon, M. (2016). Virtual reality exposure therapy for anxiety disorders: Small samples and no controls? *Frontiers in Psychology*, *7*. Advance online publication. doi:10.3389/fpsyg.2016.00326 PMID:27014137

Panda, A. K., Nanda, S., & Panda, P. (2021). Working Capital Management, Macroeconomic Impacts, and Firm Profitability: Evidence from Indian SMEs. *Business Perspectives and Research*, *9*(1), 144–158. doi:10.1177/2278533720923513

Pandey, N., Nayal, P., & Rathore, A. S. (2020). Digital marketing for B2B organizations: Structured literature review and future research directions. *Journal of Business and Industrial Marketing*, *35*(7), 1191–1204. doi:10.1108/JBIM-06-2019-0283

Papagiannidis, S., Bourlakis, M., & Li, F. (2008). Making real money in virtual worlds: MMORPGs and emerging business opportunities, challenges and ethical implications in metaverses. *Technological Forecasting and Social Change*, *75*(5), 610–622. doi:10.1016/j.techfore.2007.04.007

Park, S. M., & Kim, Y. G. (2022). A Metaverse: Taxonomy, Components, Applications, and Open Challenges. *IEEE Access : Practical Innovations, Open Solutions*, *10*, 4209–4251. doi:10.1109/ACCESS.2021.3140175

Parviainen, P., Kaariainen, J., Tihinen, M., & Teppola, S. (2017). Tackling the digitalization challenge: How to benefit from digitalization in practice. *International Journal of Information System and Project Management*, *5*(1), 63–77. doi:10.12821/ijispm050104

Peeters, D. (2019). Virtual reality: A game-changing method for the language sciences. Psychonomic Bulletin &Amp. *RE:view*, *26*(3), 894–900. doi:10.3758/s13423-019-01571-3 PMID:30734158

Pereira, A. C., & Romero, F. (2017). A review of the meanings and the implications of the industry 4.0 concept. *Procedia Manufacturing*, *13*, 1206–1214. doi:10.1016/j.promfg.2017.09.032

Peres, R., Schreier, M., Schweidel, D. A., & Sorescu, A. (2023). Blockchain meets marketing: Opportunities, threats, and avenues for future research. [). Elsevier.]. *International Journal of Research in Marketing*, *40*(1), 1–11. doi:10.1016/j.ijresmar.2022.08.001

Petrigna, E., & Musumeci, M. (2022). Metaverseand Its Impact on Healthcare: A Systematic Literature Review. *Journal of Healthcare Engineering*, *12*(1), 20220002.

Plangger, K., & Campbell, C. L. (2022). Managing in an era of falsity: Falsity from the metaverse to fake news to fake endorsement to synthetic influence to false agendas. *Business Horizons*, *65*(6), 713–717. doi:10.1016/j.bushor.2022.08.003

PlechatáA.HielkemaM.MerklL.MakranskyG.FrostM. (2023). Shifting from information- to experience-based climate change communication increases pro-environmental behaviour. doi:10.21203/rs.3.rs-2338078/v3

Plechatá, A., Morton, T. A., Pérez-Cueto, F. J., & Makransky, G. (2022). A randomized trial testing the effectiveness of virtual reality as a tool for pro-environmental dietary change. *Scientific Reports*, *12*(1), 14315. Advance online publication. doi:10.1038/s41598-022-18241-5 PMID:35995946

Porter, M. E., & Heppelmann, J. E. (2014). How smart, connected products are transforming competition. *Harvard Business Review*, *92*(11), 64–88.

Porwol, L., & Dumas, C. (2022). Transforming eparticipation: vr-dialogue – building and evaluating an aisupported framework for next-gen vr-enabled e-participation research. Transforming Government: People. *Process and Policy*, *17*(2), 233–250. doi:10.1108/TG-12-2021-0205

Pot-Kolder, R., Veling, W., Geraets, C., & van der Gaag, M. (2016). Effect of virtual reality exposure therapy on social participation in people with a psychotic disorder (VRETp): Study protocol for a randomized controlled trial. *Trials*, *17*(1), 25. doi:10.1186/s13063-015-1140-0 PMID:26762123

Powers, M. B., & Emmelkamp, P. (2008). Virtual reality exposure therapy for anxiety disorders: A meta-analysis. *Journal of Anxiety Disorders*, *22*(3), 561–569. doi:10.1016/j.janxdis.2007.04.006 PMID:17544252

Prados-Castillo, J. F., Torrecilla-García, J. A., & Liébana-Cabanillas, F. (2024). Metaverse as a booster of tourism transformation towards virtual management strategies. *Tourism Review*. Advance online publication. doi:10.1108/TR-10-2023-0750

Priyono, A., Moin, A., Aini, V. N., & Putri, O. (2020). Identifying Digital Transformation Paths in the Business Model of SMEs during the COVID-19 Pandemic. *Journal of Open Innovation*, *6*(4), 104. Advance online publication. doi:10.3390/joitmc6040104

Pu, Q., & Xiang, W. (2022). *The Metaverse and Its Impact and Transformation on Human Society. Journal of Chongqing University: Social Science Edition, 19(21).*

Purcărea, T. (2018). The future of retail impacted by the smart Phygital era. *Erişim TArihi*, *11*, 2021.

Pusceddu, G., Moi, L., & Cabiddu, F. (2023). Do they see eye to eye? Managing customer experience in phygital high-tech retail. *Management Decision*. Advance online publication. doi:10.1108/MD-05-2022-0673

Puspitasari, I. N. N. (2021). Combination of synchronous and asynchronous models in online learning. *Jurnal Pendidikan Islam Indonesia*, *5*(2), 198–217. doi:10.35316/jpii.v5i2.301

Putra, D. T., Mahmudin, T., Wiartha, N. G. M., Adnyana, I. M. S., & Septiviari, A. I. M. (2024). The Existence Of The Metaverse Tourism In Indonesia: Between Opportunities And Threats. *Reslaj: Religion Education Social Laa Roiba Journal*, *6*(3), 2291–2300. doi:10.47467/reslaj.v6i3.6162

PWC. (n.d.). Retrieved from https://www.pwc.in/research-and-insights-hub/embracing-the-metaverse.html

Qin, J., Liu, Y., & Grosvenor, R. (2016). A categorical framework of manufacturing for industry 4.0 and beyond. *Procedia CIRP*, *52*, 173–178. doi:10.1016/j.procir.2016.08.005

Qiu, Y., Isusi-Fagoaga, R., & García-Aracil, A. 2023. Perceptions and use of metaverse in higher education: A descriptive study in China and Spain. Computers and Education: Artificial Intelligence.

Queiroz, M. M., Fosso Wamba, S., Pereira, S. C. F., & Chiappetta Jabbour, C. J. (2023). The metaverse as a breakthrough for operations and supply chain management: Implications and call for action. *Int. J. Oper. Prod. Manag*. Retrieved from https://www.statista.com/statistics/1290160/projected-metaverse-use-reach-globalconsumers-businesses/

Queiroz, M., Wamba, S., Pereira, S., & Jabbour, C. (2023). The metaverse as a breakthrough for operations and supply chain management: Implications and call for action. *International Journal of Operations & Production Management*, *43*(10), 15391553. doi:10.1108/IJOPM-01-2023-0006

Quintana, M. G. B., & Fernández, S. M. (2015). A pedagogical model to develop teaching skills. The collaborative learning experience in the Immersive Virtual World TYMMI. *Computers in Human Behavior*, *51*, 594–603. doi:10.1016/j.chb.2015.03.016

Rahman, M. S., Chamikara, M. A. P., Khalil, I., & Bouras, A. (2022). Blockchain-of-blockchains: An interoperable blockchain platform for ensuring IoT data integrity in smart city. *Journal of Industrial Information Integration*, *30*, 100408. doi:10.1016/j.jii.2022.100408

Rajawat, A. S., Goyal, S. B., Goyal, A., Rajawat, K., Raboaca, M. S., Verma, C., & Mihaltan, T. C. (2023, June). Enhancing Security and Scalability of Metaverse with Blockchain-based Consensus Mechanisms. In 2023 15th International Conference on Electronics, Computers and Artificial Intelligence (ECAI) (pp. 1-6). IEEE. 10.1109/ECAI58194.2023.10194035

Ramos, M. E., Azevedo, A., Meira, D., & Malta, M. C. (2022). Cooperatives and the Use of Artificial Intelligence: A Critical View. *Sustainability (Basel)*, *15*(1), 1–17. doi:10.3390/su15010329

Rana, S., Anand, A., Prashar, S., & Haque, M. M. (2022). A perspective on the positioning of Indian business schools post COVID-19 pandemic. *International Journal of Emerging Markets*, *17*(2), 353–367. doi:10.1108/IJOEM-04-2020-0415

Ratan, R., Beyea, D., Li, B. J., & Graciano, L. (2020). Avatar characteristics induce users' behavioral conformity with small-to-medium effect sizes: A meta-analysis of the proteus effect. *Media Psychology, 23*(5), 651-675.S. G. Moore and K. C. Lafreniere, 'How online word-of-mouth impacts receivers'. *Consumer Psychology Review*, *3*(1), 34–59.

Rauschnabel, P. A., Babin, B. J., Tom Dieck, M. C., Krey, N., & Jung, T. (2022). What is augmented reality marketing? Its definition, complexity, and future. *Journal of Business Research*, *142*, 1140–1150. doi:10.1016/j.jbusres.2021.12.084

Reeves, B., & Malone, T. (2017). Leadership in the Age of the Quick Fix. *Harvard Business Review*.

Reilly, P., & Dawson, I. (2021). Track and Trace, and Other Collaborative Art/Archaeology Bubbles in the Phygital Pandemic. *Open Archaeology*, *7*(1), 291–313. doi:10.1515/opar-2020-0137

Renshaw, T., Sonnenfeld, N. A., & Meyers, M. (2016). Fundamentals for a turing test of virtual reality. *Proceedings of the Human Factors and Ergonomics Society Annual Meeting*, *60*(1), 2113–2117. doi:10.1177/1541931213601478

Riedl, R. (2022). On the stress potential of videoconferencing: Definition and root causes of Zoom fatigue. *Electronic Markets*, *32*(1), 153–177. doi:10.1007/s12525-021-00501-3 PMID:35600914

Riva, G., & Serino, S. (2020). Virtual reality in the assessment, understanding and treatment of mental health disorders. *Journal of Clinical Medicine*, *9*(11), 3434. doi:10.3390/jcm9113434 PMID:33114623

Rizzo, A., & Koenig, S. T. (2017). Is clinical virtual reality ready for primetime? *Neuropsychology*, *31*(8), 877–899. doi:10.1037/neu0000405 PMID:29376669

Rizzo, A., Thomas Koenig, S., & Talbot, T. B. (2019). Clinical results using virtual reality. *Journal of Technology in Human Services*, *37*(1), 51–74. doi:10.1080/15228835.2019.1604292

Roach, J. (2021). Mesh for Microsoft Teams aims to make collaboration in the 'metaverse'personal and fun. *Microsoft*, (November), 2.

Roblox Corporation. (2022, February 15). *Roblox reports fourth quarter and full year 2021 financial results*. Author.

Rodeck, D., & Benjamin, C. (2022). What is Blockchain? *Forbes*. https://www.forbes.com/advisor/investing/cryptocurrency/ what-is-blockchain/

Rodriguez, N. (2016). Teaching virtual reality with affordable technologies. *Lecture Notes in Computer Science*, *9731*, 89–97. doi:10.1007/978-3-319-39510-4_9

Sahoo, D., & Ray, S. (2023). Metaverse in Banking: An Initiative for Banking Transformation from Emerging Country Prospective. *Academy of Marketing Studies Journal*, *27*(S4), 1–15.

Samala, A., Ambiyar, A., Bojić, L., Indarta, Y., Ipalakova, M., Denden, M., ... Dewi, I. (2023). Metaverse technologies in education: A systematic literature review using prisma. *International Journal of Emerging Technologies in Learning*, *18*(05), 231–252. doi:10.3991/ijet.v18i05.35501

Sandhu, N., & Saluja, S. (2023). *Fraud Triangle as an Audit Tool*. Management and Labour Studies., doi:10.1177/0258042X231160970

Sari, R. N., Hayati, R. S., & Rahayu, S. L. (2020, October). Heuristic Evaluation In Mobile Augmented Reality Applications In Designing Houses. In *2020 8th International Conference on Cyber and IT Service Management (CITSM)* (pp. 1-5). IEEE.

Sarıtaş, T. (2023). Systematic Literature Review on the Use of Metaversein Education. *International Journal of Technology in Education and Science*, *6*(1), 215–229.

Särmäkari, N. (2023). Digital 3D fashion designers: Cases of atacac and The fabricant. *Fashion Theory*, *27*(1), 85–114. doi:10.1080/1362704X.2021.1981657

Sarwar, M. A., Soomro, T. R., & Pervaiz, H. (2021). Decentralized Identity Management for Metaverse: Opportunities and Challenges. *IEEE Access : Practical Innovations, Open Solutions*, *9*, 32200–32210.

Savery, J. R. (2015). Overview of problem-based learning: Definitions and distinctions. Essential readings in problem-based learning: Exploring and extending the legacy of Howard S. *Barrows*, *9*(2), 5–15.

Scavuzzo, S. T. (2022). *Immersive Experience of Ancient Architectural Heritage and Related Historical Events* (Doctoral dissertation, TU Wien).

Scheer, A. W. (2023). From Process and Enterprise Architecture to Digital Enterprise Twin in the Metaverse. In *The Composable Enterprise: Agile, Flexible, Innovative: A Gamechanger for Organisations, Digitisation and Business Software* (pp. 29–49). Springer Fachmedien Wiesbaden. doi:10.1007/978-3-658-42483-1_3

Schreibman, S., Papadopoulos, C., Hughes, B., Rooney, N., Brennan, C., Mac Caba, F., & Healy, H. (2017). Phygital Augmentations for Enhancing History Teaching and Learning at School. DH.

Schumacher, A., Nemeth, T., & Sihn, W. (2019). Roadmapping towards industrial digitalization based on an Industry 4.0 maturity model for manufacturing enterprises. *Procedia CIRP*, *79*, 409–414. doi:10.1016/j.procir.2019.02.110

Schumacher, P. (2022). The metaverse as opportunity for architecture and society: Design drivers, core competencies. *Architectural Intelligence*, *1*(1), 11. doi:10.1007/s44223-022-00010-z PMID:35993030

Schwab, K., & Sala-i-Martín, X. (2016, April). *The global competitiveness report 2013–2014: Full data edition.* World Economic Forum.

Schwab, K. (2017). *The fourth industrial revolution.* Currency.

Schwebel, D., Severson, J., & He, Y. (2016). Using smartphone technology to deliver a virtual pedestrian environment: Usability and validation. *Virtual Reality (Waltham Cross)*, *21*(3), 145–152. doi:10.1007/s10055-016-0304-x PMID:29531502

Scientist. (n.d.). Retrieved from https://www.newscientist.com/article/2295438-why-has-facebook-changedits-name-to-meta-and-what-is-the-metaverse/

Seattle, S. (2022, June 20). *Nike's New Flagship Store is a Powerhouse of Experience-Driven Retail.* Retrieved from Future stores: https://futurestores.wbresearch.com/blog/nikenew-flagship-powerhouse-experience-driven-retail

Serrano, S., Llorca, D., Daza, I., & Sotelo, M. (2022). Insertion of real agents behaviours in carla autonomous driving simulator doi:10.5220/0011352400003323

Shafiee, S., Rajabzadeh Ghatari, A., Hasanzadeh, A., & Jahanyan, S. (2021). Smart tourism destinations: A systematic review. *Tourism Review*, *76*(3), 505–528. doi:10.1108/TR-06-2019-0235

Shakeri, S., & Ornek, M. A. (2023). How metaverse evolves the architectural design. *Architecture and Planning Journal*, *28*(3), 35. doi:10.54729/2789-8547.1230

Shalender, K., & Singla, B. (2024). Creator Economy in Metaverse Space: Use Cases, Adoption Challenges, and Integration Roadmap. In Creator's Economy in Metaverse Platforms: Empowering Stakeholders Through Omnichannel Approach (pp. 1-11). IGI Global.

Shalender, K., Singla, B., & Sharma, S. (2023). Understanding the Logic and Science Behind the Emerging Field of Neuromarketing. *Promoting Consumer Engagement Through Emotional Branding and Sensory Marketing*, 44-51.

Sharma, A., & Bansal, A. (2023). Digital Marketing in the Metaverse: Beginning of a New Era in Product Promotion. In Applications of Neuromarketing in the Metaverse (pp. 163-175). IGI Global. doi:10.4018/978-1-6684-8150-9.ch012

Sharma, R. (2022). *Non-Fungible Token (NFT): What it Means and How it Works*. Investopedia. https://www.investopedia.com/non-fungible-tokens-nft-5115211

Sharma, A., & Bansal, A. (2023). An Assessment of Money Laundering and Terrorism Financing on the Indian Economy. In *Smart Analytics, Artificial Intelligence and Sustainable Performance Management in a Global Digitalised Economy* (Vol. 110, pp. 123–130). Emerald Publishing Limited. doi:10.1108/S1569-37592023000110B007

Shen, B., Tan, W., Guo, J., Zhao, L., & Qin, P. (2021). How to promote user purchase in the metaverse? A systematic literature review on consumer behavior research and virtual commerce application design. *Appl. Sci., 11*, 11087.

Sherman, W. R., & Craig, A. B. (2003). Understanding virtual reality—Interface, application, and design. *Presence (Cambridge, Mass.)*, *12*(4), 441–442. doi:10.1162/105474603322391668

Sherrill, A. M., Rothbaum, A. O., McSweeney, L. B., & Rothbaum, B. O. (2019). Virtual reality exposure therapy for posttraumatic stress disorder. *Psychiatric Annals*, *49*(8), 343–347. doi:10.3928/00485713-20190716-02

Shin, D., & Biocca, F. (2017). Exploring immersive experience in journalism. New Media &Amp. *New Media & Society*, *20*(8), 2800–2823. doi:10.1177/1461444817733133

Shin, H., & Kang, J. (2020). Reducing perceived health risk to attract hotel customers in the COVID-19 pandemic era: Focused on technology innovation for social distancing and cleanliness. *International Journal of Hospitality Management*, *91*, 102664. doi:10.1016/j.ijhm.2020.102664 PMID:32921871

Shin, H., & Kang, J. (2024). How does the metaverse travel experience influence virtual and actual travel behaviors? Focusing on the role of telepresence and avatar identification. *Journal of Hospitality and Tourism Management*, *58*, 174–183. doi:10.1016/j.jhtm.2023.12.009

Shryock, A., & Smail, D. L. (2011). *Deep history: The architecture of past and present*. Univ of California Press. doi:10.1525/9780520949669

Sigala, M., Kumar, S., Donthu, N., Sureka, R., & Joshi, Y. (2021). A bibliometric overview of the Journal of Hospitality and Tourism Management: Research contributions and influence. *Journal of Hospitality and Tourism Management*, *47*, 273–288. doi:10.1016/j.jhtm.2021.04.005

Singh, J., & Nijjer, S. (2024). Metaverse in Psychological Treatments: Is MEDverse the Next Normal? In Entrepreneurship and Creativity in the Metaverse (pp. 20-25). IGI Global.

Singh, J., Malhotra, M., & Sharma, N. (2022). Metaverse in education: An overview. *Applying metalytics to measure customer experience in the metaverse*, 135-142.

Slater, M., Usoh, M., & Steed, A. (1994). Depth of presence in virtual environments. *Presence (Cambridge, Mass.)*, *3*(2), 130–144. doi:10.1162/pres.1994.3.2.130

Smith, A. (1998). *An inquiry into the nature and causes of the wealth of nations*. Cofide.

Smith, A. (2020). *Navigating the Metaverse: A User's Guide to Virtual Reality*. Digital Publishers.

Smith, M., & … . (2021). Spatial Computing and Immersive Technologies: A Comprehensive Guide for Entrepreneurs. *Journal of Virtual Innovation*, *12*(3), 134–150.

Smith, S. A. (2019). Virtual reality in episodic memory research: A review. *Psychonomic Bulletin & Review*, *26*(4), 1213–1237. doi:10.3758/s13423-019-01605-w PMID:31037605

Sood, K., Dhanaraj, R. K., Balusamy, B., Grima, S., & Uma Maheshwari, R. (Eds.). (2022). *Big Data: A game changer for insurance industry*. Emerald Publishing Limited. doi:10.1108/9781802626056

Soowook, L. & Oh, Y. S. (2016). Study on virtual reality and e-commerce. *The International Journal of Advanced Culture Technology, 4*(4), 70-74. doi:10.17703/IJACT.2016.4.4.70

Sopher, H., & Lescop, L. (2023). Learning in metaverse: The immersive atelier model of the architecture studio. *Archnet-IJAR: International Journal of Architectural Research*, *17*(3), 536–553. doi:10.1108/ARCH-10-2022-0213

Spydra. (2023) Everything you need to know about cryptography in Blockchain, LinkedIn. Available at: https://www.linkedin.com/pulse/everything-you-need-knowcryptography-blockchain-spydra/

Sriram, G. K. (2022). A comprehensive survey on metaverse. *International Research Journal of Modernization in Engineering Technology*, *4*(2), 772–775.

Stankov, U., & Gretzel, U. (2020). Tourism 4.0 technologies and tourist experiences: A human-centered design perspective. *Information Technology & Tourism*, *22*(3), 477–488. doi:10.1007/s40558-020-00186-y

Stanoevska-Slabeva, K. (2022). Opportunities and challenges of metaverse for education: a literature review. *EDULEARN22 Proceedings*, 10401–10410. 10.21125/edulearn.2022.2527

Statista. (2023). Retrieved from https://www.statista.com/

Steinkuehler, C., & Duncan, S. (2008). Scientific Habits of Mind in Virtual Worlds. *Journal of Science Education and Technology*, *17*(6), 530–543. doi:10.1007/s10956-008-9120-8

Stephenson, N. (1992). *Snow Crash*. Academic Press.

Stephenson, N. (1992). *Snow Crash*. Bantam Books.

Stephenson, N. (2003). *Snow Crash: A Novel*. Random House Publishing Group.

Stöhr, C., Demazière, C., & Adawi, T. (2020). The polarizing effect of the online flipped classroom. *Computers & Education*, *147*, 103789. doi:10.1016/j.compedu.2019.103789

Stokel-Walker, C. (2021). *Why has Facebook changed its name to Meta and what is the metaverse?* Academic Press.

Strahilevitz, M. A., & Loewenstein, G. (1998). The Effect of Ownership History on the Valuation of Objects. *The Journal of Consumer Research*, *25*(3), 276–289. doi:10.1086/209539

Suda, Y., Fukuhara, K., Sato, K., & Higuchi, T. (2022). Improved walking through an aperture in a virtual environment transfer to a real environment: Introduction of enriched feedback and gradual increase in task difficulty. *Frontiers in Sports and Active Living*, *4*, 844436. Advance online publication. doi:10.3389/fspor.2022.844436 PMID:35308597

Sulmont, E., Patitsas, E., & Cooperstock, J. R. (2019). What is hard about teaching machine learning to non-majors? Insights from classifying instructors' learning goals. *ACM Transactions on Computing Education*, *19*(4), 1–16. doi:10.1145/3336124

Sun, J., Gan, W., Chao, H. C., & Yu, P. S. (2022). Metaverse: Survey, applications, security, and opportunities. *arXiv preprint arXiv:2210.07990.*

Sun, X., Lin, S., Sjöberg, V., & Jie, J. (2021). How to Exploit a DeFi Project. In Financial Cryptography and Data Security. FC 2021 International Workshops: CoDecFin, DeFi, VOTING, and WTSC, Virtual Event, March 5, 2021, Revised Selected Papers 25 (pp. 162-167). Springer Berlin Heidelberg. doi:10.1007/978-3-662-63958-0_14

Sun, Z., Zhu, M., Shan, X., & Lee, C. (2022). Augmented tactileperception and haptic-feedback rings as human-machine interfaces aiming for immersive interactions. *Nature Communications*, *13*(1), 5224. Advance online publication. doi:10.1038/s41467-022-32745-8 PMID:36064838

Švec, M., & Madleňák, A. (2017). Legal frameworks for the phygital concept. *European Journal of Science and Theology*, *13*(6), 209–217.

Swaminathan, V., Sorescu, A., Steenkamp, J. E. M., O'Guinn, T. C. G., & Schmitt, B. (2020). Branding in a Hyperconnected World: Refocusing Theories and Rethinking Boundaries. *Journal of Marketing*, *84*(2), 24–46. doi:10.1177/0022242919899905

Swan, M. (2015). *Blockchain: Blueprint for a New Economy*. O'Reilly Media.

Takahashi, D. (2021). *Roblox CEO Dave Baszucki believes users will create the metaverse*. VentureBeat. Available at: https://venturebeat.com/2021/01/27/roblox-ceo-dav e -baszucki-believes-users-will-create-the-metaverse/

Tapscott, D., & Tapscott, A. (2019). *Blockchain*. Rewolucja, Wydawnictwo PWN.

Teng, Z., Cai, Y., Zhang, X., & Li, X. (2022). Factors affecting learners' adoption of an educational metaverse platform: An empirical study based on an extended utaut model. *Mobile Information Systems*, *15*, 1–15. Advance online publication. doi:10.1155/2022/5479215

Tiernan, B. (2000). E-tailing. Chicago.

Tokarev, A., Skobelin, I., Tolstov, M., Tsyganov, A., & Pak, M. (2021). Development of VR educational instruments for school pre-professional education in a research university. *Procedia Computer Science*, *190*, 750–754. doi:10.1016/j.procs.2021.06.088

Torraco, R. J. (2005). *Writing integrative literature reviews: Guidelines and examples*. Human Resource.

Torres, G. C. (2022). *Phygital Approaches and Intangible Cultural Heritage as a Tourism Experience Enhancer. Tradition and Innovation for a 21st Century Academic Museum of the University of Coimbra* (Doctoral dissertation, Universidade de Coimbra).

Truong, V., Le, L., & Niyato, D. (2023). Blockchain meets metaverse and digital asset management: A comprehensive survey. *IEEE Access : Practical Innovations, Open Solutions*, *11*, 26258–26288. doi:10.1109/ACCESS.2023.3257029

Tsekleves, E., Gradinar, A., Darby, A., & Smith, M. (2014, October). Active Parks:'Phygital'urban games for sedentary and older people. In *Games for Health 2014: Proceedings of the 4th conference on gaming and playful interaction in healthcare* (pp. 140-143). Wiesbaden: Springer Fachmedien Wiesbaden.

Tuente, S K., Bogaerts, S., IJzendoorn, S V., & Veling, W. (2018, August 6). *Effect of virtual reality aggression prevention training for forensic psychiatric patients (VRAPT): study protocol of a multi-center RCT*. Academic Press.

Turco, M. L., & Giovannini, E. C. (2020). Towards a phygital heritage approach for museum collection. *Journal of Archaeological Science, Reports*, *34*, 102639. doi:10.1016/j.jasrep.2020.102639

Tyni, H., Kultima, A., & Mäyrä, F. (2013, October). Dimensions of hybrid in playful products. In *Proceedings of International Conference on Making Sense of Converging Media* (pp. 237-244). 10.1145/2523429.2523489

Unali, M., Caffio, G., & Zollo, F. (2023). Towards a Virtual Museum of Ephemeral Architecture: Methods, Techniques and Semantic Models for a Post-digital Metaverse. In *Beyond Digital Representation: Advanced Experiences in AR and AI for Cultural Heritage and Innovative Design* (pp. 191–207). Springer Nature Switzerland.

Usmani, S., Sharath, M., & Mehendale, M. (2022). Future of mental health in the metaverse. *General Psychiatry*, *35*(4), e100825. doi:10.1136/gpsych-2022-100825 PMID:36189180

Van Nuenen, T., & Scarles, C. (2021). Advancements in technology and digital media in tourism. *Tourist Studies*, *21*(1), 119–132. doi:10.1177/1468797621990410

Veleva, S. S., & Tsvetanova, A. I. (2020). Characteristics of the digital marketing advantages and disadvantages. *IOP Conference Series. Materials Science and Engineering*, *940*(1), 012065. doi:10.1088/1757-899X/940/1/012065

Vigneron, F., & Johnson, L. W. (2004). Measuring Perceptions of Brand Luxury. *Journal of Brand Management*, *11*(6), 484–506. doi:10.1057/palgrave.bm.2540194

Volchek, K., & Brysch, A. (2023, January). Metaverse and Tourism: From a New Niche to a Transformation. In *Information and Communication Technologies in Tourism 2023: Proceedings of the ENTER 2023 eTourism Conference, January 18-20, 2023* (pp. 300-311). Cham: Springer Nature Switzerland.

Vondráček, M., Baggili, I., Casey, P., & Mekni, M. (2023). Rise of the metaverse's immersive virtual reality malware and the man-in-the-room attack & defenses. *Computers & Security*, *127*, 102923. doi:10.1016/j.cose.2022.102923

Vora, J., Italiya, P., Tanwar, S., Tyagi, S., Kumar, N., Obaidat, M. S., & Hsiao, K. F. (2018, July). Ensuring privacy and security in e-health records. In 2018 International conference on computer, information and telecommunication systems (CITS) (pp. 1-5). IEEE. 10.1109/CITS.2018.8440164

Wahlster, H., Helbig, J., Hellinger, A., & Wahlster, W. (2013). *Recommendations for implementing the strategic initiative INDUSTRIE 4.0. Securing the future of German manufacturing industry; final report of the Industrie 4.0.* Working Group. Forschungsunion. Retrieved from: http://forschungsunion.de/pdf/industrie_4_0_final_report.pdf

Wang, B., Liu, H., Liu, C., Yang, Z., Ren, Q., Zheng, H., & Lei, H. (2021, May). Blockeye: Hunting for defi attacks on blockchain. In *2021 IEEE/ACM 43rd International Conference on Software Engineering: Companion Proceedings (ICSE-Companion)* (pp. 17-20). IEEE.

Wang, D., & Fesenmaier, D. R. (2013). Transforming the travel experience: The use of smartphones for travel. In *Information and Communication Technologies in Tourism 2013: Proceedings of the International Conference in Innsbruck, Austria, January 22-25, 2013* (pp. 58-69). Springer Berlin Heidelberg.

Wang, M., Asian, S., Wood, L. C., & Wang, B. (2020). Logistics innovation capability and its impacts on the supply chain risks in the Industry 4.0 era. *Modern Supply Chain Research and Applications*, *2*(2), 83–98. doi:10.1108/MSCRA-07-2019-0015

Wang, T., & Lu, S. (2003). *Digital Marketing*. China Textile & Apparel Press.

Wang, X., Liu, X., Cheng, C. T., Deng, L., Chen, X., & Xiao, F. (2021). A joint user scheduling and trajectory planning data collection strategy for the UAVassisted WSN. *IEEE Communications Letters*, *25*(7), 2333–2337. doi:10.1109/LCOMM.2021.3067898

Wang, Y., Su, Z., Ni, J., Zhang, N., & Shen, X. (2021). Blockchain-empowered space-air-ground integrated networks: Opportunities, challenges, and solutions. *IEEE Communications Surveys and Tutorials*, *24*(1), 160–209. doi:10.1109/COMST.2021.3131711

Wang, Y., Su, Z., Zhang, N., Xing, R., Liu, D., Luan, T. H., & Shen, X. (2022). A survey on metaverse: Fundamentals, security, and privacy. *IEEE Communications Surveys and Tutorials*.

Waters, M. (2020). Why Video Games are the Next Retail Frontier. *Modern Retail*.

Wei, W. (2024). A buzzword, a phase or the next chapter for the Internet? The status and possibilities of the metaverse for tourism. *Journal of Hospitality and Tourism Insights*, *7*(1), 602–625. doi:10.1108/JHTI-11-2022-0568

Weking, J., Desouza, K. C., Fielt, E., & Kowalkiewicz, M. (2023). Metaverse-enabled entrepreneurship. *Journal of Business Venturing Insights*, *19*, e00375. doi:10.1016/j.jbvi.2023.e00375

Westerman, G., Bonnet, D., & McAfee, A. (2014). *Leading digital: Turning technology into business transformation*. Harvard Business Press.

Westerveld, P., Fielt, E., Desouza, K. C., & Gable, G. G. (2023). The business model portfolio as a strategic tool for value creation and business performance. *The Journal of Strategic Information Systems*, *32*(1), 101758. doi:10.1016/j.jsis.2023.101758

What are smart contracts on Blockchain? IBM. (n.d.).https://www.ibm.com/topics/smart-contracts

Wheeler, D., & Natarajan, B. (2023). Engineering semantic communication: A survey. *IEEE Access : Practical Innovations, Open Solutions*, *11*, 13965–13995. doi:10.1109/ACCESS.2023.3243065

Whitfield, B. (2023, March 23). What is a consensus mechanism? Built In. https://builtin.com/blockchain/consensus-mechanism

Willis, J. (2006). *Based Strategies to Ignite Student Learning: Insights from a Neurologist and Classroom Teacher*. ASCD.

Wilson, C., & Soranzo, A. (2015). The use of virtual reality in psychology: A case study in visual perception. *Computational and Mathematical Methods in Medicine*, *2015*, 1–7. doi:10.1155/2015/151702 PMID:26339281

Winkler, N., Roethke, K., Siegfried, N., & Benlian, A. (2020). Lose yourself in vr: exploring the effects of virtual reality on individuals' immersion. *Proceedings of the Annual Hawaii International Conference on System Sciences*. 10.24251/HICSS.2020.186

Wu, H., Ai, C., & Cheng, C. (2019). Virtual reality experiences, attachment and experiential outcomes in tourism. *Tourism Review*, *75*(3), 481–495. doi:10.1108/TR-06-2019-0205

Wulf, G., & Lewthwaite, R. (2016). Optimizing performance through intrinsic motivation and attention for learning: The optimal theory of motor learning. Psychonomic Bulletin &Amp. *RE:view*, *23*(5), 1382–1414. doi:10.3758/s13423-015-0999-9 PMID:26833314

Wu, P., & Ho, A. T. (2022). Full article: Metaverse: Literature Review, Synthesis and Future Research Agenda. *Journal of Management Analytics*, *11*(3), 521–544.

Wu, T., & Hao, F. (2023). Edu-Metaverse: Concept, architecture, and applications. *Interactive Learning Environments*, 1–28.

Wyssenbach, T., Zeballos, M., Loosli, S., & Schwaninger, A. (2021). Nonverbal behaviour of interviewers influences the competence ratings of observers in recruitment interviews: A study investigating social influence using 360-degree videos with virtual reality and 2d screen displays. *Virtual Reality (Waltham Cross)*, *26*(2), 669–686. doi:10.1007/s10055-021-00540-3

Xiang, A., Gao, S., Peng, J., & Shen, Y. (2021). Knowledge Reorganization and Scene Re-configuration: A Meta-Universe for Digital Resource Management. *Library Information Knowledge*, *42*, 6–10.

Xiang, Z., Tussyadiah, I., & Buhalis, D. (2015). Smart destinations: Foundations, analytics, and applications. *Journal of Destination Marketing & Management*, *4*(3), 143–144. doi:10.1016/j.jdmm.2015.07.001

Xia, Q., Sifah, E. B., Smahi, A., Amofa, S., & Zhang, X. (2017). BBDS: Blockchain-based data sharing for electronic medical records in cloud environments. *Information (Basel)*, *8*(2), 44. doi:10.3390/info8020044

Xu, M., Guo, Y., Hu, Q., Xiong, Z., Yu, D., & Cheng, X. (2023). A trustless architecture of blockchain-enabled metaverse. *High-Confidence Computing, 3*(1), 100088.

Xue, J. (2021). *Exploration and Application of Metaverse in Broadcast Industry.* ABP.

Xu, Y., Liu, W., He, T., & Tsai, S. B. (2023). Buzzword or fuzzword: An event study of the metaverse in the Chinese stock market. *Internet Research.*

Yang, D., Zhou, J., Chen, R., Song, Y., Song, Z., Zhang, X., ... & Bai, C. (2022). Expert consensus on the metaverse in medicine. Clinical eHealth, 5, 1-9.

Yang, T. T., Ruan, W. Q., Li, Y. Q., & Zhang, S. N. (2023). Virtual tourist motivation: The differences between virtual tourism and on-site tourism. *Tourism Review*, *78*(5), 1280–1297. doi:10.1108/TR-07-2022-0331

Yaqoob, I., Salah, K., Jayaraman, R., & Omar, M. (2023). Metaverse applications in smart cities: Enabling technologies, opportunities, challenges, and future directions. *Internet of Things : Engineering Cyber Physical Human Systems*, *23*, 100884. doi:10.1016/j.iot.2023.100884

Yawised, K., Apasrawirote, D., & Boonparn, C. (2022). From traditional business shifted towards transformation: The emerging business opportunities and challenges in 'Metaverse' era. *The International and National Conference on Business Administration and Accountancy 2022 (INCBAA 2022)*, 162-175.

Yawised, K., Apasrawirote, D., & Boonparn, C. (2022). From traditional business shifted towards transformation: The emerging business opportunities and challenges in 'Metaverse'era. *Incbaa*, *2022*, 162–175.

Yee, N., & Bailenson, J. (2007). The Proteus effect: The effect of transformed self-representation on behavior. *Human Communication Research*, *33*(3), 271–290. doi:10.1111/j.1468-2958.2007.00299.x

Yelowitz, A. (2014). Bitcoins as An Investment or Speculative Vehicle? A First Look. *Applied Economics Letters*, *21*(6), 406–409.

Yemenici, A. D. (2022). Entrepreneurship in the world of metaverse: Virtual or real? *Journal of Metaverse*, *2*(2), 71–82. doi:10.57019/jmv.1126135

Ye, Y., & Xu, Z. (2022). The Metaverse: A New Paradigm for the Internet. *IEEE Network*, *36*(2), 28–33.

Yoo, K., Welden, R., Hewett, K., & Haenlein, M. (2023). The merchants of meta: A research agenda to understand the future of retailing in the metaverse. *Journal of Retailing*, *99*(2), 173–192. doi:10.1016/j.jretai.2023.02.002

Yu, G., & Geng, X. (2021). What is the "Metaverse": The Future Ecological Landscape of the Mediated Society. *Journal of Xinjiang Normal University: Philosophy and Social Science Edition, 2.*

Yüce, M., Filiztekin, E., & Özkaya, K. G. (2021). COVID-19 diagnosis—A review of current methods. *Biosensors & Bioelectronics*, *172*, 112752. doi:10.1016/j.bios.2020.112752 PMID:33126180

Yu, K., Tan, L., Aloqaily, M., Yang, H., & Jararweh, Y. (2021). Blockchainenhanced data sharing with traceable and direct revocation in IIoT. *IEEE Transactions on Industrial Informatics, 17*(11), 7669–7678. doi:10.1109/TII.2021.3049141

Zaczkiewicz, A. (2019). *Louis Vuitton and Banana Republic also scored high on an assessment conducted by NewStore.* Academic Press.

Zelealem, F. (2021, November 30). *South Korea's KB Bank enters metaverse space.* Academic Press.

Zhai, Asmi, Zhou, Ahmad, Anwar, Saneinia, & Li. (2020). Investigating the Mediation and Moderation Effect of Students' Addiction to Virtual Reality Games: A Perspective of Structural Equation Modeling. Discrete Dynamics in Nature and Society. doi:10.1155/2020/5714546

Zhang, H., Lee, S., Lu, Y., Yu, X., & Lu, H. (2023). A Survey on Big Data Technologies and Their Applications to the Metaverse: Past, Current and Future. *Mathematics, 11*(96), 1–28. doi:10.3390/math11010096

Zhang, K., Wang, J., Zhang, J., Wang, Y., & Zeng, Y. (2024). Exploring the impact of location-based augmented reality on tourists' spatial behavior, experience, and intention through a field experiment. *Tourism Management, 102*, 104886. doi:10.1016/j.tourman.2024.104886

Zhang, Q., Jiang, X., & Zheng, Y. (2023). Blockchain adoption and gray markets in a global supply chain. *Omega, 115*, 102785. doi:10.1016/j.omega.2022.102785

Zhang, X., Chen, Y., Hu, L., & Wang, Y. (2022). The metaverse in education: Definition, framework, features, potential applications, challenges, and future research topics. *Frontiers in Psychology, 13*, 6063. doi:10.3389/fpsyg.2022.1016300 PMID:36304866

Zhao, Y. (2019, July). Practical aggregate signature from general elliptic curves, and applications to blockchain. In *Proceedings of the 2019 ACM Asia Conference on Computer and Communications Security* (pp. 529-538). 10.1145/3321705.3329826

Zheng, Z., Xie, S., Dai, H. N., Chen, W., Chen, X., Weng, J., & Imran, M. (2020). An overview on smart contracts: Challenges, advances and platforms. *Future Generation Computer Systems, 105*, 475–491. doi:10.1016/j.future.2019.12.019

Zhou, Y. (2015). *Luxury Brand Management.* University of International Business and Economics Press.

Zhu, C., Wu, D. C. W., Hall, C. M., Fong, L. H. N., Koupaei, S. N., & Lin, F. (2023). Exploring non-immersive virtual reality experiences in tourism: Empirical evidence from a world heritage site. *International Journal of Tourism Research, 25*(3), 372–383. doi:10.1002/jtr.2574

Zhukova, G., Ono, M., & Lavrova, S. (2021). Arts education ecosystem: Digital restrictions and phygital solutions. In *EDULEARN21 Proceedings* (pp. 9572-9578). IATED.

Zimmermann, D., Wehler, A., & Kaspar, K. (2023). Self-representation through avatars in digital environments. *Current Psychology (New Brunswick, N.J.), 42*(25), 21775–21789. doi:10.1007/s12144-022-03232-6

Zuckerberg, M. (2021). *Meta: founder's letter, 2021.* https://about.fb.com/news/2021/10/founders-letter/

Zulfiqar, M., Syed, F., Khan, M. J., & Khurshid, K. (2019). Deep face recognition for biometric authentication. *2019 International Conference on Electrical, Communication, and Computer Engineering (ICECCE)*, 1–6.

Zurlo, F., Arquilla, V., Carella, G., & Tamburello, M. C. (2018). Designing acculturated phygital experiences. In *Cumulus Conference Proceedings Wuxi 2018 Diffused Transition & Design Opportunities* (pp. 153-164). Academic Press.

Related References

To continue our tradition of advancing information science and technology research, we have compiled a list of recommended IGI Global readings. These references will provide additional information and guidance to further enrich your knowledge and assist you with your own research and future publications.

Abdul Razak, R., & Mansor, N. A. (2021). Instagram Influencers in Social Media-Induced Tourism: Rethinking Tourist Trust Towards Tourism Destination. In M. Dinis, L. Bonixe, S. Lamy, & Z. Breda (Eds.), *Impact of New Media in Tourism* (pp. 135-144). IGI Global. https://doi.org/10.4018/978-1-7998-7095-1.ch009

Abir, T., & Khan, M. Y. (2022). Importance of ICT Advancement and Culture of Adaptation in the Tourism and Hospitality Industry for Developing Countries. In C. Ramos, S. Quinteiro, & A. Gonçalves (Eds.), *ICT as Innovator Between Tourism and Culture* (pp. 30–41). IGI Global. https://doi.org/10.4018/978-1-7998-8165-0.ch003

Abir, T., & Khan, M. Y. (2022). Importance of ICT Advancement and Culture of Adaptation in the Tourism and Hospitality Industry for Developing Countries. In C. Ramos, S. Quinteiro, & A. Gonçalves (Eds.), *ICT as Innovator Between Tourism and Culture* (pp. 30–41). IGI Global. https://doi.org/10.4018/978-1-7998-8165-0.ch003

Abtahi, M. S., Behboudi, L., & Hasanabad, H. M. (2017). Factors Affecting Internet Advertising Adoption in Ad Agencies. *International Journal of Innovation in the Digital Economy*, *8*(4), 18–29. doi:10.4018/IJIDE.2017100102

Afenyo-Agbe, E., & Mensah, I. (2022). Principles, Benefits, and Barriers to Community-Based Tourism: Implications for Management. In I. Mensah & E. Afenyo-Agbe (Eds.), *Prospects and Challenges of Community-Based Tourism and Changing Demographics* (pp. 1–29). IGI Global. doi:10.4018/978-1-7998-7335-8.ch001

Agbo, V. M. (2022). Distributive Justice Issues in Community-Based Tourism. In I. Mensah & E. Afenyo-Agbe (Eds.), *Prospects and Challenges of Community-Based Tourism and Changing Demographics* (pp. 107–129). IGI Global. https://doi.org/10.4018/978-1-7998-7335-8.ch005

Agrawal, S. (2017). The Impact of Emerging Technologies and Social Media on Different Business(es): Marketing and Management. In O. Rishi & A. Sharma (Eds.), *Maximizing Business Performance and Efficiency Through Intelligent Systems* (pp. 37–49). Hershey, PA: IGI Global. doi:10.4018/978-1-5225-2234-8.ch002

Ahmad, A., & Johari, S. (2022). Georgetown as a Gastronomy Tourism Destination: Visitor Awareness Towards Revisit Intention of Nasi Kandar Restaurant. In M. Valeri (Ed.), *New Governance and Management in Touristic Destinations* (pp. 71–83). IGI Global. https://doi.org/10.4018/978-1-6684-3889-3.ch005

Alkhatib, G., & Bayouq, S. T. (2021). A TAM-Based Model of Technological Factors Affecting Use of E-Tourism. *International Journal of Tourism and Hospitality Management in the Digital Age*, *5*(2), 50–67. https://doi.org/10.4018/IJTHMDA.20210701.oa1

Altinay Ozdemir, M. (2021). Virtual Reality (VR) and Augmented Reality (AR) Technologies for Accessibility and Marketing in the Tourism Industry. In C. Eusébio, L. Teixeira, & M. Carneiro (Eds.), *ICT Tools and Applications for Accessible Tourism* (pp. 277-301). IGI Global. https://doi.org/10.4018/978-1-7998-6428-8.ch013

Anantharaman, R. N., Rajeswari, K. S., Angusamy, A., & Kuppusamy, J. (2017). Role of Self-Efficacy and Collective Efficacy as Moderators of Occupational Stress Among Software Development Professionals. *International Journal of Human Capital and Information Technology Professionals*, *8*(2), 45–58. doi:10.4018/IJHCITP.2017040103

Aninze, F., El-Gohary, H., & Hussain, J. (2018). The Role of Microfinance to Empower Women: The Case of Developing Countries. *International Journal of Customer Relationship Marketing and Management*, *9*(1), 54–78. doi:10.4018/IJCRMM.2018010104

Antosova, G., Sabogal-Salamanca, M., & Krizova, E. (2021). Human Capital in Tourism: A Practical Model of Endogenous and Exogenous Territorial Tourism Planning in Bahía Solano, Colombia. In V. Costa, A. Moura, & M. Mira (Eds.), *Handbook of Research on Human Capital and People Management in the Tourism Industry* (pp. 282–302). IGI Global. https://doi.org/10.4018/978-1-7998-4318-4.ch014

Arsenijević, O. M., Orčić, D., & Kastratović, E. (2017). Development of an Optimization Tool for Intangibles in SMEs: A Case Study from Serbia with a Pilot Research in the Prestige by Milka Company. In M. Vemić (Ed.), *Optimal Management Strategies in Small and Medium Enterprises* (pp. 320–347). Hershey, PA: IGI Global. doi:10.4018/978-1-5225-1949-2.ch015

Aryanto, V. D., Wismantoro, Y., & Widyatmoko, K. (2018). Implementing Eco-Innovation by Utilizing the Internet to Enhance Firm's Marketing Performance: Study of Green Batik Small and Medium Enterprises in Indonesia. *International Journal of E-Business Research*, *14*(1), 21–36. doi:10.4018/IJEBR.2018010102

Asero, V., & Billi, S. (2022). New Perspective of Networking in the DMO Model. In M. Valeri (Ed.), *New Governance and Management in Touristic Destinations* (pp. 105–118). IGI Global. https://doi.org/10.4018/978-1-6684-3889-3.ch007

Atiku, S. O., & Fields, Z. (2017). Multicultural Orientations for 21st Century Global Leadership. In N. Baporikar (Ed.), *Management Education for Global Leadership* (pp. 28–51). Hershey, PA: IGI Global. doi:10.4018/978-1-5225-1013-0.ch002

Atiku, S. O., & Fields, Z. (2018). Organisational Learning Dimensions and Talent Retention Strategies for the Service Industries. In N. Baporikar (Ed.), *Global Practices in Knowledge Management for Societal and Organizational Development* (pp. 358–381). Hershey, PA: IGI Global. doi:10.4018/978-1-5225-3009-1.ch017

Atsa'am, D. D., & Kuset Bodur, E. (2021). Pattern Mining on How Organizational Tenure Affects the Psychological Capital of Employees Within the Hospitality and Tourism Industry: Linking Employees' Organizational Tenure With PsyCap. *International Journal of Tourism and Hospitality Management in the Digital Age*, *5*(2), 17–28. https://doi.org/10.4018/IJTHMDA.2021070102

Ávila, L., & Teixeira, L. (2018). The Main Concepts Behind the Dematerialization of Business Processes. In M. Khosrow-Pour, D.B.A. (Ed.), Encyclopedia of Information Science and Technology, Fourth Edition (pp. 888-898). Hershey, PA: IGI Global. https://doi.org/ doi:10.4018/978-1-5225-2255-3.ch076

Ayorekire, J., Mugizi, F., Obua, J., & Ampaire, G. (2022). Community-Based Tourism and Local People's Perceptions Towards Conservation: The Case of Queen Elizabeth Conservation Area, Uganda. In I. Mensah & E. Afenyo-Agbe (Eds.), *Prospects and Challenges of Community-Based Tourism and Changing Demographics* (pp. 56–82). IGI Global. https://doi.org/10.4018/978-1-7998-7335-8.ch003

Baleiro, R. (2022). Tourist Literature and the Architecture of Travel in Olga Tokarczuk and Patti Smith. In R. Baleiro & R. Pereira (Eds.), *Global Perspectives on Literary Tourism and Film-Induced Tourism* (pp. 202-216). IGI Global. https://doi.org/10.4018/978-1-7998-8262-6.ch011

Barat, S. (2021). Looking at the Future of Medical Tourism in Asia. *International Journal of Tourism and Hospitality Management in the Digital Age*, *5*(1), 19–33. https://doi.org/10.4018/IJTHMDA.2021010102

Barbosa, C. A., Magalhães, M., & Nunes, M. R. (2021). Travel Instagramability: A Way of Choosing a Destination? In M. Dinis, L. Bonixe, S. Lamy, & Z. Breda (Eds.), *Impact of New Media in Tourism* (pp. 173-190). IGI Global. https://doi.org/10.4018/978-1-7998-7095-1.ch011

Bari, M. W., & Khan, Q. (2021). Pakistan as a Destination of Religious Tourism. In E. Alaverdov & M. Bari (Eds.), *Global Development of Religious Tourism* (pp. 1-10). IGI Global. https://doi.org/10.4018/978-1-7998-5792-1.ch001

Bartens, Y., Chunpir, H. I., Schulte, F., & Voß, S. (2017). Business/IT Alignment in Two-Sided Markets: A COBIT 5 Analysis for Media Streaming Business Models. In S. De Haes & W. Van Grembergen (Eds.), *Strategic IT Governance and Alignment in Business Settings* (pp. 82–111). Hershey, PA: IGI Global. doi:10.4018/978-1-5225-0861-8.ch004

Bashayreh, A. M. (2018). Organizational Culture and Organizational Performance. In W. Lee & F. Sabetzadeh (Eds.), *Contemporary Knowledge and Systems Science* (pp. 50–69). Hershey, PA: IGI Global. doi:10.4018/978-1-5225-5655-8.ch003

Bechthold, L., Lude, M., & Prügl, R. (2021). Crisis Favors the Prepared Firm: How Organizational Ambidexterity Relates to Perceptions of Organizational Resilience. In A. Zehrer, G. Glowka, K. Schwaiger, & V. Ranacher-Lackner (Eds.), *Resiliency Models and Addressing Future Risks for Family Firms in the Tourism Industry* (pp. 178–205). IGI Global. https://doi.org/10.4018/978-1-7998-7352-5.ch008

Bedford, D. A. (2018). Sustainable Knowledge Management Strategies: Aligning Business Capabilities and Knowledge Management Goals. In N. Baporikar (Ed.), *Global Practices in Knowledge Management for Societal and Organizational Development* (pp. 46–73). Hershey, PA: IGI Global. doi:10.4018/978-1-5225-3009-1.ch003

Bekjanov, D., & Matyusupov, B. (2021). Influence of Innovative Processes in the Competitiveness of Tourist Destination. In J. Soares (Ed.), *Innovation and Entrepreneurial Opportunities in Community Tourism* (pp. 243–263). IGI Global. https://doi.org/10.4018/978-1-7998-4855-4.ch014

Bharwani, S., & Musunuri, D. (2018). Reflection as a Process From Theory to Practice. In M. Khosrow-Pour, D.B.A. (Ed.), Encyclopedia of Information Science and Technology, Fourth Edition (pp. 1529-1539). Hershey, PA: IGI Global. doi:10.4018/978-1-5225-2255-3.ch132

Bhatt, G. D., Wang, Z., & Rodger, J. A. (2017). Information Systems Capabilities and Their Effects on Competitive Advantages: A Study of Chinese Companies. *Information Resources Management Journal*, *30*(3), 41–57. doi:10.4018/IRMJ.2017070103

Bhushan, M., & Yadav, A. (2017). Concept of Cloud Computing in ESB. In R. Bhadoria, N. Chaudhari, G. Tomar, & S. Singh (Eds.), *Exploring Enterprise Service Bus in the Service-Oriented Architecture Paradigm* (pp. 116–127). Hershey, PA: IGI Global. doi:10.4018/978-1-5225-2157-0.ch008

Bhushan, S. (2017). System Dynamics Base-Model of Humanitarian Supply Chain (HSCM) in Disaster Prone Eco-Communities of India: A Discussion on Simulation and Scenario Results. *International Journal of System Dynamics Applications*, *6*(3), 20–37. doi:10.4018/IJSDA.2017070102

Binder, D., & Miller, J. W. (2021). A Generations' Perspective on Employer Branding in Tourism. In V. Costa, A. Moura, & M. Mira (Eds.), *Handbook of Research on Human Capital and People Management in the Tourism Industry* (pp. 152–174). IGI Global. https://doi.org/10.4018/978-1-7998-4318-4.ch008

Birch Freeman, A. A., Mensah, I., & Antwi, K. B. (2022). Smiling vs. Frowning Faces: Community Participation for Sustainable Tourism in Ghanaian Communities. In I. Mensah & E. Afenyo-Agbe (Eds.), *Prospects and Challenges of Community-Based Tourism and Changing Demographics* (pp. 83–106). IGI Global. https://doi.org/10.4018/978-1-7998-7335-8.ch004

Biswas, A., & De, A. K. (2017). On Development of a Fuzzy Stochastic Programming Model with Its Application to Business Management. In S. Trivedi, S. Dey, A. Kumar, & T. Panda (Eds.), *Handbook of Research on Advanced Data Mining Techniques and Applications for Business Intelligence* (pp. 353–378). Hershey, PA: IGI Global. doi:10.4018/978-1-5225-2031-3.ch021

Boragnio, A., & Faracce Macia, C. (2021). "Taking Care of Yourself at Home": Use of E-Commerce About Food and Care During the COVID-19 Pandemic in the City of Buenos Aires. In M. Korstanje (Ed.), *Socio-Economic Effects and Recovery Efforts for the Rental Industry: Post-COVID-19 Strategies* (pp. 45–71). IGI Global. https://doi.org/10.4018/978-1-7998-7287-0.ch003

Borges, V. D. (2021). Happiness: The Basis for Public Policy in Tourism. In A. Perinotto, V. Mayer, & J. Soares (Eds.), *Rebuilding and Restructuring the Tourism Industry: Infusion of Happiness and Quality of Life* (pp. 1–25). IGI Global. https://doi.org/10.4018/978-1-7998-7239-9.ch001

Bücker, J., & Ernste, K. (2018). Use of Brand Heroes in Strategic Reputation Management: The Case of Bacardi, Adidas, and Daimler. In A. Erdemir (Ed.), *Reputation Management Techniques in Public Relations* (pp. 126–150). Hershey, PA: IGI Global. doi:10.4018/978-1-5225-3619-2.ch007

Buluk Eşitti, B. (2021). COVID-19 and Alternative Tourism: New Destinations and New Tourism Products. In M. Demir, A. Dalgıç, & F. Ergen (Eds.), *Handbook of Research on the Impacts and Implications of COVID-19 on the Tourism Industry* (pp. 786–805). IGI Global. https://doi.org/10.4018/978-1-7998-8231-2.ch038

Bureš, V. (2018). Industry 4.0 From the Systems Engineering Perspective: Alternative Holistic Framework Development. In R. Brunet-Thornton & F. Martinez (Eds.), *Analyzing the Impacts of Industry 4.0 in Modern Business Environments* (pp. 199–223). Hershey, PA: IGI Global. doi:10.4018/978-1-5225-3468-6.ch011

Buzady, Z. (2017). Resolving the Magic Cube of Effective Case Teaching: Benchmarking Case Teaching Practices in Emerging Markets – Insights from the Central European University Business School, Hungary. In D. Latusek (Ed.), *Case Studies as a Teaching Tool in Management Education* (pp. 79–103). Hershey, PA: IGI Global. doi:10.4018/978-1-5225-0770-3.ch005

Camillo, A. (2021). *Legal Matters, Risk Management, and Risk Prevention: From Forming a Business to Legal Representation.* IGI Global. doi:10.4018/978-1-7998-4342-9.ch004

Căpusneanu, S., & Topor, D. I. (2018). Business Ethics and Cost Management in SMEs: Theories of Business Ethics and Cost Management Ethos. In I. Oncioiu (Ed.), *Ethics and Decision-Making for Sustainable Business Practices* (pp. 109–127). Hershey, PA: IGI Global. doi:10.4018/978-1-5225-3773-1.ch007

Chan, R. L., Mo, P. L., & Moon, K. K. (2018). Strategic and Tactical Measures in Managing Enterprise Risks: A Study of the Textile and Apparel Industry. In K. Strang, M. Korstanje, & N. Vajjhala (Eds.), *Research, Practices, and Innovations in Global Risk and Contingency Management* (pp. 1–19). Hershey, PA: IGI Global. doi:10.4018/978-1-5225-4754-9.ch001

Charlier, S. D., Burke-Smalley, L. A., & Fisher, S. L. (2018). Undergraduate Programs in the U.S: A Contextual and Content-Based Analysis. In J. Mendy (Ed.), *Teaching Human Resources and Organizational Behavior at the College Level* (pp. 26–57). Hershey, PA: IGI Global. doi:10.4018/978-1-5225-2820-3.ch002

Chumillas, J., Güell, M., & Quer, P. (2022). The Use of ICT in Tourist and Educational Literary Routes: The Role of the Guide. In C. Ramos, S. Quinteiro, & A. Gonçalves (Eds.), *ICT as Innovator Between Tourism and Culture* (pp. 15–29). IGI Global. https://doi.org/10.4018/978-1-7998-8165-0.ch002

Dahlberg, T., Kivijärvi, H., & Saarinen, T. (2017). IT Investment Consistency and Other Factors Influencing the Success of IT Performance. In S. De Haes & W. Van Grembergen (Eds.), *Strategic IT Governance and Alignment in Business Settings* (pp. 176–208). Hershey, PA: IGI Global. doi:10.4018/978-1-5225-0861-8.ch007

Damnjanović, A. M. (2017). Knowledge Management Optimization through IT and E-Business Utilization: A Qualitative Study on Serbian SMEs. In M. Vemić (Ed.), *Optimal Management Strategies in Small and Medium Enterprises* (pp. 249–267). Hershey, PA: IGI Global. doi:10.4018/978-1-5225-1949-2.ch012

Daneshpour, H. (2017). Integrating Sustainable Development into Project Portfolio Management through Application of Open Innovation. In M. Vemić (Ed.), *Optimal Management Strategies in Small and Medium Enterprises* (pp. 370–387). Hershey, PA: IGI Global. doi:10.4018/978-1-5225-1949-2.ch017

Daniel, A. D., & Reis de Castro, V. (2018). Entrepreneurship Education: How to Measure the Impact on Nascent Entrepreneurs. In A. Carrizo Moreira, J. Guilherme Leitão Dantas, & F. Manuel Valente (Eds.), *Nascent Entrepreneurship and Successful New Venture Creation* (pp. 85–110). Hershey, PA: IGI Global. doi:10.4018/978-1-5225-2936-1.ch004

David, R., Swami, B. N., & Tangirala, S. (2018). Ethics Impact on Knowledge Management in Organizational Development: A Case Study. In N. Baporikar (Ed.), *Global Practices in Knowledge Management for Societal and Organizational Development* (pp. 19–45). Hershey, PA: IGI Global. doi:10.4018/978-1-5225-3009-1.ch002

De Uña-Álvarez, E., & Villarino-Pérez, M. (2022). Fostering Ecocultural Resources, Identity, and Tourism in Inland Territories (Galicia, NW Spain). In G. Fernandes (Ed.), *Challenges and New Opportunities for Tourism in Inland Territories: Ecocultural Resources and Sustainable Initiatives* (pp. 1-16). IGI Global. https://doi.org/10.4018/978-1-7998-7339-6.ch001

Delias, P., & Lakiotaki, K. (2018). Discovering Process Horizontal Boundaries to Facilitate Process Comprehension. *International Journal of Operations Research and Information Systems*, *9*(2), 1–31. doi:10.4018/IJORIS.2018040101

Denholm, J., & Lee-Davies, L. (2018). Success Factors for Games in Business and Project Management. In *Enhancing Education and Training Initiatives Through Serious Games* (pp. 34–68). Hershey, PA: IGI Global. doi:10.4018/978-1-5225-3689-5.ch002

Deshpande, M. (2017). Best Practices in Management Institutions for Global Leadership: Policy Aspects. In N. Baporikar (Ed.), *Management Education for Global Leadership* (pp. 1–27). Hershey, PA: IGI Global. doi:10.4018/978-1-5225-1013-0.ch001

Deshpande, M. (2018). Policy Perspectives for SMEs Knowledge Management. In N. Baporikar (Ed.), *Knowledge Integration Strategies for Entrepreneurship and Sustainability* (pp. 23–46). Hershey, PA: IGI Global. doi:10.4018/978-1-5225-5115-7.ch002

Dezdar, S. (2017). ERP Implementation Projects in Asian Countries: A Comparative Study on Iran and China. *International Journal of Information Technology Project Management*, *8*(3), 52–68. doi:10.4018/IJITPM.2017070104

Domingos, D., Respício, A., & Martinho, R. (2017). Reliability of IoT-Aware BPMN Healthcare Processes. In C. Reis & M. Maximiano (Eds.), *Internet of Things and Advanced Application in Healthcare* (pp. 214–248). Hershey, PA: IGI Global. doi:10.4018/978-1-5225-1820-4.ch008

Dosumu, O., Hussain, J., & El-Gohary, H. (2017). An Exploratory Study of the Impact of Government Policies on the Development of Small and Medium Enterprises in Developing Countries: The Case of Nigeria. *International Journal of Customer Relationship Marketing and Management*, *8*(4), 51–62. doi:10.4018/IJCRMM.2017100104

Durst, S., Bruns, G., & Edvardsson, I. R. (2017). Retaining Knowledge in Smaller Building and Construction Firms. *International Journal of Knowledge and Systems Science*, *8*(3), 1–12. doi:10.4018/IJKSS.2017070101

Edvardsson, I. R., & Durst, S. (2017). Outsourcing, Knowledge, and Learning: A Critical Review. *International Journal of Knowledge-Based Organizations*, *7*(2), 13–26. doi:10.4018/IJKBO.2017040102

Edwards, J. S. (2018). Integrating Knowledge Management and Business Processes. In M. Khosrow-Pour, D.B.A. (Ed.), Encyclopedia of Information Science and Technology, Fourth Edition (pp. 5046-5055). Hershey, PA: IGI Global. doi:10.4018/978-1-5225-2255-3.ch437

Eichelberger, S., & Peters, M. (2021). Family Firm Management in Turbulent Times: Opportunities for Responsible Tourism. In A. Zehrer, G. Glowka, K. Schwaiger, & V. Ranacher-Lackner (Eds.), *Resiliency Models and Addressing Future Risks for Family Firms in the Tourism Industry* (pp. 103–124). IGI Global. https://doi.org/10.4018/978-1-7998-7352-5.ch005

Eide, D., Hjalager, A., & Hansen, M. (2022). Innovative Certifications in Adventure Tourism: Attributes and Diffusion. In R. Augusto Costa, F. Brandão, Z. Breda, & C. Costa (Eds.), *Planning and Managing the Experience Economy in Tourism* (pp. 161-175). IGI Global. https://doi.org/10.4018/978-1-7998-8775-1.ch009

Ejiogu, A. O. (2018). Economics of Farm Management. In *Agricultural Finance and Opportunities for Investment and Expansion* (pp. 56–72). Hershey, PA: IGI Global. doi:10.4018/978-1-5225-3059-6.ch003

Ekanem, I., & Abiade, G. E. (2018). Factors Influencing the Use of E-Commerce by Small Enterprises in Nigeria. *International Journal of ICT Research in Africa and the Middle East*, *7*(1), 37–53. doi:10.4018/IJICTRAME.2018010103

Ekanem, I., & Alrossais, L. A. (2017). Succession Challenges Facing Family Businesses in Saudi Arabia. In P. Zgheib (Ed.), *Entrepreneurship and Business Innovation in the Middle East* (pp. 122–146). Hershey, PA: IGI Global. doi:10.4018/978-1-5225-2066-5.ch007

El Faquih, L., & Fredj, M. (2017). Ontology-Based Framework for Quality in Configurable Process Models. *Journal of Electronic Commerce in Organizations*, *15*(2), 48–60. doi:10.4018/JECO.2017040104

Faisal, M. N., & Talib, F. (2017). Building Ambidextrous Supply Chains in SMEs: How to Tackle the Barriers? *International Journal of Information Systems and Supply Chain Management*, *10*(4), 80–100. doi:10.4018/IJISSCM.2017100105

Fernandes, T. M., Gomes, J., & Romão, M. (2017). Investments in E-Government: A Benefit Management Case Study. *International Journal of Electronic Government Research*, *13*(3), 1–17. doi:10.4018/IJEGR.2017070101

Figueira, L. M., Honrado, G. R., & Dionísio, M. S. (2021). Human Capital Management in the Tourism Industry in Portugal. In V. Costa, A. Moura, & M. Mira (Eds.), *Handbook of Research on Human Capital and People Management in the Tourism Industry* (pp. 1–19). IGI Global. doi:10.4018/978-1-7998-4318-4.ch001

Gao, S. S., Oreal, S., & Zhang, J. (2018). Contemporary Financial Risk Management Perceptions and Practices of Small-Sized Chinese Businesses. In I. Management Association (Ed.), Global Business Expansion: Concepts, Methodologies, Tools, and Applications (pp. 917-931). Hershey, PA: IGI Global. doi:10.4018/978-1-5225-5481-3.ch041

Garg, R., & Berning, S. C. (2017). Indigenous Chinese Management Philosophies: Key Concepts and Relevance for Modern Chinese Firms. In B. Christiansen & G. Koc (Eds.), *Transcontinental Strategies for Industrial Development and Economic Growth* (pp. 43–57). Hershey, PA: IGI Global. doi:10.4018/978-1-5225-2160-0.ch003

Gencer, Y. G. (2017). Supply Chain Management in Retailing Business. In U. Akkucuk (Ed.), *Ethics and Sustainability in Global Supply Chain Management* (pp. 197–210). Hershey, PA: IGI Global. doi:10.4018/978-1-5225-2036-8.ch011

Gera, R., Arora, S., & Malik, S. (2021). Emotional Labor in the Tourism Industry: Strategies, Antecedents, and Outcomes. In V. Costa, A. Moura, & M. Mira (Eds.), *Handbook of Research on Human Capital and People Management in the Tourism Industry* (pp. 73–91). IGI Global. https://doi.org/10.4018/978-1-7998-4318-4.ch004

Giacosa, E. (2018). The Increasing of the Regional Development Thanks to the Luxury Business Innovation. In L. Carvalho (Ed.), *Handbook of Research on Entrepreneurial Ecosystems and Social Dynamics in a Globalized World* (pp. 260–273). Hershey, PA: IGI Global. doi:10.4018/978-1-5225-3525-6.ch011

Glowka, G., Tusch, M., & Zehrer, A. (2021). The Risk Perception of Family Business Owner-Manager in the Tourism Industry: A Qualitative Comparison of the Intra-Firm Senior and Junior Generation. In A. Zehrer, G. Glowka, K. Schwaiger, & V. Ranacher-Lackner (Eds.), *Resiliency Models and Addressing Future Risks for Family Firms in the Tourism Industry* (pp. 126–153). IGI Global. https://doi.org/10.4018/978-1-7998-7352-5.ch006

Glykas, M., & George, J. (2017). Quality and Process Management Systems in the UAE Maritime Industry. *International Journal of Productivity Management and Assessment Technologies*, *5*(1), 20–39. doi:10.4018/IJPMAT.2017010102

Glykas, M., Valiris, G., Kokkinaki, A., & Koutsoukou, Z. (2018). Banking Business Process Management Implementation. *International Journal of Productivity Management and Assessment Technologies*, *6*(1), 50–69. doi:10.4018/IJPMAT.2018010104

Gomes, J., & Romão, M. (2017). The Balanced Scorecard: Keeping Updated and Aligned with Today's Business Trends. *International Journal of Productivity Management and Assessment Technologies*, *5*(2), 1–15. doi:10.4018/IJPMAT.2017070101

Gomes, J., & Romão, M. (2017). Aligning Information Systems and Technology with Benefit Management and Balanced Scorecard. In S. De Haes & W. Van Grembergen (Eds.), *Strategic IT Governance and Alignment in Business Settings* (pp. 112–131). Hershey, PA: IGI Global. doi:10.4018/978-1-5225-0861-8.ch005

Goyal, A. (2021). Communicating and Building Destination Brands With New Media. In M. Dinis, L. Bonixe, S. Lamy, & Z. Breda (Eds.), *Impact of New Media in Tourism* (pp. 1-20). IGI Global. https://doi.org/10.4018/978-1-7998-7095-1.ch001

Grefen, P., & Turetken, O. (2017). Advanced Business Process Management in Networked E-Business Scenarios. *International Journal of E-Business Research, 13*(4), 70–104. doi:10.4018/IJEBR.2017100105

Guasca, M., Van Broeck, A. M., & Vanneste, D. (2021). Tourism and the Social Reintegration of Colombian Ex-Combatants. In J. da Silva, Z. Breda, & F. Carbone (Eds.), *Role and Impact of Tourism in Peacebuilding and Conflict Transformation* (pp. 66-86). IGI Global. https://doi.org/10.4018/978-1-7998-5053-3.ch005

Haider, A., & Saetang, S. (2017). Strategic IT Alignment in Service Sector. In S. Rozenes & Y. Cohen (Eds.), *Handbook of Research on Strategic Alliances and Value Co-Creation in the Service Industry* (pp. 231–258). Hershey, PA: IGI Global. doi:10.4018/978-1-5225-2084-9.ch012

Hajilari, A. B., Ghadaksaz, M., & Fasghandis, G. S. (2017). Assessing Organizational Readiness for Implementing ERP System Using Fuzzy Expert System Approach. *International Journal of Enterprise Information Systems, 13*(1), 67–85. doi:10.4018/IJEIS.2017010105

Haldorai, A., Ramu, A., & Murugan, S. (2018). Social Aware Cognitive Radio Networks: Effectiveness of Social Networks as a Strategic Tool for Organizational Business Management. In H. Bansal, G. Shrivastava, G. Nguyen, & L. Stanciu (Eds.), *Social Network Analytics for Contemporary Business Organizations* (pp. 188–202). Hershey, PA: IGI Global. doi:10.4018/978-1-5225-5097-6.ch010

Hall, O. P. Jr. (2017). Social Media Driven Management Education. *International Journal of Knowledge-Based Organizations, 7*(2), 43–59. doi:10.4018/IJKBO.2017040104

Hanifah, H., Halim, H. A., Ahmad, N. H., & Vafaei-Zadeh, A. (2017). Innovation Culture as a Mediator Between Specific Human Capital and Innovation Performance Among Bumiputera SMEs in Malaysia. In N. Ahmad, T. Ramayah, H. Halim, & S. Rahman (Eds.), *Handbook of Research on Small and Medium Enterprises in Developing Countries* (pp. 261–279). Hershey, PA: IGI Global. doi:10.4018/978-1-5225-2165-5.ch012

Hartlieb, S., & Silvius, G. (2017). Handling Uncertainty in Project Management and Business Development: Similarities and Differences. In Y. Raydugin (Ed.), *Handbook of Research on Leveraging Risk and Uncertainties for Effective Project Management* (pp. 337–362). Hershey, PA: IGI Global. doi:10.4018/978-1-5225-1790-0.ch016

Hass, K. B. (2017). Living on the Edge: Managing Project Complexity. In Y. Raydugin (Ed.), *Handbook of Research on Leveraging Risk and Uncertainties for Effective Project Management* (pp. 177–201). Hershey, PA: IGI Global. doi:10.4018/978-1-5225-1790-0.ch009

Hawking, P., & Carmine Sellitto, C. (2017). Developing an Effective Strategy for Organizational Business Intelligence. In M. Tavana (Ed.), *Enterprise Information Systems and the Digitalization of Business Functions* (pp. 222–237). Hershey, PA: IGI Global. doi:10.4018/978-1-5225-2382-6.ch010

Hawking, P., & Sellitto, C. (2017). A Fast-Moving Consumer Goods Company and Business Intelligence Strategy Development. *International Journal of Enterprise Information Systems, 13*(2), 22–33. doi:10.4018/IJEIS.2017040102

Hawking, P., & Sellitto, C. (2017). Business Intelligence Strategy: Two Case Studies. *International Journal of Business Intelligence Research, 8*(2), 17–30. doi:10.4018/IJBIR.2017070102

Hee, W. J., Jalleh, G., Lai, H., & Lin, C. (2017). E-Commerce and IT Projects: Evaluation and Management Issues in Australian and Taiwanese Hospitals. *International Journal of Public Health Management and Ethics, 2*(1), 69–90. doi:10.4018/IJPHME.2017010104

Hernandez, A. A. (2018). Exploring the Factors to Green IT Adoption of SMEs in the Philippines. *Journal of Cases on Information Technology, 20*(2), 49–66. doi:10.4018/JCIT.2018040104

Hollman, A., Bickford, S., & Hollman, T. (2017). Cyber InSecurity: A Post-Mortem Attempt to Assess Cyber Problems from IT and Business Management Perspectives. *Journal of Cases on Information Technology, 19*(3), 42–70. doi:10.4018/JCIT.2017070104

Ibrahim, F., & Zainin, N. M. (2021). Exploring the Technological Impacts: The Case of Museums in Brunei Darussalam. *International Journal of Tourism and Hospitality Management in the Digital Age, 5*(1), 1–18. https://doi.org/10.4018/IJTHMDA.2021010101

Igbinakhase, I. (2017). Responsible and Sustainable Management Practices in Developing and Developed Business Environments. In Z. Fields (Ed.), *Collective Creativity for Responsible and Sustainable Business Practice* (pp. 180–207). Hershey, PA: IGI Global. doi:10.4018/978-1-5225-1823-5.ch010

Iwata, J. J., & Hoskins, R. G. (2017). Managing Indigenous Knowledge in Tanzania: A Business Perspective. In P. Jain & N. Mnjama (Eds.), *Managing Knowledge Resources and Records in Modern Organizations* (pp. 198–214). Hershey, PA: IGI Global. doi:10.4018/978-1-5225-1965-2.ch012

Jain, P. (2017). Ethical and Legal Issues in Knowledge Management Life-Cycle in Business. In P. Jain & N. Mnjama (Eds.), *Managing Knowledge Resources and Records in Modern Organizations* (pp. 82–101). Hershey, PA: IGI Global. doi:10.4018/978-1-5225-1965-2.ch006

James, S., & Hauli, E. (2017). Holistic Management Education at Tanzanian Rural Development Planning Institute. In N. Baporikar (Ed.), *Management Education for Global Leadership* (pp. 112–136). Hershey, PA: IGI Global. doi:10.4018/978-1-5225-1013-0.ch006

Janošková, M., Csikósová, A., & Čulková, K. (2018). Measurement of Company Performance as Part of Its Strategic Management. In R. Leon (Ed.), *Managerial Strategies for Business Sustainability During Turbulent Times* (pp. 309–335). Hershey, PA: IGI Global. doi:10.4018/978-1-5225-2716-9.ch017

Jean-Vasile, A., & Alecu, A. (2017). Theoretical and Practical Approaches in Understanding the Influences of Cost-Productivity-Profit Trinomial in Contemporary Enterprises. In A. Jean Vasile & D. Nicolò (Eds.), *Sustainable Entrepreneurship and Investments in the Green Economy* (pp. 28–62). Hershey, PA: IGI Global. doi:10.4018/978-1-5225-2075-7.ch002

Joia, L. A., & Correia, J. C. (2018). CIO Competencies From the IT Professional Perspective: Insights From Brazil. *Journal of Global Information Management*, *26*(2), 74–103. doi:10.4018/JGIM.2018040104

Juma, A., & Mzera, N. (2017). Knowledge Management and Records Management and Competitive Advantage in Business. In P. Jain & N. Mnjama (Eds.), *Managing Knowledge Resources and Records in Modern Organizations* (pp. 15–28). Hershey, PA: IGI Global. doi:10.4018/978-1-5225-1965-2.ch002

K., I., & A, V. (2018). Monitoring and Auditing in the Cloud. In K. Munir (Ed.), *Cloud Computing Technologies for Green Enterprises* (pp. 318-350). Hershey, PA: IGI Global. https://doi.org/ doi:10.4018/978-1-5225-3038-1.ch013

Kabra, G., Ghosh, V., & Ramesh, A. (2018). Enterprise Integrated Business Process Management and Business Intelligence Framework for Business Process Sustainability. In A. Paul, D. Bhattacharyya, & S. Anand (Eds.), *Green Initiatives for Business Sustainability and Value Creation* (pp. 228–238). Hershey, PA: IGI Global. doi:10.4018/978-1-5225-2662-9.ch010

Kaoud, M. (2017). Investigation of Customer Knowledge Management: A Case Study Research. *International Journal of Service Science, Management, Engineering, and Technology*, *8*(2), 12–22. doi:10.4018/IJSSMET.2017040102

Katuu, S. (2018). A Comparative Assessment of Enterprise Content Management Maturity Models. In N. Gwangwava & M. Mutingi (Eds.), *E-Manufacturing and E-Service Strategies in Contemporary Organizations* (pp. 93–118). Hershey, PA: IGI Global. doi:10.4018/978-1-5225-3628-4.ch005

Khan, M. Y., & Abir, T. (2022). The Role of Social Media Marketing in the Tourism and Hospitality Industry: A Conceptual Study on Bangladesh. In C. Ramos, S. Quinteiro, & A. Gonçalves (Eds.), *ICT as Innovator Between Tourism and Culture* (pp. 213–229). IGI Global. https://doi.org/10.4018/978-1-7998-8165-0.ch013

Kinnunen, S., Ylä-Kujala, A., Marttonen-Arola, S., Kärri, T., & Baglee, D. (2018). Internet of Things in Asset Management: Insights from Industrial Professionals and Academia. *International Journal of Service Science, Management, Engineering, and Technology*, *9*(2), 104–119. doi:10.4018/IJSSMET.2018040105

Klein, A. Z., Sabino de Freitas, A., Machado, L., Freitas, J. C. Jr, Graziola, P. G. Jr, & Schlemmer, E. (2017). Virtual Worlds Applications for Management Education. In L. Tomei (Ed.), *Exploring the New Era of Technology-Infused Education* (pp. 279–299). Hershey, PA: IGI Global. doi:10.4018/978-1-5225-1709-2.ch017

Kővári, E., Saleh, M., & Steinbachné Hajmásy, G. (2022). The Impact of Corporate Digital Responsibility (CDR) on Internal Stakeholders' Satisfaction in Hungarian Upscale Hotels. In M. Valeri (Ed.), *New Governance and Management in Touristic Destinations* (pp. 35–51). IGI Global. https://doi.org/10.4018/978-1-6684-3889-3.ch003

Kożuch, B., & Jabłoński, A. (2017). Adopting the Concept of Business Models in Public Management. In M. Lewandowski & B. Kożuch (Eds.), *Public Sector Entrepreneurship and the Integration of Innovative Business Models* (pp. 10–46). Hershey, PA: IGI Global. doi:10.4018/978-1-5225-2215-7.ch002

Kumar, J., Adhikary, A., & Jha, A. (2017). Small Active Investors' Perceptions and Preferences Towards Tax Saving Mutual Fund Schemes in Eastern India: An Empirical Note. *International Journal of Asian Business and Information Management*, *8*(2), 35–45. doi:10.4018/IJABIM.2017040103

Latusi, S., & Fissore, M. (2021). Pilgrimage Routes to Happiness: Comparing the Camino de Santiago and Via Francigena. In A. Perinotto, V. Mayer, & J. Soares (Eds.), *Rebuilding and Restructuring the Tourism Industry: Infusion of Happiness and Quality of Life* (pp. 157–182). IGI Global. https://doi.org/10.4018/978-1-7998-7239-9.ch008

Lavassani, K. M., & Movahedi, B. (2017). Applications Driven Information Systems: Beyond Networks toward Business Ecosystems. *International Journal of Innovation in the Digital Economy*, *8*(1), 61–75. doi:10.4018/IJIDE.2017010104

Lazzareschi, V. H., & Brito, M. S. (2017). Strategic Information Management: Proposal of Business Project Model. In G. Jamil, A. Soares, & C. Pessoa (Eds.), *Handbook of Research on Information Management for Effective Logistics and Supply Chains* (pp. 59–88). Hershey, PA: IGI Global. doi:10.4018/978-1-5225-0973-8.ch004

Lechuga Sancho, M. P., & Martín Navarro, A. (2022). Evolution of the Literature on Social Responsibility in the Tourism Sector: A Systematic Literature Review. In G. Fernandes (Ed.), *Challenges and New Opportunities for Tourism in Inland Territories: Ecocultural Resources and Sustainable Initiatives* (pp. 169–186). IGI Global. https://doi.org/10.4018/978-1-7998-7339-6.ch010

Lederer, M., Kurz, M., & Lazarov, P. (2017). Usage and Suitability of Methods for Strategic Business Process Initiatives: A Multi Case Study Research. *International Journal of Productivity Management and Assessment Technologies*, *5*(1), 40–51. doi:10.4018/IJPMAT.2017010103

Lee, I. (2017). A Social Enterprise Business Model and a Case Study of Pacific Community Ventures (PCV). In V. Potocan, M. Ünğan, & Z. Nedelko (Eds.), *Handbook of Research on Managerial Solutions in Non-Profit Organizations* (pp. 182–204). Hershey, PA: IGI Global. doi:10.4018/978-1-5225-0731-4.ch009

Leon, L. A., Seal, K. C., Przasnyski, Z. H., & Wiedenman, I. (2017). Skills and Competencies Required for Jobs in Business Analytics: A Content Analysis of Job Advertisements Using Text Mining. *International Journal of Business Intelligence Research*, *8*(1), 1–25. doi:10.4018/IJBIR.2017010101

Levy, C. L., & Elias, N. I. (2017). SOHO Users' Perceptions of Reliability and Continuity of Cloud-Based Services. In M. Moore (Ed.), *Cybersecurity Breaches and Issues Surrounding Online Threat Protection* (pp. 248–287). Hershey, PA: IGI Global. doi:10.4018/978-1-5225-1941-6.ch011

Levy, M. (2018). Change Management Serving Knowledge Management and Organizational Development: Reflections and Review. In N. Baporikar (Ed.), *Global Practices in Knowledge Management for Societal and Organizational Development* (pp. 256–270). Hershey, PA: IGI Global. doi:10.4018/978-1-5225-3009-1.ch012

Lewandowski, M. (2017). Public Organizations and Business Model Innovation: The Role of Public Service Design. In M. Lewandowski & B. Kożuch (Eds.), *Public Sector Entrepreneurship and the Integration of Innovative Business Models* (pp. 47–72). Hershey, PA: IGI Global. doi:10.4018/978-1-5225-2215-7.ch003

Lhannaoui, H., Kabbaj, M. I., & Bakkoury, Z. (2017). A Survey of Risk-Aware Business Process Modelling. *International Journal of Risk and Contingency Management, 6*(3), 14–26. doi:10.4018/IJRCM.2017070102

Li, J., Sun, W., Jiang, W., Yang, H., & Zhang, L. (2017). How the Nature of Exogenous Shocks and Crises Impact Company Performance?: The Effects of Industry Characteristics. *International Journal of Risk and Contingency Management, 6*(4), 40–55. doi:10.4018/IJRCM.2017100103

Lopez-Fernandez, M., Perez-Perez, M., Serrano-Bedia, A., & Cobo-Gonzalez, A. (2021). Small and Medium Tourism Enterprise Survival in Times of Crisis: “El Capricho de Gaudí. In D. Toubes & N. Araújo-Vila (Eds.), *Risk, Crisis, and Disaster Management in Small and Medium-Sized Tourism Enterprises* (pp. 103–129). IGI Global. doi:10.4018/978-1-7998-6996-2.ch005

Mahajan, A., Maidullah, S., & Hossain, M. R. (2022). Experience Toward Smart Tour Guide Apps in Travelling: An Analysis of Users’ Reviews on Audio Odigos and Trip My Way. In R. Augusto Costa, F. Brandão, Z. Breda, & C. Costa (Eds.), *Planning and Managing the Experience Economy in Tourism* (pp. 255-273). IGI Global. https://doi.org/10.4018/978-1-7998-8775-1.ch014

Malega, P. (2017). Small and Medium Enterprises in the Slovak Republic: Status and Competitiveness of SMEs in the Global Markets and Possibilities of Optimization. In M. Vemić (Ed.), *Optimal Management Strategies in Small and Medium Enterprises* (pp. 102–124). Hershey, PA: IGI Global. doi:10.4018/978-1-5225-1949-2.ch006

Malewska, K. M. (2017). Intuition in Decision-Making on the Example of a Non-Profit Organization. In V. Potocan, M. Üngan, & Z. Nedelko (Eds.), *Handbook of Research on Managerial Solutions in Non-Profit Organizations* (pp. 378–399). Hershey, PA: IGI Global. doi:10.4018/978-1-5225-0731-4.ch018

Maroofi, F. (2017). Entrepreneurial Orientation and Organizational Learning Ability Analysis for Innovation and Firm Performance. In N. Baporikar (Ed.), *Innovation and Shifting Perspectives in Management Education* (pp. 144–165). Hershey, PA: IGI Global. doi:10.4018/978-1-5225-1019-2.ch007

Marques, M., Moleiro, D., Brito, T. M., & Marques, T. (2021). Customer Relationship Management as an Important Relationship Marketing Tool: The Case of the Hospitality Industry in Estoril Coast. In M. Dinis, L. Bonixe, S. Lamy, & Z. Breda (Eds.), Impact of New Media in Tourism (pp. 39-56). IGI Global. https://doi.org/ doi:10.4018/978-1-7998-7095-1.ch003

Martins, P. V., & Zacarias, M. (2017). A Web-based Tool for Business Process Improvement. *International Journal of Web Portals, 9*(2), 68–84. doi:10.4018/IJWP.2017070104

Matthies, B., & Coners, A. (2017). Exploring the Conceptual Nature of e-Business Projects. *Journal of Electronic Commerce in Organizations, 15*(3), 33–63. doi:10.4018/JECO.2017070103

Mayer, V. F., Fraga, C. C., & Silva, L. C. (2021). Contributions of Neurosciences to Studies of Well-Being in Tourism. In A. Perinotto, V. Mayer, & J. Soares (Eds.), *Rebuilding and Restructuring the Tourism Industry: Infusion of Happiness and Quality of Life* (pp. 108–128). IGI Global. https://doi.org/10.4018/978-1-7998-7239-9.ch006

McKee, J. (2018). Architecture as a Tool to Solve Business Planning Problems. In M. Khosrow-Pour, D.B.A. (Ed.), Encyclopedia of Information Science and Technology, Fourth Edition (pp. 573-586). Hershey, PA: IGI Global. doi:10.4018/978-1-5225-2255-3.ch050

McMurray, A. J., Cross, J., & Caponecchia, C. (2018). The Risk Management Profession in Australia: Business Continuity Plan Practices. In N. Bajgoric (Ed.), *Always-On Enterprise Information Systems for Modern Organizations* (pp. 112–129). Hershey, PA: IGI Global. doi:10.4018/978-1-5225-3704-5.ch006

Meddah, I. H., & Belkadi, K. (2018). Mining Patterns Using Business Process Management. In R. Hamou (Ed.), *Handbook of Research on Biomimicry in Information Retrieval and Knowledge Management* (pp. 78–89). Hershey, PA: IGI Global. doi:10.4018/978-1-5225-3004-6.ch005

Melian, A. G., & Camprubí, R. (2021). The Accessibility of Museum Websites: The Case of Barcelona. In C. Eusébio, L. Teixeira, & M. Carneiro (Eds.), *ICT Tools and Applications for Accessible Tourism* (pp. 234–255). IGI Global. https://doi.org/10.4018/978-1-7998-6428-8.ch011

Mendes, L. (2017). TQM and Knowledge Management: An Integrated Approach Towards Tacit Knowledge Management. In D. Jaziri-Bouagina & G. Jamil (Eds.), *Handbook of Research on Tacit Knowledge Management for Organizational Success* (pp. 236–263). Hershey, PA: IGI Global. doi:10.4018/978-1-5225-2394-9.ch009

Menezes, V. D., & Cavagnaro, E. (2021). Communicating Sustainable Initiatives in the Hotel Industry: The Case of the Hotel Jakarta Amsterdam. In F. Brandão, Z. Breda, R. Costa, & C. Costa (Eds.), *Handbook of Research on the Role of Tourism in Achieving Sustainable Development Goals* (pp. 224-234). IGI Global. https://doi.org/10.4018/978-1-7998-5691-7.ch013

Menezes, V. D., & Cavagnaro, E. (2021). Communicating Sustainable Initiatives in the Hotel Industry: The Case of the Hotel Jakarta Amsterdam. In F. Brandão, Z. Breda, R. Costa, & C. Costa (Eds.), *Handbook of Research on the Role of Tourism in Achieving Sustainable Development Goals* (pp. 224-234). IGI Global. https://doi.org/10.4018/978-1-7998-5691-7.ch013

Mitas, O., Bastiaansen, M., & Boode, W. (2022). If You're Happy, I'm Happy: Emotion Contagion at a Tourist Information Center. In R. Augusto Costa, F. Brandão, Z. Breda, & C. Costa (Eds.), *Planning and Managing the Experience Economy in Tourism* (pp. 122-140). IGI Global. https://doi.org/10.4018/978-1-7998-8775-1.ch007

Mnjama, N. M. (2017). Preservation of Recorded Information in Public and Private Sector Organizations. In P. Jain & N. Mnjama (Eds.), *Managing Knowledge Resources and Records in Modern Organizations* (pp. 149–167). Hershey, PA: IGI Global. doi:10.4018/978-1-5225-1965-2.ch009

Mokoqama, M., & Fields, Z. (2017). Principles of Responsible Management Education (PRME): Call for Responsible Management Education. In Z. Fields (Ed.), *Collective Creativity for Responsible and Sustainable Business Practice* (pp. 229–241). Hershey, PA: IGI Global. doi:10.4018/978-1-5225-1823-5.ch012

Monteiro, A., Lopes, S., & Carbone, F. (2021). Academic Mobility: Bridging Tourism and Peace Education. In J. da Silva, Z. Breda, & F. Carbone (Eds.), *Role and Impact of Tourism in Peacebuilding and Conflict Transformation* (pp. 275-301). IGI Global. https://doi.org/10.4018/978-1-7998-5053-3.ch016

Muniapan, B. (2017). Philosophy and Management: The Relevance of Vedanta in Management. In P. Ordóñez de Pablos (Ed.), *Managerial Strategies and Solutions for Business Success in Asia* (pp. 124–139). Hershey, PA: IGI Global. doi:10.4018/978-1-5225-1886-0.ch007

Murad, S. E., & Dowaji, S. (2017). Using Value-Based Approach for Managing Cloud-Based Services. In A. Turuk, B. Sahoo, & S. Addya (Eds.), *Resource Management and Efficiency in Cloud Computing Environments* (pp. 33–60). Hershey, PA: IGI Global. doi:10.4018/978-1-5225-1721-4.ch002

Mutahar, A. M., Daud, N. M., Thurasamy, R., Isaac, O., & Abdulsalam, R. (2018). The Mediating of Perceived Usefulness and Perceived Ease of Use: The Case of Mobile Banking in Yemen. *International Journal of Technology Diffusion, 9*(2), 21–40. doi:10.4018/IJTD.2018040102

Naidoo, V. (2017). E-Learning and Management Education at African Universities. In N. Baporikar (Ed.), *Management Education for Global Leadership* (pp. 181–201). Hershey, PA: IGI Global. doi:10.4018/978-1-5225-1013-0.ch009

Naidoo, V., & Igbinakhase, I. (2018). Opportunities and Challenges of Knowledge Retention in SMEs. In N. Baporikar (Ed.), *Knowledge Integration Strategies for Entrepreneurship and Sustainability* (pp. 70–94). Hershey, PA: IGI Global. doi:10.4018/978-1-5225-5115-7.ch004

Naumov, N., & Costandachi, G. (2021). Creativity and Entrepreneurship: Gastronomic Tourism in Mexico. In J. Soares (Ed.), *Innovation and Entrepreneurial Opportunities in Community Tourism* (pp. 90–108). IGI Global. https://doi.org/10.4018/978-1-7998-4855-4.ch006

Nayak, S., & Prabhu, N. (2017). Paradigm Shift in Management Education: Need for a Cross Functional Perspective. In N. Baporikar (Ed.), *Management Education for Global Leadership* (pp. 241–255). Hershey, PA: IGI Global. doi:10.4018/978-1-5225-1013-0.ch012

Nedelko, Z., & Potocan, V. (2017). Management Solutions in Non-Profit Organizations: Case of Slovenia. In V. Potocan, M. Üngan, & Z. Nedelko (Eds.), *Handbook of Research on Managerial Solutions in Non-Profit Organizations* (pp. 1–22). Hershey, PA: IGI Global. doi:10.4018/978-1-5225-0731-4.ch001

Nedelko, Z., & Potocan, V. (2017). Priority of Management Tools Utilization among Managers: International Comparison. In V. Wang (Ed.), *Encyclopedia of Strategic Leadership and Management* (pp. 1083–1094). Hershey, PA: IGI Global. doi:10.4018/978-1-5225-1049-9.ch075

Nedelko, Z., Raudeliūnienė, J., & Črešnar, R. (2018). Knowledge Dynamics in Supply Chain Management. In N. Baporikar (Ed.), *Knowledge Integration Strategies for Entrepreneurship and Sustainability* (pp. 150–166). Hershey, PA: IGI Global. doi:10.4018/978-1-5225-5115-7.ch008

Nguyen, H. T., & Hipsher, S. A. (2018). Innovation and Creativity Used by Private Sector Firms in a Resources-Constrained Environment. In S. Hipsher (Ed.), *Examining the Private Sector's Role in Wealth Creation and Poverty Reduction* (pp. 219–238). Hershey, PA: IGI Global. doi:10.4018/978-1-5225-3117-3.ch010

Obicci, P. A. (2017). Risk Sharing in a Partnership. In *Risk Management Strategies in Public-Private Partnerships* (pp. 115–152). Hershey, PA: IGI Global. doi:10.4018/978-1-5225-2503-5.ch004

Obidallah, W. J., & Raahemi, B. (2017). Managing Changes in Service Oriented Virtual Organizations: A Structural and Procedural Framework to Facilitate the Process of Change. *Journal of Electronic Commerce in Organizations, 15*(1), 59–83. doi:10.4018/JECO.2017010104

Ojo, O. (2017). Impact of Innovation on the Entrepreneurial Success in Selected Business Enterprises in South-West Nigeria. *International Journal of Innovation in the Digital Economy, 8*(2), 29–38. doi:10.4018/IJIDE.2017040103

Okdinawati, L., Simatupang, T. M., & Sunitiyoso, Y. (2017). Multi-Agent Reinforcement Learning for Value Co-Creation of Collaborative Transportation Management (CTM). *International Journal of Information Systems and Supply Chain Management, 10*(3), 84–95. doi:10.4018/IJISSCM.2017070105

Olivera, V. A., & Carrillo, I. M. (2021). Organizational Culture: A Key Element for the Development of Mexican Micro and Small Tourist Companies. In J. Soares (Ed.), *Innovation and Entrepreneurial Opportunities in Community Tourism* (pp. 227–242). IGI Global. doi:10.4018/978-1-7998-4855-4.ch013

Ossorio, M. (2022). Corporate Museum Experiences in Enogastronomic Tourism. In R. Augusto Costa, F. Brandão, Z. Breda, & C. Costa (Eds.), Planning and Managing the Experience Economy in Tourism (pp. 107-121). IGI Global. https://doi.org/ doi:10.4018/978-1-7998-8775-1.ch006

Ossorio, M. (2022). Enogastronomic Tourism in Times of Pandemic. In G. Fernandes (Ed.), *Challenges and New Opportunities for Tourism in Inland Territories: Ecocultural Resources and Sustainable Initiatives* (pp. 241–255). IGI Global. https://doi.org/10.4018/978-1-7998-7339-6.ch014

Özekici, Y. K. (2022). ICT as an Acculturative Agent and Its Role in the Tourism Context: Introduction, Acculturation Theory, Progress of the Acculturation Theory in Extant Literature. In C. Ramos, S. Quinteiro, & A. Gonçalves (Eds.), *ICT as Innovator Between Tourism and Culture* (pp. 42–66). IGI Global. https://doi.org/10.4018/978-1-7998-8165-0.ch004

Pal, K. (2018). Building High Quality Big Data-Based Applications in Supply Chains. In A. Kumar & S. Saurav (Eds.), *Supply Chain Management Strategies and Risk Assessment in Retail Environments* (pp. 1–24). Hershey, PA: IGI Global. doi:10.4018/978-1-5225-3056-5.ch001

Palos-Sanchez, P. R., & Correia, M. B. (2018). Perspectives of the Adoption of Cloud Computing in the Tourism Sector. In J. Rodrigues, C. Ramos, P. Cardoso, & C. Henriques (Eds.), *Handbook of Research on Technological Developments for Cultural Heritage and eTourism Applications* (pp. 377–400). Hershey, PA: IGI Global. doi:10.4018/978-1-5225-2927-9.ch018

Papadopoulou, G. (2021). Promoting Gender Equality and Women Empowerment in the Tourism Sector. In F. Brandão, Z. Breda, R. Costa, & C. Costa (Eds.), Handbook of Research on the Role of Tourism in Achieving Sustainable Development Goals (pp. 152-174). IGI Global. https://doi.org/ doi:10.4018/978-1-7998-5691-7.ch009

Papp-Váry, Á. F., & Tóth, T. Z. (2022). Analysis of Budapest as a Film Tourism Destination. In R. Baleiro & R. Pereira (Eds.), *Global Perspectives on Literary Tourism and Film-Induced Tourism* (pp. 257-279). IGI Global. https://doi.org/10.4018/978-1-7998-8262-6.ch014

Patiño, B. E. (2017). New Generation Management by Convergence and Individual Identity: A Systemic and Human-Oriented Approach. In N. Baporikar (Ed.), *Innovation and Shifting Perspectives in Management Education* (pp. 119–143). Hershey, PA: IGI Global. doi:10.4018/978-1-5225-1019-2.ch006

Patro, C. S. (2021). Digital Tourism: Influence of E-Marketing Technology. In M. Dinis, L. Bonixe, S. Lamy, & Z. Breda (Eds.), *Impact of New Media in Tourism* (pp. 234-254). IGI Global. https://doi.org/10.4018/978-1-7998-7095-1.ch014

Pawliczek, A., & Rössler, M. (2017). Knowledge of Management Tools and Systems in SMEs: Knowledge Transfer in Management. In A. Bencsik (Ed.), *Knowledge Management Initiatives and Strategies in Small and Medium Enterprises* (pp. 180–203). Hershey, PA: IGI Global. doi:10.4018/978-1-5225-1642-2.ch009

Pejic-Bach, M., Omazic, M. A., Aleksic, A., & Zoroja, J. (2018). Knowledge-Based Decision Making: A Multi-Case Analysis. In R. Leon (Ed.), *Managerial Strategies for Business Sustainability During Turbulent Times* (pp. 160–184). Hershey, PA: IGI Global. doi:10.4018/978-1-5225-2716-9.ch009

Perano, M., Hysa, X., & Calabrese, M. (2018). Strategic Planning, Cultural Context, and Business Continuity Management: Business Cases in the City of Shkoder. In A. Presenza & L. Sheehan (Eds.), *Geopolitics and Strategic Management in the Global Economy* (pp. 57–77). Hershey, PA: IGI Global. doi:10.4018/978-1-5225-2673-5.ch004

Pereira, R., Mira da Silva, M., & Lapão, L. V. (2017). IT Governance Maturity Patterns in Portuguese Healthcare. In S. De Haes & W. Van Grembergen (Eds.), *Strategic IT Governance and Alignment in Business Settings* (pp. 24–52). Hershey, PA: IGI Global. doi:10.4018/978-1-5225-0861-8.ch002

Pérez-Uribe, R. I., Torres, D. A., Jurado, S. P., & Prada, D. M. (2018). Cloud Tools for the Development of Project Management in SMEs. In R. Perez-Uribe, C. Salcedo-Perez, & D. Ocampo-Guzman (Eds.), *Handbook of Research on Intrapreneurship and Organizational Sustainability in SMEs* (pp. 95–120). Hershey, PA: IGI Global. doi:10.4018/978-1-5225-3543-0.ch005

Petrisor, I., & Cozmiuc, D. (2017). Global Supply Chain Management Organization at Siemens in the Advent of Industry 4.0. In L. Saglietto & C. Cezanne (Eds.), *Global Intermediation and Logistics Service Providers* (pp. 123–142). Hershey, PA: IGI Global. doi:10.4018/978-1-5225-2133-4.ch007

Pierce, J. M., Velliaris, D. M., & Edwards, J. (2017). A Living Case Study: A Journey Not a Destination. In N. Silton (Ed.), *Exploring the Benefits of Creativity in Education, Media, and the Arts* (pp. 158–178). Hershey, PA: IGI Global. doi:10.4018/978-1-5225-0504-4.ch008

Pipia, S., & Pipia, S. (2021). Challenges of Religious Tourism in the Conflict Region: An Example of Jerusalem. In E. Alaverdov & M. Bari (Eds.), *Global Development of Religious Tourism* (pp. 135-148). IGI Global. https://doi.org/10.4018/978-1-7998-5792-1.ch009

Poulaki, P., Kritikos, A., Vasilakis, N., & Valeri, M. (2022). The Contribution of Female Creativity to the Development of Gastronomic Tourism in Greece: The Case of the Island of Naxos in the South Aegean Region. In M. Valeri (Ed.), *New Governance and Management in Touristic Destinations* (pp. 246–258). IGI Global. https://doi.org/10.4018/978-1-6684-3889-3.ch015

Radosavljevic, M., & Andjelkovic, A. (2017). Multi-Criteria Decision Making Approach for Choosing Business Process for the Improvement: Upgrading of the Six Sigma Methodology. In J. Stanković, P. Delias, S. Marinković, & S. Rochhia (Eds.), *Tools and Techniques for Economic Decision Analysis* (pp. 225–247). Hershey, PA: IGI Global. doi:10.4018/978-1-5225-0959-2.ch011

Radovic, V. M. (2017). Corporate Sustainability and Responsibility and Disaster Risk Reduction: A Serbian Overview. In M. Camilleri (Ed.), *CSR 2.0 and the New Era of Corporate Citizenship* (pp. 147–164). Hershey, PA: IGI Global. doi:10.4018/978-1-5225-1842-6.ch008

Raghunath, K. M., Devi, S. L., & Patro, C. S. (2018). Impact of Risk Assessment Models on Risk Factors: A Holistic Outlook. In K. Strang, M. Korstanje, & N. Vajjhala (Eds.), *Research, Practices, and Innovations in Global Risk and Contingency Management* (pp. 134–153). Hershey, PA: IGI Global. doi:10.4018/978-1-5225-4754-9.ch008

Raman, A., & Goyal, D. P. (2017). Extending IMPLEMENT Framework for Enterprise Information Systems Implementation to Information System Innovation. In M. Tavana (Ed.), *Enterprise Information Systems and the Digitalization of Business Functions* (pp. 137–177). Hershey, PA: IGI Global. doi:10.4018/978-1-5225-2382-6.ch007

Rao, Y., & Zhang, Y. (2017). The Construction and Development of Academic Library Digital Special Subject Databases. In L. Ruan, Q. Zhu, & Y. Ye (Eds.), *Academic Library Development and Administration in China* (pp. 163–183). Hershey, PA: IGI Global. doi:10.4018/978-1-5225-0550-1.ch010

Ravasan, A. Z., Mohammadi, M. M., & Hamidi, H. (2018). An Investigation Into the Critical Success Factors of Implementing Information Technology Service Management Frameworks. In K. Jakobs (Ed.), *Corporate and Global Standardization Initiatives in Contemporary Society* (pp. 200–218). Hershey, PA: IGI Global. doi:10.4018/978-1-5225-5320-5.ch009

Rezaie, S., Mirabedini, S. J., & Abtahi, A. (2018). Designing a Model for Implementation of Business Intelligence in the Banking Industry. *International Journal of Enterprise Information Systems, 14*(1), 77–103. doi:10.4018/IJEIS.2018010105

Richards, V., Matthews, N., Williams, O. J., & Khan, Z. (2021). The Challenges of Accessible Tourism Information Systems for Tourists With Vision Impairment: Sensory Communications Beyond the Screen. In C. Eusébio, L. Teixeira, & M. Carneiro (Eds.), *ICT Tools and Applications for Accessible Tourism* (pp. 26–54). IGI Global. https://doi.org/10.4018/978-1-7998-6428-8.ch002

Rodrigues de Souza Neto, V., & Marques, O. (2021). Rural Tourism Fostering Welfare Through Sustainable Development: A Conceptual Approach. In A. Perinotto, V. Mayer, & J. Soares (Eds.), *Rebuilding and Restructuring the Tourism Industry: Infusion of Happiness and Quality of Life* (pp. 38–57). IGI Global. https://doi.org/10.4018/978-1-7998-7239-9.ch003

Romano, L., Grimaldi, R., & Colasuonno, F. S. (2017). Demand Management as a Success Factor in Project Portfolio Management. In L. Romano (Ed.), *Project Portfolio Management Strategies for Effective Organizational Operations* (pp. 202–219). Hershey, PA: IGI Global. doi:10.4018/978-1-5225-2151-8.ch008

Rubio-Escuderos, L., & García-Andreu, H. (2021). Competitiveness Factors of Accessible Tourism E-Travel Agencies. In C. Eusébio, L. Teixeira, & M. Carneiro (Eds.), *ICT Tools and Applications for Accessible Tourism* (pp. 196–217). IGI Global. https://doi.org/10.4018/978-1-7998-6428-8.ch009

Rucci, A. C., Porto, N., Darcy, S., & Becka, L. (2021). Smart and Accessible Cities?: Not Always – The Case for Accessible Tourism Initiatives in Buenos Aries and Sydney. In C. Eusébio, L. Teixeira, & M. Carneiro (Eds.), *ICT Tools and Applications for Accessible Tourism* (pp. 115–145). IGI Global. https://doi.org/10.4018/978-1-7998-6428-8.ch006

Ruhi, U. (2018). Towards an Interdisciplinary Socio-Technical Definition of Virtual Communities. In M. Khosrow-Pour, D.B.A. (Ed.), Encyclopedia of Information Science and Technology, Fourth Edition (pp. 4278-4295). Hershey, PA: IGI Global. doi:10.4018/978-1-5225-2255-3.ch371

Ryan, L., Catena, M., Ros, P., & Stephens, S. (2021). Designing Entrepreneurial Ecosystems to Support Resource Management in the Tourism Industry. In V. Costa, A. Moura, & M. Mira (Eds.), *Handbook of Research on Human Capital and People Management in the Tourism Industry* (pp. 265–281). IGI Global. https://doi.org/10.4018/978-1-7998-4318-4.ch013

Sabuncu, I. (2021). Understanding Tourist Perceptions and Expectations During Pandemic Through Social Media Big Data. In M. Demir, A. Dalgıç, & F. Ergen (Eds.), *Handbook of Research on the Impacts and Implications of COVID-19 on the Tourism Industry* (pp. 330–350). IGI Global. https://doi.org/10.4018/978-1-7998-8231-2.ch016

Safari, M. R., & Jiang, Q. (2018). The Theory and Practice of IT Governance Maturity and Strategies Alignment: Evidence From Banking Industry. *Journal of Global Information Management, 26*(2), 127–146. doi:10.4018/JGIM.2018040106

Sahoo, J., Pati, B., & Mohanty, B. (2017). Knowledge Management as an Academic Discipline: An Assessment. In B. Gunjal (Ed.), *Managing Knowledge and Scholarly Assets in Academic Libraries* (pp. 99–126). Hershey, PA: IGI Global. doi:10.4018/978-1-5225-1741-2.ch005

Saini, D. (2017). Relevance of Teaching Values and Ethics in Management Education. In N. Baporikar (Ed.), *Management Education for Global Leadership* (pp. 90–111). Hershey, PA: IGI Global. doi:10.4018/978-1-5225-1013-0.ch005

Sambhanthan, A. (2017). Assessing and Benchmarking Sustainability in Organisations: An Integrated Conceptual Model. *International Journal of Systems and Service-Oriented Engineering, 7*(4), 22–43. doi:10.4018/IJSSOE.2017100102

Sambhanthan, A., & Potdar, V. (2017). A Study of the Parameters Impacting Sustainability in Information Technology Organizations. *International Journal of Knowledge-Based Organizations, 7*(3), 27–39. doi:10.4018/IJKBO.2017070103

Sánchez-Fernández, M. D., & Manríquez, M. R. (2018). The Entrepreneurial Spirit Based on Social Values: The Digital Generation. In P. Isaias & L. Carvalho (Eds.), *User Innovation and the Entrepreneurship Phenomenon in the Digital Economy* (pp. 173–193). Hershey, PA: IGI Global. doi:10.4018/978-1-5225-2826-5.ch009

Sanchez-Ruiz, L., & Blanco, B. (2017). Process Management for SMEs: Barriers, Enablers, and Benefits. In M. Vemić (Ed.), *Optimal Management Strategies in Small and Medium Enterprises* (pp. 293–319). Hershey, PA: IGI Global. doi:10.4018/978-1-5225-1949-2.ch014

Sanz, L. F., Gómez-Pérez, J., & Castillo-Martinez, A. (2018). Analysis of the European ICT Competence Frameworks. In V. Ahuja & S. Rathore (Eds.), *Multidisciplinary Perspectives on Human Capital and Information Technology Professionals* (pp. 225–245). Hershey, PA: IGI Global. doi:10.4018/978-1-5225-5297-0.ch012

Sarvepalli, A., & Godin, J. (2017). Business Process Management in the Classroom. *Journal of Cases on Information Technology*, *19*(2), 17–28. doi:10.4018/JCIT.2017040102

Saxena, G. G., & Saxena, A. (2021). Host Community Role in Medical Tourism Development. In M. Singh & S. Kumaran (Eds.), *Growth of the Medical Tourism Industry and Its Impact on Society: Emerging Research and Opportunities* (pp. 105–127). IGI Global. https://doi.org/10.4018/978-1-7998-3427-4.ch006

Saygili, E. E., Ozturkoglu, Y., & Kocakulah, M. C. (2017). End Users' Perceptions of Critical Success Factors in ERP Applications. *International Journal of Enterprise Information Systems*, *13*(4), 58–75. doi:10.4018/IJEIS.2017100104

Saygili, E. E., & Saygili, A. T. (2017). Contemporary Issues in Enterprise Information Systems: A Critical Review of CSFs in ERP Implementations. In M. Tavana (Ed.), *Enterprise Information Systems and the Digitalization of Business Functions* (pp. 120–136). Hershey, PA: IGI Global. doi:10.4018/978-1-5225-2382-6.ch006

Schwaiger, K. M., & Zehrer, A. (2021). The COVID-19 Pandemic and Organizational Resilience in Hospitality Family Firms: A Qualitative Approach. In A. Zehrer, G. Glowka, K. Schwaiger, & V. Ranacher-Lackner (Eds.), *Resiliency Models and Addressing Future Risks for Family Firms in the Tourism Industry* (pp. 32–49). IGI Global. https://doi.org/10.4018/978-1-7998-7352-5.ch002

Scott, N., & Campos, A. C. (2022). Cognitive Science of Tourism Experiences. In R. Augusto Costa, F. Brandão, Z. Breda, & C. Costa (Eds.), Planning and Managing the Experience Economy in Tourism (pp. 1-21). IGI Global. https://doi.org/ doi:10.4018/978-1-7998-8775-1.ch001

Seidenstricker, S., & Antonino, A. (2018). Business Model Innovation-Oriented Technology Management for Emergent Technologies. In M. Khosrow-Pour, D.B.A. (Ed.), Encyclopedia of Information Science and Technology, Fourth Edition (pp. 4560-4569). Hershey, PA: IGI Global. doi:10.4018/978-1-5225-2255-3.ch396

Selvi, M. S. (2021). Changes in Tourism Sales and Marketing Post COVID-19. In M. Demir, A. Dalgıç, & F. Ergen (Eds.), *Handbook of Research on the Impacts and Implications of COVID-19 on the Tourism Industry* (pp. 437–460). IGI Global. doi:10.4018/978-1-7998-8231-2.ch021

Senaratne, S., & Gunarathne, A. D. (2017). Excellence Perspective for Management Education from a Global Accountants' Hub in Asia. In N. Baporikar (Ed.), *Management Education for Global Leadership* (pp. 158–180). Hershey, PA: IGI Global. doi:10.4018/978-1-5225-1013-0.ch008

Sensuse, D. I., & Cahyaningsih, E. (2018). Knowledge Management Models: A Summative Review. *International Journal of Information Systems in the Service Sector, 10*(1), 71–100. doi:10.4018/IJISSS.2018010105

Seth, M., Goyal, D., & Kiran, R. (2017). Diminution of Impediments in Implementation of Supply Chain Management Information System for Enhancing its Effectiveness in Indian Automobile Industry. *Journal of Global Information Management, 25*(3), 1–20. doi:10.4018/JGIM.2017070101

Seyal, A. H., & Rahman, M. N. (2017). Investigating Impact of Inter-Organizational Factors in Measuring ERP Systems Success: Bruneian Perspectives. In M. Tavana (Ed.), *Enterprise Information Systems and the Digitalization of Business Functions* (pp. 178–204). Hershey, PA: IGI Global. doi:10.4018/978-1-5225-2382-6.ch008

Shaqrah, A. A. (2018). Analyzing Business Intelligence Systems Based on 7s Model of McKinsey. *International Journal of Business Intelligence Research, 9*(1), 53–63. doi:10.4018/IJBIR.2018010104

Sharma, A. J. (2017). Enhancing Sustainability through Experiential Learning in Management Education. In N. Baporikar (Ed.), *Management Education for Global Leadership* (pp. 256–274). Hershey, PA: IGI Global. doi:10.4018/978-1-5225-1013-0.ch013

Shetty, K. P. (2017). Responsible Global Leadership: Ethical Challenges in Management Education. In N. Baporikar (Ed.), *Innovation and Shifting Perspectives in Management Education* (pp. 194–223). Hershey, PA: IGI Global. doi:10.4018/978-1-5225-1019-2.ch009

Sinthupundaja, J., & Kohda, Y. (2017). Effects of Corporate Social Responsibility and Creating Shared Value on Sustainability. *International Journal of Sustainable Entrepreneurship and Corporate Social Responsibility, 2*(1), 27–38. doi:10.4018/IJSECSR.2017010103

Škarica, I., & Hrgović, A. V. (2018). Implementation of Total Quality Management Principles in Public Health Institutes in the Republic of Croatia. *International Journal of Productivity Management and Assessment Technologies, 6*(1), 1–16. doi:10.4018/IJPMAT.2018010101

Skokic, V. (2021). How Small Hotel Owners Practice Resilience: Longitudinal Study Among Small Family Hotels in Croatia. In A. Zehrer, G. Glowka, K. Schwaiger, & V. Ranacher-Lackner (Eds.), *Resiliency Models and Addressing Future Risks for Family Firms in the Tourism Industry* (pp. 50–73). IGI Global. doi:10.4018/978-1-7998-7352-5.ch003

Smuts, H., Kotzé, P., Van der Merwe, A., & Loock, M. (2017). Framework for Managing Shared Knowledge in an Information Systems Outsourcing Context. *International Journal of Knowledge Management, 13*(4), 1–30. doi:10.4018/IJKM.2017100101

Sousa, M. J., Cruz, R., Dias, I., & Caracol, C. (2017). Information Management Systems in the Supply Chain. In G. Jamil, A. Soares, & C. Pessoa (Eds.), *Handbook of Research on Information Management for Effective Logistics and Supply Chains* (pp. 469–485). Hershey, PA: IGI Global. doi:10.4018/978-1-5225-0973-8.ch025

Spremic, M., Turulja, L., & Bajgoric, N. (2018). Two Approaches in Assessing Business Continuity Management Attitudes in the Organizational Context. In N. Bajgoric (Ed.), *Always-On Enterprise Information Systems for Modern Organizations* (pp. 159–183). Hershey, PA: IGI Global. doi:10.4018/978-1-5225-3704-5.ch008

Steenkamp, A. L. (2018). Some Insights in Computer Science and Information Technology. In *Examining the Changing Role of Supervision in Doctoral Research Projects: Emerging Research and Opportunities* (pp. 113–133). Hershey, PA: IGI Global. doi:10.4018/978-1-5225-2610-0.ch005

Stipanović, C., Rudan, E., & Zubović, V. (2022). Reaching the New Tourist Through Creativity: Sustainable Development Challenges in Croatian Coastal Towns. In M. Valeri (Ed.), *New Governance and Management in Touristic Destinations* (pp. 231–245). IGI Global. https://doi.org/10.4018/978-1-6684-3889-3.ch014

Tabach, A., & Croteau, A. (2017). Configurations of Information Technology Governance Practices and Business Unit Performance. *International Journal of IT/Business Alignment and Governance*, *8*(2), 1–27. doi:10.4018/IJITBAG.2017070101

Talaue, G. M., & Iqbal, T. (2017). Assessment of e-Business Mode of Selected Private Universities in the Philippines and Pakistan. *International Journal of Online Marketing*, *7*(4), 63–77. doi:10.4018/IJOM.2017100105

Tam, G. C. (2017). Project Manager Sustainability Competence. In *Managerial Strategies and Green Solutions for Project Sustainability* (pp. 178–207). Hershey, PA: IGI Global. doi:10.4018/978-1-5225-2371-0.ch008

Tambo, T. (2018). Fashion Retail Innovation: About Context, Antecedents, and Outcome in Technological Change Projects. In I. Management Association (Ed.), Fashion and Textiles: Breakthroughs in Research and Practice (pp. 233-260). Hershey, PA: IGI Global. https://doi.org/ doi:10.4018/978-1-5225-3432-7.ch010

Tantau, A. D., & Frăţilă, L. C. (2018). Information and Management System for Renewable Energy Business. In *Entrepreneurship and Business Development in the Renewable Energy Sector* (pp. 200–244). Hershey, PA: IGI Global. doi:10.4018/978-1-5225-3625-3.ch006

Teixeira, N., Pardal, P. N., & Rafael, B. G. (2018). Internationalization, Financial Performance, and Organizational Challenges: A Success Case in Portugal. In L. Carvalho (Ed.), *Handbook of Research on Entrepreneurial Ecosystems and Social Dynamics in a Globalized World* (pp. 379–423). Hershey, PA: IGI Global. doi:10.4018/978-1-5225-3525-6.ch017

Teixeira, P., Teixeira, L., Eusébio, C., Silva, S., & Teixeira, A. (2021). The Impact of ICTs on Accessible Tourism: Evidence Based on a Systematic Literature Review. In C. Eusébio, L. Teixeira, & M. Carneiro (Eds.), *ICT Tools and Applications for Accessible Tourism* (pp. 1–25). IGI Global. doi:10.4018/978-1-7998-6428-8.ch001

Trad, A., & Kalpić, D. (2018). The Business Transformation Framework, Agile Project and Change Management. In M. Khosrow-Pour, D.B.A. (Ed.), Encyclopedia of Information Science and Technology, Fourth Edition (pp. 620-635). Hershey, PA: IGI Global. https://doi.org/ doi:10.4018/978-1-5225-2255-3.ch054

Trad, A., & Kalpić, D. (2018). The Business Transformation and Enterprise Architecture Framework: The Financial Engineering E-Risk Management and E-Law Integration. In B. Sergi, F. Fidanoski, M. Ziolo, & V. Naumovski (Eds.), *Regaining Global Stability After the Financial Crisis* (pp. 46–65). Hershey, PA: IGI Global. doi:10.4018/978-1-5225-4026-7.ch003

Trengereid, V. (2022). Conditions of Network Engagement: The Quest for a Common Good. In R. Augusto Costa, F. Brandão, Z. Breda, & C. Costa (Eds.), *Planning and Managing the Experience Economy in Tourism* (pp. 69-84). IGI Global. https://doi.org/10.4018/978-1-7998-8775-1.ch004

Turulja, L., & Bajgoric, N. (2018). Business Continuity and Information Systems: A Systematic Literature Review. In N. Bajgoric (Ed.), *Always-On Enterprise Information Systems for Modern Organizations* (pp. 60–87). Hershey, PA: IGI Global. doi:10.4018/978-1-5225-3704-5.ch004

Vargas-Hernández, J. G. (2017). Professional Integrity in Business Management Education. In N. Baporikar (Ed.), *Management Education for Global Leadership* (pp. 70–89). Hershey, PA: IGI Global. doi:10.4018/978-1-5225-1013-0.ch004

Varnacı Uzun, F. (2021). The Destination Preferences of Foreign Tourists During the COVID-19 Pandemic and Attitudes Towards: Marmaris, Turkey. In M. Demir, A. Dalgıç, & F. Ergen (Eds.), *Handbook of Research on the Impacts and Implications of COVID-19 on the Tourism Industry* (pp. 285–306). IGI Global. https://doi.org/10.4018/978-1-7998-8231-2.ch014

Vasista, T. G., & AlAbdullatif, A. M. (2017). Role of Electronic Customer Relationship Management in Demand Chain Management: A Predictive Analytic Approach. *International Journal of Information Systems and Supply Chain Management, 10*(1), 53–67. doi:10.4018/IJISSCM.2017010104

Vieru, D., & Bourdeau, S. (2017). Survival in the Digital Era: A Digital Competence-Based Multi-Case Study in the Canadian SME Clothing Industry. *International Journal of Social and Organizational Dynamics in IT, 6*(1), 17–34. doi:10.4018/IJSODIT.2017010102

Vijayan, G., & Kamarulzaman, N. H. (2017). An Introduction to Sustainable Supply Chain Management and Business Implications. In M. Khan, M. Hussain, & M. Ajmal (Eds.), *Green Supply Chain Management for Sustainable Business Practice* (pp. 27–50). Hershey, PA: IGI Global. doi:10.4018/978-1-5225-0635-5.ch002

Vlachvei, A., & Notta, O. (2017). Firm Competitiveness: Theories, Evidence, and Measurement. In A. Vlachvei, O. Notta, K. Karantininis, & N. Tsounis (Eds.), *Factors Affecting Firm Competitiveness and Performance in the Modern Business World* (pp. 1–42). Hershey, PA: IGI Global. doi:10.4018/978-1-5225-0843-4.ch001

Wang, C., Schofield, M., Li, X., & Ou, X. (2017). Do Chinese Students in Public and Private Higher Education Institutes Perform at Different Level in One of the Leadership Skills: Critical Thinking?: An Exploratory Comparison. In V. Wang (Ed.), *Encyclopedia of Strategic Leadership and Management* (pp. 160–181). Hershey, PA: IGI Global. doi:10.4018/978-1-5225-1049-9.ch013

Wang, J. (2017). Multi-Agent based Production Management Decision System Modelling for the Textile Enterprise. *Journal of Global Information Management, 25*(4), 1–15. doi:10.4018/JGIM.2017100101

Wiedemann, A., & Gewald, H. (2017). Examining Cross-Domain Alignment: The Correlation of Business Strategy, IT Management, and IT Business Value. *International Journal of IT/Business Alignment and Governance*, *8*(1), 17–31. doi:10.4018/IJITBAG.2017010102

Wolf, R., & Thiel, M. (2018). Advancing Global Business Ethics in China: Reducing Poverty Through Human and Social Welfare. In S. Hipsher (Ed.), *Examining the Private Sector's Role in Wealth Creation and Poverty Reduction* (pp. 67–84). Hershey, PA: IGI Global. doi:10.4018/978-1-5225-3117-3.ch004

Yablonsky, S. (2018). Innovation Platforms: Data and Analytics Platforms. In *Multi-Sided Platforms (MSPs) and Sharing Strategies in the Digital Economy: Emerging Research and Opportunities* (pp. 72–95). Hershey, PA: IGI Global. doi:10.4018/978-1-5225-5457-8.ch003

Yaşar, B. (2021). The Impact of COVID-19 on Volatility of Tourism Stocks: Evidence From BIST Tourism Index. In M. Demir, A. Dalgıç, & F. Ergen (Eds.), *Handbook of Research on the Impacts and Implications of COVID-19 on the Tourism Industry* (pp. 23–44). IGI Global. https://doi.org/10.4018/978-1-7998-8231-2.ch002

Yusoff, A., Ahmad, N. H., & Halim, H. A. (2017). Agropreneurship among Gen Y in Malaysia: The Role of Academic Institutions. In N. Ahmad, T. Ramayah, H. Halim, & S. Rahman (Eds.), *Handbook of Research on Small and Medium Enterprises in Developing Countries* (pp. 23–47). Hershey, PA: IGI Global. doi:10.4018/978-1-5225-2165-5.ch002

Zacher, D., & Pechlaner, H. (2021). Resilience as an Opportunity Approach: Challenges and Perspectives for Private Sector Participation on a Community Level. In A. Zehrer, G. Glowka, K. Schwaiger, & V. Ranacher-Lackner (Eds.), *Resiliency Models and Addressing Future Risks for Family Firms in the Tourism Industry* (pp. 75–102). IGI Global. https://doi.org/10.4018/978-1-7998-7352-5.ch004

Zanin, F., Comuzzi, E., & Costantini, A. (2018). The Effect of Business Strategy and Stock Market Listing on the Use of Risk Assessment Tools. In *Management Control Systems in Complex Settings: Emerging Research and Opportunities* (pp. 145–168). Hershey, PA: IGI Global. doi:10.4018/978-1-5225-3987-2.ch007

Zgheib, P. W. (2017). Corporate Innovation and Intrapreneurship in the Middle East. In P. Zgheib (Ed.), *Entrepreneurship and Business Innovation in the Middle East* (pp. 37–56). Hershey, PA: IGI Global. doi:10.4018/978-1-5225-2066-5.ch003

About the Contributors

Shivani Inder has done Ph.D. in finance. She is a certified Cost and Management Accountant (CMA). She has done M.B.A (finance) and M.F.C. She is currently working as Associate Professor at Chitkara Business School, Chitkara University, Punjab, India. Her domain areas are corporate finance, accounting and entrepreneurship. She has more than ten years of teaching experience. She is associated with professional bodies and review for reputed journals.

Shuchi Dawra is Professor, Chitkara Business School, Chitkara University, Punjab, India. She is a Doctorate in in the domain of human resource management and organizational behaviour from Panjab University, Chandigarh, India. She has varied experience of 16 years in industry and academia with expertise in HRM practices, work-life balance (WLB), TQM, CSR and HR analytics. She is M Com, MBA(HR), UGC(NET); and is HR analytics certified from the IIM, Rohtak. Her area of expertise include Global Practices in HRM, Organizational Behaviour & Research. She has successfully supervised two doctoral research on TQM in Higher Education in Engineering and Work Life Balance; at present she is mentoring 4 Phd Research Scholars(Senior Corporate Executives and academicians) in the Research domains of Self efficacy and Internships, CSR & leadership; and Work life Balance.She has her research publication in reputed international and national journals. She is also a reviewer, and has chaired sessions in the conferences.

Sandhir Sharma is Ph.D. in Strategic Management with nearly 22 years of experience in higher education and 5 years in Telecom industry. With more than 43 research papers to his credit published in various journals and conferences at national & international level, Dr. Sharma has developed his core expertise in the area of Strategy formulation. His research has widely published in various newspapers. Currently, he is serving as Dean, Chitkara Business School & visiting faculty to Binus University, Indonesia and University of Applied Sciences, Osnabruck, Germany. He has been instrumental in scaling Chitkara Business School operations from 60 students & one program to 1200 plus students & more than 12 programs with in span of 8 years. In his last assignment, Dr. Sharma set up a B-School in Ludhiana and was instrumental in taking that B-School to pinnacle of glory in the region.

* * *

Sumit Agarwal is Professor at Delhi Institute of Higher Education, Greater Noida West, India. He had more than 15 years of experience of working with various universities. He has got published various research papers in reputed journals and participated in conferences/seminars on critical issues relating to the management.

Khalida Akbar, from 2018 to 2023, served as a Post-Doctoral Fellow at the Durban University of Technology (DUT) within the Faculty of Research Innovation and Engagement. During this time, she specialized in the intersection of acquired brain injury and human resource management . Dr.Akbar achieved the remarkable distinction of graduating with a Ph.D. from the University of KwaZulu-Natal at the age of 26. Teaching and Supervision: Dr.Akbar 's passion for education is reflected in her ten-year tenure as a part-time lecturer at the University of KwaZulu-Natal. She has delivered lectures across various disciplines, including Human Resource Management, Entrepreneurship, Public Governance, and Industrial Organizational and Labour Studies. Dr.Akbar has also provided guidance to numerous honours, master's, and Ph.D. students, further contributing to the development of the next generation of scholars. International Engagement: Dr.Akbar has showcased her research prowess on a global stage, attending and presenting at international conferences in countries such as South Africa, France, Germany, and Mauritius. Her participation in collaborative research projects with Germany underscores her commitment to cross-border knowledge exchange and collaboration. Research Interests: Dr.Akbar 's research interests encompass a wide spectrum, including Higher Education and Development, Cognitive Function/ Brain Injury, Human Resource Management, Entrepreneurship, and Management, with a particular focus on sustainability. Her multidisciplinary approach to research showcases her versatility and dedication to addressing critical issues in academia and society. Inspirational Quote:"In a world where you can be anything, be kind." Dr.Akbar embodies this ethos through her contributions to academia, research, and her unwavering commitment to making a positive impact in the lives of others. Her exemplary career trajectory and dedication to knowledge dissemination make her a respected figure in her field. Dr.Akbar continues to inspire and lead by example, leaving an indelible mark on the academic landscape.

Sawssen Ayadi is a doctor in marketing at University of Sfax in Tunisia. Her PhD thesis is about environment thematization of experience touristic and the effects of attraction for thematization on consumer experience. Her research areas concern environment of experience, consumer experience, immersive experience, metaverse in tourism experience and the phygital experience in retail marketing.

Ajit Bansal is a Professor and Program Head (Sports Management) at Chitkara Business School, Chitkara University, Punjab, India, responsible for mentoring and administering courses since 2018. He was awarded a doctorate by HPU Shimla in 2011, and he has master's degrees in management and commerce. He has over 25 years of experience working with various reputed industries and educational institutions like Graphic Era University, Dehradun, Shoolini University Solan, MAU, Solan, etc., imparting management education in India. His research interests are in the fields of Corporate Finance, Taxation, Cultural Tourism, and Microfinance. He has published various research papers in reputed journals and participated in conferences/seminars on critical issues relating to management.

Anu Bansal is Guest faculty in Chitkara Business School, Chitkara University, Punjab, India responsible to mentor and administer UG and PG courses since 2018. She was awarded a Doctorate degree by The Glocal University, UP, in 2023, and she has master's degrees in Management and Commerce. She has a vast experience of over 10 years of working with various reputed industries and educational institutions. Her research interests are in the field of Finance, Tourism, and Microfinance. He has got published various research papers in reputed journals and participated in conferences/seminars on critical issues relating to the management.

Oindrila Chakraborty is a gold medalist in her MBA programme from University of Calcutta. She has 15 years of teaching experience in management education. She has completed her PhD from University of Calcutta and has several publications to furnish in National and International Journals of high repute.

Sachin Dev, a man of letters, completed his MBA from Lovely Institute of Technology, Jalandhar in 2009. Thereafter, he obtained Ph.D. degree from IKG Punjab Technical University, Jalandhar specializing in "Terms Insurance", has been serving full time as Assistant Professor in Management at Baba Farid College of Management & Technology, Bathinda (Punjab) since 2009 and having additional charge of Vice-Principal of the College since 2014. He also served 01 year as Agency Manager in Bharti Axa Life Insurance Company, Jalandhar from 2008 to 2009. After working in the industry, he returned to his first love, teaching. During his career, he has published 19 research papers on the subject in reputed National and International journals. He also presented 18 research papers in National and International Conferences. 03 students are doing Ph.D under his supervision at Punjabi University, Patiala. He has contributed in organizing 07 International/National conferences at Baba Farid College of Management & Technology. He has chaired 10 technical sessions in National and International Conferences. His skills include teaching, curriculum development, program planning, case management, administration, community relations and editorial consulting. He is a talented editor with experience in creative, inspirational, academic and publications. He is the editor of 02 books. He brings these experiences to the classroom and encourages students to bring their experiences.

Nomita Dey is a Researcher and Educator originally from Incredible India. She has a bachelor's in Chemistry and an M.Com in Business and Finance, national & international along with certificate in Chartered Accountancy (Intermediate). After completing her Master, she qualified UGC-NET & pursuing Ph.D. She is serving for last 17 years in commerce & management. She embarked upon a career as an auditor, writer, educator & researcher. She has a keen interest in the area of Innovation, Sustainability, Business and Finance.

Suganya G. is a Ph.D in Management Sciences. Currently she is associated with Kumaraguru College of Liberal Arts and Science, Coimbatore as Assistant Professor. Previously, she has an industrial experience of 4 years in textiles and automobile sector and has been in the field of research and teaching for 5 years. She has been associated as a researcher in a number of collaborative project conducted by University of Leeds (UK) and the Goa Institute of Management (Goa) from 2017 which was funded by: University of Leeds and British Academy in the year 2018 – 2019, AHRC Modern Slavery Policy and Evidence Centre COVID-10 SPF 2020 in the year 2020 – 2021 and UK's Arts and Humanities Research Council (AHRC) in the year 2022. She has organized a number of events and scenario workshops during her tenure. She has been associated as Research Assistant in a project which was sponsored by Indian Council of Social Science Research (ICSSR), Impactful Policy Research in Social Science (IMPRESS).

Sushant Garg is a student in Christ (Deemed to be University), Delhi, NCR.

Trisha Govender, equipped with a BSc. Degree in Chemical Engineering from the University of Kwa Zulu-Natal, embarked on a trajectory that transitioned from traditional chemical engineering to the dynamic realm of Artificial Intelligence. Prior to her tenure at SIDT, Trisha steered a series of entrepreneurial ventures spanning a wide array of fields including coding and robotics, machine learning consultancy, digital marketing, web development, and education. Her noteworthy contributions earned her recognition, being featured twice in The South African Institute of Chemical Engineers Blog for her entrepreneurial accomplishments in 2021 and 2022, as well as in Mech Chem Africa Magazine in 2021. As the Manager of MANCOSA School of Information and Digital Technology (SIDT), Trisha is fervently dedicated to propelling innovation and equipping individuals with the requisite skills for success in this burgeoning digital age. Her core mission is to mold present and future digital leaders who not only spearhead successful digital transformations but also possess a keen awareness of the cyber risks inherent in cutting-edge technology.

Nidhi Gupta is an Associate Professor in School of Engineering and Technology, Department of Computer Science and Engineering, Sharda University, Greater Noida. She has more than 16 years of academic experience. She received her Ph.D. in Computer Science Engineering from Jaypee Institute of Information technology, Noida, India. She has broad research interests in Machine Learning, Information Retrieval and Databases. She has published more than 15 research papers in various SCI/WOS/Scopus and UGC-Care journals.

Palak Gupta, Head of Department, IT, is currently associated with Delhi Institute of Higher Education, Greater Noida West. DIHE is a part of JIMS Group. Dr. Palak has many publications in reputed National & International Journals and has specialization in domains of Business Analytics, Big Data, Cloud Computing, DW&DM.

Vandana Gupta is Associate Professor, Delhi Institute of Higher Education, Greater Noida West, India. She is HOD of PGDM program. She had experience of over 21 years.. Her research interests are in the field of Marketing, Sales management and consumer behaviour. She has got published various research papers in reputed journals and participated in conferences/seminars on critical issues relating to the management.

Babita Jha is working as an Associate Professor in Christ (Deemed to be University), Delhi-NCR.

Priyanshu Kumar is a B.Tech student in Sharda University. He worked on various projects as a freelancer. His expertise is in databases, AR and VR.

Shivam Kumar is a B.Tech Student in Sharda University. He worked on various projects.

Supriya Lamba Sahdev is a certified trained academician, researcher, certified coach and trainer with 11+ years of experience in the field of Marketing and International Business, is Assistant Professor at ISBR Business School, Bengaluru, Karnataka, India. She has done her double bachelors- in Commerce and Education and her double masters- in Commerce and Education. She is Ph.D. in Management where she had worked for almost 6 years on area of open Innovation in Indian Food Processing SMEs. She has a journey of almost 11+ years in academia. Started her academic carrier with Amity University as Assistant professor and Programme Leader of 3Continent program in 2012. Later she joined ISBR business school as Assistant professor and international programs manager in 2022. She is consistently striving to create a challenging and engaging learning environment where students become life-long scholars and learners. Imparting lectures using different teaching strategies, she is an avid teacher, researcher, and mentor. She is also involved in the course and syllabus designing and developing on various Management topics, including analytics, wellbeing and management curriculum. She started her career in as Assistant Professor in Amity University, leading university in Pan Asia. Having an enriched research portfolio with the peer-reviewed publication, book chapter, and conference presentations across top tier journals in management. Presently has to her credit more than 50 plus Research Papers in UGC and SCOPUS publications in reputed national and international journals accompanied with hundreds of Research participation in International/National Conferences including FDP, MDP and Symposiums. She is serving as a member of review committee for conferences and journals. She is the Research Coordinator with ISBR Business School and is the lead organizer for conducting International Conferences, IEEE Conferences. She has almost conducted more than 2 International Conferences. She is acting as the special session-conference chair for International Conference on Intelligent and Innovative Technologies in Computing, Electrical and Electronics (ICIITCEE 2023) () which is indexed in the IEEE and Scopus. And Was the Session Chair & Core Committee Member -ICIEM Conference, Amity University-London 2020(. She is also acting as the Lead Editor for IJASRET-Editorial Board Members, , ISSN: 2456-0774; Impact Factor: 4.530 and Ecronicon -Editorial Board Members, . She has also delivered several invited talks and seminars at several platforms of national and international repute. She has successfully Filed Design Application - 372208-00. Has got 25+ certifications- few of them are from International Trade Centre, Geneva, Atal Academy and ADBI to name a few. Her area of interest includes International Business, Fusion of Technology with International Marketing, Open Innovation, Sustainability, International Management and Cross-Cultural Management, International Trade Management, Entrepreneurship Development, Role of New Age Technologies. She is a member of different Societies and professional bodies including member of World Economic Association, Member of CII, IICCI, SEPC, FIEO, AIMA and many more. She has presented her research accomplishments at international level at London. She has been to London for three continent programmes under Amity University where she had delivered many talks to global students. She acts to lead and liaise between the student community and the industry delegates, with a keen interest in training. She got patent published in Feb, 2022, , Application Number: 202241000071. Patent Journal Certificate URL: .

Bhavuk Mahindru has done Ph.D. in marketing. He has done M.B.A. (finance & marketing). He is currently working as Associate Professor at Department of Business Management Multani Mal Modi college, Patiala, Punjab, India. His domain areas are Consumer Behaviour, Digital marketing, Financial Accounting, Portfolio Management. He has more than ten years of teaching experience. He is associated with professional bodies and review for reputed journals.

Vicent Mbonye is a dedicated information technology specialist with a keen interest in the transformative power of technology on both societal and organizational levels. Currently pursuing a PhD in Information Systems and Technology at the University of KwaZulu-Natal (UKZN), Vincent holds a Master's degree and Bachelor of Commerce Honours degree in Information Systems and Technology from UKZN, along with a Bachelor's degree in Information Technology, with honors, from Kampala International University in Uganda. With a strong foundation in academia and a proven track record of professional success, Vincent has been recognized for his analytical skills, teamwork, and ability to excel under pressure. As an Emerging Researcher Award recipient and a member of the Golden Key International Honour Society, Vincent is committed to driving innovation and making meaningful contributions to the field of information systems and technology.

Sathish Pachiyappan is currently serving as Assistant Professor at CHRIST(deemed), Bannerghatta Road Campus, Bengaluru. He has eight years teaching and three years research experience. He has done his doctoral degree from VIT (deemed), Vellore. He is specialized in Finance and Accounting, doing his research in the same area. He has completed MBA from Anna University and B,Com from SRM University, Chennai. Currently, as a part of his Research work, he had published articles in peer reviewed journals which includes Scopus Indexed Journals; Web of Science Indexed Journals, Australian Business Deans Council (ABDC) listed Journals and EBSCO host Journals. Also, published book chapter in Elsevier, Springer and IGI global. Presented research papers in national and international conferences and also attended Faculty development programmes and workshops which are related to SPSS, AMOS and Econometrics. He went as resource person for various FDP, Guest Lecture, Session Chair for Conference and Workshop to various reputed colleges. He is well versed in handling SPSS,RSTATCRAFT, E-Views (Econometrics) for financial data analysis in research area. He is gold medalist and earned first rank in B.Com at SRM University, Chennai and also earned Class topper in MBA and 39th Rank Holder in Anna University. He received Research Award-2017 for publications in VIT University, Vellore. Recently, received award for "Best Researcher-2020" conducted by Pondicherry Research Society in Pondicherry.

Sabyasachi Pramanik is a professional IEEE member. He obtained a PhD in Computer Science and Engineering from Sri Satya Sai University of Technology and Medical Sciences, Bhopal, India. Presently, he is an Associate Professor, Department of Computer Science and Engineering, Haldia Institute of Technology, India. He has many publications in various reputed international conferences, journals, and book chapters (Indexed by SCIE, Scopus, ESCI, etc). He is doing research in the fields of Artificial Intelligence, Data Privacy, Cybersecurity, Network Security, and Machine Learning. He also serves on the editorial boards of several international journals. He is a reviewer of journal articles from IEEE, Springer, Elsevier, Inderscience, IET and IGI Global. He has reviewed many conference papers, has been a keynote speaker, session chair, and technical program committee member at many international conferences. He has authored a book on Wireless Sensor Network. He has edited 8 books from IGI Global, CRC Press, Springer and Wiley Publications.

J. Joshua Selvakumar is an Associate Professor at the School of Business and Management at Christ University, Bangalore. He is a marketing management educator and administrator with national and international front-line sales experience with companies such as Mahindra & Mahindra, TTK Healthcare and Excel International in Doha, Qatar. He has 18+ years of teaching in leading Business schools like PSG Institute of Management Coimbatore and others. He served as the Centre Head for PSG Institutions In-House advertising and communication division for over a decade. He has over 42 publications to his credit. He is passionate about integrated marketing communication and sales Management and has published a book titled "Dimensions of Integrated Marketing Communications" with Lambert Publishing, Germany. He has visited several Universities abroad and is currently an adjunct faculty at the University of Toledo, Ohio, USA and a Collaborator with Taylor's University, Malaysia.

Kirti Sharma is a Visionary Research Scholar and Educator. Holding a Master's degree in Commerce and Management (Finance), she furthered her academic journey by completing a B.Ed. (Commerce) and qualifying NTA UGC-NET and CTET. Currently pursuing Ph.D. in commerce. With a commendable eight years of professional experience, she has dedicated about six years to teaching and rest of the tenure to administrative work. Her enthusiasm for education is reflected in her optimistic outlook and enduring commitment. Kirti's adaptability to diverse environments positions her to excel in challenging roles. Being a research enthusiast she has published six papers altogether out of which three has been published under UGC CARE-listed journals and one in Scopus indexed journals remaining in the conference preceding books. Her expertise spans finance, encompassing areas such as working capital management and the emerging Metaverse. Additionally, she has presented her research at four national and international conferences. Her belief in producing optimal results, coupled with a strong academic record, defines Kirti as a valuable asset in the field of higher education.

Rshi Shukla is an Associate Professor AIT-Management, Centre of Excellence Chandigarh University Chandigarh, India

Jashandeep Singh is a gregarious, enthusiastic and promising young man who has a passion for teaching. He obtained his PhD from M.M. University, Haryana and MBA in Marketing Management from RIMT, Punjab. He possesses 12 years of work experience in the field of academics, academic administration and research in premier institutions of Punjab and Haryana. He is IKGPTU's certified resource person in Human Values and Ethics. He has been trained at IIM Kozhikode, SPJIMR, IIM Ahmedabad, and IIM Rohtak, and attended several workshops and development programs at various institutions of repute. He has published numerous research papers and a book as well. He has also been appointed as an editorial board member and reviewer for numerous refereed journals. He has also served as a resource person at MGSIPA, Punjab and SEBI for imparting financial literacy among various sections of society. He is a resource person for Value Ideas Investment and a freelance Personality development trainer too. He has filed 10 patents so far. He has completed many Pro-Bono projects for the upliftment of society. He has been a member of Nasha Mukt Abhiyan, Punjab (Punjab Govt run) team.

Tushar Singhal is a student in Christ (Deemed to be University), Delhi, NCR.

Sanjay Taneja is currently an Associate Professor in Research at Graphic Era University, Dehradun, India. His significant thrust areas are Banking Regulations, Banking and Finance (Fin Tech, Green Finance), Risks, Insurance Management, Green Economics and Management of Innovation in Insurance. He holds a double master's degree (MBA &M.Com.) in management with a specialization in Finance and Marketing. He received his PG degrees in Management (Gold Medalist) from Chaudhary Devi University, Sirsa, India in 2012. He earned his Doctor of Philosophy (Sponsored By ICSSR) in Banking and Finance entitled "An Appraisal of financial performance of Indian Banking Sector: A Comparative study of Public, Private and Foreign banks in 2016 from Chaudhary Devi University, Sirsa, India. He received his Post Doctoral Degree from faculty of Social Sciences, Department of Banking and Insurance, Usak University, Turkey entitled on "Impact of the European Green Deal on Carbon (CO2) Emission in Turkey" in 2023. He has published research papers in reputed SCOPUS/Web of Science/SCI/ABDC/UGC Care Journals. Prof. Taneja has more than fifty publications in total (Scopus/ABDC/Web of Science- 27).

Muhammad Usman Tariq has more than 16+ year's experience in industry and academia. He has been working as a consultant and trainer for industries representing six sigma, quality, health and safety, environmental systems, project management, and information security standards. His work has encompassed sectors in aviation, manufacturing, food, hospitality, education, finance, research, software and transportation. He has diverse and significant experience working with accreditation agencies of

ABET, ACBSP, AACSB, WASC, CAA, EFQM and NCEAC. Additionally, Dr. Tariq has operational experience in incubators, research labs, government research projects, private sector startups, program creation and management at various industrial and academic levels. He is Certified Higher Education Teacher from Harvard University, USA, Certified Online Educator from HMBSU, Certified Six Sigma Master Black Belt, Lead Auditor ISO 9001 Certified, ISO 14001, IOSH MS, OSHA 30, and OSHA 48. He is member of Harvard Business Review Advisory Council.

Neha Verma is Assistant Professor, Delhi Institute of Higher Education, Greater Noida West, India.. She had experience of over 10 years. Her research interests are in the field of Finance. She has got published various research papers in reputed journals and participated in conferences/seminars on critical issues relating to the management.

Mini Verma has an academic experience of 18 years, she did PhD in Operations research, MSc Maths. Her area of interest is Business Statistics, Quantitative techniques, Business Mathematics and Operations research. She has presented her research paper in various National and international journal. She is an Author of 4 books of statistics.

Abir Zouari is a doctor in marketing at University of Sfax in Tunisia. Actually, she has an academic experience of over 5 years. Her PhD thesis is related to the role of institutional orientation on export performance. Her research interests are in international marketing, green marketing and CSR, and digital marketing and new technologies. She published her works in reputed journals and participated in conference at national and international level.

Index

www.ingramcontent.com/pod-product-compliance
Lightning Source LLC
LaVergne TN
LVHW060425300926
849162LV00006B/1526